GAY AND LESBIAN EDUCATORS

To Joyce:
Keep up the great work
in creating just and
compassionate schools!
Nice to meet you —
Best wishes,
Karen Harbeck
10/97

EARLY PRAISE FOR *GAY AND LESBIAN EDUCATORS: PERSONAL FREEDOMS, PUBLIC CONSTRAINTS*

Karen Harbeck has written a fascinating and dramatic chronicle of the history of gay and lesbian educators in America. *Gay and Lesbian Educators: Personal Freedoms, Public Constraints* unearths and eloquently portrays both the tragedies and the triumphs of teachers struggling to maintain their integrity in an oppressive climate. Through a style that is both forceful and compassionate, Harbeck sheds a powerful light on these moving accounts of the struggle for personal freedoms by gay and lesbian educators.

Gay and Lesbian Educators: Personal Freedoms, Public Constraints is a must for all teachers who value the ideals of intellectual honesty and diversity in the classroom. This book also is a must for the generation of lesbian and gay youth growing up in America today, youth who for too long have been denied the truth about the history of gay and lesbian people.

— **David LaFontaine** is Chairman of the Massachusetts Governor's Advisory Commission on Gay and Lesbian Youth, the first commission of its kind in the nation. Mr. LaFontaine is a member of the English Department faculty at Massasoit Community College, where he teaches composition and literature.

With the experience of a lawyer, the insight of an historian, the ability of a researcher, the energy and commitment of an activist, and the intelligence and compassion of an educator, Karen Harbeck takes us on an epic and emotional journey of the lesbian, gay, bisexual and transgender educator — from Puritan times into modern times, from coast to coast and crucial points in between. She eloquently documents shifts in the landscape between personal and academic freedom and the status quo, between progressive social change and outdated notions of the past, from a time when people were forced to remain in a stifling and dank classroom closet of denial, silence, and fear, then up through the shadows, and inevitably into the glow of the sun. This important work provides a context for current debates and fills a critical gap in our understanding of the place of GLBT educators in the educational, social, and legal history of our country.

— **Warren Blumenfeld** is an educator, and editor of the quarterly *Journal of Gay, Lesbian, and Bisexual Identity*, co-author of *Looking at Gay and Lesbian Life,* and editor of *Homophobia: How We All Pay the Price*.

For those of us parents that have been thrust unexpectedly into the gay rights movement because of our love for our children, *Gay and Lesbian Educators: Personal Freedoms, Public Constraints* is a must read. Dr. Harbeck gives an objective perspective on the experiences and courage of GLBT educators from Socrates to the recent Amendment 2 decision in Colorado. I look forward to the second volume of this work when our history will include the efforts of parents advocating in schools and demanding rights for our children and GLBT educators.

> — **Sally Morse** is Vice President of Chapter Development for Parents, Families/Friends of Lesbians and Gays (P-FLAG) and the Chair of the Regional Director's Council for P-FLAG nationally. She is a Mormon mother of a gay son.

With this new study, Karen Harbeck continues her groundbreaking contributions to the cause of equal rights in education. *Coming Out of the Classroom Closet* was the first major publication on the topic of gay and lesbian issues in education; *Gay and Lesbian Educators: Personal Freedoms, Public Constraints* is a worthy follow-up. All educators, regardless of sexual orientation, should listen carefully to her message. Until all adults in education feel empowered and free from arbitrary and unfair treatment, GLBT youth will continue as victims of intolerance and bigotry, with relatively few resources for assistance. On a larger scale, the entire society will continue to pay broad penalties as a result of political and cultural demagoguery and the perpetuation of archaic stereotypes and unforgivable discrimination.

> — **Boyd Bosma**, Ed.D, National Education Association Office of Human and Civil Rights, Senior Professional Associate (retired). Boyd Bosma, now retired, has served as coordinator for civil liberties and integrated education and as a senior professional associate for the National Education Association in Washington, D.C. for several decades. In this capacity, he made numerous contributions to the cause of human and civil rights of educators and students across the nation, including developing the first national training program on issues of gay and lesbian students, *Affording Equal Opportunity to Gay and Lesbian Students through Teaching and Counseling.*

GAY AND LESBIAN EDUCATORS:

PERSONAL FREEDOMS, PUBLIC CONSTRAINTS

Karen M. Harbeck, PhD, JD

Amethyst Press and Productions, Malden, Massachusetts

GAY AND LESBIAN EDUCATORS:
PERSONAL FREEDOMS, PUBLIC CONSTRAINTS

Copyright © 1997 by Karen M. Harbeck, PhD, JD.

Published by
Amethyst Press & Productions
P.O. 249-B, Malden, MA 02148 USA
Order Number: 0748

Printed in the United States of America
First printing, 1997.

Library of Congress Cataloging-in-Publication Data
Harbeck, Karen M., 1951-
Gay and Lesbian Educators: Personal Freedoms, Public Constraints by
Karen M. Harbeck. – 1st ed
p. 400 cm. xvii
Includes bibliographical references, appendices, historical timeline,
and index..
ISBN: 1-889393-48-7 (CH: acid free).
1. Homosexuality and education — United States. 2. Gays — educa-
tion — United States. 3. Gay educators—United States. 4. Lesbian
educators —United States. 5. Homosexuality—United States—
Employment. 6. Homosexuality—United States—Law and Policy.
I. Title
LC 96-85545 1997

Material quoted from article, "Should Gays Teach School," by Max
Rafferty reprinted with permission of the Phi Delta Kappan (Oct. 1977,
pp. 91-92).

Editorial assistance and computer production by Claire A. Murray of
Murray Learning Associates. Cover design by Diana C. Coe of k̄o
Design.

Dedicated with love and appreciation
to all my teachers, and
to one in particular,
Jodie Wigren

ALSO BY KAREN M. HARBECK AND FRIENDS

Harbeck, Series Editor, *Gay and Lesbian Youth: A Matter of Justice and Compassion*, Amethyst Press, 1997.

Harbeck, *Gay and Lesbian Youth: A Matter of Justice and Compassion: Vol. I, Advocacy*, Amethyst Press, 1997.

Harbeck and Al Ferreira, *Gay and Lesbian Youth: A Matter of Justice and Compassion: Vol. II, School-based Change*, Amethyst Press, 1997.

Harbeck, *Gay and Lesbian Youth: A Matter of Justice and Compassion: Vol. III, Law and Policy*, Amethyst Press, 1997.

Harbeck, Sally Morse, and Friends, *Gay and Lesbian Youth: A Matter of Justice and Compassion: Vol. IV, The Kansas Model*, Amethyst Press, 1997.

Harbeck and Carol C. Barnes, *Gay and Lesbian Youth: A Matter of Justice and Compassion: Vol. V, Counseling and Family Intervention*, Amethyst Press, 1997.

Harbeck, Editor and Senior Author, *Coming Out of the Classroom Closet: Gay and Lesbian Students, Teachers, and Curricula*, Haworth Press, 1992.

FOR MORE INFORMATION

Amethyst Press and Productions specializes in books, videotapes and audiotapes pertaining to GLBT concerns in education from preschool through graduate school levels and about both students and educators. We also develop educational materials for youth and adults interested in understanding legal issues in their everyday lives, such as discrimination, negligence, sexual harassment, contracts, and criminal law. Please call or write for our mailing information.

Karen M. Harbeck offers lectures, seminars, and program consultation concerning GLBT students and educators and school policy. She may be contacted at: Amethyst Press and Productions, P.O. 249-B, Malden, MA 02148 USA.

Amethyst Press and Productions materials are available at discount rates for bulk purchases for conference, fundraising, and educational purposes. Special books or book excerpts can be created to suit specific needs. Contact the publisher for additional information.

About the Author

Karen M. Harbeck, PhD, JD, is an educator, author, and attorney. She is recognized nationally as an expert on the concerns of gay, lesbian, bisexual, and transgender (GLBT) youth and the employment rights of GLBT educators. Dr. Harbeck earned her doctorate from Stanford University's Graduate School of Education with the completion of her two-volume study, *Personal Freedoms/Public Constraints: An Analysis of the Controversy Over the Employment Rights of Gay and Lesbian School Teachers*, which serves as the basis of this book. She also holds a doctorate in law from the University of Santa Clara and two master's degrees.

Dr. Harbeck is the senior author and editor of *Coming Out of the Classroom Closet: Gay and Lesbian Students, Teachers, and Curricula* (Haworth Press). She co-chairs both the Education and Higher Education committees of the Massachusetts Governor's Advisory Commission on Gay and Lesbian Youth.

While maintaining a private law practice focusing on the needs of GLBT clients, she teaches law and education at Boston College. Dr. Harbeck serves on the National Editorial Board of the *Journal of Homosexuality* and as its Book Review Editor for both law and education. She is Executive Director of the National Institute for Gay, Lesbian, Bisexual, and Transgender Concerns in Education, Inc., a non-profit organization committed to assisting individuals and institutions interested in the rights and needs of GLBT youth and educators. She lectures nationwide on GLBT issues and consults to schools, universities, unions, and numerous state departments of Education and Human Services.

ACKNOWLEDGEMENTS

I believe that the acknowledgement section may be the most frequently read and enjoyed aspect of any book. Certainly there are few opportunities in life to indelibly thank friends and family for the many gifts of themselves that they have shared with the author. Thus, as I revel in the completion of this endeavor, I, too, wish to pause and express my love and appreciation to the people who have made unique and very personal contributions to my life in general and this book in particular.

The staff of the following organizations were kind enough to permit me to use their files: The National Gay and Lesbian Task Force, Gay Rights Advocates, The Lesbian Herstory Archives, The American Civil Liberties Union, and The National Education Association. Also, dozens of attorneys across the country provided documents, news clippings, and personal accounts of their legal involvement in GLBT educator case law. My doctoral advisors at Stanford University, David Tyack, Estelle Freedman, and David Rosenhan, served as mentors for this endeavor, and Boyd Bosma, Warren Blumenfeld, Sally Morse, David Tyack, and David LaFontaine provided editorial comments.

Many of you have been special sources of support and strength for me. On days of discouragement and isolation, invariably I received a letter stating how much *Coming Out of the Classroom Closet* or some other effort has affected you. By sharing your stories you remind me of the importance of this work, and you keep me going. Thank you.

To my delight, my list of loving and supportive colleagues, friends, and family members is long. While it is impossible to thank you all here, I hope that each of you knows how much I have appreciated your unique contributions to this study and to my life. Remaining undaunted by the impossible, however, I wish to conclude this acknowledgment with an expression of gratitude to some very special contributors.

My mother, Clara R. Harbeck, was a school teacher and administrator for over 40 years. Her gifts to me were many, and include my love of learning and my admiration for those who can teach. I also wish to acknowledge the importance of the support of my sisters, Linda and Anita, and their children, Brian, Christine, Kevin, Elizabeth, David, Jennifer, and Robert. I know that my personal and academic activism has been difficult for them. I hope that some day, when my very special little nephews and nieces come to understand their Aunt Karen's work, they will realize the passion and necessity that drives me — and how much I treasure their love and respect.

Katy McNair-Collins, Chuck Collins, Al Ferreira, Joanne Kliejunas, Mary Kiely, Jeff Song, Mary Lou Balbaky Erickson, Christine Cronk, Ed Wilmsen, Janice Keller, Kay Rorer, Pat Ferguson, Carolyn Stack, Nancy Hendrie, Judy Jones, Diana Bailey, Anita Kunhardt, Liz Gregory, Pinky Hope, Lynne Tabor, Valerie Moore, Chuck Colbert, Barbara Toscano, Jim Duffy, Elaine Duffy, and Kim Crawford Harvie are special friends. Claire Murray and the late Grace Loerch brought their editing expertise and unwavering support of me to this endeavor and thereby improved it greatly.

Carol C. Barnes has shared her love, friendship, and wisdom with me for seven very special years. She has been the voice outside of me urging me to write — and to get to bed on time! Without her encouragement and our daily telephone calls, this project might never have been completed.

I also wish to acknowledge the love and support of Jodie Wigren. Her contributions to me and to this effort are many, and they have provided me with the stones to build a foundation of hope, acceptance, peace, and connection.

I work to help create schools that are safe and supportive of GLBT youth and educators. Thanks to the profound examples of Jodie and Carol, I also work to create schools that celebrate loving gay and lesbian parents and their remarkable children.

WARNING/DISCLAIMER

In light of the recent litigation filed against the authors of *The Courage to Heal: A Guide for Women Survivors of Child Sexual Abuse*, it has become apparent that if an author wants to provide information and inspiration to members of her communities, she also must shield herself from readers who have suffered from the hurts that we wish to alleviate. Unfortunately, all too often we end up harming each other rather than confronting the institutions and individuals that are the source of our pain.

The issues about the rights of GLBT educators are complicated. The personalities and actions of the teacher, administrators, students, the press, attorneys, and community members, as well as the state legal entitlements and the political climate all play a significant role in the outcome. I believe many more GLBT people and our heterosexual allies must come out of the closet so all of us can enjoy our civil rights and protect ourselves and GLBT youth from hardship. I also realize that some of us will suffer immediate reprisals for our acts of courage. Hopefully, our communities will rally to support these individuals so they do not have to face the hardship alone. May we all learn some lessons from this book and, thus, more successfully assert our civil and employment rights.

Nevertheless, please remember that, despite the legal implications of this study, neither the author nor the publisher can provide or are providing individuals or entities with legal or professional services. If you need such assistance, please seek the aid of reliable experts who are informed about the unique employment circumstances of GLBT people. Do not rely on this book for such professional advice.

I have made a tremendous effort in this volume to provide accuracy of information, the broadest range of materials, and cautious interpretations of our rights and strategies to take in relation to them. Mistakes can occur both in content and interpretation, so be forewarned. Also, as the 1994 national elections clearly demonstrated, the winds of political fortune and tolerance can change swiftly, so the timeliness of the material may be limited to the printing date.

Because of these complexities and local nuances, the author and the publisher hereby disclaim any liability or responsibility to any person, entity, or institution with respect to any loss (including but not limited to personal, professional, and/or financial), damage, or hardships caused or alleged to be caused, either directly or indirectly, by the information or material set forth in the volume. If you do not agree with this warning/disclaimer, and you are not prepared to abide by the terms of this disclaimer, please return this volume to the publisher for a full refund.

TABLE OF CONTENTS

PART IV: HISTORICAL CONTEXT OF HOMOSEXUALITY AND EDUCATION TO 1950

PART I

SIGNIFICANCE OF GAY AND LESBIAN ISSUES TO EDUCATION

In the End
We will conserve only what we love,
We will love only what we understand,
We will understand only what we are taught.

— *Baba Dioum*

INTRODUCTION

If anyone asked "Mary Kelly" why she loved to teach third grade, she answered that she enjoyed the innocence and joyful expressiveness of her young students.[1] Her image of elementary school students changed the day she learned that little eight-year-old "Michael" had slashed his wrists and was in critical condition at a local hospital. While Mary, Michael's parents, and school professionals tried to comprehend the reason for Michael's actions, no explanation was forthcoming. Years later, while participating in a required inservice training session on the needs of gay and lesbian youth, Mary was struck with the realization of the cause of Michael's pain.

October, 1993. Like so many gay and lesbian youth, "Paul" found the transition into high school to be an unbearable torture of verbal and physical abuse by his peers. Despite his constant wariness and planning, he was relentlessly harassed and threatened by gangs of youth as he moved from classroom to classroom. The worst acts of violence occurred in isolated long corridors and stairwells leading from the gym to the main classrooms, places he could not avoid. If Paul saw his harassers waiting for him, he sometimes took the long way around the building, but this often placed him in even more isolated and dangerous areas where no one would notice the violence against him.

While the abuse was frightening, Paul was equally upset by the name-calling and faggot jokes that occurred in front of his teachers, who did nothing to intervene. If Paul did defend himself, teachers sent him to the Principal's office as a disciplinary problem. Yet, no one ever disciplined the students who conducted a constant campaign of harassment and assault against him and his friends.

While Paul's experience of high school and junior high reflect the norm for most "out" or apparent gay, lesbian, bisexual, or transgender students, his courageous response to this situation was unique. Paul kept a detailed diary of his daily life at this large, progressive high school in a liberal East Coast community. After several weeks of documenting the harassment and abuse, Paul and his parents met with the Superintendent of Schools and presented him with Paul's diary. The Superintendent read the diary into the early hours of the morning. He returned to school and informed Paul that he was shocked and moved by Paul's account of a school that differed so completely with the Superintendent's own impressions. On that day, the Superintendent vowed that sexual orientation protections and educational efforts would be implemented extensively into all levels of education in the system.

As citizens and as educators, most of us believe in the principles of equal educational opportunity, safe schools, child centered-learning, and diversity. And yet, when gay, lesbian, bisexual, and transgender (GLBT) concerns in education surface, many educators and community members fall back on stereotypes and prejudices that blatantly compromise the very principles for which they labor.[2]

Supposedly, everyone in our society has a right to an education. In fact, we compel school attendance. Yet for GLBT youth our schools are often places of violence and humiliation. The message to young people is perfectly clear — it is open season on anyone who is perceived to be gay, lesbian, bisexual, or transgendered.

Not surprisingly, our research suggests that school environments that are hostile and insensitive to GLBT issues respond similarly to issues of race, gender, sexual harassment, physical disability, child abuse, and the wide variety of other differences and difficulties that young people face. In moments of distress and confusion, many students know that their education and health care providers cannot be trusted to respond in a compassionate, non-judgmental manner.

Despite this treatment, GLBT adolescents and young adults have finally begun to be visible in our social and educational institutions. Visible, most powerfully and poignantly, because of their suffering. For example, PROJECT 10 was started at Fairfax High School in Los Angeles in 1985 after the school conducted a mandatory examination of the dropout history of an African-American student. It turned out that "Chris" was gay, and he was homeless because his parents had rejected him. Chris had tried to enroll in five different high schools during the first few months of the academic year. He was driven away from each school by verbal and physical assaults from students and verbal harassment from teachers because of his sexual orientation.[3] Although unable to help Chris, Dr. Virginia Uribe and her colleagues at Fairfax High School began PROJECT 10 to offer support to GLBT youth and educate the entire school community about the high price of abuse and intolerance.

Recent research documents the consequences of this injustice. It demonstrates that GLBT youth face home and school environments that can lead to extraordinarily high rates of at-risk circumstances.[4] For example, 26 percent of GLBT youth face homelessness in early adolescence due to parental rejection and conflict.[5] In fact, studies suggest that GLBT youth may comprise one quarter to one half of the young people living on the streets in

America. Approximately 28 percent of GLBT youth drop out of school.[6] Other at-risk consequences of societal rejection include high rates of alcoholism,[7] child abuse by parents and peers, HIV/AIDS infection,[8] sexual promiscuity (in part for economic sustenance),[9] low self-esteem, feelings of isolation, thoughts of suicide, more violent suicide attempts, and more numerous actual suicides.[10]

The most ominous visibility of GLBT youth has come in some recent studies of suicides committed by adolescents and young adults (ages 15 to 24). The studies estimate that as much as 30 percent of the 5,000 youth suicides annually can be attributed to distress over issues of sexual orientation.[11] The problem with this statistical finding, however, is that those who use it often do not go one step further and clarify why GLBT youth face such a high risk of ending their lives. It is not *being* gay, lesbian, bisexual, or transgender that causes one to consider suicide. GLBT youth are not inherently more suicidal or depressed than their heterosexual peers. But living in our society is stressful, for both adults and youth. Facing society's hostility is stressful. Being in the closet and "living a lie" is stressful, as is coming out of the closet and facing the risks of job loss, rejection, child custody challenges, and violence. Being different or being a member of a minority group is stressful. Our three most important social institutions that are charged with the welfare of youth — family, school, and church/synagogue — are often sources of harm and rejection. In the face of these conditions, it is not difficult to imagine why some youth cope, some excel, and some succumb. More specifically, if you examine the general studies of youth at risk, you see that the youth most vulnerable to suicide are those who have no one to listen to them and provide them with guidance and support as they struggle to find themselves in this world. As Jacobs stated in his volume, *Adolescent Suicide*, "Adolescent suicide attempts result from the adolescent feeling that he has been subject to a progressive isolation from meaningful social relationships."[12]

Few youth populations fit this description as perfectly as GLBT youth. I am not arguing that GLBT oppression is worse than racism or other forms of oppression; merely that it is different. If I was an African-American child living in a white community, the odds are high that I would go home to parents who were themselves African-American. They would teach me to be proud of my race. They would educate me about my traditions and cultural uniqueness, and they would teach me to contextualize discrimination as a societal failure and not my personal failure. They would not reject me because I was Black — they would celebrate my being.

But for most GLBT youth, this relational mirroring and acceptance is not forthcoming. We grow up in shame, invisibility, and isolation in both social and self-knowledge (cognitive) contexts. Once we have the insight and courage to realize who we really are as human beings, we begin to live in fear of rejection by our parents and peers. Often we can pass as heterosexual, but the high cost of passing is shame. If we "come out of the closet" we may face discrimination and abuse. Thus we constantly struggle within the continuum of secrecy/self-denial and openness/rejection. In fact, a recent study of 194 GLBT youth under the age of 21 revealed that 42 percent had attempted suicide between 1 and 15 times. The mental health predictors of these suicide attempts were low self-esteem, substance abuse problems, relationship difficulties, and the negative responses of peers or family members to the disclosure of the young person's sexual orientation.[13]

The GLBT youth most targeted in schools are those who realize their sexual orientation at an early age and those who challenge traditional gender roles in our society. For example, more than four percent of children born annually display some sort of anatomical or genetic difference that challenges our dichotomous assumptions about maleness and femaleness. The students refer to these transgendered peers (transsexuals and transvestites) as "gender benders." While some school climates accept rather radical self-expression, more often those male students who act feminine and those female students who act masculine face extreme abuse that is compounded by the sexism prevalent in our society.[14] Since the negative responses of peers and family members have such a strong predictive relationship to GLBT youth suicide attempts, it is imperative that we train the entire student population of every school about sexual orientation issues and the dire power of the language of hate. In January of 1995, for example, I was in Nebraska lecturing on GLBT youth in education. The day before I arrived a young Hispanic boy had hanged himself after encountering unbearable hatred in an Omaha high school. In talking about EJ's suicide, several students involved in the harassment apparently stated, "I just called him faggot like I always did. What's his problem? I didn't know that he would go off and kill himself." But the abuse at school was much too high a burden for a young boy who was homeless because of parental rejection. Every child has a right to an education. Every child has a right to be treated with respect and dignity in our nation's schools. EJ is just one of the many victims who suffer in our schools because adults fail to act honorably to protect the welfare of all youth.

Our society has obligated the institutions of family, church/-synagogue, school, and government to nurture our youth. Yet these very institutions are active agents of harm to all youth by fostering environments of rejection, abuse, ignorance, and intolerance. While GLBT youth may comprise only 10 percent to 18 percent of the school population,[15] we may account for a significantly higher percentage of the young people in need of intervention services. Nevertheless, until recently, we have been an invisible minority population in our schools, as have the GLBT educators and heterosexual allies who must be able to advocate on our behalf.

As this book documents, because of the threat of loss of employment and community rejection, GLBT educators and heterosexual allies historically have been both unable and unwilling to assert their own rights and to protect the welfare of their young charges. Even today, in this time of greater public acceptance, educators often fail to respond.

Thanks to the recent research by James T. Sears, we now know something about educators' responses to GLBT issues in education.[16] In his survey sample of teachers and school guidance counselors, many acknowledged that they had GLBT youth in their classrooms. They also knew that their national unions, professional licensing requirements, and even some school districts mandated they serve the needs of this population. When asked if they did serve these students' needs, the majority of the teachers and counselors said, "No." The three reasons given are of special importance to this book. The first was that they had not been provided with an adequate education by their professional training programs.[17] The second was that they had feelings of homophobia, so they did not know how to handle the issue.[18] The third and most common reason for failing to assist GLBT youth was fear that their colleagues would think that they were gay or lesbian, which might compromise their own reputations and employment.

This is one educational issue in which the children are leading the adults. Young people are taking the risks of honestly sharing who they are and of raising community awareness of sexual orientation concerns. Meanwhile, adults charged with their welfare often stand by in silence, ignorance, and fear. One reason for this age-related response disparity may be the changing sexual mores of our society. Issues of sex and sexuality are much more prevalent in schools and other arenas of young adults' lives today, while the older generations cling to images of discretion, silence, and restraint. These major lifestyle changes are radically affecting the educational context. For example, studies suggest that approximately 10 years ago adults recognized their sexual orientation as gay or lesbian between the average ages of 26 and 28.[19] Young people today are coming out at a much younger age, often between 15 and 17, while still in school.[20] Thus, issues that might have been ignored a decade ago now are actively played out within the school context. Despite this generational complication, then, all adults must obtain the knowledge that will compel them to act responsibly towards all students so the principles of diversity, equality, nonviolence, and individual educational excellence can flourish.

Despite the compelling circumstances of GLBT youth that demand the American educational systems address their concerns, the battle wages on. In March of 1994, Congress passed the Goals

2000 education reform program that contains a major commitment to the creation of safe schools. Numerous private and federal studies demonstrate that one of the most victimized populations in American schools is GLBT youth.

In May of 1994, for example, when I lectured to the U.S. Dept. of Education, Office of Civil Rights, staff members realized that many of the results of their recent federal study on sexual harassment in schools pointed to issues of sexual orientation discrimination as several of the worst incidences of sexual harassment. Since they had been unaware of GLBT concerns in education, these findings were not highlighted in the results. A more overt form of policy failures occurred when, in August of 1994, the U.S. Senate passed the Elementary and Secondary Education Act by a 94 to 6 vote. This Act included an amendment, advanced by Conservative Senator Jesse Helms (R–NC), demanding that federal monies be prohibited from schools that teach acceptance of homosexuality. The vote to retain the specific language of the Helms Amendment was 63 to 36, however, Senator Edward Kennedy (D–MA) included a rider that permitted a rewording of the amendment in the final legislation. The rewording prohibited the use of federal dollars from programs that "promote or encourage sexual activity" of any kind, whether heterosexual or homosexual.

Chapter Conclusion

Until adults feel empowered to openly discuss these issues and take constructive action, GLBT youth will continue to be victims of bigotry, ignorance, and violence. Resources to create truly equitable educational institutions will remain scarce, as will the mechanisms for helpful intervention. Thus, an accurate assessment of the rights of GLBT educators and our heterosexual allies is critically important. The well-being of tens of thousands of people is at stake — not just GLBT youth but heterosexual youth with GLBT family members, GLBT parents, GLBT educators, and all other youth and adult members of our communities. Prejudice, hatred, ignorance, and violence hurt us all, especially if they occur in our major social institutions of family, school, and church. As my colleague, Al Ferreira, often says, "You can measure the health of an institution by how it protects its most vulnerable members."

As you join me in this exploration of the history of the rights of GLBT educators, may I provide you with a quote from Plato (427 B.C.) that places this debate in the continuum of the struggle for full social acceptance for gay, lesbian, bisexual and transgender individuals:

> Wherever it has been established that it is shameful to be involved in homosexual relationships, this is due to evil on the part of legislators, to despotism on the part of the rulers, and to cowardice on the part of the governed.

Any truth creates a scandal.

— *Marguerite Yourcenar*

CHAPTER 1

GLBT EDUCATORS

AN OVERVIEW

April, 1992. "Carol Miller" teaches sociology and coaches women's sports at a high school in Montgomery County, Maryland. As the reader will learn in later chapters, Montgomery County was the setting for a prominent 1973 gay teacher dismissal case, <u>Acanfora v. Board of Education of Montgomery County</u>.[1] Although the judge in the case stated that Montgomery County school officials' actions were unconstitutional, they still brag that they successfully removed a gay educator and could do it again if necessary.

One day, the school psychologist approached Carol with her concern about two male students who seemed suicidal over sexual orientation concerns and peer harassment. The psychologist admitted she had no idea how to help these students and that the situation was serious. Carol decided that something needed to be done. She approached the school principal and received approval to include a lesson on sexual orientation in her curriculum. The lesson would start by showing the film, *The Life and Times of Harvey Milk*, followed by two speakers from the local gay/lesbian speakers bureau.

In response to this curriculum inclusion, Carol was targeted by Concerned Women of America, Inc., an ultra-conservative organization with national offices located nearby in the Washington, D.C., beltway. Concerned Women of America boasts a membership of over 600,000 individuals and support from Ronald Reagan, George Bush, and Jack Kemp. Although no member of Concerned Women had a student in Carol's class, they filed grievances with the Montgomery County School Board and fought to have Carol Miller fired. During a hearing, Concerned Women leaders were represented by two attorneys, while Carol had none. They questioned her about her fitness to teach and her personal life. One question was, "What kind of a person could locate gay/lesbian speakers to come into her school?" Another was, "What kind of person knows people who have died of AIDS?" At the time, Carol was overwhelmed and offered no reply. In retrospect she states, "What kind of educator is not resourceful enough to develop her curriculum?" and, "What kind of individual has not been touched by the AIDS crisis?"

Privately, Carol's superiors offered her an arrangement to protect her job if she would say she had not obtained proper approval for every aspect of her curriculum beforehand — something rarely required of her colleagues and almost completely adhered to in this situation. In return, to appease Concerned Women of America, the administrators agreed to place a letter of reprimand in her file and not to terminate her tenured employment status. Since that resolution, Concerned Women of America closely monitored Carol's classroom, despite having no legal basis for their presence in the school. Carol experienced depression, upset at the lack of support afforded her, and the dissolution of her primary relationship.

Recent update: One year later, after attending a lecture I gave on the rights of GLBT educators, Carol Miller came out to her students and colleagues at work. Everyone has been extremely supportive. Some of her colleagues expressed dismay that they had not realized the significance of the attack on her employment status the year before. They said had they known she was a lesbian they would have protected her. Carol's personal life has improved. While Concerned Women of America remains active on a national level, its presence in Carol's school has dwindled.

Despite all of the pressing social, political, and economic issues before the voting public in the 1992 national elections, the issue of gay and lesbian rights was the political "hot button." From the Republican National Convention to the Congressional hearings on gays and lesbians in the military, polar views have been presented about homosexuality. One side argues that tolerance for homosexuality is destroying our families and social fabric. The other side argues that providing anti-discrimination protections for gays and lesbians is the natural outgrowth of a commitment to civil rights and personal privacy.

Challenging the traditional hierarchy of the American military system and demanding equal employment rights for GLBT people were controversial actions. We probably have experienced only the tip of the iceberg in these debates. The State Supreme Court of Hawaii seems poised to grant same-sex marital rights equivalent to those granted to heterosexuals. This extension of full marital rights to all citizens was previously almost unimaginable and would create a ripple effect of national debate. As this book goes to press, the U.S. House of Representatives has voted to ban same-sex marriages. President Clinton and Republican presidential candidate Bob Dole have both announced that they would support the conservative's federal "Defense of Marriage Act" if it passes in the Senate. Such a law would ban federal marital entitlements although, theoretically, the other 49 states could respond by establishing their own policies on this issue in light of the full faith and credit concept of the United States Constitution. Under U.S. constitutional law, states traditionally recognize other states' actions. Hawaii's same-sex marriages might then be legally recognized in other jurisdictions, just as recent recognition of same-sex marriages in Denmark,

Greenland, Norway, Sweden and Iceland has forced their political neighbors to struggle to define the rights of GLBT people in nearby countries. Thus, if the controversies have been intense and emotional before now, the upcoming debates conceivably will be transformational on both individual and societal levels.

While real issues must be addressed in these debates, the controversy also is being used to fuel public sentiment for political purposes. For example, the controversy over gays and lesbians in the military is a frequent focus for newspaper and talk show discussion. Conservative leadership has expressed new delight in exploiting the topic to rebuild its power base. As noted recently by William Schneider, analyst at Cable News Network and the American Enterprise Institute, gays and taxes are "two new hot button issues, and gays is the hotter because so far we haven't seen people erupt over the proposed tax increases."

Note that I said, "new delight in exploiting the topic to rebuild its power base." As this book reveals, Conservative leadership has actively promoted hostility towards gays and lesbians since the late 1970s. Then, Anita Bryant demonstrated that targeting gays and lesbians as scapegoats of society's ills translated into significant tax-free donations and increased membership in Far Right organizations. In fact, former California State Senator John Briggs stated he learned this from the Anita Bryant Dade County, Florida, crusade. After he personally observed the crusade, he calculated that some radical action against homosexuals, coupled with strong support for the death penalty, would be the political platform to assure him the Governorship of California after Ronald Reagan left office.[2] Briggs decided upon a massive referendum campaign against educators who discussed topics pertaining to homosexuality in California public schools. The referendum campaign became known as Proposition 6 in the 1978 elections. In a personal interview in 1989, John Briggs informed me that he did not know any homosexuals before launching the Proposition 6 Campaign, nor had he encountered stories about teachers engaging in inappropriate behavior related to sexual orientation. His sole basis for opposition was the knowledge that this issue upset some people so intensely that it would translate into votes and campaign contributions.

Significance

Presently, there are approximately 2,787,000 teachers employed in the United States in public and private elementary and secondary educational settings.[3] Using Kinsey's outdated but often-quoted estimate of 10 percent, there are at least 278,700 GLBT educators currently employed in schools around the nation — a number equal to the entire teaching staff of the states of California and Washington combined. Another perspective on this figure is that the average number of teachers per school is 25.5, thus it is statistically probable there are two or more GLBT educators in every school in the nation.[4] In fact, the numbers may be much higher if one considers two important facts. The lesbian and gay rights movement occurred after the original 1948 estimate of the homosexual population, so numbers of GLBT people may be higher. Similarly, teaching is an occupation that historically has attracted single women and non-traditional men, thus self-selecting in a manner that encourages higher-than-expected numbers of GLBT people.

For those who find these numbers shocking, note that GLBT teachers have been a feature of the landscape of most educational settings throughout American history. Very little information is available, however, concerning the teachers who quietly resigned or quickly left town in the face of accusations concerning their sexual orientation. Throughout American history, the potential consequences of GLBT teachers challenging the system alone were extreme. Homosexuals have faced social pressures ranging from subtle expectations to act like heterosexuals to open hostility and overt persecution.[5] Alternately in history, homosexuality has been perceived as a sin, a mental disorder, and/or a criminal activity.[6] Numerous social and legal restrictions have been placed upon the expression of homosexual behavior. Sometimes the consequences of infractions have been as severe as execution or imprisonment.

Society has been confronted with the issue of the homosexual school teacher since at least 450 B.C., when the most famous male homosexual educators, Socrates and Plato, educated Greek youth. Now, 25 centuries later, Americans are debating this issue with a ferocity previously reserved for issues of race relations and abortion. Claiming great urgency, several state and local jurisdictions in the United States of America have declared it necessary to establish policies to deal with this long-standing social phenomenon. Why communities attempt to enact these policies for the first time is a major focus of this book.

Over the past 20 years, for example, communities have debated legislation that would prohibit lesbians and gay men from teaching school. They also have attempted to prohibit school-based discussions concerning sexual orientation. Over that same period, national professional unions have called for GLBT employment protections and domestic partner benefits. Similarly, the District of Columbia and nine states (Wisconsin, Massachusetts, Vermont, New Jersey, Hawaii, California, Connecticut, Minnesota, and Rhode Island) have enacted strong sexual orientation anti-discrimination statutes in employment and public accommodations. Furthermore, the states of Wisconsin, Massachusetts, Vermont, Florida, and Washington have moved to protect the rights of GLBT youth in educational settings. In fact, due in part to the efforts of this author, as of October 1, 1994, all higher education institutions in Massachusetts that conduct certification programs for teachers, administrators, school guidance counselors, and school psychologists must provide training about the needs of GLBT youth.[7] Additionally, on October 14, 1994, the Massachusetts State Board of Education presented a referendum to the bylaws of the National Association of State Boards of Education, amending the anti-discrimination protections for all students in all 50 states to include sexual orientation. By a two-thirds majority, the 50 State Boards of Education voted that:

> State boards should provide leadership in eliminating the stereotypes and discrimination on the basis of sex, age, disability, race, religion, *sexual orientation*, ethnic background or national origin in curriculum materials, counseling methods and other education processes.

The State of Georgia seconded the motion, and it passed by much more than the 51 percent vote needed when liberal states were joined by "yes" votes from the states of Georgia, Texas, Oklahoma, Mississippi, Arkansas, and Arizona. This resolution mirrors similar protections recently enacted by the National School Board Association, which represents 17,000 local school boards nationwide. Thus, while the late-1994 political tide favored conservative beliefs, the late-1994 educational tide favored extensive protections for GLBT youth and the adults who assist them.

CHANGING TRADITIONAL VALUES

Historically, American educational institutions have been used to advance majority views. Because their purposes have been in concert, society usually has permitted the educational system to regulate itself. Political and judicial leaders have deferred to school administrators in most matters of governance, policy, educational content, and personnel selection. At certain times of intense social conflict, however, these internal features of control within the school system are challenged. An appeal is made to other social institutions, such as the legal or political systems, for guidance and resolution.

Over the past few decades our society has experienced radical social and technological change. New values and beliefs have been asserted about individual freedom, minority rights, human relationships, and global involvement. Schools are a major arena of social conflict: one group asserts traditional values, and the other demands that children be prepared for changes in technology, society, and the environment. One major issue that exemplifies this conflict within the educational system is the employment controversy over GLBT school teachers. Through an analysis of case law, administrative decisions, political action, personal interviews, and community commentary, this book reveals the gradual weakening of consensus in the educational system. The traditional powers of school administrators have been challenged. Both sides of the conflict have resorted to the legal and political arenas for additional power to establish their perspectives as the social norm. Thus, this book is also a study of the role of the American legal system as a mechanism for balancing the competing rights of groups and individuals.

Since the late 1800s, there has been a growing sense of personal, political, and collective identity within the gay and lesbian population.[8] But this population remained relatively hidden from the mainstream of society until the late 1960s. The case law on homosexual school teachers from the 1950s and 1960s reveals evidence of these covert subcultures. It also reveals the consequences of exposure. In the environment of greater personal freedom over the past few decades, however, lesbians and gay men have asserted their right to personal liberties and freedom from the sanctions of the heterosexual majority.

The teaching profession has experienced a similar transformation regarding personal freedoms. Traditionally, the lifestyle of educators also was curtailed severely by community attitudes and sanctions. Teachers were viewed as role models for impressionable youth and as community employees. As such, they faced a wide variety of forbidden behaviors such as prohibitions on "smoking, drinking, dancing, theatre going, loitering downtown in ice cream stores, automobile rides on weekday nights, and leaving town without permission of the chairman of the school board."[9] Other personal liberties relating to free speech, political involvement, dating, marriage, sex, and pregnancy also have been regulated at various times. In the past few decades, teachers have challenged the community's right to control free speech, political association, personal appearance, dress codes, and marital status. This willingness by teachers to assert that they have rights is further evidence of recently liberalized social, educational, political, legal, and legislative arenas where issues of greater personal freedoms are debated. This teacher advocacy, when combined with the greater visibility, militancy, and collective action of lesbians and gay men, has pushed the issue of personal freedom to the very edge of American social tolerance, as the debate over the employment of gay and lesbians as school teachers and university professors reveals.

Much of this increase in personal freedom can be attributed to the resurgence of civil libertarian ideals in this country during the 1960s and 1970s. Quite probably, the Vietnam War protest acted as a catalyst for individuals asserting their opposition to government opinion and intrusion. The 1960s were a time of individual militancy and group affiliation. The intent was to counter, more effectively, the powers of the status quo, whether social, political, governmental, educational, or parental. In unprecedented numbers, individuals asserted their rights through personal, administrative, and legal challenges. They were assisted in the cost of these struggles by an emergent group of politicized legal aid organizations and special interest groups. The individual rights of teachers were successfully expanded during this period through the efforts of such groups as the National Education Association (NEA), the American Federation of Teachers (AFT), and the American Civil Liberties Union (ACLU). The ACLU also assisted the gay and lesbian rights movement, as did The National Gay and Lesbian Task Force (NGTLF), Gay Rights Advocates (GRA), and The Lesbian Rights Project.[10]

Since the late 1970s, however, this country has undergone a reassertion of more traditional values and beliefs concerning the regulatory powers of the state, the primacy of the family, and the subjugation of personal freedoms for the public good. To counter the emergent acceptability of liberal attitudes and perspectives, the New Right has demanded a return to more traditional American values. Currently, very divergent perspectives are struggling for public acceptance and social dominance. Both sides are appealing to the public. And, both sides are appealing to our institutions of social influence and control, such as the legal system, educational system, the media, governmental bodies, and religious organizations. The employment of gays and lesbians as school teachers has become an important debate in the public press and in these institutions. In fact, one Conservative leader called the homosexual teacher controversy the "hottest social issue since Reconstruction."[11] Each side seeks to legitimize and strengthen its influence over public sentiment. The legally complex, highly emotional issues relating to the employment of gays and lesbians as school teachers have proven to be a volatile battleground.

BATTLE LINES

On January 14, 1985, the United States Supreme Court heard oral arguments in the case of The National Gay Task Force v. The Board of Education of the City of Oklahoma City, State of Oklahoma.[12] This case challenged a 1978 law enacted by the Oklahoma Legislature concerning the State's alleged right to dismiss or refuse employment to any public school teacher, teacher's aide, or student teacher who engaged in "public homosexual conduct or activity" which might come to the attention of school children or school employees. Although the exact meaning and breadth of the statute was under debate, the State of Oklahoma's position was that the statute pertained to both public and private homosexual activity and to any conduct that "advocates, solicits, imposes, encourages, or promotes public or private homosexual activity."[13]

Those who favored legislation prohibiting homosexual conduct or activity by school teachers based their case on majority rule, moral codes, the public good, and a state's right to regulate behavior and to provide public education. Those who opposed legislation like that adopted in Oklahoma based their arguments on First Amendment freedoms of speech and association, individual civil liberationist perspectives, minority rights, privacy rights, and other federal and state Constitutional freedoms.

The emotionally intense and legally complex battle lines were drawn. Neither perspective held a clear advantage, as evidenced by the Supreme Court's 4 to 4 decision in NGTF v. Oklahoma, announced on March 26, 1985, during the illness of Justice Powell.[14] Furthermore, controversies over the dismissal of teachers for being homosexual and/or bisexual are gaining national attention as school boards and community members assert their views on what is appropriate behavior for local school teachers.

The 1989 release of the U.S. Department of Health and Human Services, "Report of the Secretary's Task Force on Youth Suicide," demonstrated the high cost of society's prejudice against GLBT people. Teen suicide has increased 200 percent since 1950, while adult suicide rates increased only 20 percent during this same period.[15] Between 1980 and 1992, the suicide rate of children between the ages of 10 and 14 has risen 120 percent.[16] Educators who believe in equal educational opportunity, safe schools, and the value of every child have been moved to respond to the needs of GLBT youth. As mentioned earlier, for example, boards of education on local and state levels are calling for the inclusion of sexual orientation in anti-discrimination policies to protect GLBT youth. Consequently, the employment rights of GLBT educators and heterosexual allies are gaining strength so these adults can fulfill their professional responsibilities without fear of reprisals.

THE MYTH OF POWERLESSNESS

After researching the history of GLBT individuals in American education for 20 years, I believe our nation has undergone a quiet revolution regarding the personal freedoms and professional entitlements that support openly GLBT school teachers and university professors who wish to remain in their profession. For the most part, I believe that since 1974 anyone with tenure has had the legal and social clout to be "out of the closet" and a public school educator, university faculty member, or heterosexual ally anywhere in America. The outcome of GLBT teacher dismissal cases today is based upon some very specific situational factors, such as tenure status, age of the students, how the information is revealed, and how the educator responds to any threat of dismissal. These factors, rather than any accurately perceived right to terminate employment based upon one's sexual orientation, determine the outcome. The controversy has changed, and our rights have been significantly enhanced. However, many GLBT educators and heterosexual allies remain convinced that if they become visible or act on behalf of GLBT youth their own employment will be compromised.

The information in this book provides insights into the process of successfully coming out of the closet as a GLBT educator or heterosexual ally. Moreover, it demonstrates that, at times, GLBT

23

educators have been on the forefront of the struggle for employment entitlements and personal freedoms for all workers. For example, the GLBT Florida dismissal cases in the 1950s successfully asserted the due process rights of all Florida educators and state employees.[17] Similarly, the 1969 landmark decision by the California State Supreme Court in Morrison v. State Board of Education established principles that still are asserted in wrongful dismissal cases nation-wide.[18] Thanks to the Morrison decision, employers must demonstrate a link between inappropriate personal conduct and its negative impact upon one's job responsibilities for dismissal to be legal. In reclaiming our history, we strengthen the ties that exist between all educators and other minority groups that have been disesteemed in our society. Also, since so few school administrators are familiar with legal principles, by reclaiming our past we educate a large population of individuals who are trying to "do the right thing." As the saying goes, "large scale change occurs when a lot of people change just a little." As educators, we have the tools to create that change with respect to GLBT concerns in education, although more often than not we feel helpless in the face of traditional public constraints.

Since 1974, the vast majority of our nation's teachers have enjoyed very strong employment protections. At that time, a variety of legal and social changes began to occur, such as the decriminalization of sex between consenting adults, a heightened awareness of minority rights, the formation of GLBT political action groups, and the enactment of formal mandates to provide union assistance. However, our isolation and invisibility have helped perpetuate myths that have prevented us from knowing that we have significantly greater employment entitlements. This isolation and invisibility have helped maintain the erroneous belief system of our nation's school administrators concerning the nature of sexual orientation and their supposed right to restrict and/or terminate the employment of GLBT adults who work with youth.

The specific processes for asserting these rights are of critical importance and will be discussed in the final chapters of a second volume. In general, these controversies occur in this context of mutual misinformation. A small, vocal minority from the community mobilizes in opposition to the teacher's sexual orientation. The school administrator anticipates controversy and unpleasantness and, through lack of information and training, mishandles the situation. Instead of acting in a legal and union-mandated manner, the administrator pressures the educator to remain silent or resign — or face public scrutiny. Because of misinformation and our internalized homophobia, many educators do resign.[19] This action then perpetuates the myth that administrators can dismiss employees because of their sexual orientation.

Administrators often believe this is their right. GLBT educators often believe this is their fate. But according to my research, if the educator can mobilize his or her self-worth and effectively assert his or her entitlements, the controversy dissipates. In fact, many GLBT educators find they are viewed as a unique resource if their school district starts to address the needs of GLBT youth. It is better for all parties if these controversies are resolved quickly through education and intervention. If the controversy results in litigation, the teacher may or may not retain his or her teaching position. He or she will very likely receive a monetary settlement at the expense of the local school community and its malpractice carrier, however, and this result will probably be suppressed at the school district's demand. Thus, everyone is left with impressions predicated on the initial aspects of the case rather than its ultimate resolution.

I am not saying that litigation is positive or the solution to employment discrimination involving GLBT educators. On the contrary, it is expensive, prolonged, and frustrating even if you win. My point is, we hear very little about successful acts of courage and education that lead to full acceptance of a GLBT educator by administrators, students, and parents in any given community. Furthermore, when the GLBT educator does win a lawsuit, there is usually a gag order in the settlement agreement. Thus, GLBT educators remain unaware of the successful assertion of our employment entitlements, and administrators remain unaware of their potential liability for acts of discrimination based upon sexual orientation. Compounding this picture is the media. Both the mainstream and GLBT presses seem much more likely to report sensationalism and conflict than to report positive resolution and harmony.

RESEARCH METHODOLOGY

In order to understand more fully the controversy over the employment of gay men and lesbians as school teachers and university professors, it is useful, if not imperative, to draw on interdisciplinary perspectives. Legal theory, historical analysis, and political analysis, when combined with legal case studies concerning GLBT educators, offer a valuable framework for interpreting the larger social issues of attitudinal change, social regulation, social conflict, and personal freedom in our society. They also provide insight into the role of the American legal system as a fulcrum for balancing the competing rights and interests of groups and individuals.

I researched the case law concerning GLBT educators by using LEXIS, a comprehensive computer search procedure. The search methodology highlighted appellate court decisions throughout the United States that contained the delineated key words of "homosexual," "lesbian," and/or "gay" in proximity with the words "teacher," "education," "school employee," "university," "college," or "school."[20] The LEXIS process searched cases for the United States Supreme Court from 1789 to the present. On a state level the capability varied, but I retrieved cases dating from the late 1800s to the present from all 50 states. I undertook four LEXIS searches, one each in 1981, 1986, 1990, and 1995. This was done because the LEXIS file expanded between 1981 and 1995 to include the very early cases as well as the most recent cases. Through attorney referrals, newspaper articles, and law review articles on employment discrimination against gays and lesbians, I found instances of local-level Superior and District court legal action that were not within the LEXIS database.

Overall, I found more than 200 cases to consider. By reviewing each case in the appropriate federal or state reporter, I determined its relevance to this study. Many cases could be dropped from the study because they merely referenced a prior relevant case that involved a gay or lesbian educator. Ultimately, 39 cases (39 to 1987, which encompasses the years discussed in the book) seemed appropriate, and I researched the litigation history of each.[21] After finding the case opinions, I located the attorneys involved through current and earlier volumes of the professional directory, Martindale-Hubbell.[22] I asked each attorney to send copies of the briefs filed and any other material that was not privileged communication between attorney and client. In this manner, thousands of pages of documents pertaining to GLBT educators were gathered, including press releases, newspaper articles, trial transcripts, court evidence, and expert testimony. The attorneys also answered questions about their involvement in the case, special interest group participation, case publicity, case outcome, and client circumstances. Typically, the earlier cases from the 1950s were the most difficult to research. If the attorney was located, he or she often could not remember the case details, and the files were destroyed after so many decades of inactive status.

The additional materials sent by the attorneys provided social, political, and historical information which augmented the legal details. In fact, one outcome of this study was the realization that an analysis based solely on published court opinions was biased in favor of the litigant who represented traditional interests at the expense of understanding the motivations of the minority litigant and the actual resolution of the dispute. For example, in the case of <u>Sarac v. State Board of Education</u> as reported in the court opinions, the circumstances of Sarac's arrest left little doubt about his criminal homosexual activity.[23] In contrast to this published legal account, Sarac's attorney expressed frustration that judicial prejudice against homosexuals prohibited him from challenging the details of the arrest that were the keystone to Sarac's dismissal from teaching. By broadening the sources of information on this emotionally-laden controversy, I could highlight the motivations, constraints, achievements, and defeats of the minority litigant. Thus, the information gathered from these different sources about each dismissal incident is combined in a manner that provides a more accurate look at the situation than is actually set forth in the published legal opinions. Since attorneys rely on those legal opinions when they prepare subsequent similar case briefs, minority litigants continue to be hampered in their efforts to assert their entitlements. When one brings alternative resources and an interdisciplinary perspective to bear on the matter, however, they reveal new avenues of argument and recourse.

In addition to attorneys, I asked numerous directors of relevant state and national organizations to provide information on their group's policy with respect to gay and lesbian educator employment rights. The NEA, several state education associations, the AFT, GRA, NGLTF, and the ACLU were all surveyed in this manner.

While researching the case law, I also considered local and state legislative actions concerning GLBT educators. I gathered all available position papers, public statements, press releases, newspaper articles, campaign literature, books, and legislative documentation. Three major political campaigns were my primary focus: Anita Bryant's "Save Our Children" campaign in Florida (1977), California's Proposition 6 Initiative (1978), and the Oklahoma State law (1978-1985) that prohibited homosexual conduct, activity, or advocacy by school employees. Overall, each of these movements arose from different influences and achieved varying results. Thus, an assessment of their purposes, strengths, weaknesses, and societal appeal broadened the assessment of ongoing changes in the social context relevant to the employment of homosexuals as school teachers and university professors. When possible, I interviewed the leaders of these campaigns. Anita Bryant, for example, declined to be interviewed, while California State Senator John Briggs spent three hours with me explaining his views on prohibiting GLBT people from teaching.

OVERVIEW OF CHAPTERS

When people think of the controversy over the employment of GLBT people as educators, the name "Anita Bryant" quickly emerges as a major reference point. Chapter Two describes this backlash against GLBT rights that occurred on a local level during 1977 and 1978. An emergent conservative political coalition, initially led by former Miss America finalist Anita Bryant, was very successful in Dade County, Florida; Eugene, Oregon; St. Paul, Minnesota; and Wichita, Kansas. In light of the coalitions' resounding success on a local level, they appealed to voters in California (Chapter Three) and Oklahoma (Chapter Four) to prevent the hiring and retention of GLBT school teachers and individuals who expressed support for homosexuality. In California, these referendum efforts failed. In Oklahoma, however, such a bill unanimously passed the House and Senate in 1978. It remained a state law until 1985, when the U.S. Supreme Court narrowly affirmed a lower court ruling that the statute, as written, was unconstitutional.

Chapter Two through Chapter Four establish the nature of the contemporary debate over the employment of GLBT people as university professors and school teachers. Chapter Five places these arguments within the historical context of constraints placed upon the lives of teachers in general and within the dismissal process on grounds of immorality. Chapter Six offers both a legal and sociological introduction to the social issues that have been used by the majority to place restrictions on the freedoms of the minority GLBT population. During the 1960s and 1970s, American society experienced new perspectives on personal freedom and minority rights. The Sexual Revolution, for example, gradually changed the regulatory aspects of private, consensual sexual activity. Similarly, out of the success of the Civil Rights Movement, gays and lesbians began to forge a new political identity that also demanded equality in our society.

Chapter Seven explores the nexus between homosexual educators and education, both crossculturally and in American history from the Colonial period to the 1940s. Because of the difficulties inherent in conducting historical research on a topic that, if

29

revealed, would lead to job termination, the material in Chapter Seven stands as an initial effort that, hopefully, will be expanded through additional research in the not-too-distant future.

Chapter Eight builds upon this legal and historical material and adds early litigation details to discuss the status of GLBT educators from the early 1950s to 1969. I selected this period because it provided a cohesive history of gay and lesbian school teacher cases that involved criminal sexual conduct and societal consensus about the evils of homosexuality. The typical case from this period concerned the retention of a male teacher who had been arrested for soliciting sex in a public men's room. The charges would be dropped because of criminal procedure protections, but the individual faced independent consideration of his school employment status. Local law and community values were the determinants of these cases, as expressed by the decision-making power of school authorities. The criminal behavior, combined with general societal abhorrence at the idea of a homosexual teaching school children, led to the predictable outcome of teacher dismissal.

Chapter Nine presents the litigation from 1969 to 1973. During this short period some significant changes were evident in the legal and social attitudes towards homosexuality. The California Supreme Court's decision in Morrison v. State Board of Education called for an extensive analysis of the individual's behavior in relation to his or her job responsibilities before employment dismissal was possible.[24] Furthermore, the Court announced that the status of being a homosexual was insufficient grounds for dismissal unless coupled with some related misbehavior. Despite this major advance in individual and GLBT employment rights, many courts managed to avoid the Morrison criteria because the plaintiffs still were brought into the dispute through arrests for criminal sexual activity.

Chapter Ten discusses the case law from 1973 to 1977. This was a time in which the effects of the Sexual Revolution and the legal emphasis on personal freedom, privacy, and minority rights combined with the established political effectiveness of the lesbian and gay rights movement to alter the character of GLBT educator case law. In this period, the typical case involved a male or female teacher who was exposed as a homosexual without criminal behavior, admitted his or her sexual orientation, and challenged the school system's right to abridge his/her employment freedoms solely on the basis of being gay or lesbian. Litigants during this period appealed to the Federal courts and asserted that their civil rights and constitutional freedoms were being denied through local prejudice. These lesbian and gay male educators enjoyed the financial and emotional support of special interest groups that championed GLBT rights and/or the rights of educators to personal freedoms. Also, by 1973 several states had liberalized their laws concerning sex between consenting adults. Thus, the criminal statutes that previously served as the standard for determining whether the immoral conduct was sufficient for dismissal often were no longer available to local school authorities in GLBT educator cases. The case law demonstrated growing support for the GLBT educator, although case outcomes were not consistent. There were two striking alternative pieces of evidence of this gradual social acceptance during this time. First were the municipal and school board anti-discrimination ordinances passed in support of homosexuals in general and gay and lesbian educators in particular. Second were the national mandates to protect the employment rights of GLBT educators that were passed in 1974 by the NEA. With the backing of this powerful educational union, the debate over the employment rights of GLBT educators was radically transformed. Traditionally, a powerful school board and its retained counsel dictated the terms of dismissal to a lone GLBT educator who probably could not afford an attorney since he or she was losing his or her job. With national, state, and local union support and the free legal counsel they provided, the battle over GLBT employment rights was equalized. Many school districts found it less expensive to ignore the issue than to face the potentially financially-crippling effects of extensive litigation.

By the end of Chapter Ten, the advancements made by GLBT educators help to explain the intense backlash that emerged in the Anita Bryant, Dade County, Florida campaign discussed in

Chapter Two. Emergent ideas of minority rights caused many policy-makers to assume that the natural extension of rights would include GLBT people. National unions and local school boards alike drafted new anti-discrimination policies that included protections for GLBT people. I would argue, however, that this increased acceptance of GLBT rights was not accompanied by increased educational efforts about our lives. Gay men and lesbians rarely exerted their entitlements under these new protective mandates, and we continued to remain largely invisible within our communities. When the Far Right finally organized against us, we lacked the public support and political cohesiveness to effectively assert our rights. Thus, while the current public debate over gays and lesbians in the military has been ugly and unsuccessful to date, it has had the positive effect of raising public awareness about gay, lesbian, bisexual, and transgendered individuals in American society.

This book ends where it began, with the well-known Anita Bryant anti-gay campaign in Dade County, Florida, in 1978. In another volume, the analysis continues with contemporary cases and controversies over the employment of GLBT people as educators. The book begins by exploring the issues of pedophilia and child abuse as they relate to educational settings. One of the major accusations against GLBT people is that, if given an opportunity, we seduce young children into our way of life. Contrary to such public stereotypes, the research on GLBT people and pedophilia concludes that the odds of a child being sexually abused by one of us is 0 percent to 3.1 percent.[25] Male heterosexual family members are the real perpetrators of child sexual abuse in American society.

That book also explores contemporary struggles over the employment entitlements of GLBT educators. One chapter focuses on the "mega-cases" since 1973. These cases demonstrate the threat to the hiring and retention autonomy enjoyed by school administrators if the courts require them to disregard a teacher's sexual orientation within the employment context. Because of the complexities of the legal and social issues, and because of the seemingly limitless legal and financial resources on both sides, the courts appear to have tried to avoid a direct declaration concerning whether or not homosexuals have a constitutional right to teach. Repeatedly, these cases have been remanded to lower courts in an attempt by the various state supreme courts to avoid taking the initiative on a controversial social issue.[26] Another chapter examines the very recent litigation on GLBT educator employment rights. The typical scenario is that if the educator is willing to challenge an administration's threat to his or her employment entitlements, the educator keeps his or her job and possibly receives a sum of money to compensate for the discrimination. More often than not, school districts are retreating from any overt actions that restrict the employment rights of gay and lesbian educators. Covert discrimination, such as unpleasant job assignments and negative gossip, continues to be a problem. Even in the 41 states that do not offer employment protections for GLBT people, however, administrators are cautious about taking aggressive action against a gay or lesbian educator.

The balance of the book offers a legal analysis of the factors that affect the outcome of litigation and the social and legal policy implications of the GLBT educator debate. Furthermore, it briefly explores the relationship of the AIDS (Acquired Immune Deficiency Syndrome) crisis and the increasing visibility of GLBT youth in relation to educational policy.

Also included is a recent example of controversy in a state college setting over the employment rights of a lesbian educator. Having researched the area of GLBT educator employment rights for almost 20 years, I've been "blessed" by the Universe with first-hand experience in the matter. Finally, a summary of insights provided by this study is presented in the areas of school and university administrative policy, teacher personal freedoms, GLBT rights, social change, and the relationship of law to social issues.

CHAPTER CONCLUSIONS

Despite the current intensity of the debate on federal, state, and local levels, and the apparent setback of the 1994 elections with its Republican landslide, the possibilities for addressing the needs of

GLBT people remain positive. Public debate over GLBT concerns provides opportunities to educate people. Also, studies suggest that individuals who are familiar with GLBT individuals exhibit much greater acceptance and advocacy on our behalf. This research suggests, for example, that people who hold negative attitudes about homosexuals are less likely to have had personal contact with lesbians or gay men. Further, it shows they are more likely to reside in more conservative areas like the southern and midwestern parts of the United States; be older and less well-educated; be religious and belong to a conservative church; and subscribe to traditional sex role differentiation and restrictions. These studies also suggest that the two most effective means of creating more positive attitudes towards GLBT individuals are a course in GLBT concerns, or in human sexuality in general, and increased positive contact with known lesbians and gay men.[27]

GLBT youth are at the forefront of this educational process. They are coming out of the closet at a significant rate, forcing adults to come to terms with their visibility and existence. Ironically, but not surprisingly, many GLBT educators are fearful of these public GLBT youth. After spending their lives in the closet trying to retain their reputations and employment, along comes an entire generation of young people who seem indifferent to the consequences of being public about their sexual orientation. The high cost of their being out of the closet has been documented. However, many of today's GLBT youth are willing to pay that high cost for the freedom of self-expression rather than remain silent, isolated, and invisible.

The at-risk circumstances of GLBT youth, the extreme hatred voiced by the Far Right, and the dire implications of the AIDS crisis may be the factors that ultimately help us define, in a positive manner, the rights of GLBT individuals and our heterosexual allies. Out of this great pain and loss, a broader concept of freedom may emerge.

Since today's struggle bears some resemblance to the well-known Anita Bryant campaign in 1978, starting with her story should help set the context for the struggle over the employment rights of GLBT educators. During the late 1960s, the civil rights movement expanded its influence to assert protections for all minorities, including women, GLBT individuals, and the disabled. While gaining significant entitlements, GLBT individuals did not educate the American public by being visible and vocal. Thus, the Far Right was able to label us as the embodiment of the evils of liberalism in American society. By 1978 we stood vulnerable to the Far Right's effort to reassert its dominance over American values and social institutions. Somewhat by accident, Anita Bryant served as the catalyst for this widely-followed social struggle.

PART II

STATEWIDE STRUGGLES — NATIONAL NEWS 1977–1985

Homosexuality is a sin, and if homosexuals were given carte blanche to glamorize their "deviant lifestyle" in Miami-area classrooms, the American family would be destroyed and the American way of life would disappear.

— *Anita Bryant*

CHAPTER 2

SAVE OUR CHILDREN
ANITA BRYANT AND THE FIRST CONSERVATIVE BACKLASH, 1977–1978

In January of 1977, Anita Bryant and her family attended their usual Sunday revival meeting at the North Miami, Florida, Northwest Baptist Church.[1] The sermon by Reverend William Chapman, known as "Brother Bill," focused on a proposed ordinance for the City of Miami that called for protections against discrimination in housing, employment, and public accommodation based on "sexual preference." Although the ordinance would not have applied to either public or private educational institutions, Reverend Chapman called upon his congregation to oppose the ordinance in case they were forced to hire known homosexuals as Christian school teachers. In particular, he urged Bryant to use her position as one of Miami's most notable citizens to lead the fight on God's behalf to discourage the enactment of the ordinance.[2]

As Bryant stated in her 1977 account of the Dade County struggle, *The Anita Bryant Story: The Survival of Our Nation's Families and The Threat of Militant Homosexuality*, she felt moved by God to take her first political action. "Because of my love for Almighty God, because of my love for His Word, because of my love for my country, because of my love for my children, I took a stand — one that was not popular."[3]

Anita Bryant's religious conviction that "God put a flame in my heart" to oppose homosexuality seemed sincere. Raised in the Bible Belt of rural Oklahoma and "born again" at age eight, she had spent many of her 37 years seeking signs from God to guide her career, marriage, and personal beliefs.[4] Married for 17 years to former Miami disc jockey Bob Green, who managed her career, Bryant focused her life on her appeal to religious audiences as a singer and her desire to be home with their four children. The former Miss Oklahoma and second runner-up for Miss America earned additional income from commercial endorsements for Coca-Cola, Kraft, Singer, Holiday Inn, and the Florida Citrus Commission, as well as from her annual role as commentator for the Orange Bowl Parade.[5]

Although Bryant stated she had met homosexuals in the entertainment industry, her first real awakening to the "evils of homosexuality" occurred during and shortly after Rev. Chapman's sermon. A few days later, a local police sergeant gave a presentation to Bryant's church on child pornography, complete with very graphic slides pertaining to homosexual acts with adult males. In shock and disgust, Bryant vowed to campaign against the homosexual conspiracy she felt existed to corrupt the nation's youth.

Along with her religious zeal, another personal factor contributed to Bryant's fervent leadership in the Dade County anti-gay movement. Prior to 1977, Bryant's long-time booking agent and friend, Dick Shack, asked her to tape political endorsements for his wife, Ruth, a candidate for the Dade County Metro Commission. These radio endorsements were significant to Ruth Shack's winning the election.

However, Shack and 48 other candidates for local office also were endorsed by the Dade County Coalition for the

Humanistic Rights of Gays. Dade County has a political history as a liberal community with a large gay/lesbian population. Thus, more than 65 candidates sought the Coalition's endorsement. In return for the homosexual vote, the candidates promised support for GLBT rights. Of the 49 candidates endorsed by the Coalition, 45 won in the election.[6]

Because of the tremendous support for gay rights voiced in pre-election meetings, shortly after the election Ruth Shack introduced to the county commission the anti-discrimination ordinance supporting homosexual rights. Church members who had voted for Shack because of Bryant's endorsement confronted Bryant. She admitted, "I felt ashamed to think I had influenced people to vote for someone who later proposed this ordinance. I knew I had to do something of a public nature because of that earlier endorsement."[7] Thus, on January 18, 1977, Bryant wrote each of the nine county commissioners, asking each one to vote against the ordinance. Later that month, in a heated public discussion, Bryant and others spoke in opposition to the ordinance. The County Commissioners passed the ordinance by a 5 to 3 vote.

Bryant and her followers were stunned. As she stated in her *Story*,

> I couldn't believe it. I was devastated. I sat there, and I heard the result of the vote, and I thought. <u>This is a free country, and if we present our case and we're right and if it's proven, then we should win it</u> (emphasis in original).

> That's what shocked me so badly — to think we live in a country where freedom and right are supposed to reign, a country that boasts "In God we trust" and has such a rich spiritual heritage; yet where internal decadence is all too evident, where the Word of God and the voice of the majority is sometimes not heeded at all. Has it come to this: that we are a society that in fact does glorify aberrant behavior and oppresses the rights of the majority on a moral issue?[8]

Bryant was instantly politicized to fight the "encroaching moral decay in America, and in our own city and county in particular."

With the help of her husband and "Brother Bill," Bryant formed the "Save Our Children" organization. Save Our Children immediately gathered signatures to petition for a referendum to repeal the ordinance.[9] Financial support for the organization poured in from all over the country, as it did for the groups supporting the ordinance. Dade County became the setting for the first head-to-head conflict between the fundamentalist religious movement, with Anita Bryant as its nationally-prominent spokesperson, and the as-yet rather closeted but increasingly militant GLBT population. On both a national and local level, the press referred to the Dade County election as "one of the most emotionally-charged campaigns ever to confront the American voter."[10]

With passage of the ordinance and the move by Bryant followers to revoke it, the County faced a referendum struggle that would cost its citizens almost $400,000.[11] In light of this financial reality, the nine county commissioners discussed revoking the ordinance rather than have the county fund the public vote. Gay and lesbian rights leaders faced a difficult decision. If a county-wide vote was held on the issue in this liberal community, they might win. Without a vote, it was clear that the commissioners would repeal the ordinance.

Lindsy Van Gelder's incisive brief history of the ordinance battle offers insight into the GLBT community's efforts.[12] In a unique move, the gay and lesbian leaders offered to fund as much of the election as possible to keep the ordinance on the ballot. Jack Campbell, a millionaire owner of gay bath houses and clubs, kicked off a nationwide fundraising appeal by contributing $5,000 to the county's election funds.[13] Not surprisingly, Save Our Children leaders refused to help underwrite election costs. They hoped the commissioners would revoke the ordinance. Thus, the nationwide solicitation of funds by the GLBT community helped underwrite the election costs and fund the campaign materials and media appeal supporting the ordinance.[14] According to Bryant, the "outside funding" was evidence of a nationwide homosexual "conspiracy" that she termed "a carefully disguised attempt to break down further the moral fabric of society."[15] Bryant used the conspiracy theory to spur Dade County voters to react against outside interference in local community matters.

THE HOMOSEXUAL CONSPIRACY

Bryant characterized this "conspiracy" as anti-God, anti-country, and anti-decency. In several speeches she stated, "it seems very obvious that the Communist element is a part of all this, because a lot of these people have no reverence for their country."[16] She portrayed the GLBT population as deviously powerful and capable of anything to achieve its end:

> The word gay totally belies the homosexual lifestyle. I don't even know how the word gay was attached to the homosexual lifestyle. The militant homosexuals took the word and with the power that they have, they programmed it into our modern vocabulary. That in itself is a frightening example of what they can do to a society — how they can brainwash you into using their terminology.

> It's too early to say, and I don't know what the homosexuals still have up their sleeve. They are very desperate people who will stop at nothing.[17]

With Bryant's free-flowing Biblical references, the Dade referendum became a match between the Goliath of nationally-organized deviants and the David of a small group of believers in God. Bryant's speeches and rallies suggested that, with God's aid, she and her followers would rout an evil that had seduced politicians, liberal church leaders, and average citizens into thinking that its lifestyle should be accepted.[18]

The success of Save Our Children in portraying the GLBT group as a national conspiracy was matched by its success in creating two images of itself. In some situations, the Bryant organization emphasized its local focus and the hardships faced by a small, relatively poorly financed group facing a larger national organization.[19] Bryant repeatedly emphasized that her group felt the referendum was of local importance and should, therefore, be decided by efforts from local voters using their own money. Bryant expressed pride that, despite the personal and financial hardships, the anti-ordinance group had adhered to this philosophy.[20]

At other times, however, Bryant noted the tremendous national visibility her campaign had garnered and the potential for making money by opposing homosexuality.[21] Bryant's organization raised over $200,000, most of which came from sources outside Florida.[22] Furthermore, free publicity was obtained through Bryant's appearances on local and national radio and television programs sponsored by fundamentalist religious leaders. In fact, the night before the Dade election, Anita Bryant was guest speaker on Reverend Jerry Falwell's nationwide television broadcast. Bryant called it "Divine Providence;" pro-ordinance forces called it unfair.[23] With or without Anita Bryant present, local and national fundamentalist leaders used their pulpits, radio and television programs, and mailing lists to solicit financial and political support for repealing the ordinance.

By the time of the Dade County referendum, it was apparent that the fundamentalist group had ideological cohesion and pre-existing networks on its side. In contrast, the gay and lesbian rights groups lacked organization. It was difficult to develop cohesion in a five-month period, especially when potential participants feared reprisals and were not easily identified. To make matters worse, both the structure of the arguments and the nature of gay and lesbian politics made it even more difficult to form a solid political alliance.

The Bryant organization's attack was aimed at the stereotypical, limp-wristed, seductive, crossdressing, male homosexual who was sexually interested in young boys. For example, Bryant expressed fear that if the ordinance passed the community would be helpless in the face of gay teachers "who want to wear dresses to work and flaunt their homosexuality in front of my children."[24] Since stereotypes are usually based on some essence of reality, the Bryant group succeeded in arousing the fear of straight citizens. At the same time, it divided the GLBT population. Feeling as if they were under attack, more flamboyant members of the GLBT community fought back with heightened outrageousness and visibility. They demanded their right to live without interference. More mainstream GLBT individuals wanted to disassociate themselves and their cause from the more overt aspects of GLBT expression. Quite correctly, they feared that it would prove unpalatable to the voters. As one frustrated lesbian feminist stated, "We're going to lose our rights because of these guys and their god-damned drag-queen/fist-fucking/chicken-hawk/ leather-bar image."[25]

Although gays and lesbians were asking for their civil rights and to be free of discrimination, the image projected was a demand for the freedom to behave outrageously. This enabled the Bryant organization to successfully co-opt the issue of civil rights by contrasting the demand for immoral license with a parent's right to protect his or her children from harm.

Other divisive issues in the gay and lesbian community were sexism and sexual politics. According to Van Gelder, strong anti-Bryant sentiments caused many gay men to cross the fine line between condemnation and crudeness. Sexist comments against Bryant exposed a larger "misogynistic attitude." Given the almost entirely male leadership of the Coalition, and their overt unwill-ingness to include lesbian leadership, the charge that sexism was "absolutely rampant" in the Coalition was well founded.[26] Lesbians found themselves supporting the cause of gay men in order to advance their own rights, despite an awareness that these same men had not supported their campaign for the Equal Rights Amendment (ERA) in Florida and other issues important to lesbian feminists.[27]

Despite the political and personal differences between lesbians and gay men in the Dade County struggle, Anita Bryant capital-ized on lesbian participation in the ERA, to the harm of both causes. When speaking in opposition to the ERA, Anita Bryant expressed that there was "frightening" evidence of a conspiracy by the lesbian task force of the National Organization of [sic] Women to finance the entire gay rights movement, in part because the ERA and NOW were fronts for lesbianism.[28]

The Bryant organization's use of communist-hunting, McCarthyesque tactics frustrated the efforts of the pro-ordinance forces. While alleging that they held evidence of a conspiracy to harm children, families, country, God, and the American way, Bryant forces were able to make extreme statements about the nature and practice of homosexuality. Pro-ordinance forces found themselves combating sensationalist rhetoric with mundane statistics, denying a conspiracy while trying to organize forces, and defending themselves from charges of criminal and immoral behavior.

Bryant's organization considered the mere visibility of a homosexual to be an affront to decency. The fact that lesbians and gay men had organized themselves and requested legal protections was characterized as an aggressive act of hostility towards God and American society — proof that the past few decades of liberal humanism had culminated in the ultimate threat of social destruction. But, according to Bryant,

> God is allowing America one last space to repent. If the parents of American children had stood by God's Word...the destruction of America's moral fiber wouldn't have happened. They've seen how so called humanism works.[29]

Bryant's followers were encouraged to rise up, repeal the evil incarnate, and, finally, eliminate it either through redemptive or punitive means. Otherwise, God's anger over this social decadence would cause Him to destroy America either through war or environmental disasters. Their view seemed to be that homosexuality could be tolerated by society only if those who practiced it kept quiet. Realistically, Bryant and her followers acknowledged there always would be a few homosexuals in society, but these people should not have a chance to increase their numbers through seduction or recruitment. Only the invisible, silent lesbian or gay man could be an acceptable member of the local community, and she or he would have no need for extraordinary legal privileges. These views were premised on the belief that those who wished to have such privileges intended to use them to assert their lifestyle on the majority. Recognizing the presence of homosexuals in society and granting them rights equaled acceptance and legitimization of the sexual practice. Visibility, acceptance, and protection provided lesbians and gay men with the opportunity to increase their numbers. Spouses would leave their families, children would turn against their parents, and the whole foundation of society would crumble as the American family was destroyed. In her interview with *Playboy Magazine*, Anita Bryant stated:

> Homosexuality is a sin, and if homosexuals were given carte blanche to glamorize their "deviant lifestyle" in

Miami-area classrooms, the American family would be destroyed and the American way of life would disappear.[30]

Ironically, the conservative fundamentalists' view of homosexuality contained an interesting, internal inconsistency. On one hand, it was despicable. On the other hand, it was so desirable that few people could refrain from it if they were exposed to the experience. As Bryant noted:

> The homosexual act is just the beginning of the depravity. It then leads to . . . sado-masochism, alcohol, drugs . . . and ends up with suicide. The worst thing is that these days, so many married men with children who don't have a happy marriage are going into the homosexual bars for satisfaction — if they're not careful, they're going to get caught up in it totally.[31]

While some might view this need to find satisfaction outside the marriage as an indictment of the American family, conservative leaders portrayed the homosexual alternative as evidence of the attractiveness of Satan's seductions. Although adults might be corrupted, it would be an isolated loss. The possibility of wholesale recruitment and corruption existed where young, impressionable children were gathered to learn under the instruction of a trusted adult role model. The Far Right encouraged this perception. In the referendum struggle in Dade County and elsewhere they shifted the focus to the issue of employment of homosexual school teachers.

HOMOSEXUALITY, ACCORDING TO BRYANT

In her interview with *Playboy Magazine*, Bryant admitted that her knowledge of homosexuality was almost non-existent until 1977. Then, she first learned the "nitty-gritty" of homosexuality, and her abhorrence was based upon Biblical references. For example, she believed God called homosexuality an "abomination," because:

> . . . homosexuals eat spermatozoa, the building block of blood, so, therefore, homosexuals are swallowing, and presumably digesting, the essence of life. Homosexuality is hideous because it is anti-life, degenerative.[32]

When confronted with the argument that heterosexuals also eat sperm, Bryant stated that this "abominable practice" had spread from the homosexual community. Asked whether she believed that birth control also was an abomination, Bryant said, "No, because you are not wasting the sperm."[33]

Referring to her own children, Bryant stated, "I'd rather my child be dead than be a homosexual."[34] She stated further that, while she could never condone what her child did, she would still love him. She did say that in the sex education of her children she had explained the depravity and unnaturalness of homosexuality by telling them that "even barnyard animals don't do what homosexuals do."[35]

In addition to their religious objections to homosexuality, Save Our Children members emphasized the potentially dire legal circumstances faced by Dade voters if they allowed the ordinance to exist. Parents would be helpless as homosexuals issued demands to be included in every aspect of American society. One Minneapolis incident was used as a frequent example of the homosexual desire to infiltrate in order to recruit.

In 1974, shortly after the passage of the Minneapolis anti-discrimination ordinance, a gay man volunteered to be a Big Brother for a fatherless boy. Directors of the Big Brothers program tried to prevent the man from working with boys but were told that this would not be possible because of the city ordinance. Next, the organization sent information to the mothers of boys who might be assigned to the man, informing them that their child might have a homosexual counselor. This practice was stopped after a court determined that it violated the civil rights of the gay volunteer. In fact, the Minneapolis Department of Civil Rights apparently encouraged the organization to actively recruit more gay men as Big Brothers. In response, the Executive Director of the Minneapolis Big Brothers organization wrote Anita Bryant praising her "gumption to stand up and speak out." Bryant supporters published this letter along with the headlines "Would you want a homosexual 'Big Brother' for your fatherless boy?"[36]

Parental legal helplessness in the face of militant, violent, immoral, and debased people would have been intolerable for

Dade voters. The Bryant organization emphasized this as the authentic image of homosexuals. Reverend Jerry Falwell told *Newsweek Magazine* that it was common knowledge that homosexuals would "just as soon kill you as look at you."[37] Educator Max Rafferty offered his expert opinion, based on his years as superintendent of public instruction in California, "I do assure you, we took for granted the self-evident proposition that a homosexual in a school job was as preposterously out of the question as a heroin mainliner working in the local drugstore."[38] Moreover, according to Bryant, 50 percent of the nation's suicides and homicides in large cities were because of homosexuality. In Los Angeles alone, Bryant told of 30,000 children under the age of 12 being "recruited and sexually abused by homosexuals."[39] Evidence of this link in an even larger nationwide ring of homosexual child pornographers supposedly had been uncovered by the *Los Angeles Times* and the *Chicago Tribune*, according to Bryant campaign literature. The "national goals" of the "homosexual conspiracy" were to eliminate the age of consent and to gain "special legal privileges" in order to seduce, corrupt, and harm the nation's children.[40] The "special privileges" that the homosexual community were requesting in Dade County, in Bryant's opinion, "violated the state law of Florida, not to mention God's law."[41]

Worse yet, if Dade voters allowed homosexuals to have "special privileges," then every other deviant group would have legal grounds for inclusion under anti-discrimination ordinances. Bryant told *Playboy Magazine* that,

> Under the proposed ordinance every sexual deviation would have been legally acceptable among schoolteachers . . . a man who has a Great Dane as his lover . . . whores . . . ad infinitum. . . . If [homosexuals are] a legitimate minority group, then so are nail biters, dieters, fat people, short people, and murderers.[42]

Despite their extreme image of homosexuals, Bryant and her followers denied having hateful and un-Christian motives in opposing the ordinance. Rather, they maintained that their position was one of love for the homosexual. As Bryant told *Today's Student*, "I love the homosexuals. If you have a friend that you love, you love them enough to tell them the truth."[43] Fundamentalist leaders argued that their mission was like Christ's; to go among the sinners and show them the error of their ways. One Virginia church leader who specialized in converting homosexuals stated, "God is merciful. He loves the homosexual like He loves the murderer or the rapist. I want to offer these people a chance . . . to find Jesus."[44] Although their motives may have been Christian, their rhetoric against homosexuals aroused an unparalleled level of violence.

CAMPAIGN OF VIOLENCE

Fueled by the vicious comments about homosexuals, youths in Florida and California ganged up to harass identifiable lesbians and gay men. In Dade County, cars sported bumper stickers with the slogan, "Kill a queer for Christ." Evidence of violence included the bombing of a gay activist's car after he participated in a radio talk show about the ordinance and the shooting of a gay man as he left a pro-ordinance fundraising dance. Coalition members offered rewards for the conviction of perpetrators. They repeatedly called upon the Save Our Children leadership to discourage violence and hatred, although without apparent success.[45] In San Francisco, gay-owned businesses in the Castro district were cherry bombed, and a gay man was beaten to death by four young men shouting, "Here's one for Anita." The mother of the slain gay man filed suit against Bryant, California State Senator John Briggs, and the Save Our Children organization, charging that they had conspired to incite physical violence against homosexuals.[46]

In addition to the overt acts of violence, an immeasurable amount of psychological harm resulted. Several suicides and suicide attempts were directly linked to the intense anti-gay atmosphere in the Dade County area.[47] Ironically, Bryant's assessment that homosexuality led to suicide was verified to some small extent, as lesbians and gay men faltered in their struggle to exist in an oppressive and hateful environment.

On the anti-ordinance side, Bryant reportedly experienced several threats on her life. These were enough to cause tight security measures wherever she went. Rumors of these threats caused Dade County citizens to call Coalition headquarters and threaten that, "If anything happens to Anita Bryant there'll be a homosexual hanging from every tree in the country."[48] Members of the Ku Klux Klan committed themselves to protecting Bryant during her public appearances.[49]

Additionally, Bryant faced what became known as a "gaycott;" a boycott of Florida orange juice products endorsed by Bryant in her contract with the Florida Citrus Commission. It is difficult to assess the effectiveness of the gaycott. Bryant's comments on the issue ranged from expressions of serious financial harm to the Commission, and to herself, to delight at a backlash that had caused a "25 percent increase in sales." According to Bryant, however, her participation in the ordinance struggle caused her to lose over 70 percent of her bookings and commercial endorsements.[50]

THE VOTE

On June 7, 1977, after a five-month campaign, voters in Dade County rendered the first decision by popular vote on homosexual rights. The ordinance supporting gay and lesbian housing and employment protections was repealed by a vote of 69 percent to 31 percent, with over 300,000 people participating in the election.[51] During the post-election press interview, Anita Bryant announced that Save Our Children would conduct a national campaign against homosexuality. Its first two targets would be the pro-gay rights bills under consideration in both the Massachusetts legislature and the United States Congress. The latter bill had been introduced by then-New York Congressman Edward Koch and would have amended the 1964 Civil Rights Act to include protections for homosexuals.[52] In addition to these two major campaigns, Bryant expressed interest in initiating repeal efforts against local anti-discrimination ordinances in St. Paul, Minnesota; San Antonio, Texas; and Washington, D.C.[53] Just before the Dade vote, Bryant told the press:

> It is a battle of the agnostic, the atheists, and the ungodly
> on one side, and God's people on the other. We're going
> to have to stand once and for all.[54]

> All America and all the world will hear what people (in Miami) have said, and with God's continued help, we will prevail in our fight to repeal similar laws throughout the nation which attempt to make legitimate a lifestyle that is both perverse and dangerous.[55]

In her victory speech after the election Bryant stated, "Tonight, the laws of God and the cultural values of men have been vindicated."[56] Homosexuals across the nation expressed their opposing view by staging impromptu marches and candlelight vigils in San Francisco, Chicago, Boston, New York, and other cities. Pro-ordinance gay and lesbian leaders in Dade County expressed dismay at such a resounding defeat in their normally liberal community, especially in light of Bryant's announcement to undertake a nationwide campaign against homosexual rights.[57]

Despite the Bryant victory, however, the GLBT community had reason to remain optimistic. Gay and lesbian rights had become a national issue. The Dade County campaign had caused countless numbers of lesbians and gay men to step "out of the closet" and into the mainstream of American society and politics. Increased political activity meant increased visibility and the chance to educate the public about homosexuality. The stereotypical images fostered by isolationism and dehumanization could be challenged by direct experience with normal people who were gay or lesbian. Equally important, men and women who were attracted to members of their own sex found a haven of similarity, solidarity, and acceptance within this emergent subculture.

THE ONGOING WAR

All concerned parties knew that the issue had not been resolved in Dade County. Fundamentalist supporters had won the first battle in a political war that continues to date. Shortly after Dade County, subsequent battles would be fought in the cities of St. Paul, Eugene, and Wichita. Conservatives would emerge victorious again. Some elements of conservative success would be eroded, however, as the campaign spread beyond its source in Dade County.

Although Bryant was active to some extent in subsequent referendum struggles, she did not conduct the nationwide campaign she had announced the night of the Dade County victory. In her interview with *Playboy Magazine* and in her autobiographical account of the elections, she spoke of the tremendous potential for political power and national fundraising through opposition to homosexual rights. But, despite her own eagerness to continue the battle and the readiness of Save Our Children, God had not given her a sign to take her opposition nationwide. And so, the same adherence to religious direction that caused Bryant to lead the repeal efforts now dictated her withdrawal. She told *Playboy*,

> There's a revival beginning in America now. What happened in Dade County is happening all over the country. We could fill up every auditorium in America. If we had done so after our victory in Dade County, we could have gotten such a momentum going that we could have wiped the homosexual out. That was a very real possibility. We realized that. We could have made a lot of money too. . . . but we needed a rest and I had no leading of the Lord to do it. All the people we'd been working with were chomping at the bit to go national, but I just did not have a direct leading of the Lord to continue in that light. I prayed and I prayed and wanted direction from God to do that and it wasn't coming.[58]

Other motives included career considerations, the needs of her children, and the impending dissolution of her marriage to Bob Green. Bryant's participation in the ordinance repeal had given conservative leadership a tremendously popular national figure. In fact, in a 1977 poll by *Good Housekeeping* magazine, Bryant was voted the most popular woman in America.[59] Her motives for participating in the repeal efforts suggested a deeply religious concern for society and a mother's concern for the well-being of her children. In contrast, subsequent conservative leadership, such as State Senator and gubernatorial candidate John Briggs of California, appeared motivated by personal political gain.[60]

Another blow to the conservative campaign was its waning claim to local representation. Despite national funding and participation by numerous outside religious leaders, Anita Bryant's residency in Dade County helped legitimize the image of localism in the campaign. After Dade County, it became clear that the network opposing gay rights was no more local in character than the pro-gay rights groups. Voters who chaffed at the idea of outside interference from homosexual groups now faced outside interference from conservative groups as well. Opposition to gay rights began to look more and more like a "witch-hunt." Even the conservative press, which had congratulated Bryant on her "vote of confidence" in Dade County, warned that the vote was "not a flaming sword" for extremism.[61]

Ultimately, "messianic madness" could be "a greater threat to this society" than homosexuality, according to an article by Carl Rowan that was read into the *Congressional Record* on June 17, 1977. Bryant's appeal to "gullible and unsophisticated Americans" might cause serious harm to our concepts of liberty, justice, and civil rights. As long as conservative leaders focused on ordinance repeals, however, they could claim that they were preventing gay men and lesbians from gaining "special legal privileges" at the expense of other citizens. Most voters were not willing to elevate gays and lesbians to the same level of legal protections from discrimination as African-Americans, other minorities, and religious practitioners. On the other hand, as set forth in the next chapter, voters also were not willing to revoke civil liberties from individuals because of their sexual orientation.

LOCAL REFERENDA AFTER DADE COUNTY

Two major implications arose out of the Dade County repeal efforts. First, a large, well-organized, and financially affluent political coalition of fundamentalist ministers and political leaders was firmly established as the opposition. Second, the emotionally-charged issues surrounding sexual orientation, particularly concerning the employment of gay and lesbian school teachers, had attracted the attention of average citizens. It had motivated them to rally locally as a conservative voting block. Fundamentalist leaders had found an issue that gathered political support and a mechanism of local referenda that gave their voice significant impact. The initial success of the Dade County movement mushroomed into a series of local victories against GLBT rights. By late 1978, Baptist religious leaders in St. Paul, Wichita, Eugene, and Seattle had created local organizations. These local organizations quickly gathered enough signatures to place the gay rights ordinances in those cities on the ballot for public reconsideration.[62]

Faced with potential revocation of the anti-discrimination clauses, local lesbians and gay men formed coalitions with other minority, feminist, religious, and political special interest groups. The diversity of these coalitions depended on the strength of liberal ideology in the particular community. For example, in the rather liberal community of St. Paul, Minnesota, the mayor, other city officials, and religious leaders of the predominantly Catholic community joined labor unions, teachers' unions, Black organizations, and women's groups to support civil rights for gays and lesbians.[63] In the more conservative community of Wichita, Kansas, Catholic religious leaders actively petitioned their members to oppose gay rights, and local city officials avoided involvement in the referendum struggle.[64]

Opponents of gay and lesbian rights continued their effective rhetoric of characterizing the ordinances as condoning immoral behavior and guaranteeing special privileges to homosexuals. For example, Lynn H. Greene, 25, a leader of the anti-homosexual movement in Eugene, Oregon, stated:

> The ordinance would encourage homosexuals to kiss, caress and dance in public, slap fannies, ask heterosexuals for dates at places of employment or in bars, and will even allow the occasional touching of the genitals.[65]

Moreover, opponents felt these anti-discrimination laws would be followed quickly by affirmative action demands and that gays and lesbians would soon have greater rights than the average citizen. Anti-gay literature distributed in St. Paul stated that, under the ordinance, a landlord would be legally required by law to rent to an otherwise undesirable tenant, merely because he/she was homosexual, or face a fine and three months in jail.[66] Campaign literature distributed in Eugene stated that landlords could discriminate against heterosexual couples with children, but homosexuals would be protected completely against housing discrimination.[67]

The threat of molestation and recruitment of young children remained the most powerful emotional conservative themes. Eugene opposition materials stated that parents on outings with their children would not be able to protect them from exposure to "offensive homosexual behavior."[68] Thus, upstanding citizens would lose the right to condemn and prohibit behavior that they felt was sinful, immoral, and mentally ill.[69] Not only would the community be rendered powerless in the face of homosexual demands, but other undesirable groups would rely on the ordinances to seek protection and influence. As Anita Bryant stated during a Topeka rally, "Next you will have thieves, prostitutes and people who have relations with St. Bernards asking for the same rights."[70]

Certainly the most powerful rallying issue of the Far Right campaign was its comments about the dangers of homosexual school teachers. Despite frequent clarifications by local political officials and the press that a city ordinance about gay and lesbian rights protections did not pertain to school policy, it was still rumored that homosexuals would be free to flaunt their lifestyle in classrooms.[71] Conservatives claimed the anti-discrimination laws would force teachers to present homosexuality as an acceptable alternative lifestyle, and the community would have to tolerate homosexual school teachers who would be free to affect the minds of local children. Three themes about GLBT teachers emerged repeatedly in the referendum campaign material and newspaper articles: molestation, recruitment, and violence. Probably the most sensationalist commentary on these fears was printed by the *National Enquirer* in January of 1979. The editorial began and ended with the question: "Do YOU want a homosexual teaching YOUR children?" It detailed the Chicago molestations and killings of dozens of boys by John Gacy and the Houston sex-and-torture murders of 27 boys by Elmer Wayne Henly, Jr. According to the *Enquirer* and its panel of psychological "experts" (all of whom were affiliated with the Bryant organization), these two men (who were not educators) typified the ethos of all homosexual educators. One panelist stated that homosexuals "are more dangerous than normal people because of a perverted hatred for their parents," while several other "experts" stated that homosexuals are "paranoid and prone to violence."

Thus, by allowing homosexuals to teach, children were being exposed "to an emotional time bomb" that could go off at any minute — raping, killing, or seducing young children.[72]

Proponents of gay and lesbian rights attempted to demonstrate that the ordinances were about basic civil rights and had not caused any harmful consequences. In the face of the highly emotional appeal of the anti-gay movement, these efforts were largely ineffective. Although it was acknowledged that the debate concerned civil rights, Arizona Senator Dennis Deconcini (R–AZ) stated a common response. Civil rights were important, but the larger social imperative was that "each community should be able to decide on the morality of that community."[73] A vote for gay and lesbian rights was categorized as a vote for the continued breakdown of American society. Even some conservative supporters, however, eventually became concerned about the extreme charges by the "New Right."

For several months during the referendum campaign, the editorial pages of *The Wichita Eagle* and *The Beacon* were filled with anti-gay rights essays and letters to the editor. In late April of 1978, just before the May 9 vote, the paper announced that it favored keeping the city ordinance in support of gay and lesbian rights. In commenting on its changed perspective, the paper criticized the Concerned Citizens group for misleading the public, printing lies, and arousing the emotions of the voters with "rhetorical and emotional overkill." The paper concluded that the ordinance was a necessary and very "straightforward" statement of civil rights, rather than some plot to corrupt society by granting homosexuals special privileges. Further, the paper stated that thoughtful voters would realize the need for the ordinance, but that "the ordinary voter" may not take the time to educate himself about the initiative, and thus would fall victim to the untruths of the anti-gay group.[74]

In their public speaking engagements nationwide, religious leaders of the New Right denied their role in influencing the local referendum initiatives. While in Wichita participating in a "Revive America" rally, several Baptist religious leaders preached violently anti-gay sermons. When it was her turn to speak, Anita Bryant denied that the rally had been organized in a place and time that would gather support for the recall efforts. Bryant stated, "I am not attempting to sway people here concerning this issue. I feel that it has to be the community's choice and we have not tried to intervene." In Topeka, one day before the rally, however, Bryant blasted the gay rights ordinance as granting special privileges and opening the doors to "thieves, prostitutes . . . etc."[75] These large revival meetings granted the New Right the excuse to bring in nationally-known fundamentalist religious leaders who would comment on the local gay and lesbian rights referendum struggle in the community and urge the audience to vote against the measures.

In addition, these organizations provided personnel and financial assistance to the local fundamentalist groups challenging the gay rights initiatives. Bryant's Save Our Children lobbying group contributed over $20,000 to the Wichita and St. Paul elections. In fact, the Eugene, Oregon, referendum drive was notable as the only anti-gay local effort to forego funding assistance from the nationally-organized Bryant group.[76]

Not everyone was delighted with this national-level interference. As one editorial stated, "Miss Bryant should stay home. Other communities are quite capable of writing or overthrowing their own legislation and of coping with their homosexual subgroups."[77] The editorial further commented that, as a concerned citizen, Bryant had every right to react strongly to a perceived threat to her own community. If she carried the issue nationwide, however, that amounted to a "witch-hunt."

By the end of 1978, several lopsided victories had been achieved by these fundamentalist groups. Following the 2 to 1 victory in Dade County, St. Paul repealed its non-discrimination protections in April of 1978 by the same margin. Wichita followed suit in early May of that same year with a 5 to 1 repeal vote. In late May, the voters of Eugene, Oregon, also defeated the protections by a 63 percent majority.

CHAPTER CONCLUSIONS

After over a year of successfully influencing local politics on the issue of gay and lesbian rights and the community's right to determine local morality, the Far Right felt confident that it would win the first statewide struggle, particularly if the focus was the prohibition of gays and lesbians from the classroom. Conservative energies focused on California and the Briggs Initiative. California's penchant for starting national trends guaranteed extensive publicity. It also presented the strong likelihood that success in opposing GLBT school teachers in California would lead to a national policy change supporting the conservative perspective. Former State Superintendent of Public Instruction (CA), Max Rafferty, set out the moral imperatives for prohibiting GLBT educators in the following manner in one of his weekly columns on education that appeared in more than 100 U.S. newspapers:

> The ancient Jews who wrote the Torah used an interesting term to identify the act of sodomy: "confusion." That's what it is, you know. Confusion of the sex roles. Confusion of the biological purpose behind the sex act. Confusion of masculinity with femininity. Confusion thrice confounded.

> My point is this connection: American classrooms are currently perplexed, bewildered, befogged, jumbled, and muddled enough, Lord knows, without being forced to undergo the ultimate injection of super-confusion in the persons of homosexual teachers who will willy-nilly escalate existing obfuscation into total chaos.[78]

If we wait to speak until we are not afraid,
we will be speaking from our graves.

— *Audre Lorde*

CHAPTER 3

RIDDING THE SCHOOLS OF HOMOSEXUAL EDUCATORS

CALIFORNIA'S PROPOSITION 6, 1977–1978

As a young graduate student in California in 1977, I found the public bandwagon for Proposition 6 frightening. Conservative State Senator John Briggs was constantly in the press discussing the evils of homosexuality. His main argument was that gay and lesbian individuals intentionally entered the teaching profession to seduce young students into a homosexual lifestyle. Thus, Proposition 6 was necessary to curb this conspiracy of corruption.

I was distressed that the statements of hate presented descriptions so different from the honorable, hardworking, kind individuals whom I had met in the gay and lesbian communities of northern California. Their integrity made me delight in the realization that I, too, was a lesbian and an educator. Proposition 6 politicized me and stirred within me a lifelong commitment to writing and researching about GLBT issues in education. Like so many of my peers in 1977, I distributed information opposing Proposition 6 at the local supermarkets. Invariably, the shoppers who expressed hostility for homosexuals also admitted that they had never met one. We would let them know that we were gay or lesbian in an attempt to humanize the debate with real faces of normalcy. One tactic involved coming out of the closet in everyday transactions by handing out business cards that stated, "You have just conducted business with a homosexual individual, please oppose Proposition 6."

John Briggs grew to represent my image of an insane and power-hungry individual who cared nothing about the people he hurt. Imagine my feelings when, in 1988, I interviewed him for over three hours about the Proposition 6 campaign and his race for the California Governorship. He knew nothing of GLBT life. For example, when I introduced myself and stated that I was "out" at work as a university professor, he gave me his condolences for "being out of a job." In answer to the question whether he knew any GLBT individuals, he noted that the reporter who covered him for the *San Francisco Chronicle*, Randy Shilts, had become one homosexual acquaintance. I was now one of the few others that he had ever spoken with directly. His two motivating forces were a wish to be Governor and a repulsion at the idea of two men engaging in sex together. In his sexist logic, he cared nothing about "what you girls do in bed. Women just don't get this issue." He had no grasp of the people he hurt and the hatred he fostered. To this day, I marvel at his bizarre logic, his lack of knowledge about GLBT people, and his extreme wish that I would like him as a person.

CALIFORNIA'S PROPOSITION 6

The scenario the press most often portrays of the beginning of the Proposition 6 Initiative in California is a shift from local politics to a statewide campaign. It portrays this shift as occurring after the significant victories by fundamentalist leaders in Dade County, St. Paul, Eugene, and Wichita. In fact, the Proposition 6 campaign was launched during the Dade County debate and thus preceded any subsequent conservative repeal victories. Additionally, the Proposition 6 campaign began a new precedent in the GLBT teacher debate since it was fought in the legal arena at several junctures. It included an attempt to determine the constitutionality of the Initiative before, rather than after, voter approval.

In June of 1977, California State Senator John Briggs (R-Fullerton) introduced an Initiative to "rid the schools of homosexual teachers."[1] This Initiative was to be placed on the November 1977 ballot for statewide election consideration. In October of 1977, The Pride Foundation, a gay rights organization, filed suit in the California Supreme Court seeking the withdrawal of the Initiative on the grounds that it violated the California Election Code. The day before the Supreme Court was to render its decision, Briggs withdrew the Initiative, citing the need to avoid expensive litigation.[2] Two days after withdrawing the Initiative, Briggs refiled an identical version to be placed on the November 1978 ballot.

Advocates of Proposition 6 argued that the Initiative did not forbid school systems from hiring homosexual school teachers; it merely gave them the option not to do so.[3] The decision would be made by local school boards. For example, Rev. Bill Sheldon explained that under the law "the San Francisco school board could decide that it was all right for homosexuals to teach in the public schools while the Bakersfield school board could decide they were unfit for the schools there."[4] Although this arrangement may have been the intent of Proposition 6 proponents, it actually had a much stronger mandate.

In part, Proposition 6 would have amended the California State Education Code with the following language:

> One of the most fundamental interests of the state is the establishment and the preservation of the family unit. Consistent with this interest is the state's duty to protect its impressionable youth from influences which are antithetical to this vital interest. This duty is particularly compelling when the state undertakes to educate its youth, and, by law, requires them to be exposed to the state's chosen educational environment throughout their formative years.

> A schoolteacher, teacher's aide, school administrator or counselor has a professional duty directed exclusively towards the moral as well as intellectual, social and civic development of young and impressionable students.
>
> As a result of continued close and prolonged contact with schoolchildren, a teacher, teacher's aide, school administrator or counselor becomes a role model whose words, behavior and actions are likely to be emulated by students coming under his or her care, instruction, supervision, administration, guidance and protection.
>
> For these reasons, the state finds a compelling interest in refusing to employ and in terminating the employment of a schoolteacher, a teacher's aide, a school administrator or a counselor, subject to reasonable restrictions and qualifications, who engages in public homosexual activity and/or public homosexual conduct directed at, or likely to come to the attention of, school children or other school employees.
>
> This proscription is essential since such activity and conduct undermines the state's interest in preserving and perpetuating the conjugal family unit.[5]

Critics of the Initiative, including former California Governor Ronald Reagan, argued that its overbroad definition of "homosexual conduct" rendered the Initiative unconstitutional.[6] "Homosexual conduct" was defined as "advocating, soliciting, imposing, encouraging, or promoting of private or public homosexual activity directed at, or likely to come to the attention of schoolchildren and/or other employees." Thus, under this broad definition, a wide range of behaviors would be grounds for termination or non-hiring. Certainly, a homosexual teacher who discussed his or her lifestyle and presented this way of life as a positive alternative to students would come under the Initiative's mandate. Also, any heterosexual teachers who expressed tolerance of homosexuality to a small group of friends at a private party could come under the Initiative's scrutiny, with the argument that their comments advocated, promoted and encouraged GLBT activity. This possible extension of the Initiative would be a direct and unconstitutional intrusion into First Amendment freedoms of protected speech and association.

Additional criticisms of the Initiative targeted the review and dismissal process, which gave local school boards unlimited authority to define standards of conduct and gather information against the school employee. These unrestrained powers were contrary to federal and state constitutional limitations and would have directly violated state constitutional requirements of separation of powers. They also violated emerging but well-regarded privacy protections established on both a federal and state level.

Proponents of Proposition 6 responded that the Initiative would not deny homosexuals their human rights because "there is no inherent right for an individual to hold a teaching position."[7] They argued that teaching, in contrast to other forms of employment, was "a public position" and, as such, "is a privilege, not a right."[8] Arguing that they were not campaigning against a minority, Briggs stated, "I am for normal people having their rights. If they want to lead quiet, decent lives, playing cards in their bedrooms or doing other things quietly, they would not be affected."[9]

In his own letter to the homosexual community, published in the gay newspaper, *Coast To Coast Times*, John Briggs asked for the opportunity to "correct the record" about Proposition 6:

> I believe that private rights end where public injury begins. Society has the right and the power to prohibit behavior by individuals which is injurious to it . . . .
>
> Homosexuality is not simply an alternative lifestyle, but is a direct assault on the institution of the family. Apparently, attacking the family unit is an inherent part of the drive to make homosexuality totally acceptable, if the numerous articles and statements I've read in homosexual publications is any indication. The party line is that heterosexuals are dull, uncreative, sexually repressed child molesters. Ironically, the latest Kinsey study of homosexuality says that the most stable and rewarding homosexual relationships are to be found in situations which come closest to the family and marriage.

The family unit is the glue which holds our society together for everyone's benefit — including the homo-sexual community. When it begins to break down, the social costs are immense. We all suffer from increased crime, drug addiction, venereal disease, welfare and all the other problems that tend to come from children raised in broken homes.

This is a public injury which society has a right and duty to prevent, even if in doing so we limit private rights . . . .

I submit to you that the mere physical activity carried on by homosexuals in private should not be cause for public concern. Although I personally consider such conduct immoral and repulsive, it does not by itself constitute that public injury which we in government should seek to stop. Rather, it is the flaunting of the homosexual lifestyle and the attempt to convert and recruit when impression-able young children are involved that creates a threat.[10-]

THE CALIFORNIA CONTEXT

Before discussing further the Proposition 6 campaign, it might prove helpful to discuss the status of homosexual teachers in California before the Briggs' action. Contrary to the general image of northern Californians as accepting of alternative lifestyles, the status of lesbian and gay male teachers was not good.

Dr. Max Rafferty, an ultra-conservative, was State Superintendent of Public Instruction for the California school system in the early 1970s. He believed that all homosexuals were criminals because sodomy was against the law. It was in this mindset that he chaired the California statewide credentials commission for eight years, which, as he stated in a later publication "was to decide each month whether certain teachers were morally fit to be allowed to teach in California schools."[11] In the same article, he further addressed his views on the inappropriateness of GLBT educators:

And considering our declining and falling posture in all the opinion polls, fellow educators, we simply can't afford the luxury of urging the hard-pressed taxpayers to pay criminals to teach their children. Really, we can't.

Oh, it's not because I want any American citizen denied his or her constitutional rights. But, let's face it. Nobody has a constitutional right to be a schoolteacher.

And it's not because I particularly enjoy being beastly to the bisexual or nasty to the nance. No, it's because children, especially young children, reason this way more often than not:

"Mom and Dad tell me to mind Teacher, to listen carefully to what she tells me. So what she does and what she is must be okay, fine and dandy."

But what the homosexual does and is are most emphatically not okay, fine or dandy, at all. Such people, whether willingly or unwillingly, are abnormal by the very definition of the word; that is, if you concede that the word "abnormal" has any meaning any more.

Thus, Rafferty believed it was his duty, and critical for the survival of the education profession and our society, to "automatically" revoke the credential "of any teacher who was proven to be gay" during his period of leadership.[12] Although Rafferty's staff subsequently admitted that he lacked the authority to take this action, this threat of job loss, when combined with an environment of local prejudice, caused GLBT teachers in California to remain in the closet until the mid 1970s.

By 1975, gay leaders in the San Francisco school system estimated that over one-third of the district's 4,400 teachers were gay or lesbian and that the district's policy was to ignore sexual orientation as long as the teachers were silent and discreet. By 1974, however, in a few school-related incidents, teachers had spoken out about homosexuality and their sexual orientation. One teacher was threatened with dismissal. It was ultimately decided that his nine years of excellent service and the lack of any grounds on which to fire him warranted his retention.[13]

In 1975, however, controversy arose in the San Francisco School District because the School Board refused to allow the Gay Teachers Caucus to print its meeting notices in the district newsletter. Also, the Board refused to include "sexual preference" in the list of anti-discrimination categories adopted in its 1975 employment procedures.[14]

Because of the School Board's action, several more teachers revealed their sexual orientation and lobbied for recognition and acceptance within the district. Support was gathered from the California Federation of Teachers and from Assemblyman John Foran, who introduced an employment gay rights bill in the state legislature.

In a letter to the district, Foran wrote, "It appears to me that we would all be dealing more effectively with gay people if we stopped pretending they don't exist."[15] Foran informed the board of the experiences reported in Washington D.C. since the enactment of its 1972 resolution preventing discrimination against homosexual teachers. President of the Washington School Board, Marion Barry, Jr., wrote:

> This resolution met with a limited amount of community opposition and there has been no opposition to this resolution within the public school system itself. Passage of this resolution has not resulted in any problems . . . .[16]

In another such letter, dated April 1, 1977, sent to the Mayor of Miami, Florida, Barry wrote,

> Washington, D. C. has nearly five years of experience with regulations which prohibit discrimination against gay citizens. With this experience in mind, it is especially important to note that none of the negative consequences that were said to be likely from legislation of this sort have materialized. Specifically, I know of no case in which our regulations have encouraged "child recruitment" into homosexuality, "child molestation," or proselytizing by our gay citizens toward young people that the homosexual life-style is a superior one. I know of no improper or offensive behavior by teachers that has resulted from these regulations.
>
> On the contrary, what has become clear is that our gay citizens are approaching positively their individual roles in the economic and political life of the city . . . .

By 1977, GLBT teachers in San Francisco succeeded in adding "sexual preference" to the list of anti-discrimination clause features of their union contract, thus bypassing a direct vote of inclusion by the school board. Despite their success and the relative environment of tolerance in the San Francisco district, one teacher in 1978 commented that he knew his declaration of being a homosexual teacher automatically precluded him from advancing into administration. In fact, by 1978, despite the large numbers of homosexual teachers in the district, only about 20 attended the Gay Teacher Coalition meetings. Very few of those who attended felt comfortable being "out."[17] Thus, the Proposition 6 campaign was launched essentially during a time of continued silence and invisibility within the homosexual teacher community.

THE BRIGGS' CAMPAIGN

The most significant actor in the Proposition 6 story was John Briggs. As a state representative of one of the most conservative districts in California and the son of a fundamentalist minister, Briggs' personal, political, and religious leanings placed him squarely in support of the New Right ideology. When Willie Brown, the very liberal, African-American Speaker of the California Senate, went to Florida to speak out against Anita Bryant's Dade County campaign, John Briggs was upset. He felt that Brown (elected in late 1995 as Mayor of San Francisco) was trying to represent himself as speaking for all the people of California — and trying to gather national attention. With Ronald Reagan retiring as Governor of California, the seat was open to the individual who could portray him- or herself as a national-level player. John Briggs wanted to be the next Governor of California.[18]

Upon arriving in Florida, Briggs and his wife began campaigning with Anita Bryant. Briggs quickly noted that the Bryant forces were disorganized and failing to reach out into the Hispanic communities. Since his wife was Mexican and spoke fluent Spanish, they concentrated much of their efforts in the minority communities, urging them to vote against homosexual legal protections.

On the night of the Dade County vote, John Briggs sat with Anita Bryant and her followers and watched their prediction of overwhelming success come true. According to Briggs, the success of the Bryant campaign in capturing voter emotions — and voter dollars — was not lost upon himself or other Conservative religious leaders in the campaign. Briggs credited Anita Bryant with the discovery of the power of this particular theme with conservative voters. Briggs admits that he, Jerry Falwell, San Diego preacher Tim LeHay, and other evangelical ministers quickly capitalized on the debate. As he stated during our interview, "It was great to go to church and pray, but there wasn't any big, burning issue. Anita Bryant slayed the dragon, and it was a great Bible-thumping exercise for preachers on Sunday."

Briggs returned from Florida with the realization that the emotional and financial appeal of this specific "hot button" — homosexual educators — could make him Governor. He called it his "Panama Canal," his ticket to larger political fame.[19] The Proposition 6 campaign provided Briggs with an inroad to three objectives he had hitherto lacked in California political circles — respect within the political community, issues to heighten his visibility, and financial backing. Until the Proposition 6 Initiative, when Briggs announced he was a "credible" Republican candidate for governor, one colleague responded, "John, you wear lifts on your shoes and contact lenses, your teeth are capped and you've had a hair transplant. That's credible?"[20]

Later, a probe was conducted of Briggs' questionable use of funds for his unsuccessful gubernatorial campaign. It was revealed that, apparently, he diverted $317,956 from the California Defend Our Children Initiative fund as well as money from another Initiative he sponsored broadening the use of the death penalty.[21] Thus, sponsoring the Proposition 6 Initiative provided Briggs with a high level of political visibility and access to funds from conservative supporters, although any personal use of such Initiative money violated state election laws. Early in 1978, Briggs withdrew from the Republican race for governor. He had consistently trailed fifth out of five candidates and gathered only 3 percent of the primary votes.[22]

Briggs' stated opposition to homosexuals stemmed from his concern for the family rather than any direct experience of harm from the lesbian and gay male community. A former real estate broker and the father of three grown children,[23] Briggs converted to Catholicism when he married. But he felt that the Catholics were "no help" in his Proposition 6 battles. Rather, his support came from "born-again Christians who . . . shared his abhorrence of gays who infest the school system."[24]

To Briggs, homosexuals were criminals who were "living an immoral lifestyle, committing an infamous crime against nature." As long as they were discreet about it, however, Briggs did not mind. In fact, he was questioned about the dilemma faced by homosexual teachers who might choose to lie to the school board about their sexual orientation. Briggs replied, "In politics, you tell the truth — but not always the whole truth."[25] Thus, Briggs' direct concern was the more open, politicized homosexual, because he or she presented a viable alternative lifestyle to the traditional, heterosexual nuclear family. As Briggs stated in one speech, "the central issue here in Proposition 6 is the question of role modeling and parents' rights. . . . An open and avowed homosexual is not a good role model."[26]

Briggs and his followers were aware that many lesbians and gay men were teaching in the California schools but were not easily identified as homosexual. In a speech with Briggs in Healdsburg, California, the president of the school board stated, "there are lesbians, homosexuals in every school district now and they keep their lives to themselves."[27] But those who have "come out of the closet" and present their lifestyles as normal and healthy are a direct threat to the moral fiber of the nation.

When questioned directly about the Proposition 6 campaign, Briggs admitted that he had no evidence of homosexuals harming children in schools. He called it, "A man thing. Women in California did not perceive it to be a threat to them, but men got it automatically." Briggs further stated that what two women did in bed was of no interest or offense to him, but all men agreed that two men in bed was repulsive. It was this repulsion that required passage of Proposition 6 — to save young boys from being seduced into that activity.

Briggs then admitted that he had not even known any homosexuals, although he later found out that some of his legislative colleagues were gay. In fact, when pressed during a nationally-televised debate to prove if he even knew a homosexual, Briggs floundered for a moment, then pointed to the reporter who had been assigned to cover him for the *San Francisco Chronicle*. Randy Shilts had not come out of the closet publicly before that evening. Shilts subsequently gained national attention as the award-winning author of *And The Band Played On: Politics, People, and the AIDS Epidemic* and *Conduct Unbecoming: Gays and Lesbians in the U.S. Military*.[28]

POISED FOR VICTORY

By late May of 1978, the "Briggs' Initiative" took on new significance. By then the victories in Dade County, St. Paul, Eugene, and Wichita were political realities. Confidence in a victory in California seemed warranted. Those opposed to Proposition 6 felt that they had to prohibit the Initiative from the November ballot through legal action or prepare to fight its constitutional validity after the election. Defeat by public vote looked doubtful.[29]

On May 2, 1978, Briggs filed the signatures of registered voters required to place Proposition 6 on the November ballot. Starting at the San Francisco County Registrar's Office, Briggs filed only 1,000 voter signatures, but commenced the action there because it was "the moral garbage dump of homosexuality in this country."[30] Later that day, in Los Angeles County and other counties around the state, Briggs filed another 500,000 signatures. However, the exact number of valid signatures may have been closer to the 312,000 required to qualify the Initiative.[31]

During the Los Angeles filing, Briggs announced, "We had the preliminary back in St. Paul, back in Dade County. And now the main event is here in California." Political observers agreed, noting that whether it passed or failed Proposition 6 had the "potential for setting national trends."[32] Success seemed certain. Analyses by pollsters suggested that almost a quarter of California's voters had some ties to conservative Christian churches, the backbone of the political activity for the Initiative.[33] An initial poll by Mervin Field taken in late August of 1978 showed the Initiative passing by a 61 percent to 31 percent margin.[34] By late September, however, the Initiative only held a two-point advantage, and an even later poll showed it trailing by 14 points.[35] This abrupt change of public sentiment appeared to result from the emerging visibility of opposition to the Initiative by public figures and political leaders.

Los Angeles Mayor Thomas Bradley characterized Proposition 6 as "the kind of measure that might have been introduced by Adolf Hitler."[36] Dr. Benjamin Spock, Governor Edmund Brown, and then-President Gerald Ford also warned that the Initiative would "invite abusive invasions of privacy."[37] After voting 6 to 1 to oppose the Initiative, the San Francisco Board of Education described it as a "serious threat to the civil liberties of all Americans . . . which would repress the freedom of speech of teachers and other staff, and would permit legal discrimination against any public school employee who supported gay rights."[38]

To oppose the Initiative, the AFT, with a California membership of 32,000, united with the California Teachers Association (CTA) and its 157,000 members. The Assembly of the NEA adopted a statement declaring that the organization was committed to defeat all laws and initiatives that discriminated against teachers and other school employees.[39]

The greatest influence opposing Proposition 6 was former Governor Ronald Reagan. In commenting on the Initiative, Reagan said that it had "the potential for real mischief." Students might blackmail their teachers with threats of accusations of homosexuality. "Innocent lives could be ruined."[40] Reagan stated:

> Whatever else it is, homosexuality is not a contagious disease like measles. Prevailing scientific opinion is that an individual's sexuality is determined at a very early age and that a child's teachers do not really influence this . . . .[41]

Furthermore, Reagan noted that existing California laws were sufficient to punish any teacher who flaunted his or her homosexual lifestyle or harmed children, and they provided adequate procedures for investigating and fairly determining charges of teacher misconduct.[42] In one statewide editorial, Reagan noted the measure would involve enormous governmental activity and cost incalculable amounts of public funds for enforcement. He concluded the editorial by calling for a "No" vote on Proposition 6, so that "the old line, as California goes, so goes the nation," would mean less government involvement and the prevention of a nationwide witch-hunt against homosexuals.[43]

When questioned about Reagan's role in defeating Proposition 6, John Briggs stated, "they cut me off at the knees." Apparently Briggs had met with Reagan to ask his endorsement, and Reagan initially expressed support. Briggs stated he knew his cause was lost when Reagan said he would have to ask Nancy Reagan and his staff before giving an endorsement. Given all of Nancy's homosexual Hollywood friends and hairdressers, and Reagan's national campaign for the Presidency, Briggs knew that Reagan would not be permitted to give a statement favoring the proposition. Briggs, however, did not expect Reagan to make such a strong statement opposing the Initiative.

Reagan's public statements of opposition were significant because of his leadership role in the Conservative realm of California politics. According to the pollsters, a significant shift away from support for Proposition 6 occurred after the comments of Ronald Reagan and other political leaders. Their opinions cut into the support base of those who advocated the Initiative.

In commenting upon the apparent lack of support for the Initiative from political leaders and the non-fundamentalist religious organizations, John Briggs stated, "all of the pandering politicians have veered off to the left because there is money over there. . . . So I stand almost alone, but I think I have God on my side."[44] Perseverance was necessary, according to several fundamentalist leaders, because Proposition 6 was the key to their continuing battles against "homosexuality, abortion, Satanism, and humanism."[45]

DESPERATE TO DEFEAT

Since the Proposition initially looked as if it would pass at the polls, groups opposing Proposition 6 felt their best strategy to protect homosexual rights was to eliminate the Initiative before the election. This two-pronged legal attack on the Initiative involved challenging the validity of its qualifications and its constitutionality.

Charges of voter fraud around the Initiative immediately surfaced. One student at California State University, Long Beach, said she answered an employment ad posted at the university calling for someone who could transfer printed material to hand-written material in different writing styles. Claudia Long said a man named Bill Crosby handed her a list of computer printouts of voter registration rolls and several empty Briggs' Initiative petitions. He told her to transfer the voter information onto the petition forms. When she questioned the legality of this action, Crosby told her that the voters had given their permission by phone. According to Long, she later telephoned several of the people listed, and they denied any knowledge of the petition efforts. Long later informed the Huntington Beach Police Department and the District Attorney in Orange County.[46]

In other fraud charges, petition circulators were accused of telling people they did not have to be registered voters to sign the petition and that the petition was a bill to "prevent homosexuals from enticing children."[47] State election codes require that the wording of the Initiative be incorporated into the petition to inform the public of its specific content. However, many complaints surfaced about invalid petitions and inaccurate information. Part of the concern over the validity of the signatures was that the Briggs' forces paid people who circulated the petitions between $.35 and $.50 per name — an unusual action. Opponents felt this action gave circulators an incentive to deceive voters and to gather an inordinate number of signatures.[48]

Although numerous charges of voter fraud surfaced around Proposition 6, Secretary of State March Fong Eu decided that enough signatures were valid to qualify the Initiative. ACLU attorneys protested that the Los Angeles County District Attorney's Office handled the complaints of petition fraud in a "disinterested fashion," and concluded that little would come of the supposed investigations.[49]

Since efforts to challenge the validity of qualifying signatures failed, opponents asserted other legal tactics to prevent the Initiative's placement on the November ballot. In late May of 1978, two lawsuits filed in the California Supreme Court charged the Initiative was unconstitutional and, therefore, should be barred from the ballot.

The CFT and the Metropolitan Community Church (MCC), joined with an *amicus curiae* brief ("friend of the Court" — an additional legal perspective on the issue under consideration) by the Northern California Chapter of the ACLU, argued that the California Supreme Court should strike the Initiative from the ballot before the election. They urged the Court to take this unusual step because of the numerous unconstitutional characteristics of the Initiative. They charged that the Initiative was overbroad because it would punish homosexual or heterosexual teachers who expressed facts or opinions that might differ with local school officials. Further, they argued that the Initiative "lends itself to arbitrary, discriminatory and erratic enforcement."[50]

The group charged that the Initiative violated freedoms of speech, assembly, and association, as well as rights of due process, equal protection, and privacy. The MCC suit further argued that the Initiative violated the establishment of religion clause of the First Amendment and the free exercise clause. Their view was that it imposed the views of certain fundamentalist sects on all California school teachers, and it limited the freedom of those teachers to worship in the MCC homosexual environment.[51]

In a summary of their position, the petitioners stated that since the Briggs' Initiative was a clear abridgement of U.S. Constitutional protections, such as freedoms of speech and association, a public vote on the matter should not be permitted. Majority rule should have nothing to do with unconstitutional laws.[52]

In early July of 1978, the California Supreme Court refused to grant the relief requested, without stating an opinion. Donald Solomon, an attorney for Gay Rights Advocates (GRA), a San Fransisco legal aid organization for homosexuals, which represented the California Federation of Teachers, expressed disappointment but not surprise at the outcome. "The Supreme Court has not intervened in pre-election matters except for a handful of times."[53] The traditional role of the Court is to await the outcome of such an election and then rule on the constitutionality of such a measure, rather than interfere with the voting process.

Because of the threat of a McCarthyesque blacklisting, groups organized to oppose Proposition 6 faced a difficult time gathering both personal and financial support. Not surprisingly, GLBT school teachers in California felt caught in a "Catch 22" situation regarding their political involvement against the Initiative. Not working to defeat Proposition 6 left them vulnerable to the possibility of its passage. Working against the Initiative potentially exposed them as homosexual, which further threatened their job security whether or not the Initiative succeeded. In fact, members of the California Save Our Children Committee were quick to expose GLBT teachers who were working in opposition to the Initiative.[54]

In Healdsburg, California, for example, second-grade school teacher Larry Berner publicly opposed Proposition 6 in a letter to the school board. Somehow, his homosexuality became public knowledge. A petition was circulated immediately and presented to the school board demanding that Berner be fired. Because sex between consenting adults was legalized in California in 1975, there were no criminal grounds on which to remove Berner from his teaching post. In protest of Berner's retention, 15 parents removed their children from the school. With this action, the school board argued that Berner should be fired on the grounds that he was costing the school revenue and causing parental upset.

In a public hearing to consider Berner's dismissal, over 300 protesters gathered to oppose the school board's action. Numerous parents mentioned that Berner was an excellent teacher. Two Chicano mothers stated they did not want their children to "grow up to be bigots."[55] Speaking in support of Berner's dismissal, one mother stated that children who had been in his classes "wiggled and minced" their way to the school bus.[56] Considering the threats by the opposition protesters to remove their children from the school, however, the Healdsburg School Board voted to retain Berner.

Throughout the Proposition 6 campaign, John Briggs referred to the frustration of the Healdsburg School Board and its legal inability to remove an openly homosexual teacher from its staff. Proposition 6, in Briggs' opinion, was the only mechanism for again establishing "automatic grounds" for removal since the 1975 law changed concerning sex between consenting adults.

The day after the Healdsburg School Board was forced to retain Berner, Briggs and the board chairperson, Mrs. Lee, appeared in a press conference in Los Angeles. She stated it was because of people like Berner that Proposition 6 needed to be passed. Briggs commented:

> If you'd put a second-grade child with a homosexual, you're off your gourd.

> We don't allow necrophiliacs to be morticians. We've got to be crazy to allow homosexuals who have an affinity for young boys to teach our children.

> We're not here to say that homosexuals can't teach. We're saying that public homosexuality shouldn't be tolerated.[57]

Berner attempted to prevent Briggs from repeatedly naming GLBT teachers in his speeches and written materials. He filed suit charging Briggs with singling out these individuals for vilification by portraying them as child molesters and with being violent and mentally ill.[58] Fear of these consequences, however, effectively kept much of the teaching population of California publicly silent on the issue.

School teachers were not the only Californians leery of publicly opposing Proposition 6. Some of the greatest fear was expressed in the entertainment industry, usually a source of tremendous support for liberal causes. Receptions and fundraisers gained only slight attendance, as celebrities feared they would be labeled homosexual if they attended a "No-on-6" event. At one such event in Southern California, when a television crew arrived to report on the celebrity attendance, almost everyone left the hotel rather than be filmed.[59]

Similar difficulties arose in relation to soliciting contributions. Under the 1974 Political Reform Act, donors contributing $50.00 or more to any political campaign must give their name, address, occupation, and place of employment. This policy had been instituted in response to the Watergate scandals, which revealed that corporations were donating large contributions to candidates in return for support of their special interests. To avoid disclosure, contributors opposing Proposition 6 would limit their support to $49.00 in cash. The need for this secrecy was heightened when it was revealed that Briggs' San Francisco office had obtained documents listing contributors who had given more than the $50.00 limit. In response to the fear and potential intimidation, attorneys for the ACLU filed petitions with the California Court of Appeals, requesting that contributors opposing the Initiative not be required to give their names. Precedent for this exemption was established when the Communist Party was exempted from the Reform Acts requirements, also because of blacklisting and threats of reprisals.[60]

Activities of the anti-initiative forces focused on two strategies. One was voter registration, in a direct attempt to outnumber conservative representation at the polls. The other tactic was community education. This latter process was very difficult for many lesbian and gay men because it forced them to expose themselves to their colleagues and to strangers as homosexuals. One attitudinal study undertaken during the Initiative revealed that if a voter knew one homosexual, he or she was likely to vote in opposition to Proposition 6.[61] Thus, lesbians and gay men all over California took the courageous stand of informing people whom they knew that any sort of anti-gay legislation would affect them personally. Working with the theme of "we're no different than you," well-dressed teams of a lesbian and a gay man canvassed neighborhoods in support of gay rights. In areas that might be more hostile, the gay team would be joined by two heterosexuals as they canvassed.[62] Some of this heterosexual support came from staff members of various candidates for public office, who hoped to benefit from the predicted large number of gay voters turning out for the November elections.[63]

To counter the growing support in opposition to the Initiative, Briggs tried to characterize the need for the Initiative as an attempt to stop a homosexual conspiracy. Briggs warned parents that, "a coalition of homosexual teachers and their allies are trying to use the vast power of our school system to impose their own brand of nonmorality on your children."[64]

As evidence of the conspiracy and that homosexuals were intent upon recruiting young children, the California Defend Our Children literature listed demands stated in a 1972 convention platform of the National Coalition of Gay Organizations. Apparently the Coalition called for a repeal of all laws governing the age of sexual consent; federal support for sex education material and courses that included homosexuality in a positive format; and the enactment of legislation that removed sexual orientation as a bar to child custody, adoption, visitation, and foster parenting.[65] Conservatives felt that homosexuals intended to totally destroy the American family.[66] As Briggs noted, "How many more letters must Los Angeles and San Francisco papers print from wives and husbands whose marriages collapsed because the spouse became homosexual, before we begin to see that homosexuality is undermining America's families?"[67]

Another theme in the campaign literature paralleled the Puritan belief that God would punish all of society if individuals were allowed to behave in a manner that caused displeasure. Because of the homosexual affront, God would punish the nation with earthquakes, storms, freezing weather, and other disasters. In his "Letter of Warning to the Homo's," Donald Chesney wrote a long analysis of the dangers of homosexuality. Although his writing is grammatically incorrect, his sentiments echoed those of many fundamentalist believers:

> Homosexuality is one of the worst sins our nation will be punished for — it is so much against our God and Mankind!!!! This madness has to stop before our whole country is submerged into hell — this is civil suicide!!

> Our Government is supposed to be for the people and ruled by the majority of the people! The abnormals have no voice in it. This is all very wrong in Gods eyes and in His Laws!! Humans never made our laws, that this Universe is suposed to be controled by — our Heavenly Father made these — no one else!!!

> Do you people not have enough love for yourselves, enough respect, enough morals and enough love for country to stop all this, immorality, before you bring hell down on all of our heads! Cannot you see that conditions are getting worse and worse!! Don't any of you have an ounce of wisdom?? But you have seen nothing yet as to what our God can do, if you do not stop these evil acts of yours!! Did you not see the movie, "Earthquake"? Well,

that could be mild, compared to what our God can really do and will do if people do not strighten themselves out and turn back to Him!!

And you know in your hearts — that because mostly of homos and prostitution and pornography; San Fran is now one of the most wicked cities in the world and over-ripe for a destruction — and if it were not for Christians pleading and praying to our God; He would have probably destroyed it a long time ago — just another reason why all people should be so thankful that there are praying Christians!!

Ours is about the only Christian Country in the Universe, that I know of — and as we drift away from Him; So it is the very reason why we have lost so much of that power and prestige that we used to have, only a few short years ago. . . . And as we drift further and further from Him; so goes the freedom for all of us — a person with only half a brain can see this and know that we do not have the freedoms that we used to have.

So if you people do not come <u>to grips with reality</u>; come to our <u>Lord Jesus Christ</u>; and throw off Satan — were all doomed!!! It wasn't funny, a long time ago; but now it is sickening!![68]

CHAPTER CONCLUSIONS

Finally, on November 7, 1978, California voters defeated the Briggs' Initiative by a 2 to 1 margin.[69] For the first time, supporters of homosexual rights had won an election against the conservatives. In fact, they may have won their most important election. With the loss in California, Conservative leaders abandoned the tactic of statewide propositions for popular consideration that had been so successful on the local level. By November of 1978, the new avenue of success against homosexual teachers appeared as bills, which contained the same wording as California's Proposition 6, introduced directly to a state's House and Senate. Attention now turned to the State of Oklahoma and its enactment of such a law against homosexual teachers.

It may be better to live under robber barons than under omnipotent moral busybodies.

— *C. S. Lewis*

CHAPTER **4**

OKLAHOMA AND THE U.S. SUPREME COURT

A STANDOFF ON EMERGENT STATES' RIGHTS, 1978–1985

As the local organizer for GLBT concerns in Oklahoma City, "Sam White" was devastated by the rapid passage of the Proposition 6-type legislation that opposed any positive portrayal of homosexual issues in public educational settings. Sam knew the only mechanism for challenging the legislation was litigation concerning the constitutionality of the bill. As always, there were the significant obstacles of establishing community support and financial assistance to undertake the litigation. But of greater concern in this instance was the challenge of finding individuals who were willing to risk their employment and lifetime teaching credentials to serve as petitioners to the court in opposing the legislation.

After months of hard work, Sam convinced seven teachers employed in public schools in Oklahoma to stand as petitioners. They agreed, provided they could do so anonymously to avoid job loss, threats of violence, and verbal harassment. Anonymous petitions to American courts is an established legal entitlement in circumstances of hardship and repercussions to the petitioners if their identities become known. Sam felt hopeful that now the litigation could move forward smoothly and relatively quickly. But the collusion of the Oklahoma judicial system with the state legislature helped cause a seven-year delay in resolving the dispute. The Court prohibited the anonymous petitions by denying that any threat to the petitioners existed if their identities were known to their employers or the public. Thus, all of the anonymous petitioners withdrew from the litigation.

Eventually, Sam located one gay man in Oklahoma who held a state teaching credential and was willing to challenge the litigation publicly. Stan Easter took this courageous step and withstood the repercussions for several months. Eventually, he too withdrew from the litigation and left the State of Oklahoma. However, his initial courageous act served as the basis for the legal challenge of the Oklahoma statute that ultimately led to the United States Supreme Court.

During the final months before the popular vote on California's Proposition 6, the Oklahoma House and Senate were presented with House Bill 1629. It was an exact duplicate of the Briggs' Initiative against "public homosexual conduct" by school teachers. John Monks (D-Muskogee) introduced the measure in the House of Representatives in February of 1978. The House passed the measure by a vote of 88 to 2 with no debate. Once sent to the Senate for consideration, the Bill was in the hands of its major sponsor, Senator Mary Helm (R-Oklahoma City), for whom it was named. On April 6 of 1978, the Oklahoma Senate passed the Helm's Bill by a vote of 42 to 0, again with no debate. Governor David Boren immediately signed it into law.[1]

Since the Helm's Bill was a replica of the Briggs' Initiative, its content will not be discussed further. Instead, of interest here is the political history in Oklahoma and the legal maneuvering that eventually led the United States Supreme Court to consider the law in January of 1985.

THE KLAN CAMPAIGN

Conservative Oklahoma was a predictable setting for statewide legislation against homosexual school teachers during the 1977-1978 anti-homosexual campaigns. Anita Bryant was the former Miss Oklahoma and a Miss America finalist. She remained a popular religious and commercial figure in the state. In fact, after the 1977 Dade County campaign, the Oklahoma Senate unanimously passed a resolution praising Anita Bryant for her stand against homosexuals. Sponsored by Senator Mary Helm, the resolution was in response to the perception of "an apparent national movement to discredit our beloved Anita Bryant."[2] The resolution commended Bryant for leading a movement to protect children against "insidious forces more interested in gratifying their own personal desires than guarding the children and families. . . . the basic foundation of our great nation." Supporters of Anita Bryant and the Helm's Bill viewed these efforts as an attempt to stop the "trend that was singling out homosexuals for special rights."[3]

Another significant factor in the Oklahoma campaign was the strong presence of the John Birch Society and the Ku Klux Klan, particularly within the public high schools. In May of 1977, Grand Wizard David Duke and several Oklahoma high school students publicly discussed the Klan's recruitment efforts and the battle against homosexuals. Duke noted that the Klan's belief in "one's race, one's self, the Constitution, and God" held great potential for male students. Thus, to further direct these young men on the Klan path, homosexuals must be barred from teaching children and flaunting their ways in society. Comments from the male students stressed that the modern Klan was not only against Blacks, but against girls, Jews, Catholics, dope smokers, and gays. They admitted organizing a violent "campaign of terror" against homo-sexuals. This included attacks with baseball bats and knives on the grounds that "this activity (homosexuality) is morally and socially wrong."[4] Klan meetings were held to arouse student hatred and plan raids on homosexual clubs and gatherings. Furthermore, Klan supporters acted as bodyguards for Anita Bryant and other conser-vative leaders during anti-homosexual rallies.

Although it is a broad leap from Klan and student activities to the Oklahoma State House, they shared common views against homosexuals. This manifested itself as almost unanimous disap-proval of anyone, heterosexual or homosexual, who expressed acceptance of the lifestyle and certainly against anyone who engaged in same-sex activity. The goal, according to Representative Monks, was to keep "these sick, deranged people from affecting our precious treasures, our children." "Word would get around about any queers or lesbians" who were a substantial risk to children because of their teaching employment, and the legislation would be in place to permit their dismissal.[5]

EMPOWERED CONSERVATIVE ADMINISTRATORS

Even before the Helm's Bill became law in Oklahoma, some superintendents of schools around the State took action against GLBT educators. They based their authority upon the Dade County campaign and a recent homosexual educator case the United States Supreme Court had refused to reconsider. In Gaylord v. Tacoma School District, a high school teacher had been dismissed from employment because a former student had mailed a letter to the school accusing him of being a homosexual.[6] Gaylord admitted to school authorities that he was a homosexual, so the District felt entitled to terminate his employment despite frequent excellent evaluations.

In a similar context, Superintendent Thomas Smith of Oklahoma City announced that disciplinary action would be taken against homosexuals if their activities interrupted normal teaching duties. Since, in his opinion, role modeling was an important function of teaching, teachers' behavior that deviated from that norm would be scrutinized closely. Smith further stated that his district was comparatively liberal in its attitude towards homosexuals. It had no set policy about dismissing homosexuals just because of their lifestyle and would weigh any improper conduct against an individual's teaching responsibilities.[7]

PUBLIC PARALYSIS

The lack of public response to the Bill might suggest that the majority of Oklahomans favored action against homosexual educators. Another interpretation might be that people opposed to the Bill, such as some school employees, believed that overt criticism of this law would jeopardize their employment. In Norman, Oklahoma, for example, John Mehring of the University of Oklahoma's Gay Activist Alliance spoke on behalf of "innumerable" educators concerned that the Helm's Bill was overbroad and vague. Mehring characterized both homosexual and heterosexual teachers as fearful of a witch-hunt if they spoke up against this limitation on their civil rights.[8]

Another outspoken critic of the Helm's Bill was Steve Keller, also a member of the Alliance. Keller labeled the Bill "fundamentally unconstitutional" and openly discussed the role of the Ku Klux Klan in organizing high school students to attack homosexuals. He encouraged the Oklahoma Education Association to take action, demanding that they adhere to the NEA's stated policy concerning its opposition to discrimination on the basis of sexual orientation. Richard Morgan, Executive Director of the Oklahoma Education Association, said he could not confirm Keller's statement about NEA policies since it "has floated back and forth over the years" and was unclear to him at that time. Morgan did express strong opposition to the law, however. He called it an "election-year bill" that infringed upon the due process rights of teachers.[9] Although Morgan and the Oklahoma Education Association did not "condone or support homosexual activity by teachers," in their opinion the current education code was sufficient to deal with any problem that might arise.[10]

Ultimately, the Oklahoma Education Association elected not to participate in the litigation because its membership did not believe in non-discrimination on the basis of sexual orientation. Weldon Davis, a subsequent director of the organization, said the law was "clearly discriminatory." Davis said he expected it to be "struck down once it got outside of Oklahoma" and that his organization was quite willing to let others make the hard decisions for them.[11]

Because of the strong support for the Helm's Bill, and the fear of negative consequences if one publicly opposed it, efforts to organize a visible counter-movement barely materialized. Homosexual leaders of the Gay Activist Alliance sought legal support from GRA and from the ACLU.[12] Thus began the seven-year legal struggle to have the Helm's Bill declared unconstitutional. Due to the statute's broad, vague language and its potential to infringe upon First Amendment freedoms of speech and association, defeat seemed imminent. What stands out, however, are the great lengths to which the majority used the legal system to frustrate minority efforts and the precarious balance between civil rights and homosexual expression.

LEGAL MANEUVERING

To commence litigation against the Bill in the federal court in Oklahoma City, GRA and ACLU attorneys had to identify plaintiffs who were willing to step forward and litigate their rights. Since the law had not been applied to a specific person, some teachers in Oklahoma affected by the Bill had to state that their First Amendment rights of free speech, association, and religion and their due process and equal protection rights were "chilled" by the presence of the law on the books. Finding suitable plaintiffs was not an easy process. Heterosexual or homosexual school employees who stepped forward faced harassment and possible dismissal. Some willing litigants had less-than-perfect teaching records, which would provide the State with the argument that their dismissal was on grounds not pertaining to the Helm's Bill. Eventually, seven people were identified as litigants.[13]

To protect the seven litigants' identities, they filed a brief as anonymous plaintiffs, providing affidavits explaining how the law adversely affected their rights. This procedure had been affirmed by the courts in situations where identified plaintiffs faced potential harm.[14] Despite the need and the precedence concerning anonymous plaintiffs, the plaintiffs were concerned that the defendant, the Oklahoma Board of Education, would challenge the use of the procedure. This would delay the litigation by as much as two years. In fact, the Oklahoma school system did choose that tactic.[15]

Although it was predictable that the Board of Education would use this legal maneuver, no one assumed that it would prevail in its argument that the plaintiffs faced no potential harm. When the case of Mikki Moe, Jane Roe, Darlene Doe, Paula Doe, John Doe, Mary Moe, and Robert Roe v. The State Board of Education of the State of Oklahoma came before federal District Court Judge Luther Eubanks, he ruled that the use of anonymous plaintiffs was inappropriate and unnecessary in this instance. Since none of the plaintiffs felt safe about revealing his or her identity, Eubanks dismissed the suit. Subsequent appeals concerning the legality of anonymous plaintiffs and later motions to seek a preliminary injunction to prohibit the enforcement of the statute also were denied.

The anticipated long delay became a reality as the search for appropriate plaintiffs continued. Throughout the life of the Helm's Bill, its supporters would argue that since it was never applied to a specific teacher, it did not violate constitutional freedoms. It is apparent, however, that the problems in finding willing plaintiffs to challenge the law stemmed from real fears about job loss and physical violence. These fears were validated by Bill Rogers, chairman of Oklahomans for Human Rights, who noted that teachers were leaving the State and the profession because of the consequences of the Helm's Bill.

THE CONSTITUTIONAL CHALLENGE

Finally, in The National Gay Task Force and Stan Easter v. The Board of Education of the City of Oklahoma City, State of

Oklahoma, opponents of the Helm's Bill restated their challenges. Lobbying efforts to encourage the NEA to join as a plaintiff had failed. The anti-Helm's leaders feared their standing to sue might prove to be vulnerable again.[16] Stan Easter, who was certified to teach in Oklahoma, had never even applied for a teaching position.

As before, the Board of Education argued that no actual harm had occurred to an identifiable plaintiff in the lawsuit. Although the Court ruled in favor of the National Gay Task Force's (NGTF) right to proceed as a plaintiff, the issue was complicated further when Stan Easter withdrew his name from the litigation. Easter felt he lacked standing to sue in the matter since he had never applied for a teaching position.[17] Despite this setback, the litigation proceeded with NGTF as the sole plaintiff on behalf of all homosexual educators.

On June 29, 1982, Judge Eubanks issued his opinion in favor of the Board of Education of Oklahoma City. Eubanks determined that if a teacher was declared unfit under the Helm's statute he or she would "materially and substantially" disrupt normal school activities. Thus, Eubanks found firm support for the position of the school board over the rights of free speech of an individual teacher related to the issue of homosexuality. Furthermore, Eubanks held that unreasonable fears were the basis of any "chilling" effect that the law might have on freedoms of speech and association. The arguments of overbreadth and vagueness were countered by the comment that "a man of reasonable intelligence can certainly view the statute and determine which acts he should avoid." Finally, Eubanks held that there were no privacy, equal protection, due process, or establishment clause protections that would apply to same-sex behavior.[18]

In response to the Eubanks decision, anti-Helm's litigants appealed to the United States Court of Appeals, 10th Circuit. There, by a vote of 2 to 1, they prevailed.[19] The holding in this instance was important because it was upheld later by the United States Supreme Court, which in this case granted a *writ of certiorari* to consider homosexuality as the central issue.[20]

The focus of the 10th Circuit opinion was the statutory phrases "public homosexual activity" and "public homosexual conduct." The Court reasoned that indiscreet acts, such as oral or anal sex, were grounds for dismissal. They determined that the statute did not invade privacy rights or freedom of association because, as written, it did not pertain to homosexual behavior in private between consenting adults. On the other hand, in the Court's opinion the phrase "public homosexual conduct" posed significant constitutional problems of overbreadth and vagueness.

As defined by the Helm's Bill, "public homosexual conduct" meant:

> . . . advocating, soliciting, imposing, encouraging or promoting public or private homosexual activity in a manner that creates a substantial risk that such conduct will come to the attention of school children or school employees.[21]

The court noted that, in <u>Brandenburg v. Ohio</u>, the United States Supreme Court had determined that First Amendment protections extended to the advocacy of lawless behavior unless it was intended and likely to incite imminent lawless action.[22] Because of the extreme to which freedom of speech is protected, teacher discussions of homosexuality could not be limited. As written, the Helm's Bill would infringe upon the liberties of any school employee who publicly or privately spoke in favor of legal or social change regarding homosexuality. Since the Court could not ascertain a constitutionally appropriate, narrow construction of the language of the Bill concerning conduct, particularly in terms of freedom of speech, it held that portion of the law was unconstitutional. Nevertheless, it upheld the remaining sections. The Court commented that the equal protection clause was not compromised because of the state's compelling interest in "not allowing public homosexuals or public advocacy of homosexuality to influence school children." This interest was based upon the state's obligation to provide public education that prepared individuals for citizenship and preserved the values of society.

The 10th Circuit Court of Appeals concluded that the Helm's Bill, minus the section on "public homosexual conduct," still served as the effective deterrent intended by the Oklahoma legislature. However, the Board of Education felt its powers had been severely curtailed. The Board petitioned the United States Supreme Court on a *writ of certiorari* to reconsider the 10th Circuit's opinion. Since the Supreme Court had refused to hear other cases pertaining to homosexual rights over the past few decades, its acceptance of the Oklahoma matter for consideration raised conservatives' hopes for a decision in their favor. Court watchers predicted the Supreme Court would vacate the Appeals Court decision on procedural grounds and avoid ruling on the merits of the case altogether. This would ensure the continued existence of the law during the long process of reconsideration.

THE SUPREME COURT NON-DECISION

On January 14, 1985, oral arguments were held in <u>Board of Education of Oklahoma City v. NGTF</u>. Laurence Tribe, Harvard University's constitutional law scholar, spoke on behalf of the Task Force, while Dennis Arrow represented the Board of Education. Justice Lewis F. Powell was absent from the hearing because he was recovering from prostate surgery. Powell did have the option to review the testimony and vote with the other eight justices.

Arguments were raised about the Task Force's standing to sue and the possible lack of ripeness of the issue since the law had not been applied to any specific individual. The central focus of the debate, however, was the phrase "public homosexual conduct." This issue was complicated by the fact that sodomy was a crime in Oklahoma and 21 other states. Thus, expressions of support or acceptance of the homosexual lifestyle, by extension, were acts of encouraging criminal conduct. As Laurence Tribe noted, the problem was not that teachers "get up on soapboxes and say 'sodomy now.'" Instead, any educator who tried to provide students with a more complicated view of human sexuality, or who advocated for the legalization of homosexual behavior during their non-school hours, faced restrictions upon their freedom of speech.

Tribe also pointed out to the Court that, in 1981, the Task Force agreed to drop the litigation if the Board of Education would limit application of the statute to anyone who intentionally and directly encouraged school-aged children to commit sodomy. The Board of Education refused this offer because it desired to retain control over the broadest possible range of behavior. During questioning by the justices, Arrow admitted that the Board of Education might apply the statute to situations where a teacher was a homosexual and a role model, to public or private statements of support for homosexuality, or to efforts to educate children about homosexuality.[23]

Both parties agreed that the Supreme Court's decision would be a central, precedent-setting determination of educators' freedom of speech rights. Attorney Arrow emphasized the long history of constraints upon teachers and their responsibilities as role models for children. Ultimately, in his opinion, the state's interest in public education as a mechanism to provide "an introduction to traditional, fundamental cultural values" would be threatened *sui generis* (by its very nature) by homosexual advocacy. Furthermore, the psychological welfare of the state's children was at risk.

Attorney Tribe focused his arguments on the long history of minority struggles for civil rights and the great lengths to which the government protected free speech. His references to the Brandenburg criteria about freedom to advocate the violent overthrow of the government met with a strong reaction by one of the justices, as it had with a member of the 10th Circuit. Both justices stated their belief that homosexuality was more evil than promoting the violent overthrow of the government. Ironically, in defense of the argument that homosexuals recruited children, Tribe referred to the 1978 statements made by then-President of the United States, Ronald Reagan, in opposition to Proposition 6. Reagan had stated that common sense made it obvious that homosexuality was not a threat and that current legislation was adequate to deal with any instance in which a teacher molested or enticed a student. Reagan further characterized the Proposition 6 legislation as too costly, too much government intrusion, and too open for the possibilities of witch-hunts within the schools.

93

On March 26, 1985, the United States Supreme Court announced its decision in Board of Education of Oklahoma City v. NGTF. The vote was 4 to 4, with Justice Powell abstaining from the matter. The identities of the justices on each side of the issue were not revealed. However, observers speculated that justices Brennan, Marshall, Blackmun, and Stevens had voted to affirm the unconstitutionality of the law, while justices Rehnquist, O'Connor, White, and Burger had voted to reverse the 10th Circuit opinion. Because of the split decision, the holding of the 10th Circuit was upheld. The issue still is not resolved. Due to the absence of the deciding vote of one justice, the Supreme Court may reconsider the matter if it arises again.

Justice Powell's voting record would suggest that had he participated in the Oklahoma v. NGTF decision, he would have voted with the conservatives. For example, in Bowers v. Hardwick, Justice Powell initially indicated that he would vote in favor of decriminalization of Georgia's sodomy statute, but he ultimately voted along with the conservative majority. Michael Hardwick had been fined for holding an open can of beer on a city street. Although he had paid the fine and the case was resolved, the City of Atlanta erroneously issued an arrest warrant. The police came to Hardwick's apartment and were let into the home — and into Hardwick's bedroom — by a house-mate. The police then arrested Hardwick for violating the state's sodomy statute because he was engaged in consensual homo-sexual sex when they entered his bedroom. The City of Atlanta dropped all charges, but Hardwick proceeded with litigation with the intent of having the courts rule that Georgia's sodomy statute was an unconstitutional intrusion into privacy rights and discriminatory because only same-sex couples were prosecuted. Unfortunately, the 5 to 4 decision by the U.S. Supreme Court is still used today to justify the legality of the sodomy laws in various states.[24]

In a 1990 seminar with law students at New York University, then-retired Justice Powell was asked how he could support privacy rights in Roe v. Wade (women's right to an abortion, 1973) but not support privacy rights within private consensual sex situations. "I think I probably made a mistake with that one," Powell replied, stating that he had thought Hardwick was "a frivolous case," and that he did not realize the larger legal implications of changing his vote to support the conservative majority. In fact, Powell stated that he reread the court's opinion a few months after the decision because it had bothered him, and he realized then that "the dissent had the better of the arguments."[25]

Thus, despite the fact that states such as Texas and Georgia have looked to the <u>Hardwick</u> decision to enforce their sodomy statutes, esteemed constitutional scholar and Harvard Law professor Lawrence H. Tribe placed Justice Powell's admission of error in a significant constitutional context:

> The fact that a respected jurist who is indispensable to the majority conceded that on a sober second-thought he was probably wrong certainly will affect the way that future generations look at the decision.[26]

VOICES OF VICTORY

With the announcement of the Supreme Court's split decision, both sides proclaimed victory. Attorneys for the Board of Education expressed confidence the State would rewrite the legislation and narrow the definition of "conduct" so it would pass subsequent judicial scrutiny. Given the increasingly conservative makeup of the United States Supreme Court and its new leanings towards the rights of each state to define its own laws, observers predicted that a similar hearing on the matter might favor the Board of Education. When asked by NBC Nightly News to comment on the outcome, state Rep. Monks argued that the Supreme Court's decision did not matter because he was sure school boards would continue to get "these people" out of the schools.

Attorney Tribe commented that although the outcome was not definitive, it was a signal "that there will be no green light from this court for laws silencing" speech about homosexuality.[27] Former executive director of the Task Force, Virginia M. Apuzzo, stated:

> In our view the Court has affirmed that gay men and lesbians have the same First Amendment free speech rights as other Americans. It is gratifying to me that justice has been done, but I am appalled that there are four members of the nation's highest court who would deny lesbian and gay citizens their basic Constitutional rights. Clearly, our community cannot relax its vigil, and we must remind our friends outside the gay and lesbian community that we need their continued support.[28]

Certainly the 4 to 4 non-decision of the Supreme Court failed to resolve the matter. In fact, the close vote seemed to convince conservatives that, with a little rewriting, similar legislation would be approved by the Court. Thus, Oklahoma legislators redrafted their legislation to permit administrators to refuse employment or to dismiss school teachers who have engaged in "criminal sexual activity" that impairs their effectiveness as public school employees. Since consensual homosexual sex is illegal in Oklahoma, this law does affect the personal freedoms of educators in the state.[29]

In several other jurisdictions, including North Carolina,[30] Nevada,[31] Texas,[32] and Arkansas,[33] state legislators began considering the enactment of laws similar to the Helm's Bill and the revised Oklahoma provision. In Idaho, a bill prohibiting public school employees from teaching that "homosexuality is a normal or acceptable form of behavior" was drafted in response to the Idaho Education Association's legal support of homosexual rights during the Oklahoma litigation. It was passed by the House of Representatives but killed in the Senate Education Committee.[34]

CHAPTER CONCLUSIONS

The intense conflict over the employment of homosexuals as educators stems from the intersection of three important social issues that have undergone tremendous change recently: homosexuality, the family, and the rights of teachers. By using the legal system to prohibit homosexuals from teaching, conservatives mustered a major resource of the majority in its opposition to the wishes of the minority. Stopping lesbians and gay men from teaching school was equated with stopping the tide of change in traditional cultural values. The move was an effort to preserve the role of the school teacher as one who loyally inculcated these traditional social beliefs.

The state legislative campaigns in California and Oklahoma demonstrate the majority's use of traditional institutional power. Conservative politicians and judges substantiated most of the delaying tactics used by their colleagues in an effort to frustrate the legal efforts of the supporters of homosexual and teacher rights. For example, the accepted use of anonymous plaintiffs was prohibited in the Oklahoma challenge. This occurred despite public statements by conservative and liberal politicians and educators concerning teacher dismissal action and threats of physical violence, the latter by the Ku Klux Klan in particular. In fact, court observers anticipated that the United States Supreme Court also would enhance the conservative position by vacating the 10th Circuit Court's decision on procedural grounds. This would have enabled the Helm's legislation to remain in effect during the long legal battle for reconsideration.

Ironically, one may argue that the strongest weapon GLBT rights advocates had against conservative strength in the traditional institutions of politics, law, education, and religion were the brief statements issued by Ronald Reagan before he became President of the United States. As one of the most influential conservative leaders, Reagan's statement opposing the California Briggs' Initiative carried great weight, as evidenced by the dramatic shift in voter opinion polls.[35] Laurence Tribe's use of these statements in the Oklahoma case hearing before the Supreme Court was a powerful tactical move that reminded the conservative judiciary of the publicly-stated opinions of its Chief Executive.

Although President Reagan may have changed his public image to lean more towards the conservatives, he has never retracted his statements about the Briggs' legislation or called for the dismissal of homosexuals in sensitive employment settings. Neither has he aided the cause of GLBT rights beyond his powerful opposition to the legislation, ostensibly based upon his commitment to limit big government and to cut expenditures. It may be the case, however, that Reagan's many years in the entertainment industry exposed him to numerous lesbians and gay men on both a personal and professional level. Former President Reagan may serve as another example of greater acceptance of and knowledge about the GLBT lifestyle that often develops through actual interpersonal contact with any individual labeled by society as different.

The tie vote of the U.S. Supreme Court Justices in the 1985 Oklahoma case reflected the competing views of American citizens during this first national-level scrutiny of the rights of GLBT educators. Centuries of restrictions upon the personal lives of educators and homosexuals were being rapidly transformed by the emerging concepts of civil rights advanced in the late 1960s. What follows is a history of the struggle from public constraints to personal freedoms — for both educators and gay, lesbian, bisexual, or transgender people — from Colonial times to the present. Since this struggle has taken place within several societal contexts, such as law, education, religion, medicine, family, and self, chapters Five and Six are intended to provide a brief multidisciplinary overview.

Chapter Five focuses on the history of teaching, the concerns of role modeling influences on young minds, and immorality and the teacher dismissal process. Chapter Six first examines the developing legal concept of personal freedom in relation to majority rule. Then, it discusses the sociological framework of status politics where the values of the majority define social acceptance for all, often at the expense of a number of divergent minority populations. Having set these complicated but important elements within the debate over the employment entitlements of GLBT educators, Chapter Seven presents the very earliest historical evidence of the relationship of homosexuality to education.

PART III

AN INTERDICIPLINARY CONTEXT: MORALITY, PRIVACY, STIGMA

I hope to see the day when, as in the early days
of our country, we won't have any public schools.
The churches will have taken them over and
Christians will be running them.
What a happy day that will be.

— Jerry Falwell

CHAPTER 5

TEACHING
A DISESTEEMED PROFESSION

1891 — Elizabeth was raised in reasonable comfort in a small town just outside of Boston. Since young women were permitted an education within the public school system, Elizabeth's academic abilities quickly became apparent. Long after she completed her education, she dreamed of being back in the setting that had been the joy of her life. One-by-one her sisters married, and Elizabeth's parents grew more concerned over her future. One option was to travel to Chicago and work in the slums with a young woman named Jane Addams. One of Elizabeth's friends had made this decision and written back to her describing the need for others to come and assist the poor women and children. But Elizabeth knew that her dreams were in education.

Elizabeth learned of an open teaching position in a town several hours from her home. She wrote to them and was hired quickly. Due to the low pay and the significant restrictions upon her contact with members of the opposite sex, Elizabeth was informed she must live with another young woman who had just joined the school. Thank goodness, she thought, the age-old practice of boarding the school teacher around from house to house on a weekly basis was a thing of the past. Now Elizabeth and her new friend would make a home of their own. But never in her wildest dreams had she imagined the passion and love that became their lifetime commitment. She had found herself a love and a profession she would cherish for the rest of her life.

In order to understand the controversy over the employment of gay men and lesbians, one must have some idea of how teachers have been treated in American society. Whole chapters of books on teaching have been devoted to the question of whether teachers are second-class citizens.[1]   Both educational historians and teachers themselves have recognized that in our society teachers have played an important role in educating the young, but they have also been treated as members of a disesteemed profession.

COMMUNITY CONSTRAINTS

Since Colonial times, American education has emphasized religious and moral development as a primary goal. Puritan ideology asserted that individual and collective survival in this life, and salvation in the next, was possible only by ascertaining God's will and adhering to "the path of righteous conduct."[2]   But salvation was not only a personal compact with God; it also was inextricably linked with the behavior of other community members. In his wrath at an individual, God had the capacity to harm the entire community. Moreover, the misbehavior of one individual suggested that the collective had failed in its duty to inculcate and regulate Christian conduct.

Initially, the Puritans relied on the family and the church to transmit this cultural ideology and the basic knowledge necessary to function as a responsible citizen. But English tradition also included elementary schooling. In fact, the Reformation had stimulated interest in the nexus between education and religion.[3] Thus, by 1642, leaders of the Massachusetts Bay Colony passed laws requiring literacy to read the Bible and skills development for employment purposes. Although it was not formal schooling in the sense we know it today, it served a dual purpose.[4] First, it transmitted religious ideology. Second, it provided children with enough reading, writing, and math skills so they did not become financially burdensome public dependents.

In addition to this religious basis for American schools, another facet of educational history explains the strong culture of Christian conformity in the educational system. During the early Colonial period, the best-educated community members were usually the town ministers. Thus, communities enlisted the most orthodox members of society to teach and gave them control over this emergent mechanism of socialization. These ministers brought to the teaching profession their heightened sense of "strict sectarian tenets." Typically, this was beyond the community's actual collective moral precepts.[5]

By the late 1600s, leaders in the Massachusetts Bay Colony complained that communities were evading their responsibilities by relying on the town minister to teach the children in his spare time. Thus, in 1701 a law was passed that prohibited the use of the town minister as the school instructor, although he retained supervisory control over the endeavor.[6]

Two aspects of this arrangement are relevant to a discussion of constraints on teachers' personal lives. First, the ministers insisted that those who educate the young adhere to the same religious and moral codes to which they themselves were bound. Thus, the hiring process selected individuals who would comply with these demands. Second, during the Colonial period almost all of the teachers were men. Because teachers were paid poorly, the teaching profession attracted people whose professional and personal characteristics were often less than desirable. The desire to hire people who conformed to strict religious and moral codes sometimes conflicted with the reality of who was actually hired. Therefore, both the town minister and other community members felt obligated to intensely regulate the personal and professional conduct of all teachers.

Several issues were involved in the characterization of Colonial teachers as "less than desirable." Often, they lacked the rudimentary skills to teach reading, writing, and math. Also, men who were educated often thought of teaching as a temporary or secondary occupation, since the expansive economy of the New World offered much greater possibilities for monetary reward in other occupations.[7]

To deal with the shortage of teachers while avoiding large public expenditures, it was not unusual for a town to purchase an indentured servant. The servant was duty-bound to teach school for a number of years in exchange for his passage to the New World. "Too often, however, the indentured teachers were convicts shipped from English prisons to America." As one minister in Delaware wrote in 1725, "The truth is that the office and character of such a person is generally very mean and contemptible here, and it cannot be other ways 'til the public takes the Education of Children into their mature consideration."[8]

The low status of teachers in Colonial America, particularly in the Southern colonies, was evidenced by the newspaper notices pertaining to the sale of teachers. In about 1776, the *Maryland Journal* advertised the arrival of an Irish ship into Baltimore, with a cargo of "Irish commodities," including "school masters, beef, pork and potatoes."[9] A 1773 commentary on the ships into Maryland stated:

> Not a ship arrives either with redemptioners or convicts, in which schoolmasters are not as regularly advertised for sale, as weavers, tailors, or any other trade, with little other difference, that I can hear of, excepting perhaps that the former do not usually fetch so good a price as the latter.[10]

Additional press notices "gave warnings of school masters who had run away or forged papers" in a manner similar to the practice of announcing runaway slaves and wives.[11]

Not only did school authorities closely scrutinize the teacher's behavior, but community members were also involved in regulating their public servant. One mechanism for community involvement was the procedure of "boarding around" the local school master in various homes throughout the town.[12] This saved money from the public funds, and it provided opportunities for intimate scrutiny of the personality, beliefs, and behaviors of the school teacher. Townspeople felt directly involved in the regulatory process and free to complain about teacher transgressions and non-conformity in a way no other profession experienced.

Part of the success in obtaining teacher compliance with the regulations began with the hiring process. To preserve the status quo, school trustees and administrators sought teachers who exemplified the same social characteristics and values of the dominant group. Thus, minority applicants and people who might challenge the traditional values were typically unsuccessful in entering the profession. For example, during a period of intense nationalism in the schools in the 1790s, Noah Webster warned community leaders not to hire "foreign teachers and men of poor breeding who are bound to impart their vices to their students."[13] Not surprisingly, African-Americans, immigrants, and other people who were different from the majority were screened out in the hiring process, depending upon the many prejudices that arose locally and nationally during any given period of American history.

Even if a teacher successfully overcame the challenges of the hiring process, he was not completely trusted to uphold community values. Local school authorities instituted elaborate rules of conduct to govern the private lives of their employees. During the initial decades of community homogeneity, compliance was instilled through personal promise and collective watchfulness.

Part of the reason this system of teacher regulation remained effective was that teachers became predominantly female by the early 19th century.[14] Despite this new occupational niche for women in the elementary classrooms of the common school movement, the societal hierarchy of men as managers and women as workers prevailed. Women were to bring their innate skills as nurturing, maternal figures to the classroom to gently mold the personalities of their young charges. Men remained the mentally gifted, managerial wizards who would transpose the world of business onto the educational setting. Thus, much of the teaching work force was female and subservient to their superiors because of the socialization process and the general character of their hierarchical, gender-segregated society.

Furthermore, the women were marginally educated and easily controlled because of their youth. Often, they were interested in teaching as a means to make money only until a marriage proposal allowed them to withdraw from the work force. Even if they desired to retain their teaching position after marriage, the contractual agreement usually decreed that marriage was grounds for immediate termination. This meant that teacher turnover was fairly frequent. Male teachers also added to the turnover issue because other occupations were much more prestigious and financially rewarding. Many educated men obtained short-term jobs as teachers until they established themselves in other professions.

Although a lack of experienced teachers was one facet of this turnover issue, it was of marginal concern because wages were lower for beginning teachers and the community saved revenue. In terms of teachers' rights, however, this high turnover rate harmed efforts to improve the status and freedoms of teachers because it is difficult to organize transitory employees.

Another factor that aided the regulation of teachers' personal lives was that the educators themselves were a part of their community, which typically could be characterized as predominantly rural and conservative. They, too, were socialized to consider teachers above reproach. They were quite aware of the consequences of acting outside the scope of acceptable behavior. Thus, they were self-regulating to a large degree.[15] In fact, one legal advocate for teachers' rights has argued that educators have been aware of the consequences of displeasing their communities, but they have been woefully unaware of their civil liberties and constitutional rights even as late as the 1970s.[16] For example, a 1972 survey of Massachusetts teachers disclosed that the majority of them assumed their freedoms of speech and action were more constrained than were actually the circumstances under state and federal laws. Furthermore, these same teachers believed that signing their employment contract meant they had irrevocably given up the few rights of which they were aware.[17] By remaining uninformed of their rights, and by failing to challenge the educational establishment, these teachers facilitated the existence and proliferation of employment regulations concerning their personal behavior.

CONTRACTUAL CONSTRAINTS

With the advent of urbanization and industrialization during the mid-1800s, the regulation of teacher behavior through community consensus began to break down. School officials continued to assert control over teachers by routinely demanding they sign contracts that severely restricted their personal behavior. For example, one contract for a female teacher in a public school in 1915 obligated her to "not dress in bright colors, not to dye her hair, to wear at least two petticoats, and not to wear dresses more than two inches above the ankles."[18] Another contract in the 1920s mandated that the female teacher adhere to the following:

> I promise to take vital interest in all phases of Sunday-school work, donating of my time, service, and money without stint for the uplift and benefit of the community.

> I promise to abstain from all dancing, immodest dressing, and any other conduct unbecoming a teacher and a lady.

> I promise not to go out with any young men except in so far as it may be necessary to stimulate Sunday-school work.

> I promise not to fall in love, to become engaged or secretly married.

> I promise not to encourage or tolerate the least familiarity on the part of any of my boy pupils.

> I promise to sleep at least eight hours a night, to eat carefully, and to take every precaution to keep in the best of health and spirits, in order that I may be better able to render efficient service to my pupils.

> I promise to remember that I owe a duty to the towns-
> people who are paying me my wages, that I owe respect
> to the school board and the superintendent that hired me,
> and that I shall consider myself at all times the willing
> servant of the school board and the townspeople.[19]

Given these and other detailed restrictions, one teacher in 1935 noted, "How I conduct my classes seems to be of no great interest to the school authorities, but what I do when school is not in session concerns them tremendously."[20]

Although these constraints seem dated and humorous, it is sobering to realize that "until recently the courts have not afforded much solace to teachers burdened by such restrictions."[21] Only during the past three decades have the courts begun to scrutinize the efforts of school authorities to control a teacher's private life.[22] Many constraints have been determined to be unconstitutional abridgements of basic American freedoms of speech, association, religion, and privacy. Since the formation of good character and citizenship historically have been the dominant goals of schools, moral excellence has been required of those who work in schools. In fact, as late as 1980 an Arkansas court stated that not only did a school board have the right to concern itself with the behavior of its teachers, it had an affirmative obligation to the community to do so.[23] Since teachers have been construed to be the absent parent, to stand *in loco parentis* in the eyes of legal, educational, and social institutions, they have been held to the highest standard of conduct.

The restrictions articulated in these early contracts demon-strate the belief that serving as a public employee was a privilege. In light of this esteemed opportunity, and for the greater public good, the employee had to forego the personal freedoms enjoyed by other members of society. This perspective was reinforced by the legal system before the 1960s: "the Courts conceived of government employment as a privilege subject to whatever condi-tions the government wished to impose."[24]

PERSONAL FREEDOMS

With the emergent politics of minority rights in the 1960s, teachers have stepped up the process of challenging their employers. Several factors, such as population movement to urban centers that increased anonymity between home and work, stronger teacher organizations and lobbying efforts, the influence of the mass media,[25] and societal changes for minorities, facilitated these developments

By the late 1960s, the courts began to hold that the surrender of constitutional rights could not be a condition of employment in teaching.[26] Nevertheless, advocates for teachers rights suggest that this minority may be one of the least politicized and informed, especially in light of the severe constraints upon their freedoms.[27]

Now that teachers are asserting their rights, other members of the community regard this change in the status quo as a sign of the breakdown of society. For example, one woman who was shocked by local teacher strike activity, stated:

> I grew up in an era when school teachers were among the most respected members of the community. We looked up to them because of their advanced education and dignified behavior. They were considered to have high moral standards and to be genuinely interested in the welfare of their pupils.

> So the first time I heard that the teachers in a large city had gone on strike, I was shocked. Although I didn't have children in the school system, I felt personally involved. I was so shaken by this new development that I felt I must pray over the matter.[28]

This perspective that schools are the cornerstone of our moral structure is not new. Willard Waller has argued that schools have been considered by the American public to be "museums of virtue." Thus, the public has held the belief that it had the right and the duty to investigate and regulate school personnel's occupation-related and private behavior. Because of these perspectives, constraints upon teachers' personal lives have been numerous and constant over time. People entering the profession have been unconcerned by their presence and accepting of such regulation.

Howard K. Beale, on the other hand, believed that concerns about the personal freedoms of teachers have ebbed and flowed over the years.[29] Beale argued that the rights of teachers lessened and increased during various periods of social change. At first glance, the lessening of restrictions on teachers' personal lives seems difficult to document until the past three decades. There is evidence, however, to support an argument that the public has been more intensely concerned about the behavior of teachers at certain times in our national history and less intensely concerned at other times. For example, during the decades following the American Revolution, when education was thought to be the key to creating the new nation, the public was highly critical of teacher conduct.[30] Teachers also came under fire in the early 20th century, during a period of heightened nationalism in response to increased urbanization, industrialization, and immigration from southern European countries.[31] Thus, it may be more accurate to characterize the ebb and flow seen by Beale as a reflection of changing emphasis on various constraints. These constraints change accordingly as social concerns increase or decrease over certain issues. The real expansion of the rights of teachers, however, occurred in concert with the expansion of personal freedoms for all individuals during the 1960s.

Although a more complete analysis of the constraints on teachers' personal lives is beyond the scope of this book, please note that this topic has more than historical significance. Beale argued in his writings that greater freedom for teachers is a social necessity because it is one of the most important mechanisms for developing intelligent, independent-thinking citizens. He believed that periods in which constraints are imposed upon teachers are dangerous because the consequences — conformity, fear, and rigidity — could cause harm to our society. Schools become the tool for "handing down to children the views, attitudes, prejudices, and ideals of the older generation to be accepted, learned, and lived without question or analysis."[32] Furthermore, in this current period of criticism of the schools and shortages of qualified teachers, it is important to realize that, undoubtedly, some highly attractive candidates have been dissuaded from entering the teaching profession or left it because of these restrictions.[33]

Albert Shanker, President of AFT, has been active in the campaign to improve teachers' lives and the quality of the educational process. Shanker argues that over the next 30 years our nation's schools will face a tremendous demand for excellent teachers due to retirement and attrition. Current studies show that people interested in pursuing a career in education overwhelming fall within the lowest quartile in national college achievement scores. Traditional sources of high-quality teachers coming into education, such as women with few alternative job opportunities and conscientious objectors, are no longer available.[34] Studies also show that, in addition to low pay and lack of professional status, constraints on one's personal life is a very real deterrent to talented individuals who might otherwise consider entering the teaching profession. At a time of tremendous demand for excellent teachers and excellence in education, we must reflect on the status of teachers and the balance between their personal freedoms and society's needs for public constraints. Talented individuals, including the potential pool of between 10 percent and 18 percent of the nation's GLBT population, must be welcomed into the profession and encouraged to remain. The topic of GLBT educators must come out of the closet so personal and policy decisions can be made in an equitable and informed manner.

While Shanker himself expressed support of GLBT educators, he stated that his personal advocacy on this "red herring" issue would detract from the many other important educational concerns he was trying to advance. In other words, he felt the needs of many should be advanced over the concerns of a few individual teachers who wished to raise a very controversial issue within their communities.[35] While the concerns of almost 300,000 educators and their student counterparts should be sufficient numbers to warrant advocacy assistance, the reality is that educators traditionally have tried to avoid controversy within their own communities. In this instance, then, our higher moral and educational principles of equity, inclusion, excellence, and integrity are compromised on the basis of a false consensus. As is the case with issues of racial and gender equity, laws will be needed to bar discrimination in employment and educational opportunity on the basis of sexual orientation. To some extent, laws can effectively curb discriminatory behavior, but attitudes take a much longer time to be modified. Thus, real institutional change will be slow to materialize unless courageous educators firmly articulate and actualize the principles of equity and inclusion that supposedly govern American education.

SHADOW CITIZENS

In his sociological analysis of the teaching profession, Dan C. Lortie characterized teachers as having a "special but shadowed" status that, in part, explained their disesteemed professionalism, limited power, and low wages. In the Colonial period, teachers had to defer to local ministers and community leaders in all aspects of schooling. In the latter decades of the 19th century, communities became larger and more impersonal, and schools were run on a business model. Thus, school principals and other administrators became the "shadows" over the status and power of teachers, joined in later decades by college of education professors.[36]

Throughout American history, teachers have been hired for their ability to model moral and patriotic conduct exceeding that required of other members of society. Because of this requirement, they have had to answer to people who were not knowledgeable about the educational process. Similarly, during the 19th century, when business became the model for educational efficiency, the people who actually educated the students were considered to be ill-equipped for decision-making in the professional management system. Thus, it is arguable that teachers have never controlled their occupational duties in the educational setting. It could be argued, too, that this institution historically has been subject to the will of the community in a manner unlike that experienced by any other profession.

Lortie also suggested that, unlike most other professions, teaching has always been an occupation that was relatively easy to enter. State and local communities have found it beneficial to accept individuals with minimal educational backgrounds and then encourage them to further their education while employed as teachers. Widening the pool of potential teacher candidates was one way to provide incentives and entry into a remarkably low-paying occupation. On the other hand, these practices are the opposite of those taken by law, medicine, and other high-status professions that emphasize learning a specialized body of knowledge through highly selective processes of educational attainment.

One feature of professionalization that education has shared with law and medicine has been the entry-level scrutiny of personal morality. Candidates for these professions have had to file applications and recommendations that attest to their moral character, patriotism, and honesty. In her research on this review process in the legal profession, however, Deborah Rhode suggests that if a candidate was a male member of the mainstream racial, ethnic, economic, and religious grouping, the attestations of his moral uprightness were merely a perfunctory examination.[37] If the candidate was Black, female, economically underprivileged, Jewish, homosexual, or of some other less acceptable background, the morality criterion loomed as a potential barrier to entering the profession. On the other hand, unlike the teaching profession, once candidates in law and medicine were ushered into the professional body, scrutiny of their private morality lessened. In some manner, mere acceptance into the professions of law or medicine assured the admittee the protection of the occupational collective and the deference of the population at large. This has never been the case in the teaching profession.

TEACHERS AS ROLE MODELS

As the previous sections of this chapter demonstrate, clergy and community leaders have been concerned with the moral development of our nation's youth since Colonial times. For example, in 1790 Noah Webster argued that:

> Laws can only check the public effects of vicious principles; but can never reach the principles themselves; and

preaching is not very intelligible to people, till they arrive at an age when their principles are rooted, or their habits firmly established.

The only practicable method to reform mankind, is to begin with children; to banish, if possible, from their company, every low bred, drunken, immoral character. . . . The great art of correcting mankind therefore, consists in prepossessing the mind with good principles.[38]

One of the most accepted methods of "prepossessing the mind with good principles" was to expose children to people who would model exemplary behavior. It was this role-modeling function that served as the basis for demanding that teachers adhere to a virtuous lifestyle.

The concern that children be exposed to proper exemplars has been a facet of the American educational system since its inception. But it was not until the 1920s and early 1930s that scholars from several disciplines began to formulate scientific and theoretical perspectives on role modeling.[39] While analysis of this complex subject is beyond the scope of this book, the issue warrants a brief discussion because much of the anti-homosexual sentiment is based upon the belief that homosexual role models will instill children with homosexual tendencies and desires.

As is the case with other complex social and psychological topics, the subject of role modeling has gone through a long history of theoretical development and criticism. For example, in one recent essay Jeanne Speizer argued that there is no evidence to prove that children need or are affected by modeled behavior. If, in fact, role modeling is significant in development, there is no evidence available concerning why a child might select one individual over another for emulation. Furthermore, we do not know the level of interaction necessary to influence a child or whether the "sheer presence of a person is sufficient for positive or negative identification."[40] Until the late 1960s, however, both the mental health and legal professions assumed a direct correlation between exposure to homosexuality and a child's eventual sexual orientation choice as a homosexual. This cause/effect relationship has not been borne out by the evidence available to date.

It is arguable that a child's identification with his or her parent is usually the strongest role-modeling connection. Thus, if there was a nexus between exposure to homosexuality and its subsequent effect on a child's development, it would be most directly observable in that relationship. Although data must be collected over a much longer time, short-term studies undertaken by psychiatrists and social scientists have all demonstrated that exposure to homosexuality is no significant or determinable factor in a child's sexual orientation designation.[41] For example, Richard Green's research on the sexual development and sexual orientation of children raised by homosexual or transsexual parents concluded that 36 of the 37 children grew up to be heterosexual.[42] Bell's research on homosexuality concluded that children were not negatively affected by their parent's homosexual orientation.[43] A similar outcome was reached by Kirkpatrick, Roy, and Smith in their study of lesbian mothers.[44] Based on these studies, it is possible to conclude that since a parent's sexual orientation does not seem to influence the child, his or her teacher's sexual orientation is of even less relevance in his or her eventual sexual expression.

Despite the significance of the role-modeling argument in homosexual school teacher litigation, there appears to have been no professional testimony on the topic until the 1973 case of Joseph Acanfora v. Board of Education of Montgomery County.[45] During that trial, expert testimony for both parties concluded that most children's gender identity and sexual orientation identity were clearly established by the age of five or six.[46] Thus, only a few students remained "at risk" upon entering the school environment. These "vulnerable" children posed two problems if they were to be assigned a homosexual teacher, according to the experts testifying on behalf of the school board. First, the teacher, especially a very dynamic and caring personality, might serve as a role model for the "vulnerable" child to emulate. Secondly, the "vulnerable" child might be disturbed by the presence of a homosexual teacher.[47] Conversely, experts for Acanfora argued that there was little or no evidence to prove that a homosexual teacher could influence the "vulnerable" child to be homosexual and, further, that having a positive role model of homosexuality might help the child to resolve his or her sexual orientation conflict in a life-enhancing manner.

Ultimately, <u>Acanfora</u> was resolved based upon other issues. In terms of the role-modeling argument, however, the court did articulate the legal opinion that since a child's sexual orientation seemed to be established at an early age, having a lesbian or gay male school teacher would not pose any significant harm. Furthermore, the court noted the possible benefits of providing some students with diverse and sympathetic mentors.

IMMORALITY AND THE DISMISSAL PROCESS

Since education was not mentioned in the United States Constitution by our founding fathers, it is one of several public issues that falls into the realm of state prerogatives under its broad "police powers." Thus, the criteria for teacher hiring and dismissal are determined by state legislators although, given the sharing of state codes, there is remarkable similarity throughout the 50 jurisdictions. For example, in the State of California a permanent teacher may be dismissed for one or more causes enumerated in the California Education Code. These causes include the commission of criminal acts, violent political revolutionary advocacy, evident unfitness for service, physical or mental unfitness, immoral or unprofessional conduct, insubordination, incompetence, dishonesty, or moral turpitude.[48] The dismissal basis most frequently listed by the 50 states is immorality.[49]

As an earlier section of this chapter noted, issues of teacher immorality have been broadly construed to include drinking, smoking, cheating on exams, late-night courtship, criticizing school authorities or community leaders, and using vulgar language, to name a few of the behaviors. According to Davis' study of teacher dismissals, however, sex-related infractions and improprieties have been the most common reason for termination. Davis has divided the fact patterns of the sex-related dismissal cases into the following six categories:

1. Notoriety and Suspicion of Immorality:

These cases concern rumors of adultery, fathering illegitimate children, and being indicted on charges of intent to commit rape. The school board dismissed the teachers because of their damaged reputations, whether or not they were innocent.

2. Cohabitation With a Former Student:

One example of the power of school authorities was a 1966 case in which a recently-widowed junior college teacher lived with a former student until their marriage. In upholding his dismissal, the Court held that, "If adherence to a code of proper personal conduct is not essential in all callings, it is in the teaching profession."

3. Improper Display of Affection:

Most cases were situations in which male teachers or administrators made advances on female teachers and students.

4. Improper Sex Instruction:

Teachers were terminated for graphically describing sexual intercourse to students, expressing support for premarital and extra-marital sex, expressing support for birth control, and/or for telling sexually explicit jokes.

5. Conviction of a Sex Offense:

A 1955 case serves as an exemplar of the net cast by the California lewd vagrancy laws discussed further in subsequent chapters. An elementary school teacher from San Francisco was arrested in Los Angeles for lewd vagrancy and renting a room for sexual relations with one to whom he was not married. The Court sentenced him to 20 days in jail and 2 years probation. Without benefit of a hearing, he was dismissed from his job, and his life teaching credential was revoked.

6. Homosexual Behavior:

Although he does not discuss very many of the homosexual school teacher cases, Davis points out the difficulty of evading local decision-making power when the dismissal criteria includes the nebulous qualities of "good reputation," "conduct that does not arouse suspicion," and "standards of propriety of the community."

As these categories demonstrate, school authorities have been aided in their enforcement of personal codes of conduct for school teachers by the criminal legal codes and law enforcement officials. In no other profession has an arrest for drunken driving, a police call concerning domestic violence, or an arrest for non-marital sexual acts hundreds of miles from home served as the basis for immediate dismissal and revocation of professional credentials regardless of a subsequent finding of guilt or innocence. Thus, teachers have faced the general limitations of the criminal code and another level of personal limitations based upon innuendo, reputation, and vague standards of community propriety.[53]

In fact, in his essay on "Sex and The School Teacher," Michael Willemsen argued that prior to the decriminalization of sex between consenting adults in 1975, more than 70 percent of California's school teachers lived with the threat that their typical sexual activities were grounds for criminal convictions, job termination, and credential revocation.[54] Arguably, any teacher who engaged in adultery, oral sex, anal sex, non-marital sex, birth control, unmarried cohabitation, masturbation, or homosexuality offended a large segment of the community. The vast majority of teachers, therefore, faced potential professional banishment if their sexual activities — married or unmarried, heterosexual or homosexual — came under the scrutiny of school authorities or parents. The mechanism for granting this wide range of community discretion was the vague grounds for dismissal based upon "immorality," "moral turpitude," and "lack of good character and reputation."

Furthermore, these rather subjective criteria concerning immorality and impropriety have taken on more precise legal qualities as the case law has developed, with predictable outcomes, until recently. As Lawrence Goldyn commented in his dissertation on *Legal Ideology and the Regulation of Homosexual Behavior*:

> . . . although judges do render judgments about a highly subjective subject — morality — they do so in an ideological framework which makes the topic seem less subjective and the judgement less a matter of personal discretion.[55]

Judicial personal discretion is actively at issue in school employment cases. In fact, in some instances the public perception that teachers should be above reproach has led to the judicial assumption that educators cannot be criminals. For example, in a Kentucky case concerning incest, the judge held that since the father was a school teacher he could not possibly have engaged in sexual misconduct with his daughter.[56] Conversely, the myths and fears about lesbians and gay men explicitly and implicitly enter into the debate over school employment. Judges are the representatives of dominant perspectives in our society, and often they promulgate traditional values, beliefs, and prejudices. On the other hand, since the early 1970s, as our attitudes towards sexual expression have diversified, the judicial branch also has expanded its perspectives on personal freedoms. Thus, the traditional grounds for teacher dismissal have been threatened by an increasing lack of community consensus about immorality. As a consequence, laws explicitly banning homosexuals from teaching school have been advanced as public policy on a local and state level.

"Status politics" is one helpful way to think about the laws against the employment of GLBT people as schools teachers. Joseph Gusfield, for example, has argued that laws can have instrumental or symbolic purposes.[57] The instrumental effect of a law against the employment of GLBT school teachers might be to prohibit or deter homosexuals from teaching. The symbolic effect of such a law may be to create public sentiment against homosexuality, to more firmly establish heterosexuality as the acceptable societal norm, or to enhance the visibility of the special interest group itself.

One way to ascertain whether the purpose of a law is instrumental or symbolic is to assess the level and mechanisms of enforcement of the law.[58] If resources of the legal system are allocated by society for the enforcement of a law, and the sanctions established under such a law are clear and punishing, then there is a greater likelihood that such a law serves an instrumental purpose.

In the case of employment of gay and lesbian teachers, at first glance the laws appear to be largely symbolic in purpose. Most states have already established effective laws for the removal or discipline of teachers who engage in immoral or injurious conduct. Furthermore, few resources are currently allocated for the enforcement of laws against gay and lesbian teachers. This suggests that some indirect or symbolic purposes may be the prime motivating factors. By analyzing these laws in their social and historical context, however, it will be possible to determine whether the relatively recent enactment of specific laws against the employment of homosexual school teachers addresses some currently significant social concerns in an instrumental manner.

Although it is analytically useful to distinguish between the instrumental and the symbolic intent of a law, this is not to say that the symbolic purposes of any law are insignificant. The power of the majority to define what is appropriate and legal can impact all realms of one's life, including educational opportunity, employment entitlements, marriage and family experiences, and self-esteem. As Chapter Six demonstrates, this is particularly true in the area of GLBT rights, where the legal-ideological debates over homosexuality have been a major stimulus in the social, political, and legal controversies over morals enforcement and individual entitlements.

CHAPTER CONCLUSIONS

Constraints upon the private lives of teachers have been a feature of American life since the inception of our educational system. In fact, monitoring the activities of the teacher was an affirmative community responsibility rather than a mere prurient interest. Having entrusted the impressionable minds of their youth to these surrogate parents, community members felt the need to assure that their values and beliefs would be inculcated as the one moral and patriotic path. The teacher hiring process was administered in a manner that selected like-minded people who were representative of the collective ideals. Rigid codes of conduct and close scrutiny of personal behavior assured that teachers would adhere to the traditional perspectives or face swift termination from their employment situation. Since the teacher was the public servant of the community, local definitions of such vague terms as "immorality" and "moral turpitude" served as sufficient legal basis for termination.

The constraints upon teachers' personal lives seem to have been numerous and constant over time. With the advent of the minority rights movements of the 1960s, however, teachers also demanded and obtained greater professional and personal freedom. Despite having gained a wide range of liberties, the topic of sex and the school teacher still arouses public concern, especially around the issue of lesbian and gay male school teachers and university professors.

We have cooperated for a very long time in the maintenance of our own invisibility.
And now the party is over.

— *Vito Russo*

Chapter 6

Community Morality
The Debate Over Personal Freedoms

"When I was about, I don't know, 15, I guess, people at school decided I was gay. I didn't even know what they were talking about at first. They just started calling me 'faggot' this and 'fag' that, and all of the sudden I didn't have any friends anymore. Anyway, so people started calling me faggot and queer and stuff, and I thought, 'Yeah, I'm gay. That's what I am.' I saw what happened to other kids who got called queer at school. I dropped out. I got a job. My mom thought that was cool. I didn't tell her why until later, and that's when things got sort of bad."

"But really, it's better. Since AIDS, people know that we exist, at least. But they still hate us. Our parents hate us, our teachers hate us, straight kids hate us, adults hate us. . . . " His voice falters a little. Christi leans over the table and takes his hand. "But WE don't hate us, dummy. WE don't hate us."[1]

In John Stuart Mill's 1859 essay, *On Liberty*, Mill argued there was a simple principle that would successfully govern the individual in relation to society. Mill felt it was imperative for the individual to be free in both conscience and action, and the only appropriate societal control should come when the individual might harm others.[2] Our democratic society essentially has accepted Mill's perspectives on freedom of thought and the expressions of those thoughts through writing and speech. We have been less willing to accept the freedom of "harmless action."[3]

A specific focus for this debate between individual freedom of "harmless action" and society's right to regulate behavior commenced in 1957 in England with the advent of the Wolfenden Committee's report criticizing the British laws against prostitution and homosexuality. Since then, with homosexuality as the exemplar, scholars and politicians have debated the extent to which society must and/or should be allowed to intrude into individuals' private lives.[4]

In its report, the Wolfenden Committee recommended that "homosexual practices in private between consenting adults no longer be criminal."[5] The Committee asserted:

> In this field, its [the law's] function, as we see it, is to preserve public order and decency, to protect the citizen from what is offensive or injurious, and to provide sufficient safeguards against exploitation and corruption of others. . . . It is not, in our view, the function of the law to intervene in the private lives of citizens, or to seek to enforce any particular pattern of behaviour, further than is necessary to carry out the purposes which we have outlined. . . . There must remain a realm of private morality and immorality which is, in brief and crude terms, not the law's business.[6]

The Report and its conclusion sparked a debate which commenced with Lord Devlin's lecture, "The Enforcement of Morals." Devlin concluded about homosexuality:

> We should ask ourselves in the first instance whether, looking at it calmly and dispassionately, we regard it as a vice so abominable that its mere presence is an offence. If that is the genuine feeling of the society in which we live, I do not see how society can be denied the right to eradicate it.[7]

The essence of Lord Devlin's argument is thoroughly analyzed in Ronald Dworkin's book, *Taking Rights Seriously*. Some of Dworkin's assessment of the relationship of law and morals is of interest here. According to Dworkin's interpretation, Lord Devlin believed the state has a duty to serve as a "moral tutor" through the criminal legal code. Thus, "society has a right to punish conduct of which its members strongly disapprove," whether or not that conduct is harmful to others. The basis of society's right is two-fold; one is its right to protect its existence, and the second is its right to defend "its social environment from change it opposes."[8] Lord Devlin did not believe society has the right to impose its morality on every given social issue. He did believe it has that right when "public feeling is high, enduring and relentless," when, as with homosexuality, it rises to the level of "intolerance, indignation, and disgust."[9]

Thus, in Lord Devlin's perspective, passionate public disapproval is sufficient reason for criminalizing homosexual conduct whether or not such conduct is harmful to the public. This outcome is based upon the belief that if some members of society were allowed to practice freely their homosexual orientation, then society itself would change. Our concepts of family, religion, morality, and other societal norms and institutions might be profoundly affected by legalizing this one concern. According to Devlin, our society expects its elected and appointed officials to explore and monitor those issues that may affect the society. Furthermore, it expects these officials to balance the harm to society against our belief in personal freedoms.

Dworkin's difficulty with this balancing of societal good and individual rights stems from his belief that every individual has some fundamental legal rights that usually outweigh society's interests. These rights are articulated in the United States Constitution and The Bill of Rights, in the form of freedom of speech, association, and the pursuit of happiness, to name a few. Dworkin argues that these articulated freedoms stem from a fundamental societal belief in human dignity and equality. Thus, "the weaker members of a political community are entitled to the same concern and respect of their government as the more powerful members have secured for themselves."[10] The juxtaposition of personal freedom and public good is clearly at debate when one considers the right of GLBT individuals to teach in schools and colleges.

Dworkin believes this duty to balance the interests of society against the interests of the individual makes it relevant to examine what legislators or judges should consider in their evaluations. Note that Dworkin is speaking of a requisite legal morality — a firm, rational, moral basis for the formation of law — that he believes is necessary before legislation is warranted. Thus, his criteria invalidate several more emotional reasons.

Through its legislative and judicial structure, the legal system is designed to avoid the extremes of political pressure. Social uproar over an issue may be significant, but immediate demands are held in check by procedural and due process constraints. Furthermore, to make humane laws, strong public sentiment should be grounded in some higher moral principle that is not easily subject to change. Traditionally, religion, and later medicine, provided the principles that assert the immorality and sickness of homosexuality. More recently, however, the injunctions of the Bible are accepted less literally, as is the previously unquestioned belief that procreation is the only proper purpose of sexual activity. Moreover, psychiatrists have reversed themselves by removing homosexuality from the realm of a physical or mental disorder.

Another tactic has been to assert that homosexuals are evil or debilitated, as evidenced by their lifestyle. This assertion, too, appears weak in the face of social and empirical evidence. Others have asserted that everyone acknowledges the immoral nature of homosexuality. But, this belief is challenged directly by the fact that enough social disagreement exists to sustain the public debate. Conversely, the fact that a social practice is becoming more common and more acceptable does not automatically elevate the practice from immorality to morality.

Dworkin suggests that the flaw in Lord Devlin's perspective is not that "the community's morality counts, but his idea of what counts as the community morality."[11] Although all the above arguments have been asserted as moral bases, Dworkin argues that we should not confuse them with justice and principles of political morality. Rather, these arguments are "strategies of persuasion" and "facts of political life."[12] In "hard cases" where no clear rules of law exist, such as the employment of homosexuals as school teachers, Dworkin favors legal decisions based upon abstract, fundamental principles rather than policy appeals that assert a social goal. His reason for this preference is that policy can be dominated by one group or compromised to please several competing groups, but principles "rest on social values" that are fundamental to society.[13] Because of the importance of these human rights, policy should be compromised only on that rare occasion when a social "goal of special urgency" outweighs individual rights. Only in that instance should we use this criteria of principle rather than policy to determine justifiable legal constraints.

One question, then, is whether the social goals in prohibiting gays and lesbians from teaching are imperative enough to outweigh the potentially fundamental individual liberties. This balancing of interests is a process ingrained in our legal system and is articulated as the Equal Protection Clause of the 14th Amendment. It dictates that no state shall "deprive any person of life, liberty, or property, without due process of law; nor deny any person within its jurisdiction the equal protection of the laws."[14]

CONSTITUTIONAL CONSIDERATIONS

To understand the expansion of minority and individual rights in the United States, it is important to be somewhat familiar with the Equal Protection and Due Process clauses of the 14th Amendment. This section presents an oversimplified history of those legal trends that directly relate to an individual's ability to assert that he or she has rights in the face of the majority goal to place restrictions on minority entitlements.

In drafting the United States Constitution, political leaders included several clauses requiring the federal government to treat all states and their citizens equally.[15] In 1791, 10 amendments to the United States Constitution went into effect. These laws, known as "The Bill of Rights," were intended to limit governmental intrusion into the lives of private citizens. Among other things, they asserted U.S. citizens' right to bear arms, practice their religious beliefs, be free from unreasonable searches and seizures, have a speedy trial, and be represented by legal counsel in criminal proceedings. In terms of the rights of GLBT educators, the Fifth Amendment and 10th Amendment have greatly influenced the debate over personal freedoms and public constraints.

The Fifth Amendment states, in part, that no person can "be deprived of life, liberty, or property, without due process of law . . . " Thus, the federal government must follow established and fair procedures before it can limit or revoke an entitlement. An additional curb on the power of the federal government, established in the 10th Amendment, states, "The powers not delegated to the United States by the Constitution, nor prohibited by it to the states, are reserved to the states respectively, or to the people." Thus, although the federal government was intended to be a powerful, umbrella influence over the country, the 10th Amendment clearly establishes that the states retain a wide range of power to govern according to their own laws and beliefs. This concept of state authority and federal limitations is called "State's Rights."

As per these Constitutional entitlements, each state began establishing laws and defining the rights of the state in relation to its citizens. One area in which this state-level authority was clearly evident pertained to the issues of slavery and restrictions upon the rights of African-American individuals. Some states forbade slavery, yet also prohibited Blacks from attending white public schools. Some states permitted slavery and other numerous restrictions on the entitlements of racial minorities on the grounds that Blacks were property, not human beings. Obviously, our society went through a major, tragic conflict over these competing policies, as evidenced by the Civil War.

For a few years after the Civil War, Northern federal authorities demanded that the Southern states abolish slavery, permit racial minorities to vote, and eliminate laws that were discriminatory based upon race. The model for these demands that all citizens of a state be treated equally were the Constitutional demands of the Fifth Amendment that the federal government treat all states and citizens equally. Thus, the United States adopted the 14th Amendment in 1868, in which Section 1 states:

All persons born or naturalized in the United States, and subject to the jurisdiction thereof, are citizens of the United States and of the state wherein they reside. No state shall make or enforce any law which shall abridge the privileges or immunities of citizens of the United States; nor shall a state deprive any person of life, liberty, or property without due process of law; nor deny to any person within its jurisdiction the equal protection of the law.

Theoretically, then, the federal government had the right to demand that each state adhere to a standard of fairness for all its citizens. And, of course, the federal government had to establish the same standards for all states. Thus, as early as 1868 the federal government had the power to insist on civil rights for all citizens. Between 1869 and 1877, however, "white supremacy" was being re-established in the Southern states. By 1877, political deals had been made and the last of the Northern troops withdrew from the Southern states. Even if the desire for civil rights protections existed, Southern states would have needed Northern troops to enforce them. Neither the desire nor the troops were there.

Although the 14th Amendment was now law, conservative southern justices comprised the majority of the U.S. Supreme Court after the Civil War. They consistently side-stepped the application of the Amendment to state governmental affairs. In 1896, however, the justices faced a major test of whether the federal government would require equal treatment of each state's citizens. In Plessy v. Ferguson, the Court was asked to determine the constitutionality of a Louisiana law that required racial minority individuals to ride in restricted railroad cars.[16] Mr. Plessy was of 7/8ths Caucasian descent and 1/8th African-American descent. When he tried to ride in the whites only compartment, train officials arrested him. All of the Louisiana state courts validated the law as a rational restriction on the commingling of the races, so Plessy appealed to the U.S. Supreme Court. The Court ruled that each state can establish laws that segregate citizens on the basis of race as long as facilities provided to each race were substantially equal. Thus, "separate but equal" became the law of the land in terms of racial minority rights. On its face, this ruling complied with each state's obligation to maintain "equal protection" per the 14th

Amendment. In reality, the Court legalized the regressive "Jim Crow" laws that denied basic rights to African-American citizens. This analysis of a state's obligations to its minority citizens under the 14th Amendment remained the standard for almost 60 years until the U.S. Supreme Court offered a different interpretation in Brown v. Board of Education in 1954.[17]

During the first 50 years of the 20th century, individuals concerned about racial discrimination in our society were constantly hampered by the Court's acceptance of the separate but equal doctrine. Educational equity cases during this time reflect a meticulous effort to compare every aspect of a white school to those of a local Black school to demonstrate to the Court that the facilities were not equal. Sometimes the minority advocates won. More often than not, the Court ignored the disparities or ordered greater equality, but without oversight to ensure enforcement. People interested in creating greater equality on the basis of race searched for some legal analysis to challenge the entire separate but equal interpretation of the 14th Amendment.

Educational settings became the key battleground because of the emerging view that the government owed all its citizens a public education and because it was clear that inferior, segregated schooling harmed minority youth. Through the concentrated efforts of the NAACP and other advocacy groups around the country, several lawsuits were brought challenging the separate but equal doctrine in public education. Several of these cases were consolidated into Brown v. Board of Education.

In Brown v. Board of Education, Chief Justice Earl Warren and the liberal members of the Supreme Court commenced an emerging new analysis of the 14th Amendment. This new analysis dominated American legal and social life until the election of President Ronald Reagan and subsequent conservative presidents.

The "new" interpretation of the 14th Amendment created a process for balancing the state's right to enact legislation for the public good against the rights or interests of some individual or group that might be harmed by such legislation. Traditionally, to prevail in this process of balancing interests, the government merely needed to demonstrate that it had a "rational basis" for enacting the law, regardless of who or what it harmed. This standard of judicial scrutiny was minimal since any good reason was usually acceptable. Thus, if a state made a law saying the races must be segregated in educational settings because outbreaks of violence between the races would be minimized, or because it would be too costly to alter the segregated system, the reasons were considered rational and acceptable to the court.

The emerging interpretation begun in <u>Brown v. Board of Education</u> held that the "rational basis" test normally was the law of the land with respect to state action. However, the Court articulated two instances in which the standard would be changed to a "strict scrutiny" of the state's policy because the rights of the individual were so important. The first instance would be if a fundamental constitutional right were being denied to a citizen of any given state. Fundamental constitutional rights are those enumerated in the Constitution, such as freedom of speech, freedom of association, religious freedom, the right to a speedy trial, etc.

The second instance would involve the Equal Protection Clause of the 14th Amendment. Under this new analysis, Congress or the Supreme Court could articulate that certain categories of individuals have been so badly treated in our society they deserve special protections under the laws. In light of the Civil War and the treatment of African-Americans in our society, the Court determined that any classifications based upon race were likely to be unfair and discriminatory and obviously worth special scrutiny.

If the plaintiff (the individual being harmed) could prove that his or her litigation involved one of these fundamental freedoms or that he or she was a member of a "protected class," then the court would do two things to aid that individual's case against the state. First, the "burden of proof" in the case would switch from the plaintiff to the state. Normally, the plaintiff would have to prove discrimination or a restriction on a fundamental constitutional right by the state. Now, however, the state would have to prove it did not discriminate or impede a constitutional right. To put it in very simple terms, if the plaintiff could provide almost any evidence that the case concerned a restriction on a fundamental right or harmed him or her as a member of a protected class, the whole case shifted against the state. The presumption would be that the state could not engage in "whatever" activity if that activity harmed or restricted the plaintiff's rights. Suddenly the assumptions in these cases favored the harmed individual over the state's power.

Second, the state would need an "extraordinary justification" for actions that infringe upon an individual's rights. Traditional legal analysis held that if the state had a "rational basis" for its actions, it could proceed with actions that resulted in the discriminatory infringement on an individual's rights. Under the new interpretation, the presumption was that the state needed an extraordinary justification for its actions and that almost no reason justified infringing upon the individual's rights. Even if the state had an excellent justification for its action, it also was required to prove that the mechanisms it was using were the least restrictive means possible to achieve the important end. In other words, the state needed a really good excuse for its behavior, and no excuse was probably sufficient to block someone's fundamental constitutional rights or to permit discrimination based upon some group classification. The public good is presumed to be outweighed by the strong societal concern for the protection of a fundamental human right or the protection of the rights of a given group that historically has been treated poorly in our society. This demonstration or test of a higher standard is called "strict scrutiny."

In 1973, the United States Supreme Court articulated the standards for evoking strict scrutiny. Greater judicial surveillance is needed when a group has been voiceless politically, when a legislative classification has been based upon an inherent and immutable characteristic, and when discrimination against the group has been a feature of social/political life.[18] Strict scrutiny most often has been applied in cases involving racial discrimination where the classification is inherently suspect. What "suspect" means in this usage is that the court presumes discrimination probably occurred if the event was guided by racial motivation since our social history is replete with examples of discrimination based upon racial classifications. In such instances, the Court is willing to take a closer look into these cases and to presume discriminatory motives with less proof than is normally required. The burden of proof then shifts to the employer to demonstrate that its actions were not motivated by prejudicial beliefs against an entire class of individuals. Thus, it is the employer's, not the employee's, motivations that are "suspect." The description of standards for evoking strict scrutiny may fit other groups, such as women, gay men and lesbians, and children. To date, however, the federal courts have been unwilling to apply the full authority of a strict scrutiny analysis to their legal conditions.[19]

Congress has expanded the number of groups included under these special protections by passing such legislation as the Civil Rights Act of 1964, as amended, and the Americans with Disabilities Act (ADA) of 1990. If the Equal Rights Amendment had been enacted in the early 1970s, women would have enjoyed the full federal protections of redress against discrimination based upon gender classification as well. Instead, current legal analysis offers a compromise standard of "fair and substantial," which theoretically is greater than rational basis, but not as powerful as strict scrutiny. The justices have frequently commented that the Civil War demonstrates the significance of addressing racial inequities, however, no war has been fought over women's rights. Also, in the justices' view, mandating that the country function in an egalitarian manner concerning gender would be extremely costly and create sweeping social change. Since they have been unwilling to take this bold step, they have "compromised" by establishing a middle-level analysis.

Commencing in 1973, litigants mentioned in this book have asserted that GLBT individuals deserve Equal Protection under the 14th Amendment. The U.S. Supreme Court had just articulated the standards for strict scrutiny consideration for any minority group as mentioned above. Clearly, GLBT individuals were voiceless polit-ically and suffered from institutionalized discrimination. The issue under debate was whether homosexuality was a choice and a deviancy, or whether it was an immutable characteristic that quali-fied under the Court's criteria. While some lower court decisions mentioned in this volume suggested that strict scrutiny should be the legal standard of review, each stopped short of applying that higher standard because of the belief that the U.S. Supreme Court would reverse the lower Court's judicial opinion. Since having one's rulings reversed by a higher court implies judicial error and some level of incompetence, few judges are willing to assert emergent legal theories, especially if the courts of higher review would most likely react negatively to that assertion.

While the U. S. Supreme Court has not applied the strict scrutiny standard to augment GLBT rights, its recent decision in Romer v. Evans concerning Colorado's Amendment 2 referendum is of major importance with respect to state-wide attempts to prohibit GLBT people from having rights. In 1992, the citizens of Colorado passed a state-wide referendum that prohibited the legislative, judicial, and executive branches of state and local governments and school districts from enacting or enforcing any action designed to protect individuals on the basis of sexual orientation.[20] Amendment 2 stated:

> No Protected Status Based on Homosexual, Lesbian or Bisexual Orientation.

> Neither the State of Colorado, through any of its branches or departments, nor any of its agencies, political subdivisions, municipalities or school districts, shall enact, adopt or enforce any statute, regulation, ordinance or policy whereby homosexual, lesbian or bisexual orientation, conduct, practices or relationships shall constitute or otherwise be the basis of or entitle any person or class of persons to have or claim any minority status, quota preferences, protected status or claims of discrimination. This Section of the Constitution shall be in all respects self-executing.[21]

Advocates for Amendment 2 offered several rational basis arguments for the validity of the law. One concern was that, by granting GLBT individuals a status equal to other minority groups, GLBT people would enjoy more extensive legal protections than the average citizen of Colorado. An employer could fire an employee for being poorly dressed or left-handed, for example, but GLBT people could argue a special protection under the law because of their sexual orientation. Additionally, the argument was advanced that since the U.S. Supreme Court had permitted states to criminalize consenting

sexual activity between same-sex individuals in its 1986 holding in
Bowers v. Hardwick, the citizens of Colorado were merely exerting
their entitelments to regulate conduct that the majority of them found
to be immoral and criminal.[22]   As Justice Scalia stated in his
dissenting opinion in Romer v. Evans, "If it is constitutionally
permissable for a State to make homosexual conduct criminal, surely
it is constitutionally permissable for a State to enact other laws
merely disfavoring homosexual conduct."[23]

The U.S. Supreme Court did not extend Equal Protection entitlements of GLBT individuals in their 1996 decision in Romer v.
Evans. By a 6 to 3 vote, however, they did hold that Amendment
2 failed to further a proper legislative end and that it was a violation of Equal Protection of the law to prohibit an entire class of
citizens from seeking the aid of their government to redress
wrongs. Writing for the majority, Justice Kennedy stated:

> Central to both the idea of the rule of law and to our own
> Constitution's guarantee of equal protections is the prin-
> ciple that government and each of its parts remain open
> on impartial terms to all who seek its assistance. Equal
> protection of the laws is not achieved through indiscrim-
> inate imposition of inequities. . . . [24]

> Amendment 2 confounds this normal process of judicial
> review. It is at once too narrow and too broad. It identifies
> persons by a single trait and then denies them protection
> across the board. The resulting disqualification of a class
> of persons from the right to seek specific protection from
> the law is unprecedented in our jurisprudence. . . . [25]

> Amendment 2, however, in making a general announce-
> ment that gays and lesbians shall not have any particular
> protections from the law, inflicts on them immediate,
> continuing, and real injuries that outrun and belie any
> legitimate justifications that may be claimed for it. . . . [26]

> We must conclude that Amendment 2 classifies homo-
> sexuals not to further a proper legislative end but to make
> them unequal to everyone else. This Colorado cannot do.
> A state cannot so deem a class of persons strangers to its

laws. Amendment 2 violates the Equal Protection Clause, and the judgement of the Supreme Court of Colorado is affirmed.[27]

Certainly the implications of the holding in Romer v. Evans should have a substantial impact on future litigation concerning the employment entitlements of GLBT individuals. The current U.S. Supreme Court, known for its conservative, state's rights leanings, surprised many by its majority holding. It remains to be seen whether this Court will recognize sexual orientation as a protected classification and specifically extend the full federal entitlements of the Equal Protections laws to GLBT people on a nationwide basis.

Since states are free to provide their citizens with greater, but not lesser, rights than those provided under federal laws, many states have enacted legislation that extends these strict scrutiny protections to women, gay and lesbian individuals, and other minority groups. The District of Columbia, for example, enacted legislation in 1977 protecting gay men and lesbians from discrimination in employment, housing, public accommodations, and insurance. Wisconsin passed similar legislation in 1982, as did Massachusetts in 1989. To date, the District of Columbia and nine states have enacted employment protection prohibiting discrimination on the basis of sexual orientation. The states taking this action were Wisconsin (1982), Massachusetts (1989), Hawaii and Connecticut (1991), New Jersey, Vermont, and California (1992), Minnesota (1993), and, most recently, Rhode Island (1995). Basically, this legislation added sexual orientation to the already-protected categories of race, color, religious creed, national origin, sex, age, ancestry, and disability.[28] Recent efforts to pass the federal Employment Non-Discrimination Act (ENDA)· prohibiting employment discrimination on the basis of sexual orientation, have failed, despite the active support of President Clinton and a significant number of members of Congress.[29] ENDA will continue to be introduced annually because of the powerful protections offered to enumerated classes as described above.

Similar federal legislation was passed in Canada in May of 1996 under its Human Rights Act. Thus, all federal employees, plus those individuals who work in federally regulated industries, such as banking, air and rail travel, and broadcast communications, are protected on the basis of sexual orientation. Additionally, in June of 1996, Canada's human rights tribunal found that denial of same-sex partner health care benefits was a violation of the law with respect to all federal employees. These new federal protections augment entitlements provided by most Canadian provinces and territories, except Alberta, Newfoundland, the Northwest Territories, and Prince Edward Island.[30]

Gays and lesbians have tried to assert their right to strict scrutiny review because of the invidious nature of homophobia.[31] Moreover, the legal issue is also relevant to this study because of the fundamental U.S. constitutional rights involved regarding privacy, free speech, free association, marriage, and sexual expression.

Over the past 40 years, in addition to expanding the number of protected classes, the legislative and judicial bodies of federal and state governments have expanded our fundamental personal freedoms. The Supreme Court, for example, ruled unconstitutional Virginia's restrictions against interracial marriages,[32] Connecticut's law prohibiting married couples from obtaining birth control mechanisms,[33] and a state's right to prohibit abortions during the first trimester of pregnancy.[34] These additional individual rights at the expense of the state's rights are a relatively recent phenomenon. As the debate over abortion demonstrates, many individuals resent federal interference in the rights of states to make laws governing personal conduct. The Epilogue of this volume serves as a harbinger that the U.S. Supreme Court has become more cautious in the face of the hostility generated by its decision in Roe v. Wade pertaining to abortion rights. In subsequent situations where the Court could push the edges of personal freedoms over public constraints, such as in the Oklahoma gay teacher case discussed in Chapter 4, the Court has shied away from opportunities to impose alternative social policies on unwilling states and their citizens.

This retrenchment from federal restrictions on states' rights is the essence of the Democratic and Republican struggle in American politics over the past several decades. Conservatives and religious fundamentalists have been angered by the expansion of privacy and individual rights that protect sexual freedom, the rights of the mother over those of the fetus, secular public education, and gays and lesbians, among many other things. These individuals who adhere to a "strict construction" of the U.S. Constitution are called "state's rights" advocates. Under a strict construction viewpoint, if a power is not specifically and literally granted to the federal government or prohibited to the states in the Constitution, then under the 10th Amendment all rights to regulate that arena of the law are reserved for the states. Since privacy, abortion, homosexuality, consensual sex, education, and school prayer are not delineated in the Constitution, the federal government has no right to interfere with state actions on such matters.

Since <u>Brown v. Board of Education</u> in 1954, however, "expansionists" of the U.S. Constitution have argued that such clauses as the "right to life, liberty, and the pursuit of happiness," inherently entail a federal power to restrict state interference or to demand state compliance in situations the Court or the federal legislature deems appropriate. This emergent legal trend has suffered a major setback with the rise of conservative influence and control in American politics. Angered by federal dictates relative to individual freedom versus state authority, and angered by environmental protection over commercial interests, conservatives have successfully mobilized. With this mobilization, they have reconstituted federal mechanisms of control such as the U.S. Supreme Court, the presidency, and Congress.

As this volume demonstrates, one of the most powerful rallying issues for conservatives has been their anger at the increasing acceptance of gay and lesbian rights in our society. In the early 1970s, when the liberal interpretations of minority rights were expanding, many municipalities and governmental bodies included in their regulations protections on the basis of sexual orientation. This was done with the assumption that the courts and federal government would favor individual and minority rights over state's rights. Since the Conservative Right has come into power, however, this assumption is no longer clear. The Conservative Right maintains a constitutional deference to the state's rights perspective, and thus demands that any assertion of minority and individual freedom at the expense of the state's authority must be obtained through pressure on state legislative power rather than through federal power.

This is why political tactics concerning GLBT rights have been modified. It was hoped that a Democratic president and Congress would enact legislation that would create sweeping national change. Instead, advocates for the rights of GLBT people have had more success on the state level. Over the past five years, approximately two state legislatures per year have enacted employment and public accommodation protections on the basis of sexual orientation. For the foreseeable future, much of the debate over the personal freedoms of GLBT people will occur on a state and local level, even though a federal mandate would be more rapid and uniform in application for all 50 states. The current U.S. Supreme Court and the Republican-controlled Congress are weighted in favor of state's rights. Thus, while action on the state level offers less far-reaching consequences, it probably offers more opportunities for success.

Throughout this volume, then, the contrasting judicial interpretations of the Equal Protection clause of the 14th Amendment plays a critical role in the ebb and flow of minority rights in general and those of GLBT educators in particular. Both sides of the controversy direct their attention to the terse few sentences of the 14th Amendment. Each group's bias in interpreting that law, however, radically affects every individual's experience of personal freedoms and public constraints.

PERSONAL FREEDOMS

The first real announcement by the United States Supreme Court that it had adopted the emergent view of greater personal freedom came in 1965. In Griswold v. Connecticut,[35] the Supreme Court declared unconstitutional a Connecticut law prohibiting the use of contraceptives by married and unmarried people. The Court held that implicit in several Constitutional provisions was the concept of a "right of privacy" which extended to this marital intimacy. With its decision in Griswold v. Connecticut, the Supreme Court intensified the debate over personal freedom and society's right to control private behavior and morals.

A right to privacy is, itself, a bold legal precedent.[36] In their book, *Privacy: The Right To Be Let Alone*, Morris Ernst and Alan

Schwartz assert that the right of privacy is "perhaps the most personal of all legal principles."[37] They also call it the newest legal principle because only a very sophisticated society would have the interest and ability to nurture personal human dignity. On the other hand, Ernst and Schwartz argue that a legal right of privacy is "a minority concept" that, by its nature, establishes an "alienation between the individual and his society" which is the very heart of any civil liberty.[38]

The Supreme Court's recognition of a right of privacy in the marital relationship fueled the assertion of freedom from unwarranted governmental intrusion into private, intimate matters. This demand directly challenged the state's historical interest in preserving "the tone of the society, the mode, . . . the style and quality of life." The state's interest has not been limited to the physical well-being of a community.[39] Rather, it has extended to the "moral soundness of its people as well."[40]

When faced with the issue of private sexual activity between consenting adult gays and lesbians, however, the Court has ruled differently. The Doe v. Commonwealth's Attorney for the City of Richmond (1975) decision affirmed Virginia's criminal sodomy statute.[41] The High Court refused to extend the implied "right of adults to control their own sexual activities" of the Griswold decision.[42] They distinguished the Doe decisions from Griswold by suggesting that marriage was a union the state supported and legalized, so intrusion into that union should be minimal. Conversely, they reasoned that society had long condemned and criminalized homosexual behavior, so in the interest of morality and decency the state could continue to intrude into homosexual unions.

One feature of this period of legal/social change, however, is that repeated challenges are made to any articulated perspective. As mentioned earlier, in Michael Bowers v. Michael Hardwick, a 1986 challenge to Georgia's sodomy statute, the United States Supreme Court again affirmed the state's right to regulate homosexual conduct.[43] This outcome is in direct conflict with the strong legal trend that sex, in private, between consenting adults, is outside the regulatory powers of the state based on privacy rights and constitutional freedoms. Clearly, the current Supreme Court has sanctioned personal freedom in heterosexual sexual activity while denying equal protection to homosexuals. This unfair result was the reason retired Justice Powell stated that he had made a mistake in supporting the Conservative view, which was upheld by reference to the long history of societal abhorrence of homosexuality and societal commitment to preserving the heterosexual family unit.[44]

Interestingly, recently-retired Justice Harry A. Blackmun, credited with writing the majority decision in Roe v. Wade, eventually may become more famous for his strong dissent in Bowers v. Hardwick. In it, he argued that the case was about "the most comprehensive of rights and the right most valued by civilized men," namely, "the right to be let alone."[45]

The legal sequel to Bowers v. Hardwick is significant to this book and will be discussed more thoroughly a later volume. In brief, advocates of gay and lesbian school teachers' rights believed that if the Court favored individual privacy, future litigation about GLBT employment would be very successful, since this private sexual behavior would be beyond the state's scrutiny. However, if the Court favored the state's interest in regulating homosexual sex between consenting adults, then immediate and continued success in the GLBT employment area was doubtful. The Court did uphold the state's argument, which was reinforced further by the changing composition of American political influence and, by extension, the changing composition of the U.S. Supreme Court towards more conservative values. The elections of Republican presidents Nixon, Reagan, and Bush provided conservatives the opportunity to reverse the long trend of individual rights championed by the Supreme Court from the 1950s to the 1970s.

Now, issues of civil rights, personal freedoms, marital and family considerations, and minority rights have been interpreted to favor each state's perspective and not a national standard of entitlements or personal freedoms. The current U.S. Supreme Court is heavily biased in favor of conservatives and moderates who are supportive of state's rights. Thus, people hoping to advance causes relevant to individual rights may need to avoid the federal court system and its potentially harmful judicial decisions. Ironically, since state's rights are favored by the High Court, advancing personal freedoms for GLBT people and other minorities on a state-by-state level is a very promising tactic, just as it has been for women's rights.

In fact, recent actions by a conservative state court reflect this legal trend toward personal freedoms. Between 1989 and 1993, over 25 people were prosecuted under the State of Tennessee's 1989 Homosexual Practices Act.[46] While a $50 fine and 30 days in the county jail might not seem like significant punishment, many of the individuals lost their jobs, their homes, and custody of their children because of criminal prosecution of this consensual homosexual conduct. In January of 1996, the State Court of Appeals avoided any Equal Protection argument that might suggest that gay and lesbian citizens should be protected from discrimination. On the other hand, the Court embraced the right to privacy argument, stating that "the right of the plaintiffs to engage in consensual, private, non-commercial sexual conduct" involved "intimate questions of personal and family concerns" that were protected under the state's constitution. In June of 1996, the State's highest court declined to review the decision, making the sodomy law unenforceable. If courts in the State of Tennessee recognize constitutional rights of privacy for GLBT citizens, the prospects look excellent for similar rulings around the country.

SOCIOLOGICAL PERSPECTIVES

In his book, *Stigma: Notes on the Management of Spoiled Identity*, Erving Goffman analyzes the process by which an individual is "disqualified from full social acceptance."[47] According to Goffman, as socialized individuals we constantly categorize people by attributes we expect them to exhibit. This "social identity" allows us to anticipate human interactions without excessive conscious thought and nervous confusion, as we expect and demand very specific behaviors based on these characteristics.[48] Conflict arises when the individual's attributes are incongruous with those we anticipate and thus frustrate our expectations and demands. Quite often, our response to unanticipated attributes is to further categorize the individual as less desirable than individuals who conform to our social identity stereotype. The individual "is thus reduced in our minds from a whole and usual person to a tainted, discounted one."[49]

Goffman has grouped these negative characteristics into three types. The first type is the various physical "abnormalities." Second is the character disorders, such as dishonesty, weakness, or evilness; expressed through negatively-perceived behavior such as prostitution, homosexuality, drug addiction, alcoholism, unemployment, welfare dependency, and political radicalism. And third is the group stigmas based on race, color, religion, and ethnicity; usually transmitted through familial lineage and affecting all members of the family group.

Because of these perceived negative characteristics, we "tend to impute a wide range of imperfections on the basis of the original one."[50] Thus, a homosexual male is perceived as a pedophile awaiting the opportunity to molest a young boy, for example. Our beliefs about the original characteristic, plus the imputed additional negative images, allow us to self-righteously exclude and discriminate against stigmatized people. This further reduces their chances for full participation in normative social dynamics. Consequently, they are pushed to the negative fringes and suffer from lack of access to more traditionally-available resources. Then, they may adopt the negative societal context into which they have been thrust.[51] Thus, the cultural stereotype takes on a larger power that reinforces the discriminatory process. A good example of this effect on homosexuals is the often-difficult process of labeling oneself as a gay or lesbian because our image of "that type of person and that lifestyle" does not mesh with our knowledge about ourselves and our social choices.

The socialization process itself instills in each of us a desire to be normal, to belong. This power to define normalcy is the basis of the success of stigmatization since all people go through the cultural process. "The stigmatized person tends to hold the same beliefs about identity" that are held by the rest of the population.[52] Shame, fear, secrecy, and reactive efforts are all possible results of this realization of one's failure to conform or one's abnormality.

Furthermore, the individual spends effort trying to manage this "spoiled" identity. If the characteristic is readily obvious — a physical limitation, for example — the person constantly is forced to manage despite the fear of being immediately discredited, labeled, and stereotyped by his or her mental, physical, and emotional capabilities. In contrast, people whose disability is not obvious, as with gay men and lesbians, constantly must manage the information about themselves in the world. Otherwise, they must face the possibility of being discredited by both intimates who had not known of the characteristic and strangers who would also react harshly.

Full disclosure about oneself radically alters the process from information management to dealing directly with the discreditation. Greater personal and political power, however, becomes possible through confronting the stigma and realizing that others share one's attributes and manage their lives in a positive and desirable manner, in direct contrast to the negative societal identity.[53] The stigmatized identity of evil personal characteristics acted out in sordid activities and places gradually gives way to a more positive self-identity. As more and more of the "normal" members of society are confronted by these non-stereotypical individuals, the whole normative belief system about this class of people is challenged.

SOCIAL POLITICS

Goffman's analysis of deviance and stigma focuses on the individual's experience. Several authors have taken this school of analysis on deviance and cast it in a larger social and political context. For example, in his essay, "Moral Passage: The Symbolic Process in Public Designations of Deviance," Joseph Gusfield describes various classes of deviants and society's responses to them.[54] A "repentant" deviant is one who accepts the societal norm and expresses guilt and sorrow at having violated it. A "sick" deviant also poses no threat to the norm; he or she is merely unable to live up to the standard because of some personal inability. A "cynical" deviant would be someone, such as a professional criminal, who knows the norm exists and spends energy trying not to be caught and punished for willful transgressions. Historically, the least typical deviant was the "enemy." An "enemy" deviant challenges societal norms and its label of deviancy. On an individual basis, the enemy deviant could be silenced as foolhardy, a criminal, or a martyr. If a larger group identification occurs through a movement or a subculture, however, then such deviants move out of isolation into a larger collective that challenges the societal norm. "Enemy deviance flourishes where two sets of norms conflict, one official and one unofficial."[55]

When open rebellion against the norms occurs, then society has two choices. It must retaliate successfully against this challenge, or it must modify normative behavior to either incorporate the values of the enemy or be entirely replaced by those values. The ability to define and maintain norms demonstrates group power. In fact, it provides a further mechanism to enhance that power by assuring access to resources and benefits, as well as control over important outcomes, policies, and values.[56] Because of the powerful significance of being able to control societal norms and definitions, stigma contests are a very real threat to adherents of the status quo, and proportionately greater pressure is brought to bear on the enemy deviant.

Because "deviance . . . is essentially a matter of definition," a large part of the stigma contest is waged through propaganda. "What the opponent calls propaganda, the user typically labels education." Whatever the label, the intent is "the pervasive effort to influence beliefs, attitudes, and gut reactions, and the common manipulation of key symbols in furtherance of such goals."[57] Little attention need be paid to facts and truth, since arousal of an emotional, subjective response is a more dramatic and effective guarantee of full partisan support.

Once a vocal and visible support base is mobilized, its leaders can use it to appeal to the "gatekeepers" of social change. These are the legislators, judges, business people, media controllers, and political elites who have direct influence over the outcome of any individual or group conflict. In fact, it is then possible to arouse institutional normative conflict, as one institution rallies to support one perspective and another major social institution rises in opposition.

For example, the American legal system may be prepared to grant greater legal rights to gay men and lesbian women as an extension of its overall support of fundamental human rights and civil liberties at the expense of state power. However, the American educational system, as projected by school administrators, is obviously threatened on several levels if it relinquishes its hitherto almost sacrosanct right to select teachers and control their behavior based on its own standards. Given this perceived and probably real threat to the power of school administrators, any and all anti-discrimination demands by teachers are potentially dangerous. Given the propaganda need to arouse emotions and support, few topics are as volatile as that of employing homosexuals as school teachers.

CHAPTER CONCLUSION

Stigma contests are eventually resolved, usually through victory or compromise. Then, the nature of that resolution defines the current moral boundaries. If, for some new reason, another cause arouses the stigma contest, the push/pull process of power assertion and moral behavior definition starts again. Certainly, the legal history of the employment of lesbians and gay men as school teachers outlined in this book provides evidence that these conflicts are not always resolved in a linear fashion. For a time, one group's norms are accepted, eventually challenged, and manage to survive. Later, they may be modified or completely replaced by the values of a new or more powerfully organized group perspective.

In all of this discussion of norms and power, however, we must remember that the contest is not merely an intellectual conflict over ideological ideals. Social control and the power to define normalcy has, as its extension, the power to control personal actions, determine access to employment and financial security, regulate the right to have intimate relationships legitimized and supported by the government, and the power to intrude into a person's very sense of self-worth and self-respect.

PART IV

HISTORICAL CONTEXT OF HOMOSEXUALITY AND EDUCATION TO 1950

In most native cultures, gay men and lesbians held positions as healers, visionaries, and teachers.

— *Susan Beaver*

CHAPTER 7

THE HOMOSEXUAL EXPERIENCE IN EDUCATION PRIOR TO 1950

Born in 1819, Walt Whitman grew up sleeping with his brothers and, apparently, engaging in sex with them and other local boys. In fact, when visiting Whitman in 1856, Henry David Thoreau and Amos Bronson Alcott noted that Whitman still slept with his brother.

Whitman began teaching school on Long Island in 1836, while still a teenager. Up until the time of the Civil War, the practice of "boarding around" the local school teacher was a common arrangement to provide food and housing for this poorly-paid civil servant. Apparently the arrangement went even further, with the local teacher sharing a bed with the eldest same-sex child of the farmer or merchant whose turn it was to take in the teacher. Whitman seems to have taken advantage of this arrangement.

His poetry during this period tells of young boys cruising for sex in the local bars frequented by sailors and other working-class men. Whitman soon left the teaching profession under a cloud of rumors that he was much too intimate with his male students. In fact, in its 1907 printing of the "Personal

Recollections of Walt Whitman," the *Atlantic Monthly* removed all of Whitman's references to a passionate relationship between himself and a young farm boy whose father became upset over their intense arrangement.[1]

Although homosexuals have been employed as school teachers for centuries, many social and economic factors caused this to be a relatively invisible social phenomena until the 1950s and 1960s. In this chapter, several strands of the history of same-sex love are explored to set the context for the more overt stage of the American homosexual school teacher controversy.

EARLY BEGINNINGS

Throughout history theologians, philosophers, medical practitioners, legislators, social scientists, and citizens have debated the nature and causes of homosexuality. Much of this rich material is beyond the scope of this book, although some contextual setting adds an important dimension to the analysis.

At the onset, it is important to note that the attitudes about homosexuality presented in this volume are culture-bound by American social values and beliefs about human sexuality.[2] Other societies adhere to different perspectives on homosexuality that often reflect a greater acceptance of this behavior. For example, the available scholarship suggests that the intellectual elite of ancient Greece and Rome extolled the virtues of same-sex love, although the physical expression of that love was less widely supported. Homosexual conduct, however, was not against the law in ancient Greece except between certain people, such as slaves and freeborn youth. In fact, the ancient Greeks believed that their gods engaged in homosexual acts, such as Zeus with Ganymede.[3]

In their study of sexual behavior, C. S. Ford and F. A. Beach concluded that the disapproval of homosexuality expressed in America differed greatly from other societies. Of the 76 other cultures studied, 49 (64 percent) considered homosexual activities "normal and socially acceptable for certain members of the community."[4] The most notable example was that of "berdache" among the Indian tribes of North America, when a male adopted the dress, mannerisms, duties, and sexual roles of a woman. Similar conduct has been noted in Latin American Indian tribes and sub-Saharan Africa.[5] Thus, the discussion that follows concerning the abhorrent nature of homosexuality and its invisible practitioners is set in a context relevant to Judeo-Christian, European, and American cultures.

In his book, *Sexual Freedom and The Constitution*, Walter Barnett traced the religious origins of contemporary American social and legal attitudes towards homosexuality. Barnett suggested that the Jewish prohibition against same-sex relationships (as evidenced in the tale of the destruction of Sodom and Gomorrah and the harsh code of Leviticus against sodomy and bestiality) served as one means to differentiate the Jews from their pagan contemporaries.[6] Another more unconscious purpose may have been to increase the numbers of a persecuted group by forbidding non-reproductive sexual activity.

The early Christian church was confronted with pagan licentious as well, and it opted for a stoic asceticism that elevated the spirit at the expense of the body. Church leaders like Augustine, Jerome, Origen, and Tertullian emphasized that sexual desire and sexual gratification were "basically evil in themselves, redeemable only in the context of a permanent union of one man and one woman for the production of children."[7] Celibacy, virginity, and sexual restraint were viewed as holy qualities, while most other sexual matters became grievous sins.

In his *Summa Theologica*, Thomas Aquinas articulated the various sexual sins against God in order of magnitude. Bestiality, homosexual sodomy, heterosexual sodomy, and masturbation were sins against God because nonreproductive sexual gratification offended God's spiritual aspirations for man. On the other hand, lust, rape, adultery, and seduction were lesser sins to God despite the harm to neighbors.

With these religious beliefs in place, their codification as laws against sodomy and bestiality was easily accomplished. The punishment set forth in the medieval English legal system was death by burning, although some jurists felt that "the offender should be buried alive like those who had dealings with Jews or Jewesses."[8]

With the Protestant Reformation in England under Henry VIII, the powers of the ecclesiastical (church) courts were transferred to the King's courts. Thus, the close relationship between sodomy and bestiality as sin and criminal behavior was retained in the English law of 1533. These crimes often were referred to as offenses to the crown and a "high displeasure of Almighty God."[9] They were thought to be so unspeakable that Blackstone in his legal *Commentaries* referred to them only as the "crime against nature not to be named among Christians."[10]

Since the English sodomy law remained unchanged until 1861, when the death penalty was changed to life imprisonment, it was available to American colonists as they established a legal code. The typical colonial statute contained wording from both Blackstone's 1811 references and the 1533 English statute of Henry VIII. For example, North Carolina's original sodomy statute stated:

> Any person who shall commit the abominable and detestable crime against nature, not to be named among Christians, with either mankind or beast, shall be adjudged guilty of a felony, and shall suffer death without benefit of clergy.[11]

Thus, by 1776, male homosexuality was punishable by death in all of the 13 original colonies.

Lesbianism was included as a capital offense by Reverend John Cotton in 1672 when he drafted some fundamental laws for the colony at the request of the General Court of Massachusetts. Cotton's suggestion was rejected, since lesbianism had not been punished under English law, although there had been executions of women under Roman law in France and Italy.[12] Lesbianism was included as a capital offense punishable by death in the 1655 colonial laws of New Haven. This was in effect for only 10 years until the colony joined Connecticut and came under its laws.[13]

Probably the most unique response to the legal issue of homosexuality occurred in the Pennsylvania laws of 1682. Under the
leadership of William Penn, and because of the Quaker opposition
to physical violence, the sentence for sodomy was reduced to a
whipping, the loss of one third of one's estate, and six months hard
labor in the house of corrections.[14] These penalties were the most
humane sentences in American law concerning homosexuality
adopted by any state until 1961, but they were not in effect for very
long. In 1700, under pressure from the British Parliament, the
Pennsylvania legislature changed the sentence to include life
imprisonment and possible castration. The latter penalty was deleted
from the laws five years later.[15] Any Black person found guilty of
sodomy, murder, or rape of a white woman faced the death penalty.[16]

The death penalty for sodomy remained in effect in American
states until 1873, when South Carolina became the last state to
drop it from its list of capital offenses. The slow trend began in
Pennsylvania in 1776, when the new state constitution mandated
that the harsh British criminal code imposed in 1718 be modified.[17]
The Quaker influence was important, and their humane perspective was supported in the mid-1700s by legal theorists who argued
that the laws of a civilized society needed to be compassionate.
Montesquieu noted that people accused of sodomy often had been
political enemies of the church. Cesare Beccaria also noted the
political convictions on sodomy grounds, but he was more
concerned with his assessment that the educational system
fostered homosexual activity by segregating boys in same-sex
schools. Beccaria feared that by applying the death penalty for
sodomy offenses, society was punishing boys for behavior
fostered by its own educational system.[18]

According to Crompton, the trial transcripts of English-
speaking colonial America showed that at least two people were
put to death for sodomy offenses. William Cornish was burned at
the stake in Virginia in 1625, and William Plain was hanged in
Guilford in 1646. In 1646 and 1660 two men in Dutch New
Amsterdam were sentenced to death by burning at the stake and
by drowning, respectively, for sexual relations with boys. There
was no proof that the sentences were enforced. In Pennsylvania

as late as 1785, another man was executed for the "crime against nature," but it was unclear whether this entailed sodomy or bestiality.[19]

Although the actual consequences of two centuries of capital punishment for the crime of sodomy were relatively limited, its existence in American law was extremely significant. Because of the unmentionable nature of the crime, the legal records provide poor documentation. It may be that many other individuals suffered death and/or imprisonment under these laws. Equally important, people in 17th and 18th century America who were attracted to members of their own sex faced death if their expression of that love was discovered. Given this legal background, it is not surprising that the early history of homosexual educators in this country is invisible.

THE NATURE OF HOMOSEXUALITY

The early religious prohibitions against homosexuality suggested that it was a willful offense to God, caused by human evilness or possession by the devil. By the 18th century in America, the model was modified to portray homosexuality as a vice that could be cured only by public punishment and private penance. In either instance, however, for society to avoid the wrath of God, sodomy must be exorcised. The tale of Sodom and Gomorrah served as ample evidence of God's willingness to punish an entire population for its failure to prohibit and punish sodomy.

This religious perspective served as the basis for the American legal response to sodomy, as the previous section of this chapter stated. It also had independent significance in defining and controlling homosexual conduct, since religious leaders historically have been at the forefront of the debate over social norms and morality.

By the late 1800s, the religious model of homosexuality was joined by the medical model.[20] Under this analysis, homosexuality was a physiological condition and, later, a mental disorder of an identifiable group of individuals. Weeks and Faderman have argued that these medical perspectives provided individuals who were attracted to members of their own sex with a framework to clarify their own identity and to establish a collective conscious-ness as a sexual minority. Hence, they suggested that the medical models of homosexuality served the lesbian and gay male commu-nity positively by providing a framework for their self and group definition. In a different analysis of these medical models, Chauncey argued that they were promulgated by doctors who were trying to account for the increasingly visible homosexual subcultures and the changing role of women in society.[21] Chauncey suggested that the medical models were advanced by doctors eager to legitimize the heterosexual status quo and continue the subordination of women by asserting biologically-based theories that supported the existing social order.

The Victorian ideology of the late 1800s typically character-ized men as lustful and aggressive sexual beings, while women were viewed as having no sexual desires. This ideology offered additional insight into the lack of legal sanctions against lesbianism, since it was inconceivable that two women would initiate and enjoy sexual contact.[22] Under the medical models, then, for sexual gratification to occur between members of the same sex, one person had to invert his or her sexual role orienta-tion and take on the characteristics of the opposite sex. Thus, the 19th century term for homosexuality, "sexual inversion," included this role reversal as well as the same-sex attraction that has contemporary significance.[23]

Under this medical model of analysis, one party in the homosexual encounter took on the mannerisms, roles, and psychological make-up of the opposite sex. Some sexologists believed that even the anatomical attributes of the opposite sex were evident, so that a woman in the male role had an enlarged clitoris, while the male in the female role had a high-pitched voice and a slight bone structure.[24] Thus, the medical focus was upon the invert rather than on the partner who engaged in a supposedly normal sex role function, despite the fact that his or her lover was of the same sex.[25]

In his analysis of early American homosexual history, John D'Emilio argued that the shift from the religious to the medical model of homosexuality in approximately 1900 benefited lesbians and gay men in Britain and Germany.[26] Once homosexuality was characterized as a hereditary defect by the medical community, some public sentiment existed not to punish people for an inherent and immutable characteristic, so the laws of Britain and Germany were changed.[27] In the United States, however, D'Emilio suggested that the public reaction to the biological information was different. By retaining the legal and social restrictions, a person who was homosexual would be prevented or deterred from acting on those biological impulses.[28]

Thus far in the historical analysis, homosexuality has been characterized as devil possession, a sin, a crime, and/or biologically hereditary. With the advent of psychological theory in the late 1800s, homosexuality was also defined as a mental disorder and, later, a learning disorder.[29]

Under psychoanalytic theory, heterosexuality is the biological norm of all human beings, even though some people might not reach that developmental goal.[30] Since the scientific basis of these theories has been essentially untestable, and the clinical evidence has been developed from studies of people with numerous mental and emotional problems, the popularity of psychoanalytic theory has waned since the 1960s. In its place sprang new theories of the importance of learned behavior. In other words, homosexuality was a learned and acquired orientation just as other tastes and preferences were established by an individual. Through "reinforcement, punishment, modeling, contiguity (classical conditioning), and cognitive organizing," the individual learned to be either heterosexual or homosexual, with the only innate feature being the individual's need for sexual release.[31]

According to Kinsey and his colleagues, three aspects of experience — the first, the most intense, and the most recent — had the most profound influence on sexual preference development.[32] Thus, several psychological, experiential, and emotional factors coalesced at some point in the individual's life so that his or her "erotic gestalt" was homosexual.[33]

According to learning theorists, two more factors were necessary, however, before the individual assumed a completely homosexual identity. First, the individual needed to experience failure with heterosexual contacts.[34]   Second, the person needed to perform some socially "deviant" homosexual acts.[35] It was these additional criteria that supported the argument that homosexuals should not be permitted to influence young children, nor should they be permitted the opportunity for potential sexual activity with children. If a child needed a homosexual encounter to identify with a same-sex orientation, then contact with homosexuality must be prohibited. Thus, the child could not gain the learning experiences necessary to form a homosexual identity.

Because of intellectual and scientific advancements, theories about the causes of homosexuality changed over time, although their origins are easily recognizable in the models discussed above. Current scientific studies argue that the propensity for homosexuality is a genetic condition and/or linked to one's brain structure.[36] In his book, *The Sexual Brain*, for example, Simon LeVay discusses his research on that part of the brain known as the hypothalamus. LeVay argues that the brains of gay men differ from those of the heterosexual males with respect to the cells believed to be related to sexual behavior.[37] In another recent book on the subject, Dean H. Hamer, a geneticist with the National Cancer Institute in Maryland, writes that his preliminary research on a genetic basis for male homosexuality demonstrates that one or more genes on the X chromosome at Xq28 influences one's sexual orientation. "Xq28" means the DNA at the tip of the long arm (q) of the X chromosome (X) at Segment 28. This specific gene structure, however, does not equate with a "gay gene." Apparently, if a male has the genetic composition, he has a 70% chance of being homosexual and a 30% chance of not being homosexual. On the other hand, if the subject lacks the specific genetic composition, he has a 100% chance of being heterosexual. Since the relevant genetic material for homosexual males is on the X chromosome, like baldness, it is a characteristic passed through the maternal line. Preliminary genetic research on women has not correlated with the male findings, so little is known about any genetic propensity that influences lesbianism.[38]

Some members of the GLBT communities, and their family members, are delighted with these findings that suggest a genetic propensity as the cause of homosexuality. Since "immutable" characteristics are the legal basis for strict scrutiny in Constitutional arguments for individual rights, protections on the basis of sexual orientation might be expanded if it is classified as an innate characteristic like skin color, gender, or age. Similarly, after working with the Family Fellowship, a nationwide group of Mormon parents organized to support their GLBT offspring despite their harsh religious perspectives, I have noted their relief at a potential biological cause for homosexuality.[39] It removes the orientation from being a parental failure or a willful violation of religious and social edicts to being a condition created by God. As part of God's "Plan of Salvation," these previously "lost" (cast out into ever darkness) sons and daughters may now join the rest of the family in the Celestial Kingdom. Since most of the world's religions and judicial systems have several of these shared perspectives, discovery of a genetic basis for homosexuality might create world-wide reconsideration and acceptance of sexual orientation.

While many take comfort in a biological cause for homosexuality, others fear that it will become categorized as a genetic defect. Given recent advancements in prenatal screening, parents could have a fetus tested for homosexuality, as well as for potential health complications, and then opt for an abortion. In the face of so many emerging medical possibilities, our culture is grappling with the moral and ethical implications of its options. Having the right to physician-assisted suicide, genetically-engineered life, or living with and loving whomever one desires are some of the current challenges in the debate over personal freedoms and public constraints.

Although science may eventually find the cause of homosexuality, during that process it also has placed some theories in disfavor by testing sexual orientation in relation to personality, physiology, values, and mannerisms. No difference between heterosexual and homosexual self-esteem, neurosis, anxiety, emotional adjustment, personality or character disorders, or personality integration were discovered in several studies conducted in the mid-1970s.[40] Another study showed no difference in birth order or family size.[41] Other studies invalidated distinctions in psychopathology,[42] hormone levels,[43] and effeminacy and masculinity.[44] In fact, in his review of more than a dozen studies, Mark Freedman concluded that "when homosexual subjects are compared with heterosexual control groups, except for sexual preference, there is no significant difference between them."[45] It is not surprising, however, to note that in some instances when the researchers found no significant differences between heterosexuals and homosexuals, they concluded that their "test instruments were invalid, rather than their beliefs about homosexuality."[46]

In some measure, it was because of these conflicting physiological and psychological opinions and test results that the Board of Trustees of the American Psychiatric Association (APA) determined in 1974, despite some membership opposition, that:

> . . . homosexuality per se was no longer to be considered a mental disorder, although a diagnosis of "sexual orientation disturbance" could be made if a homosexual were to consult a psychiatrist either to seek heterosexual reorientation or to relieve stress caused by homosexual orientation.[47]

In fact, it may be the case that the greatest stress on the GLBT personality is not the GLBT orientation per se, but the societal reaction that has traditionally labeled it a sin, a crime, and/or a mental disorder.[48]

All the analyses presented above on the nature of homosexuality have focused on the individual's causal motivations. Another perspective does exist, however. This perspective argues that economic and societal changes that have occurred in the late 20th century have permitted men and women to identify themselves as GLBT on both an individual and collective basis. In his essay, "Capitalism and Gay Identity," John D'Emilio traces the development of capitalism in American society and its effect on the nuclear family and wage labor. For example, in Colonial times the family was the main unit of production and support for most individuals. As the United States slowly transformed to a capitalist, free labor economic system, the family began to lose its significance as a source for production of goods. On the other hand, the need for economic interdependence among family members remained. This was joined by an ideology that stressed the emotional significance of the family as a source of support and happiness. D'Emilio argues that by 1950, however, the individual began to make his or her living through wage labor and could do so independently of the nuclear family. Thus, men and women were free to seek alternative emotional arrangements based upon their attraction for members of their same sex. In concert with these economic and social changes, D'Emilio argues that scientists by the early 1900s began to formulate new theories about homosexuality as an inherent condition. Men and women began to reconceptualize their feelings about themselves and their sexual orientation in a manner that permitted the emergent, political homosexual subcultures of the late 1960s. Under this theoretical construct, then, the number of lesbians and gay men in the United States will continue to increase as more people choose emotional ties based upon affectional preference and erotic desire rather than economic or social constraints. In fact, D'Emilio suggests that the statistical disparity between the numbers of gay men and lesbians will decrease as women become more successful as independent wage earners within our economic system. Furthermore, in light of this free choice, the Conservative Right has a legitimate fear that homosexuals can "recruit" new members into its community. Thus, a conservative backlash has arisen to attempt to counteract this social and economic change by re-emphasizing the importance of the family.

DEFINITIONS OF HOMOSEXUALITY

In light of the previous material on the nature of homosexuality, it is apparent that one's definition of homosexuality may depend upon beliefs about causation and gender roles. For example, the term "sexual inversion" assumed that one individual must adopt the sexual role of the opposite sex to effect the sexual act modeled after heterosexuality. In his study of the Newport, Rhode Island, Navy sex scandal of 1919-1920, Chauncey noted that the Navy ran into difficulty sustaining charges of criminal homosexual conduct precisely because it prosecuted only one of the two parties in any homosexual encounter. In other words, the male who adopted the female sexual role of servicing the male was arrested. The other person was deemed to be engaging in permissible deviant behavior.[49]

This lopsided hostility toward the person in the homosexual couple who was perceived to be outside his or her gender role was not unique to the Newport scandal. In some Latin American countries, for example, a homosexual is defined as the person who engages in fellatio or who is penetrated during anal sex in a same-sex encounter. The other party maintains the social, moral, and legal benefits of heterosexuality while avoiding the potentially harsh consequences of being stigmatized as a homosexual.[50]

In his study of the "tearoom trade" (sex between men in public rest rooms), Laud Humphreys also noted that a surprising number of ostensibly heterosexual males engaged in sometimes daily homosexual activity in public men's rooms without considering themselves homosexual as long as they were the dominant actors in the sexual encounter.[51] Humphreys calculated that over 5 percent of the male population in his metropolitan research area participated often in the public restroom sexual activity.[52] These people, according to Humphreys, rarely adhered to a homosexual identity. In fact, the majority of them were married and lived with their wives.[53] Those who did identify as homosexual preferred more supportive haunts like gay bars and bath houses. In his conclusion, Humphreys suggested that, in fact, the participants in the tearoom trade were homosexuals who were unable to accept that aspect of their sexual makeup. He also noted that a majority of the men despised women, commitment in relationships, and prolonged intimacy and affection. The James Bond "use them and leave them" image of sex with women was a frequently-articulated ideal of the study's participants.[54]

Often, the tearoom participants had the further complication of reconciling their conservative political and religious views with their sexual practices. For example, some of the men studied were conservative clergy while others were active in the John Birch Society. According to Humphreys' analysis, these religious and political affiliations provided the tearoom participants with the public image of righteousness. They served to blind the participant's everyday "audience" by providing a "shield of super-propriety."[55]

In these images of homosexuality, a constant theme appears concerning hostility toward women and the receptive sexual role that is defined culturally as female. Historically, men who have adopted this role have been persecuted to the greatest extent. On the other hand, since women have been valued so little in most societies, lesbians have escaped much of the persecution by remaining invisible. Although these images have shaped responses toward homosexuals, they have not been useful in defining homosexuality. As scholarship on sexual expression continues, however, these rigid perspectives on the nature of homosexuality are being challenged.

In 1948, when Dr. Kinsey and his associates were studying homosexuality, they developed a seven-point scale that addressed the wide range of sexual expression possible over the course of a lifetime. Zero points reflected a person who was exclusively heterosexual with no homosexual behavior or fantasies in his or her history. Three points reflected a person who engaged in equal heterosexual and homosexual conduct. Six points reflected an individual who was exclusively homosexual in orientation.[56] With this perspective on sexual expression, it was understood that an individual could display a wider range of sexual behavior than was evidenced by the extreme categorization of either heterosexual or homosexual. Kinsey's work exposed the gray area of American sexual expression.

Due to their research in the 1940s and 1950s, which predated the emergence of politicized homosexual subcultures, Kinsey and his colleagues concluded that approximately 10 percent of

American adults were predominantly homosexual in orientation.[57] Additionally, Kinsey reported that 37 percent of the adult male population, or 2 out of every 5 males, had engaged in overt, consensual homosexual activity to the point of orgasm at least once since adolescence.[58] In light of this information, Americans had to reconsider their beliefs about homosexuality and acknowledge a growing awareness of its presence in society.

Kinsey and subsequent sex researchers and psychologists may have been closer to defining the reality of homosexuality when they considered it on a continuum of sexual expression. This perspective focused less on the causation issue and more on the details of a much wider range of sexual expression than had been considered previously. Under the Kinsey model, then, a person could be predominantly heterosexual or homosexual, or move back and forth in a less defined area of sexual expression that included both.[59]

In addition to actual sexual behavior, Kinsey and his colleagues applied the sexual continuum analysis to sexual fantasies and feelings. All three of these criteria — sexual behavior, sexual fantasies, and sexual feelings — were applied to various periods in a respondent's life. Thus, while a respondent might declare himself or herself a "6" — or "exclusively homosexual" — at this time, the individual's previous history of sexual expression was not lost in the analytical process.

The significance of this perspective on homosexuality is borne out by the case law discussed later in this book. This case law demonstrates that numerous school employees arrested for homosexual behavior denied having that sexual orientation, despite being caught in a homosexual act. Certainly the consequences of declaring one's self a homosexual in that situation were severe, so it is not surprising that a person would deny being a lesbian or a gay man. On the other hand, it may be that there is a very large "gray area" of sexual expression in American society, just as Humphreys documented in his study of men's public rest rooms. Many people who consider themselves predominantly heterosexual may have found themselves arrested during an incidence of homosexual activity. Because they were so legitimate in the heterosexual sphere, with a wife and children possibly, they may have been willing to take the public risk of challenging their dismissal from school employment because of the arrest for homosexual activity. Conversely, people who identified themselves as homosexual, without the prerogative of heterosexuality, may have accepted dismissal and left town rather than have that identity confirmed to the public. In part, this would explain the large number of cases in which the school employee denied being a homosexual.

While the psychological model of homosexuality revealed a gray area of sexual expression, the discussion above demonstrates that this is not the case in the legal model of homosexuality. In the eyes of the law, being caught in one act of homosexual sexual expression renders the perpetrator open to the full force of legal hostility against homosexuals. Under the legal model, the one arrest for homosexuality suggests an active history of criminal behavior that has eluded prosecution previously.

As the case law on gay and lesbian school teachers demonstrates, however, a few people fired from teaching for homosexual conduct have been able to assert some mitigating factors in their defense. The court has been more considerate of people who were exposed through rumor rather than arrest, had little or no history of homosexual activity, and who had tried to change their homosexual desires through therapy. Thus, although school systems adhere to the legal model of homosexuality that permits firing based upon one same-sex incident, when these firings have been challenged in court, the judicial system has been willing to consider mitigating circumstances. The case of Marc Morrison v. The State Board of Education offers the best example of the court considering these factors,[60] while Sarac v. State Board of Education offers the best example of the court ignoring them.[61]

In addition to the problems with the psychological and the legal definition of homosexuality, this book is complicated by historical research factors as well. The reality of exploring an invisible minority whose behavior is "not to be named among Christians," is that it is almost impossible to determine who is or was homosexual in his or her orientation.[62] An analysis of how the legal, educational, political, and social institutions respond to a person accused of being homosexual is possible. This information is valuable for efforts aimed at social, legal, and political change for gay men, lesbians, and other minorities. It is, however, in danger of falling short in terms of the rich history of contributions to American society made by lesbians and gay men. If the definitional focus is "did they or did they not engage in a homosexual sex act," then it includes people — such as prisoners, soldiers, and others restrained in a same-sex or dominance-dependent situation — who lack an emotional or political commitment to GLBT subcultures. Conversely, people who are committed emotionally, politically, socially, and sexually to members of their same sex may not be evidenced in such a study because of their otherwise exemplary lifestyles or because there is little evidence available to prove they acted on their strong emotional attractions. Historical research on homosexual school teachers is complicated by this latter factor. It could send the researcher off on a "did they or didn't they" search that misses the essence of whether a person was committed to members of his or her same sex at some times in his or her life.

Due to this difficulty with historical research, Carroll Smith-Rosenberg and others have presented an alternative definition of homosexuality. This definition focuses on the intense bonding and emotional commitment to same-sex relationships, whether or not the person ever acted on those feelings. Furthermore, Smith-Rosenberg's perspective takes into account a continuum of "cultural norms and arrangements" that have existed in American society. Smith-Rosenberg argues that between the mid-18th and the mid-19th centuries, for example, rigid gender-role differentiation that segregated men and women led to intense relationships between women that were socially acceptable. These "homosocial" ties were reflected in a wide range of expression — passionate letters of everlasting friendship and love, "smashes" or crushes outgrown in adulthood, lifelong relationships of support and comfort, and fully actualized homosexual commitments.[63] With this social/historical perspective, a researcher can go beyond analysis of an individual's social, psychological, and sexual developmental history and look at the larger societal context. Since individual behavior is shaped by that social context, it is possible to place the issue of homosexuality in its cultural framework of attitudes, norms, and arrangements.

One might expect to find more information about same-sex commitments that occurred during periods of greater tolerance for homosocial relationships, then, than one would find for periods of social hostility. In fact, the record may be more confusing, since a person with an attraction to members of his or her own sex might have a history of relationships with members of the opposite sex as well. Not only is the continuum of sexual expression widened for society overall, it is widened for the individual. Given the complexities of this historical research, the following section on the history of gay and lesbian educators merely serves to introduce a topic that requires much more extensive information and analysis.

THE INSTITUTIONAL CONTEXT

One cultural context that was renowned for its acceptance of homosexuality was ancient Greek civilization. Xenophon, in his contemporaneous analysis of ancient Sparta, paused to reflect on the effect of pederasty on the educational system, since it was so common.[64] As Henri Marrou discussed in his essay on "Pederasty In Classical Education," to the ancient Greeks same-sex love was considered to be the most perfect form of education. Through this love relationship, the elder person excelled in the labor of teaching, and the younger person venerated the art of learning. The laws of Sparta went so far as to hold a "lover morally responsible for the development of his beloved."[65] Thus, according to Marrou's details of Greek relationships, famous philosophers like Socrates and Plato inspired and trained their lovers, such as Xenocrates, Polemon, and Arcesilaus, as intellectual successors.[66] Famous scientists, artists, and politicians also trained their renowned successors in a similar intellectual/sexual manner.[67]

Marrou argued that this perspective on education was an outgrowth of the intensely sex-segregated features of Greek society. In fact, he argued that it was the absurd extreme of gender-role dichotomy. Since women were considered highly inferior beings fit merely for childbearing and household duties, only in the company of men could a boy learn the essentials of his gender role and class position. Thus, although the youth adopted an inferior role in the relationship, its purpose was to train him in the duties of manhood, including sexual duties, rather than to feminize him. Upon adulthood, then, the boy would perpetuate the educational process by being the teacher/lover of other young men even though he also might have a wife and children.

One outcome of this highly developed men's-club perspective was that women formed equally intense same-sex bonds and networks. By 600 B.C., Sappho of Lesbos provided a higher education for girls of affluent families during the transitional period between childhood and marriage. In academies dedicated to the goddess of culture, young women learned music, art, drama, ballet, literature, charm, and fashion. Physical prowess was also emphasized, as young women participated in athletic contests, in part for the honor of their mentors.[68]

Some of the classical idealization of homosexual love survived the Greek civilization and was evidenced in the sculpting of Michelangelo, the artistry of Leonardo de Vinci, the writing of J. A. Symonds, and the poetry of Walt Whitman. On the other hand, societal perspectives on homosexuality shifted toward greater abhorrence, so that people who loved members of their same sex faced severe personal and professional sanctions.

Another feature of Greek life that survived was the phenomenon of sex-segregated educational settings. Since the late medieval period, for example, the British have educated their young boys in boarding schools that have isolated them from their families and from females. Not only were there significant numbers of homosexual school teachers in this setting, but the institutions themselves permitted complex social practices that encouraged homosexual behavior.

In the early 19th century, for example, the British educational model mandated that boys of all ages were to be locked in their dormitories after 8:00 in the evening without adult supervision. Whatever occurred during these nighttime lockups was of no concern to adults. In an 1810 editorial, however, the British critic Sydney Smith characterized the schools as a "system of premature debauchery that only prevents men from being corrupted by the world by corrupting them before their entry into the world."[69]

In an attempt to reform the boarding schools, British head-master Thomas Arnold proposed a prefect system that placed senior boys in charge of the behavior of the younger children.[70] This arrangement institutionalized the already established private hierarchical structure that placed the younger boys at the service of the elder in terms of chores, errands, and sexual favors. C. S. Lewis described this system of "House Tarts" as second only to athletics in the hearts and minds of his school peers. At every occasion, the boys were "buzzing, tittering, hinting, whispering" about who was in favor with whom.[71]

Lewis discussed his feelings about homosexuality in the English boarding schools later in the same essay. Although he viewed homosexuality as a distasteful perversion, Lewis remained equally critical of people who labeled it the most serious of social ills; in part, because he acknowledged society's guilt in placing children in segregated, competitive, and emotionally empty boarding schools, and then condemning those same youngsters for attaining some level of human warmth. Furthermore, he asserted that love, in whatever form, retained some essence of social benefit that could not be found in other human vices.

One major value of the Lewis essay is that it discussed a common phenomenon in Western society that is rarely acknowl-edged. The public images of English boarding schools and American same-sex colleges were that no homosexual teachers were employed and no homosexuality occurred between the students. The private realities of these institutions is that they supported practices that encouraged homosexual behavior by both faculty and students.

Furthermore, this two-faced perspective can be extended to American traditions of elementary and secondary education as well.

For example, until the 1940s women teachers were prohibited, by the threat of job loss, from marrying. Some remained in teaching for a brief time and then resigned their positions to marry, and some kept their marriages a secret. The most numerous long-term female teachers, however, were the spinsters — single heterosexual or lesbian women who were disinterested in men and/or committed to their careers. In a further piece of social irony, society approved of these women doubling up as partners, ostensibly to defray living expenses and monitor their morality in terms of contact with men. Thus, although the national average of homosexuals in the population is estimated to be about ten percent,[72] it is almost assuredly the case that the teaching profession has had a disproportionately higher number of lesbians and gay men than any other profession. Some concrete evidence exists to support this statement.

In 1977, Vern and Bonnie Bullough published their study of a small lesbian community in the 1920s and 1930s. Of the 25 people studied, at least 6 were known to have been teachers.[73] Kinsey and his colleagues reported similar information in their 1953 study of the sexual behavior of women.[74] Exact numbers will never be ascertained, but it certainly is true that GLBT men and women have had a long and relatively quiet history of educating American youth.

THE INDIVIDUAL CONTEXT

In the preceding sections of this chapter, the discussion focused on the relationship of homosexuality to social institutions. During periods of extreme segregation of the sexes (such as in early Greece, and mid-18th and mid-19th century America), intense bonds between members of the same sex were an aspect of these cultural arrangements. Given the broad range of expression of this affection, it would be inappropriate to label all of these individuals as homosexual, particularly because they often participated in heterosexual marriages and families as well. On the other hand, it also is inappropriate to dismiss these significant homosocial attachments since they played a major role in the emotional and social lives of many individuals. Furthermore, if one ignores these intense relationships, the rhetoric of the dominant majority about traditional cultural norms is heightened at the expense of understanding the wider range of human behavior and minority alternatives to those norms. Despite the majority portrayal of homosexuality as a sin, crime, or mental or physical disorder, it is important to realize that numerous individuals have challenged these disapprobations and their consequences in order to express their love for members of their sex.

In this section, the relationship of these individuals to society is explored within the context of the teaching profession. The material is offered as a preliminary discussion and is not meant to serve as an exposé of who was gay or lesbian. In fact, it stands as an example of the difficulties inherent in researching non-traditional behavior and "invisible" minority populations.

Given the debate in the English press around 1810 over sex in boarding schools that was discussed in the previous section, it may not be a coincidence that the first known case in the English-speaking world concerning a homosexual school teacher occurred during this period in Scotland.[75] The case of <u>Woods and Pirie v. Dame Cummings Gordon</u> gained national attention when two women who ran a boarding school for girls sued a wealthy citizen for libel because she had accused them of having a homosexual relationship. Dame Gordon's ward, who attended the school, accused the women of being lesbians after they commenced action to expel her for disciplinary reasons. Gordon considered it her duty to warn other parents, who collectively withdrew all of their children from the school and forced it to close.

In addition to the sensationalistic details of this case, the press was drawn into the legal debate over whether two women could desire or express sexual activity between themselves. Given the cultural image of women as virtuous and without sexual desires, it was incomprehensible in both a legal and a social context that women would be sexually active without a male catalyst. Ultimately the Court ruled in favor of Woods and Pirie because of the sketchy hearsay evidence presented against them and because of the judges' own personal disbelief in the possibilities of lesbian physical love. Unfortunately, the publicity ruined their reputations, their livelihoods, and their relationship, despite receipt of a small settlement.

Because of the widespread newspaper coverage and the copious legal documentation, details of the Woods/Pirie case survived. Lillian Hellman used these in her controversial play, *The Children's Hour*, first performed in 1934.[76] Most details of the play, including the dialogue, were taken directly from the court documents — only the conclusion is substantially different. In the play, Woods and Pirie lost their libel suit, their school was closed, and their reputations were ruined. One of them committed suicide because of the realization that she did love her colleague "in that manner," and then the student revealed that she lied. With this ending, Hellman affirmed the sensibilities of her audience concerning the evil and tragedy of homosexuality and further blurred the details of real-life homosocial experience.

In using the Woods/Pirie case, Hellman changed the details for dramatic effect and to increase the popularity of the play. In a similar manner, the personal histories and literary works of several notable Americans with homosocial ties may have been changed in order to "protect" their reputations and increase their commercial success. In light of these obscured historical records, the following discussion concerning the mid-19th century American transcendentalists is provided as a preliminary basis for further research.[77]

Because of their famous literary careers, the teaching experiences of Ralph Waldo Emerson, Margaret Fuller, Elizabeth Peabody, Amos Bronson Alcott, Henry David Thoreau,[78] Henry W. Longfellow, Herman Melville, and Walt Whitman have been overshadowed. Like so many teachers in early American educational settings, none of them viewed teaching as a life-long occupation. Rather, as educated individuals, they were able to obtain the financial support that they needed at various times by teaching school. Also overshadowed is the research that suggests these notable Americans had intense same-sex relationships during periods of their adulthood, that in some instances were consummated. Certainly some of their contemporaries knew of their same-sex desires and affiliations, but the record has been blurred by efforts to protect their reputations and by the inadequate definitions of what constitutes homosexuality.

Margaret Fuller formed a special relationship with Elizabeth Peabody while they worked together at the Temple School in Boston, run by Amos Bronson Alcott. Fuller's diaries reveal strong attachments to other women, although she also married late in life. Herman Melville appears to have been in love with Nathaniel Hawthorne, to whom he dedicated *Moby Dick*. It is unclear whether or not Hawthorne returned this affection. Walt Whitman's homosexual activities were the "cause celebre" of his Long Island teaching community in the late 1830s. Henry James, who wrote about educational issues, also was known to have had intense homosexual feelings, although he was married. It is unclear whether James ever acted upon those urges, although his sister, Alice James, did act upon her homosexual desires.[79]

Ironically, the most revealing information available on a "homosexual" educator concerns Amos Bronson Alcott. Alcott, married and the father of four children, including the writer Louisa May Alcott, maintained ongoing social and intellectual relationships with most of the notable Americans mentioned above. Emerson was his friend and financial supporter. Fuller and Peabody worked for him at his school in Boston in the 1830s. Alcott introduced Thoreau and Whitman to each other during a trip to New York. Despite these close associations with people who were attracted to members of their same sex, Alcott appeared to be the heterosexual liberal who maintained these friendships for their intellectual stimulation. This perspective on Alcott has shifted, however, since Madelon Bedell released her biography of him in 1980.[80]

Before the Bedell biography, educational historians and Alcott biographers attributed his repeated firings from teaching positions to his unique educational perspectives. Alcott was infamous for ignoring the basics of reading, writing, and arithmetic. Under the influence of Rousseau, Pestalozzi, Robert Owen, and William Russell, he developed innovative learning techniques that included the Socratic question-answer method, field trips, scientific experimentation, experiential projects (such as mapping the school yard for a geography lesson), and athletic exercises. But

Bedell argues that Alcott's radical behavior included socializing with his students, inviting them to his rooms, and being physically affectionate with both male and female students. Bedell suggests that Alcott's "seductive personality" won the hearts of his students but caused conflicts. Apparently, the parents resented Alcott's influence over their children and, quite possibly, questioned the physical intimacy between teacher and students.

In 1842 Emerson paid Alcott's way to England to visit Alcott House, an innovative educational experiment named after him. There Alcott met Charles Lane, a founder of the Alcott House experiment. Lane, Alcott, and another founder, Henry Gardiner Wright, returned to America with plans to start a utopian community in Massachusetts. On a farm in Harvard, named Fruitlands, the Alcotts, Lane, and a few utopian followers, wintered in cold, crowded, and barely sustaining circumstances. According to Bedell, it was during this utopian experiment that Alcott and Lane formed an intense emotional and probably sexual involvement.

In response to her husband's relationship with Lane, Abby Alcott issued an ultimatum: she was leaving the farm, leaving Alcott, and taking the four children and all of the furniture with her. To her brother, Samuel May, she confided that Charles Lane offered, "no clean, healthy, safe course," so she was prepared to face social ruin by leaving her husband rather than remain in the situation.

In her diary of December, 1844, Louisa May Alcott, recorded that her father had decided to remain with Charles Lane. When confronted with the fate of remaining in an empty, cold, and financially ruined household, however, Charles Lane left first. Bronson Alcott became severely depressed, refused all food and water, and almost died before he rebounded from the emotional turmoil.

Although the details available concerning Bronson Alcott's life may not conclusively demonstrate that he was a homosexual educator, they certainly demonstrate some of the difficulties of labeling and interpreting behavior about this topic. His repeated failure at running schools may have been due to his innovative ideas and unusual personality, but there also is evidence to suggest that in the eyes of their parents, he was too intimate —

intellectually, emotionally, and physically — with his students. These details, combined with his network of same-sex oriented friends, provide some of the most overt, albeit meager, historical evidence available on the circumstances and consequences of an educator with strong emotional attachments to members of his own sex. Only a few other, pre-World War II, examples have been found to date.

Given the historically close association of the roles of town minister and town school teacher, the dismissal of Horatio Alger, Jr. (1832-1899) in 1866 from his Unitarian pulpit in Brewster, Massachusetts, is illustrative. After completing his education at Harvard University and Harvard Divinity School, Alger followed in his father's ministerial footsteps and accepted a position in Brewster. Although a popular minister and speaker during his 15-month tenure, in March of 1866 Alger was confronted by the town leaders with charges of "gross immorality . . . the abominable and revolting crime of unnatural familiarity with boys."[81] Alger left town that very evening, never to return to the ministry or to the town of Brewster. Alger resigned his ordinational rights immediately, upon the advice of his father and supportive church officials who felt that he should "have a chance in some other walk of life to redeem his character."[82]

The community's awareness of Alger's behavior was extensive, and numerous letters were sent to church officials concerning what action should be taken against him. Some letters were sympathetic, while some went so far as to call for the punishment set forth in Leviticus, which is death.[83] Ultimately, given Alger's resignation and retreat, and the highly-placed position of his father in the church community, the issue died down to a one-line notice in the *Christian Register* of Alger's resignation from his ministerial capacities without reference to any reason for the action.[84] In fact, had Alger not gone on to be a rather famous writer, the information concerning the reason for his dismissal essentially would have been lost to history.

In *Gay American History: Lesbians and Gay Men in the U.S.A.*, Jonathan Katz documented that a few homosexuals mentioned in his book also were teachers, but only one example went into greater detail. In 1915, there was a movement to terminate the employment of Stark Young, a gay English professor at Amherst College. The adamant leader of the anti-homosexual group was another Amherst professor, the poet Robert Frost. No legal action was taken, although the president of the college was petitioned. Young retained his faculty appointment because of the high quality of his teaching.[85]

THE 1940S AND 1950S

Given the long history of viewing homosexuality as evil, it is not surprising to find that very little information about the nexus between being homosexual and being a teacher of impressionable youth exists prior to World War II. By the late 1940s, however, more men and women began to identify themselves as homosexuals on both a personal and collective basis. Correspondingly, the details of this life experience began to emerge in the public awareness. D'Emilio argued that this increased societal consciousness of homosexuality had to do with the psychiatric screening process of World War II inductees as structured by the federal government.[86] In an unprecedented societal move, tens of thousands of Americans were questioned about their homosexual urges and actions. The medical model of homosexuality gained public prominence, although the religious and legal perspectives remained viable.

D'Emilio argued further that the screening of homosexuals in the military was ineffective due to the brief questioning and the potential to lie because of negative sanctions or patriotic fervor. Thus, the military experience isolated vast numbers of men in a sex-segregated environment, the classic medium for increased homosexual contact. To a lesser extent, many women were affected by the sex-segregated military experience as well. Also, women moved into urban settings to undertake previously male-dominated jobs to support themselves and aid the war effort. As they did this, their opportunities for same-sex involvement increased.

Thus, World War II and the post-war period evidenced tremendous social disruption. Soldiers and civilians remained in urban settings where their personal behavior was not scrutinized by family and friends. The coming out process was simplified, as homosexual men and women found kindred spirits in the increasingly numerous lesbian and gay bars. Emergent personal, social, and political identities were formed within the homosexual subcultures that supported the expression of same-sex love.

CHAPTER CONCLUSIONS

Although the anthropological and historical records reveal that some societies have accepted homosexuality, the cultural norm in the English-speaking world has viewed it as a sin, sickness, or crime. By the early 1900s, however, new scientific theories about homosexuality were advanced to explain the emerging personal and collective identification of men and women with same-sex desires as a genetic defect, mental disorder, or learning disorder. Conversely, D'Emilio argued that these social changes were allowed because individuals were freed by the capitalist economic system from dependence upon the family unit for support.

Since the late 1940s, scientific research also has been used to challenge the validity of these medical models and to reveal the wide range of sexual expression in American society. In particular, the work of Kinsey and his associates challenged the heterosexual cultural norm. It exposed the public to an undercurrent of nontraditional sexual expression practiced by numerous individuals who passed as adherents to those norms.

Despite the often severe consequences of acting on homosexual urges, historical research reveals that many individuals, including some of the intellectual elite of New England in the 1830s and 1840s, participated in a lifestyle that included strong same-sex bonds. When these relationships are placed in their wider social context, they reveal a society in which the sexes are rigidly segregated by gender. In fact, since medieval times the process of educating young males often has included isolation from families and females unless the children were very young. Historically, women's access to education has been severely limited in comparison to males, but often they, too, were educated in a sex-segregated setting. These situations encouraged the formation of strong bonds of intimacy between members of the same sex, not just for human warmth, but because of the entire social context that heightened the differences between men and women.

With this emphasis on the extreme differences between the sexes came a disparaging attitude toward and distorted image of the capabilities of each group. Men were viewed as aggressive sexual beings unable to control their desires, but dominant, managerial, and capable in the world. Women were viewed as asexual beings whose virtue and sensitivity were to be used for raising a family and making the home a desirable haven for their worldly male. Usually, each sex adhered to the cultural expectation that they marry and have children, in part for economic reasons. But throughout their lives, they may have also maintained strong same-sex bonds that ranged in expression on a continuum from affection to sexual activity. Because of this range of expression, and because of the disapprobations against homosexuality, this chapter demonstrates some of the difficulties in researching nontraditional behavior in the sensitive realms of sexual expression and "deviant" behavior.

Although the invisible nature of homosexual activity still exists today, the first indication that heterosexual cultural traditions were being challenged became evident in the 1940s. As the popularity of the medical model increased, it was brought into other institutional realms, particularly the military during World War II. Suddenly, a vast number of American citizens were being questioned about their sexual orientation and expression, while simultaneously being isolated in sex-segregated military settings. Upon returning home from the war, many individuals remained in urban areas that afforded freedom from community scrutiny and anonymity of sexual expression. Simultaneously, a strong movement arose to suppress deviant behavior and other changes that threatened traditional values. It is within this context of an emergent homosexual subculture and overt governmental hostility that the legal case law on gay and lesbian educators commences.

Your silence will not protect you.

— *Audre Lorde*

CHAPTER **8**

COMMIE, PINKO, QUEERS, AND CRIMINALS
EARLY CASE LAW AND TRADITIONAL VALUES, 1950–1968

Spring, 1957. After waiting months for this moment, "Jeffrey Lowell" felt almost calm. He should have been excited. He had just finished helping his 11th grade debating team evaluate its research for the upcoming Florida State High School Debate Championships. Yet Jeff knew that he would not be attending the debates. In fact, he thought, maybe he had attended just one too many. Jeff flinched as he recalled last year's debates and the knowing wink from the coach at "Evergreen High School," whom he recognized from the gay bars. It was clear evidence that his alias of "Kip" in the gay community had been decoded into "Jeffrey Lowell, school teacher at Smithson High."

It had to happen some time, Jeff rationalized, as he walked to the principal's office. For the past few years police hostility towards gays and lesbians had been rampant. This included raids on private parties, recording people's license plate numbers outside gay-oriented events with subsequent blackmail threats, severe beatings, harassing arrests, telephone taps, and postal searches of people's mail. It made him wonder that so many men and women continued to love members of the same sex given the pressure, harassment, and fears.

It was hard to live two lives and hope that they never intersected. All of the gay professionals Jeff knew had an alias in the gay community so their employment would not be so easily threatened. And, of course, there was that age-old dating arrangement. Jeff had attended so many school functions with his lesbian friend, Laura, over the past 10 years that people were sure a wedding announcement would be forthcoming. It benefited Laura, too, since her boss thought she was engaged to Jeff, so he asked fewer questions and made fewer sexual comments to her. But now it was all over. All of his hard work and his passion for teaching would end today, thanks to "Charley Johns Investigating Committee on Communism and Homosexuality."

Upon reaching the principal's office, Jeff was led into an empty classroom that had been designated as the interrogation room. Empty was not quite the right description. Two police officers stood by in full uniform, and there was a woman seated in front of some tape recording equipment. Finally, Jeff was introduced to Inspector R. J. Strickland, state director of the investigating committee into communism. Surely, it was too late to convince these people that communism and homosexuality were not inextricably linked. Maybe it was a case of nerves, but Jeff almost laughed aloud at the supreme irony of the situation. The rumor in the gay community was that Senator Joseph McCarthy's aide, Roy Cohn, was a notoriously sexually active homosexual.[1] What better way to divert suspicion than to have everybody looking for "Commie, pinko, queers" in government and the schools. And if Jeff "named names," the irony was that they would not believe him if he included Cohn. It was a no-win situation, so Jeff decided to just keep quiet.

This last resolve was difficult, however. Inspector Strickland informed Jeff that they knew, based upon the testimony given by other teachers, that he was a homosexual. Jeff was not swayed by the promise that "they might go easier on him" if he talked — he knew his teaching career was finished. But then Inspector Strickland told Jeff that if he did not cooperate they would subpoena him for a public in-court examination of his homosexual activities. The whole town, and maybe even Jeff's parents in Minnesota, would know the details. It was worse than Jeff had imagined. Jeff thought, maybe if he just named a few of the obvious men and women, he could avoid the public disgrace. After all, they probably had those names already. . . .

Only later did Jeff discover that the threat of public court examination was a lie. The Johns Committee lacked the legal authority to subpoena individuals. It had taken unconstitutional measures to trick lesbian and gay teachers into confessing and naming names. Unfortunately for Jeff, it had worked.

In 1956, spurred by the influence of McCarthyism and the search for communists in government, the Florida Legislature voted to institute a committee to investigate subversive activities. Since the rhetoric of the time inextricably linked "Commie, pinko, queer," as the characteristics of someone believed to be anti-country, anti-god, and anti-the-American-family, the committee believed that if it hunted down homosexuals it would be eradicating communism as well.

While many GLBT individuals might have laughed at the implication that they were Communist subversives, as with most stereotypes, the link between communism and homosexuality was not completely unfounded. One of the first groups organized to promote social contact and political awareness among homosexuals was the Mattachine Society. Founded in 1951 in Southern California, the organization was formed by men who had learned their political skills working for the Communist Party, which was sympathetic to homosexuals as an oppressed minority. The Communist Party provided the Mattachine Society with a structural model of organization that protected the identity of its membership from public exposure. Conversely, it associated the homosexual group with the intense hostility directed towards the Communist Party in the 1950s. This political connection proved detrimental to the Mattachine Society's ability to attract members and effectively organize. Also, the link added fuel to the negative stereotypes American society held about lesbians and gay men.[2]

Since many people believed that homosexual communists could not reproduce "naturally," they assumed that homosexuals recruited young minds to ensure their numbers. Thus, the Johns Committee mandate was quickly narrowed to "delve into the homosexual problem" in the state's public schools.[3] The initial focus of the Johns Committee was on public high schools in Central Florida, particularly around the Gainesville area. It was rumored that numerous homosexuals had moved into this area after World War II and that many of them taught in the public high schools. In fact, the Florida legislature estimated that more than 60,000 "deviants" were residing in its State. Through a unique arrangement with the State Superintendent of Schools, the Committee was permitted to conduct school-based investigations and demand immediate dismissal of educators. Individuals suspected of being homosexual were investigated at their school in the presence of police officers, a Committee investigator, and a tape machine operator.

The Johns Committee used two tactics when confronting educators. First, the investigator promised leniency if the educator would name his or her homosexual peers. When that failed, the investigator threatened public exposure through a subpoena to appear in court. The implication made to the educator was that if he or she did not cooperate, his or her entire private life as a homosexual would be discussed in open court. The educators did not know the Johns Committee had no subpoena power over witnesses. Thus, the threat of exposure through a public examination in court was a bluff by investigators intended to intimidate witnesses. Most often, it worked.

Once the local interrogations were completed, the investigator presented the information to the State Superintendent of Schools. The Superintendent then petitioned the State Board of Education to revoke the lifetime teaching credential of each educator under investigation. Since statutory procedures permitted a hearing before revocation of a teaching credential, some brave individuals hired attorneys to attend the hearing with them. Armed with character witnesses, affidavits, and legal counsel, some educators thought they might win their appeal before the Board. Unfortunately, the State Board of Education refused to hear from anyone in attendance, including attorneys. Instead, the only admissible evidence was a public replaying of the original interrogation tape. Each educator's lifetime teaching credential was revoked immediately; without the credential it was impossible to remain employed.

It is difficult to measure the full impact of the Johns Investigating Committee on Communism and Homosexuality on the lives of men and women teaching in Florida in the 1950s. Many teachers and administrators probably resigned immediately rather than face the scrutiny of state officials. Others may have been surprised by their inclusion in the search for communist homosexuals and their ultimate inability to defend their reputations. Being called before the interrogators was the end of one's career in education. In addition to that pain and loss, often there was the added shame of having named colleagues who would be targeted for the same fate.

Eventually, at least three individuals — William Neal, Mary Frances Bradshaw, and Anne Louise Poston — sued the State Board of Education. Their cases were consolidated and decided by the Florida State Supreme Court in 1962. Their attorneys argued that, while the state might have the authority to search out communists and homosexuals in the teaching profession, it had to comply with established statutory procedures for the dismissal of tenured teachers as stated in the Florida Education Code. Also, they argued, none of the teachers' confessions should be admissible against them since they were coerced by interrogators who knowingly lied about the extent of the Committee's subpoena power.

Attorneys for the State Board of Education argued that the due process procedures in the Code were merely guidelines the Board could modify at will. Further, they argued, even if those procedures were mandatory in their application, the dire emergency circumstances of eliminating communist homosexual educators from their positions of influence over young minds justified immediate action. This peril excused the State Board of Education from following statutory law.

The Florida State Supreme Court ruled that the due process procedures established in the Education Code required mandatory compliance under all circumstances. Thus, the Court ordered the State Board of Education to reinstate the lifetime teaching credentials of the educators. While this ruling was a victory for the employment entitlements of educators and government employees nationwide, it was a hollow victory for Neal, Bradshaw, and Poston. Subsequent paragraphs in the Court opinion urged the Board to continue its important efforts to eliminate communist homosexuals from Florida schools. It suggested that the material gathered from the Johns investigation could serve as the basis for immediate and properly administered revocation proceedings against these same educators. All evidence suggests that the Board aggressively acted upon the Court's advice and revoked the credentials through formal procedural guidelines.

While the Johns Committee's earliest efforts concentrated on public high school teachers, during its eight-year existence it quickly moved into investigating state hospitals and universities as well. In Tampa, for example, numerous gay men were reportedly employed at a state tuberculoses hospital. The process of interviewing suspected homosexuals and fraudulently forcing them to name names went even further in these investigations, according to John Loughery, who recently had the opportunity to review the Johns Committee files that have been sealed for 30 years. Loughery reports that the Committee, having targeted one physician in particular, enlisted the help of Eastern Airlines in providing information on the vacation travels of the doctor and his companions. Since this release of confidential information is illegal without a subpoena, Loughery writes that "a nervous Eastern official begged the Committee not to make public the fact that the airline had provided this service."[4]

Loughery's brief article devotes most of its attention to the Johns Committee's investigations at the University of Florida at Gainesville, which commenced in 1958. Apparently, anonymous sex in men's restrooms at the local courthouse, in the University library, and elsewhere on campus had grown to such proportions that it had become common knowledge on campus. The President of the University had held a meeting to discuss the problem, and a student reporter had considered writing an article about it. Strickland and his police decoys staked out the various restrooms, arrested suspects, and then took them for interrogations at their covert headquarters in a local hotel. Many individuals refused to name their peers, although eventually at least 16 tenured faculty members would be fired.[5] Loughery suggests that one of the major motivating forces in the University of Florida at Gainesville investigations was that the legislature viewed the faculty there as liberal "eggheads" who supported Adlai Stevenson for President and opposed loyalty oaths and the crackdown on communists.

Ironically, Loughery reports that the Johns Committee's ardor for pursuing perversion eventually led to its downfall. In 1964, the Committee published a pamphlet detailing sexual perversions in Florida and arguing against any repeal of state sodomy laws. The Model Penal Code, with its revocation of victimless crimes, was under consideration by each state's legislature at this time, and the impact of this debate is discussed later in this chapter. The apparently vivid, somewhat pornographic, photos detailed in the pamphlet led to public outcries that the "purple pamphlet" was as outrageous and harmful as the behaviors that were under investigation. According to Loughery, an embarrassed legislature issued a public apology and withdrew the publication from distribution.

Until late in 1995, the only historical evidence available concerning the Florida Legislature's crackdown on gay and lesbian educators came from the three teacher dismissal cases found in researching this book. With the recent opening of the Johns Committee's papers at the State Archives in Tallahassee, thousands of pages of our history can be reclaimed. The names of the victims may never be known since state law prohibits the release of personally identifiable information. After 30 years of state imposed invisibility and isolation, however, the process of reclaiming their stories, our history — and our heroes — has begun.

GLBT LIFE IN THE '50S AND '60S

As discussed in Chapter Seven, as society grew more aware of homosexuality during the late 1940s, it escalated its efforts to prohibit and to punish such behavior. Also, the real and imagined links between homosexuality and communism heightened the Cold War attentions of federal and state officials intent upon stamping out the Red Menace and its threats to American society. It was "obvious" to any good American that anyone who engaged in such supposedly immoral and perverse behavior was a likely source of political corruption as well.

Searching for communists and searching for sexual perverts became an indistinguishable mission for government agents. Gay and lesbian educators were viewed as the source of Communist recruitment efforts in this country, and sex was their means of enticement. Conservatives argued that liberal sexual attitudes and practices were the influence of communist ideology in American society. Thus, sex education in the schools became a major target of political scrutiny along with the search for homosexual educators. In the early 1960s, for example, the Orange County Public School System (Southern California) terminated its pioneering sex education program because the John Birch Society successfully characterized it as a Communist plot to corrupt the morals of American youth.[6]

Arguably, part of the increased hostility towards GLBT individuals stemmed from the post-war changes in sexual mores occurring in American society. Hints of these changing social and sexual values were evidenced by the American Law Institute's recommendations in the 1955 Model Penal Code that called for the legalization of all forms of sexual activity between consenting adults. Judges, attorneys, and other criminal law experts witnessed, first-hand, the consequences of criminalizing such acts as adultery, homosexuality, and non-marital sex. Lives were being ruined by arrests and criminal convictions that permanently marked individuals as felons. The police and criminal justice systems were becoming overwhelmed with "victimless crimes" while more serious offenses went unpunished due to lack of resources. Criminal justice experts who advised the states about updates to their criminal codes called for the end of prosecutions for consensual sex acts. This specific recommendation, however, was rejected by all state legislatures.[7]

Thus, local statutes prohibiting lewd vagrancy, sodomy, open and gross lewd conduct, extramarital sex, and loitering became effective mechanisms for harassment of gays and lesbians. These statutes provided police departments with legitimate reasons for decoy operations, raids on gay bars and private parties, automotive license plate surveillance, undercover operations, and entrapment procedures.[8] Cities as diverse as Boise, Idaho; Miami, Florida; Baltimore, Maryland; and Sioux City, Iowa; became havens for public abuse, anti-gay harassment, and violence. Widespread surveillance efforts were enacted that involved local police, postal employees, state and federal agents, and civilian employers.[9] Furthermore, charges of being a homosexual served the age-old function of intimidating and harming political dissenters and civil rights advocates. Local police departments were encouraged to harass suspected homosexuals in the interest of national security and moral righteousness. D'Emilio's book details the hostilities towards homosexuals during this period, including thousands of arrests, involuntary commitments to mental hospitals, physical and emotional brutality, robberies, and job terminations due to police surveillance and disclosures.[10]

Everyone caught in this web of legal, social, moral, and political turmoil faced severe consequences. Quite probably, the occupational group most harmed was lesbian and gay educators. Not only did they face the legal and social consequences of their arrest, but in most states they also faced immediate job termination, regardless of the disposition of their criminal case.

The state most actively engaged in dismissing lesbian and gay educators was California. Because of their influence in political and educational institutions, conservatives were successful in enacting extraordinary powers for the state and local boards of education. When the historical constraints upon teachers' personal lives and the fear of ideological and social corruption of youth were combined with the perceived link between communism and homosexuality, conservatives easily asserted their views in this social and legal struggle. No other occupation received this legislative mandate to purge homosexuals from its work force.

Part of the perceived need for these extraordinary powers may have stemmed from the greater leniency established within the criminal procedural process. To protect the reputations and livelihoods of people caught in the "temporal injustice" of a changing society, the criminal procedural process permitted plea bargaining and not guilty findings. As sexual mores moved toward greater individual freedom, the courts became more lenient in victimless crime arrests. Furthermore, both state and federal courts were articulating stronger protections for individuals in the criminal legal system. More and more convictions were being overturned because of police error and procedural technicalities. Meanwhile, the reporting requirement legislated by California Education Code waived all these constitutional criminal procedure protections. The Code permitted an arrest for sexual misconduct to serve as sufficient basis for dismissal whether or not the arrest and conviction were valid. This chapter presents the legal challenges to these extraordinary powers; challenges raised because of the implications for infringement upon both constitutional rights and fair employment practices.

CALIFORNIA CRIMINALS

Local police officials, particularly in the communities of Long Beach and Los Angeles, actively used two pieces of state legislation aimed at ferreting out immoral educators. Enacted after World War II, California Penal Code, Section 291, required a sheriff or chief of police to notify the state licensing board and the local superintendent of schools immediately upon the arrest of a teacher for certain enumerated criminal behaviors relating to sex and morality, even if the arrest later proved to be erroneous or unsubstantiated.[11] Immediate job suspension, and often job termination, followed. The strong constitutional protections pertaining to criminal matters applied in the arrest but not to the school employment controversy. Thus, while the criminal case against the school employee might be dropped due to lack of evidence, an illegal arrest, or a not guilty finding, all the information could be used in the job termination hearing. With this highly incriminating evidence, the usual outcome was job termination or employee resignation.

In a collateral move, in 1954 the California Legislature passed California Education Code, Section 12756, that permitted the immediate suspension of teaching credentials if an educator was convicted of any one of several statutes pertaining to sex and morality. This presumption of unfitness to teach streamlined the administrative process in the educational setting by automatically providing the grounds for teacher dismissal. Even in cases where the teacher was found not guilty, school boards used the arrest as grounds for dismissal on the presumption of unfitness to teach. Thus, "criminal conduct" arrests and dismissals have further distorted the image of lesbian and gay educators.

Perhaps California represents a wider political spectrum than most states and, consequently, is an active arena for values conflict. On one hand, the gay and lesbian population in California has been numerous and increasingly visible since the 1940s. On the other hand, the sex crime panic of the 1950s provided police officials in that state with strong legal sanctions against same-sex conduct, especially as it pertained to educators, until the mid-1970s. To date, it appears no other state required law enforcement officials to inform school authorities of teacher misconduct as did California with Penal Code Section 291. The only state that experienced a similar panic was Florida, as discussed earlier in this Chapter.

These few statutory considerations are important examples of the unique legislative deference given to the educational system. No other employer or licensing body, except religious entities, has had this preferential treatment relative to its employees' legal rights. In this effort to eliminate gay men and lesbians from the teaching profession, several major constitutional and administrative freedoms were abrogated. To retain their livelihood, individuals who were fired for conduct arguably unrelated to their teaching employment were compelled to challenge these laws. Remember, however, that although the case controversies offer insight into the social and legal history of both the teaching profession and homosexuality, case law examines the rare exceptions to the usual manner of resolving community conflict over the continued employment of someone accused of being gay or lesbian. Quite probably, many lesbians or gay men lived quietly within the educational setting, and then accepted termination upon discovery or availed themselves of the traditional response by immediately resigning their teaching post. Some evidence does exist concerning this outcome.

In 1973, Eugene Warren, counsel for the 24,000 teachers who were members of the Arkansas Education Association, was interviewed about teacher dismissal for homosexuality.[12] Warren stated he had not encountered a challenge for dismissal for homosexuality, or for any immoral act for that matter, in the 20 years he had represented the union. Although homosexuality or immorality may have been the background reason for dismissal, Warren believed that school authorities found other grounds to establish dismissals. This proved favorable for both parties by eliminating public disclosure of the immoral conduct. It also provided the school board with additional protection from costly litigation concerning burden of proof, defamation, and discrimination.

Warren's overall conclusion was that homosexual teachers in Arkansas had accepted termination on alternative grounds rather than face the public scandal and high expense of challenging the school board's decision about homosexuality and immorality. Personally, Warren expressed support for homosexual school teachers, but the practical reality of the situation suggested that lesbian or gay male teachers who challenged the system would lose their appeal.

Although termination on grounds of homosexuality seems covert, school authorities have been more overt during the hiring process. This is when they have the most subjective and legal discretion. In a 1971 interview, Bob Milne, vice-president of the Mattachine Society of New York, commented that before the Homosexual Rights Movement school authorities were willing to state their refusal to hire homosexual educators. Once the threat of civil rights litigation became a reality in the early 1970s, however, employers were more careful to establish alternative grounds for rejecting employment applications from alleged or apparent homosexuals. One problem for male applications in particular, according to Milne, was that school authorities began to rely on the draft status of applicants. Thus, a 4F or 1Y classification alerted employers to the possibility of homosexuality. Applicants were forced to sign a release for their military records to have this investigated or face immediate rejection as a potential employee.[13]

CRIMES NOT TO BE NAMED

Despite the tangible essence of the legal record, the case law concerning homosexual school teachers has been distorted by the criminal prosecution process. The full details of any criminal action are recorded at the district court level. However, at the appellate level, in highly sensitive cases the details often are referenced only by penal code section. For example, at the appellate level the case may state a person was convicted under California Penal Code Section 647, subdivision (a) public solicitation of lewd acts, rather than detail the circumstances surrounding the arrest. Everyone involved in the cases at the time, including the school board and the appellate court, would know if the solicitation was homosexual in nature. Twenty or thirty years later, however, it is extremely difficult to ascertain whether or not the criminal activity was homosexual unless some reference is made by the court.

This frustrating aspect of the historical case law research was evidenced in several of the earliest cases, such as <u>Fountain</u>, <u>Lerner v. Los Angeles City Board of Education</u>, and <u>Jarvella v.</u>

Willoughby-Eastlake City School District Board of Education,[14] which will be discussed later in this Chapter. These cases were not flagged by the computer research methodology because they did not contain the words homosexual, lesbian, or gay in the text of the court opinion. Future research in this area would require a search with LEXIS of the various state penal codes that might involve homosexual behavior. Access to the district court opinion filed in the storage areas of specific local courthouses would then help to uncover the details of these cases. This would also be the situation for appellate decisions that the court has determined should not be published, as in Amundsen v. State Board of Education.[15] When Amundsen was decided in 1971, legal scholars and activists interested in the case obtained knowledge about it as it occurred. Unfortunately, earlier cases have been lost.

Before discussing the case law, it might be helpful to explain the process by which criminal records are expunged (deleted). The ramifications of this procedural maneuver are critical to the early case law on homosexual teachers because it provided people arrested for sexual misconduct with the opportunity to suppress the information. As the criminal process became more protective of individual rights, it weakened the absolute sense of right and wrong in terms of victimless crimes. Reliance on the state and local criminal justice systems for the community's definition of "immoral conduct" was breaking down for educational systems. School administrators' response was to lobby for extraordinary legislation such as California Penal Code, Section 291, as discussed earlier. Thus, as the criminal process modified to accommodate changing sexual mores, the educational process intensified its hold on traditional values.

In the late 1940s it was possible, as it is today, to negotiate special procedures in relation to certain embarrassing but non-violent criminal charges.[16] The defendant pled not guilty to the charges and accepted a finding of guilt by the court, with the proceedings suspended. Usually, the person paid a fine and was placed on probation.[17] At the end of the probationary period, a new hearing was held. The court usually vacated its finding of guilt and dismissed the charges against the defendant. At this point, the record could be expunged, and the defendant could proceed as though no legal action had ever been taken against him or her. The process benefited the defendant by eventually clearing the record of criminal charges for victimless crimes. Such charges often were more embarrassing, and personally and professionally harmful, than charges for more serious criminal behavior. The process also served the legal system and the public, providing the right to arrest people for socially objectionable behavior, and served as both a deterrent and a basis for prosecution. The perpetrators are punished, revenue is obtained for the jurisdiction, and the punishment is modified in order not to ruin the lives of people who are not usually caught outside the boundaries of acceptable social behavior.

On the other hand, this process thwarts school administrators and parents from using the criminal legal system to gather information about the personal behavior of teachers and to issue a clear statement of the community standard of unacceptable behavior for hiring and retention decisions. These were the reasons the legislative branch of government granted unique and broad powers to the educational system, particularly in relation to the conduct of school teachers.

Overall, publicity concerning a homosexual school teacher case is a difficult issue. Legal and political activists desire the information and precedent that comes with an expanding body of material on an aspect of litigation. Further publicity, however, is usually undesirable to anyone immediately after arrest and prosecution, especially in the sensitive personal and social context of exposure for homosexuality. For school teachers found guilty of homosexuality, the emotional trauma and social stigma of the criminal process are magnified by the loss of employment and exposure of one's homosexuality to family, friends, colleagues, and strangers. Any willingness to challenge an arrest and/or the loss of employment for homosexual conduct or exposure as a homosexual carries great risk. There is potential for great and life-long financial, emotional, and even physical harm from being labeled publicly in the press and the court documents as a homosexual. Given these tremendous personal costs, it is as significant that there are so many cases concerning GLBT school teachers as it is that there are so few.

EARLY DECISIONS — CRIMINAL

The earliest known case concerning a potential homosexual school teacher was clouded by legal ambiguities surrounding criminal charges under the lewd vagrancy laws. In <u>George Fountain v. State Board of Education</u>,[18] a tenured elementary school teacher's credential was revoked in 1954 by the State Board of Education when the Board learned of a 1948 incident in which Fountain was charged with lewd vagrancy.[19] Because of the "unmentionable" nature of the crime, no explicit details are available concerning Fountain's offense, but it appears to have involved homosexual solicitation.

In <u>Fountain</u>, the question of law concerned whether or not California Education Code, Section 12756, could be applied retroactively by the Board of Education.[20] Section 12756 called for automatic dismissal for "sex offenses," giving the Board of Education power to revoke teaching credentials automatically and without a hearing. However, it was enacted in 1954, four years after the criminal incident. Fountain's legal challenge did not question the Board's right to deny due process through automatic dismissals. Rather, it questioned their right to exert that power retroactively.

The California Appellate Court ruled for Fountain. It stated that retroactive application of the statute was not ordered by the California Legislature and that Fountain might have handled his criminal trial differently had he known of the possible collateral action by the State Board of Education.[21]

Subsequently, in <u>Lerner v. Los Angeles City Board of Education</u>,[22] a similar issue arose concerning the revocation of a teaching credential under the same statute. Lerner, a tenured high school teacher, was also arrested in 1948 as a lewd vagrant under California Penal Code, Section 647, Subdivision 5. Although he maintained that he was innocent, Lerner pled guilty to the charge rather than face trial publicity which would harm his teaching career.[23] He paid a fine of $100.00 and remained on probation for six months, until the guilty plea was set aside and the case dismissed in 1949.

After enactment of Section 12756 in 1954, the State Board of Education automatically revoked Lerner's teaching credential without a hearing, based on the 1948 incident. Because the Fountain decision was handed down during the extended litigation of Lerner, the State Board of Education reinstated Lerner's credential in keeping with that ruling. The local Board of Education, however, refused to reinstate Lerner.

The issue before the California Supreme Court in Lerner was whether Lerner was barred from seeking reinstatement to his teaching position due to the long delays in litigation. By a 4-3 vote, the California Supreme Court determined that Lerner was not barred from seeking reinstatement, in particular because the court decision in Fountain and Lerner's later resolution of proceedings with the State Board did not occur until 1958. These would have had to have been completed before Lerner could approach the local Board of Education for reinstatement. Thus, the case was remanded to a lower court for a reconsideration of Lerner's right to reinstatement.

The Lerner litigation was not a major influence in the case law on homosexual school teachers. It was very significant, however, for providing one of the first opportunities for a newly-appointed member of the California Supreme Court, Justice Matthew Tobriner, to commence his life-long commitment to the rights of the individual to be "free from unnecessary social and legal barriers."[24] Through his activist efforts, Justice Tobriner sought to mitigate the negative consequences to the individual who was caught in a "temporal injustice;" that period in which the criminal laws lagged far behind the changing social mores and practices, particularly private sexual matters between consenting adults.[25] Because of his interest in personal freedom and his influence on the majority members of the California Supreme Court, probably no other single person had more influence on litigation regarding the employment of gay and lesbian educators.

195

CRIMINAL DECISIONS — CONTINUED

Donald Odorizzi was employed as an elementary school teacher in California in 1964 and under contract for 1965. During the summer break, Odorizzi was arrested by police, questioned, booked, and charged with criminal homosexual activity. Shortly after his release on bail, Odorizzi was confronted at his apartment by the district school superintendent and the principal of his school. Both men persuaded Odorizzi to sign a resignation immediately; telling him that any delay would cause the School Board to commence a public hearing to suspend him, which would cause him "to suffer extreme embarrassment and humiliation."[26] Further, they informed Odorizzi, if he resigned immediately the incident would not be used to jeopardize his chances for a teaching position in some other district. Odorizzi signed the resignation.

Later in the summer, the criminal charges against Odorizzi were dropped, and he sought to rescind his resignation. The School Board refused to reinstate Odorizzi, and they were supported in this decision by the lower courts. On appeal, however, the Appellate Court reversed the decision favoring the School Board.

Odorizzi argued that his resignation was invalid because it was obtained by threat, menace, duress, fraud, and undue influence. The Appellate Court carefully reviewed the legal elements of each factor, and concluded that there had been no threat, menace, fraud, or duress in the way that the school officials had obtained Odorizzi's resignation. The Court did find, however, that there had been undue influence. It noted several factors that contributed to such a finding, including Odorizzi's emotional upset over the police experience, the inappropriate time and place for the school officials to discuss the matter with Odorizzi, the insistence on immediacy which allowed no legal counsel, and the biased emphasis on possible consequences. Additionally, the Court noted, the school officials had been ambiguous in their discussion with Odorizzi when they failed to inform him that under California Education Code, Section 13409, they had a positive duty to initiate dismissal proceedings against him rather than a mere legal right to do so if they wished. Although the case was remanded to the lower court for further fact finding, the Appellate Court clearly stated that it did not have an opinion on the merits of Odorizzi's case, or "the propriety of his continuing to teach school."[27]

TRADITIONAL VIEW — SARAC

The case that most explicitly expressed traditional judicial views toward homosexuality was Sarac v. State Board of Education.[28] In Sarac, the California State Board of Education revoked Sarac's teaching credential upon a finding of criminal behavior. According to the facts set forth in the Court's opinion, in July of 1962, Thomas Sarac, Jr., approached an undercover officer for sex in a restroom on a public beach in Long Beach. Sarac was allowed to touch the officer's genitals before he was arrested and charged with violating the State Penal Code, Section 647, Subdivision (a) (public solicitation of lewd acts). Although public solicitation of lewd acts was a misdemeanor charge, according to Sarac's attorney, Norman G. Rudman, it was nevertheless:

> . . . deemed such a serious offense that persons convicted of it were required to register as sex offenders with the police departments of their city of residence (or the county sheriff if they resided in unincorporated areas) and to maintain that registration wherever they moved so long as they lived in the State of California or until the conviction was expunged.[29]

These sex offender registration lists were used periodically by the police to round up registered people whenever some sexual crime was under investigation. Thus, unless a person charged under Penal Code Section 647, Subdivision (a), had an air-tight defense, he or she tried to arrange a deal with the prosecutor to avoid conviction under this statute.

In September of that same year, Sarac successfully made a deal with the prosecutor to lessen the sex offender charge to a Municipal Code charge of disorderly conduct. In return, Sarac entered a plea of guilty. Under most circumstances, this was the appropriate and most common legal action to take in the face of a lewd conduct charge. Unfortunately, Sarac's criminal legal counsel either did not know or did not consider that the State Department of Education was capable of bringing credential revocation proceedings against Sarac independent of the criminal charges.[30]

Consequently, Sarac's general secondary teaching credential was revoked on the grounds that he "had committed 'a homosexual act involving moral turpitude,' that constituted both immoral and unprofessional conduct within the meaning of the State Educational Code, Section 13202."[31] Sarac appealed this finding of "unfitness for service in the public school system."[32]

Sarac's main argument was that no rational connection was established between his homosexual conduct in the restroom and his fitness to teach. His other arguments concerned the question of his guilt, which he had not contested in the original trial because of his understanding with the prosecutor. Furthermore, he argued, the Municipal Ordinance concerning disorderly conduct was unconstitutional for vagueness and uncertainty, and it was being unconstitutionally applied to his homosexual behavior because the State Penal Code laws regulating homosexual behavior preempted the municipal interest.

To Sarac's detriment, the Court opinion contained no discussion of the quality of his teaching, which in some cases appears to mitigate the circumstances in the teacher's favor. Also to his detriment, Sarac supposedly had admitted to frequent homosexual conduct, although the Court, theoretically, was obliged to focus only on the beach incident.

In March of 1967, the Appellate Court rendered its decision. Essentially, it focused on the evidence suggesting Sarac's guilt and whether that was sufficient cause to find Sarac unfit to teach. The Court very directly stated its understanding of community sentiment about homosexuality:

> Homosexual behavior has long been contrary and abhorrent to the social mores and moral standards of the people of California as it has been since antiquity to those of many other peoples. It is clearly, therefore, immoral conduct

within the meaning of Education Code, Section 13202. It may also constitute unprofessional conduct within the meaning of that same statute as such conduct is not limited to classroom misconduct with children.[33]

The Court also stated that the behavior clearly constituted evidence of unfitness for service in the public school system. Such behavior conflicted with the "appellant's statutory duty as a teacher to endeavor to impress upon the minds of the pupils the principles of morality."[34] This finding, when coupled with the "necessary close association" between teachers and their students, compelled the Court to find "an obvious rational connection" between Sarac's conduct on the beach and the finding of his unfitness to teach.[35]

According to the published Court opinion, the facts against Sarac were extreme. He had approached a police officer for sex, and he had admitted to prior homosexual activities. There apparently was no evidence given that might mitigate the outcome, such as an exemplary teaching record. Given the weighty issues against him, one could wonder why Sarac appealed the State Department of Education's revocation efforts.

Although the briefs and other Court documents were not accessible for my research, Rudman, Sarac's attorney, remembered the case quite well. Rudman's version of the Sarac trial offers a very different perspective on the case and heightens the necessity to expand research on emotional legal topics beyond the printed opinion of an involved and potentially biased Court.[36]

According to Rudman, Sarac always maintained his complete innocence, which to this date Rudman believes was the truth. Sarac did enter the Long Beach restroom, but whatever occurred merely juxtaposed Sarac's word against that of a vice officer present specifically to make such arrests. Rudman felt that Sarac's Yugoslavian background, and his rather effeminate mannerism, caused him to be charged by the officer as a homosexual. Furthermore, Rudman believed that these stereotyped mannerisms and cultural differences worked against Sarac in the trial, despite the presence of his wife, children, and parents. Also present at the hearing, according to Rudman, were numerous character witnesses, fellow teachers, and administrators (more than two dozen colleagues), who "professed confidence that the charges against him [Sarac] were untrue."[37] These witnesses also testified that Sarac was an excellent and committed teacher who had an exemplary relationship with his students, their parents, and his colleagues.[38]

To Sarac's detriment, he did admit to one homosexual encounter in his early teens. He was in his late thirties at the time of the trial. With the arrest, the trial, the Court ruling against him, and the loss of his teaching credential, Rudman characterized Sarac's life as "devastated." Rudman further commented that he remembered the Sarac case quite well because of his (Rudman's) frustration in trying to penetrate the judge's bias against homosexuality or against Sarac as a "homosexual," the miscarriage of justice, and the "sanctimonious" decision of the Appellate Court.[39]

The Rudman letter demonstrates the power of the court to isolate certain facts and base its opinion on very emotional reactions to the case. It further demonstrates the consequences of that bias on case precedent, since the reported opinion of Sarac served as the legal basis for litigation in the area of homosexual school teachers in California as well as other parts of the country.

JUDICIAL BIAS AND HOMOSEXUALITY

In his dissertation on legal ideology and the case law on homosexuality, Lawrence Goldyn analyzed judicial responses to homosexuality in United States Appellate Court decisions dating from 1926 to 1979. Goldyn found that the severity of the negative judicial response to homosexuality, as evidenced by the presence or absence of derogatory language, varied based upon three factors — "the amount of subjective moral judgement required of the court, the extent to which the case triggers homophobia by the presence of actual homosexual behavior, and the nature of the object being 'protected.' "[40]

Goldyn concluded that the traditional images of homosexuality as immoral, corrupt, sick, or criminal varied in emphasis depending on the type of case before the court. Thus, sodomy and child custody cases prompted the most negative judicial responses. Sodomy prompted a strong negative judicial response because of the overt act necessary for prosecution. Child custody elicited such a response because of the involvement of children, the possibility of corrupting influences, and the high level of judicial discretion in the equity tribunal of family court.

Early litigation regarding homosexual school teacher employment was brought to the court's attention most often through a criminal charge of sodomy. Since these cases also involved the right to teach children, they represent another area where strong negative judicial response would be expected. Indeed the themes of corruption of young children and immorality do appear, while the criminality of the behavior involved is given a secondary emphasis. It is particularly difficult to challenge themes of corruption and immorality because the basis for their existence is subjective. Scientific evidence and countervailing beliefs often are useless in the face of these deeply held perspectives.

Thus, homosexual school teacher employment cases are one of the most difficult types of cases under analysis because several of the most potent themes usually appear. Furthermore, the presence or absence of these views about homosexuality directly correspond to the outcome of the cases. During the 1950s and 1960s, when traditional beliefs about homosexuality prevailed, the chances of successfully retaining a teaching position after being accused of homosexual conduct were almost nonexistent.

LEGAL CHANGE — JARVELLA

Jarvella v. Willoughby-Eastlake City School District Board of Education[41] (Ohio) is significant to this analysis of trends in gay and lesbian school teacher case law for two reasons. First, it is an early example of the shift in legal reasoning concerning the school community's rights and the individual freedoms of the teacher. In Jarvella the Court defined "immoral conduct" in the context of whether or not it was "hostile to the welfare of the school community."[42] This perspective of balancing the community interest and the teacher's interest was very different from earlier cases. In cases such as <u>Sarac</u>, homosexuality and immorality themselves were abhorrent and, thus, sufficient grounds for dismissal. Second, <u>Jarvella</u> serves as a classic example of the problems endemic in researching a topic "not to be named by Christians."[43] At this writing, even Jarvella's attorney, John S. Nelson, does not recall whether the case involved homosexual conduct.[44] It is presented here, then, because of its unique contributions to this analysis, but it has not yet been determined to be specifically about a homosexual school teacher.

Mr. Jarvella was dismissed from his high school teaching job for "immoral conduct" because he wrote and mailed several "gross, vulgar and offensive" letters to a former male student. The student's mother found the letters and informed the School Board, which suspended Jarvella and later reinstated him. Somehow the letters were leaked to the local press, and the School Board felt that it was necessary to dismiss Jarvella.

Jarvella's suit for reinstatement was heard by the Ohio Court of Common Pleas. In its opinion, the Court balanced the school's interest in protecting students from corruption against Jarvella's United States and Ohio constitutional rights.[45] The Court also took notice of Jarvella's "exceptional merit" as a teacher, based on testimony of colleagues and the routine evaluations of Jarvella by his superiors. This positive information about his commitment to teaching apparently impressed the Court immensely. The judges found that Jarvella's letters, by themselves, were not a direct harm to the school community. Furthermore, since the letters were intended as private communications, they were protected speech under both the United States and the Ohio State constitutions.

Although the Court ruled Jarvella's letters were not a direct harm to the school community, it then had to determine whether the leak of the letters' contents to the press and school community equaled a harm that warranted Jarvella's dismissal. On this issue, they concluded there was harm to the school community, but the harm had not occurred through the misconduct of Jarvella. Rather, the Court determined there had been "unwarranted intrusion" into Jarvella's personal freedoms and those freedoms were not suspended merely because of his employment as a school teacher.

Jarvella serves as a harbinger of a change in legal perspectives to require a balancing of the school's interests against the teacher's interests and a determination of a nexus between the teacher's behavior and his or her fitness to teach. These legal perspectives are more fully advanced and developed in the very significant California case on homosexual school teachers, Marc Morrison v. The State Board of Education, discussed in Chapter Nine.

MALE AND FEMALE EDUCATORS

Because so many early cases arose through criminal misconduct, which is applied almost exclusively to men, the balance between male and female teacher representation has been distorted. Since women teachers comprise approximately 67 percent of the profession, it is statistically likely that a study of GLBT school teachers would focus on women.[46] Also, the teaching profession has favored the employment of single women since the 18th century, so it is arguable that the percentage of lesbians is disproportionately higher in teaching than in any other profession. On the other hand, of the 39 individuals involved in GLBT educator litigation to 1987, only 10 litigants (26 percent) were women. None was revealed through criminal misconduct as lesbian, although a recent civil suit has been filed by a woman who alleges that one of her teachers, a Roman Catholic nun, molested her in a Catholic girls' school in Detroit, Michigan. So much time has passed that the statue of limitations will probably preclude the local district attorney from commencing a criminal complaint against the nun. Also, three of the sensational child abuse cases since 1987 involved heterosexually-identified women charged with molesting preschoolers.[47] This under-representation of lesbians in the case law can be accounted for in several ways.

First, as Chapter Seven revealed, lesbians have been overlooked in the larger scheme of defining criminal homosexual misconduct.[48] Since women historically were viewed as passive sexual beings, there seemed little need for laws to regulate the unlikely sexual encounter between two women.

Second, lesbians appear to maintain a more monogamous, less visible lifestyle than their allegedly more sexually promiscuous male counterparts.[49] Much of this disparity is attributed to the different socialization process faced by each gender, whether heterosexual or homosexual, and the greater social acceptance of male sexual expression and female sexual repression.

Third, although the gay male community may be more visible than its lesbian counterpart, there may also be more homosexual males than females. Statistics of the numbers of gay men and lesbians in American society repeatedly suggest there are 4 percent to 5 percent more gay men than lesbians.[50] If the capitalist model of wage labor has affected sexual expression, however, then more women will be free from economic dependence upon marriage and may choose a lesbian lifestyle. Thus, under D'Emilio's analysis, the numerical disparity between gay men and lesbians should lessen over time.

And fourth, it is arguable there is a major disparity between the public's emotional reaction to a gay male teacher than to a lesbian teacher. This has heightened the chances of dismissal and ensuing litigation for men.[51] A greater portion of societal reaction against the GLBT educator has focused on the stereotype of the effeminate male homosexual or the sexually active and seductive male pedophile.[52] Furthermore, greater cultural conflicts appear over the issue of the sexual orientation of a male child. These may have economic origins concerned with continuing the family name and fortune, or they may stem from the generally patriarchal, male-oriented, anti-female aspects of this society. The combination of these factors with the gay male reputation for extensive public, promiscuous sexual activity has raised the ire of American society. Currently, this existing disapprobation is being combined with actual fear of mortal danger from AIDS contamination because the general public still often equates homosexuality with AIDS.

CHAPTER CONCLUSIONS

According to the analysis of cultural norms discussed in Chapter Six, the case law on gay and lesbian educators in the decades before the emergent homosexual rights movement should reflect the dominance of heterosexuality as a cultural indicator. In fact, this is the case. No visible homosexual subculture had emerged. No powerful "enemy" deviants existed to challenge long-standing traditional values. Homosexual subcultures existed on the fringe of society, but people who engaged in same-sex relationships did so with an individual, rather than a collective, political identity. People accused of homosexual conduct litigated their cases as individuals accused of a crime, not as members of a minority group with financial, emotional, and legal support from like-minded people or special interest groups.

In fact, during this period, the criminal status of homosexual conduct exposed school teachers to the sanctions of both the legal and educational systems. The typical case of the 1950s and 1960s involved a male school teacher arrested in a public restroom for lewd acts. His defense focused on the legality of the arrest and the clarity of the statutes, rather than on individual rights to privacy or equal protection. Success in the legal realm was possible because of strong social concern for the fair treatment of those accused of a crime, as evidenced by the procedural protections and assumption of innocence. In the educational realm, however, the institution focused concern on the protection of children and the powers of the school administration. Once accused of criminal homosexual conduct, a teacher had little chance of retaining a teaching position because of the dual onus of the criminal and homosexual labels.

Despite the criminal system's procedural protections, those accused of homosexual conduct were considered in the case law of this period mentally or physically sick or morally reprehensible. If they chose to repent or combat their illness, the dominant majority could afford to deal sympathetically with them. However, if the homosexual deviant continued his or her minority behavior, the mechanisms of social control were there to deter and/or punish willful violations of the norm.

Judicial opinions of this period reflect the power of traditional values. Because heterosexuality was the only culturally acceptable sexual practice, little legal and social analysis was needed by the Court to label homosexual behavior as deviant. Community consensus, societal tradition, group morality, and common sense were powerful sources of legitimization.

Because of society's consensus about the evils of homo-sexuality, there was little argument that local officials were free to dismiss a lesbian or gay male teacher from his or her employ-ment. However, the added and very severe consequence of credential revocation caused some plaintiffs to challenge any procedural failing by the state. Otherwise, their livelihood as educators was terminated. If, in their zeal to eradicate homo-sexuals from the schools, administrators and state officials failed to follow established procedural guidelines, the GLBT educator had a viable challenge to dismissal or credential revo-cation. On the other hand, these cases also demonstrated that the legal system permitted — in fact encouraged — subsequent re-enactment of dismissal or revocation proceedings as long as the state guidelines were followed. Thus, if a teacher won on appeal it did not mean he or she retained the teaching credential or was reinstated in a teaching position.

In 1967, however, an Ohio court in Jarvella v. Willoughby-Eastlake City School District Board of Education articulated a decision that enhanced the rights of teachers in general and served as a harbinger of future trends that might favor gay and lesbian school teachers in particular. In that case, the Court determined that the interests of the school and the community would not prevail automatically. Despite the extreme power of the state and local boards of education, or maybe because of it, by the late 1960s some courts had begun to articulate support for the rights of the individual teacher. Chapter Nine will describe this transitional period from 1969 to 1973, when the power of the alliance between the educational and criminal systems was still firmly in place, but emergent doctrines of individual and minority rights were prepared to challenge the absolute power of the traditional perspectives. Also, in the late 1960s the rights of teachers were enhanced because of the growing legal doctrine of employment protection, so gay and lesbian educators benefited as well. Eventually, the GLBT school teacher employment issue would challenge the boundaries of this emergent concept of individual rights in employment settings.

Courage faces fear and thereby masters it.
Cowardice represses fear and is thereby
mastered by it.

— *Martin Luther King, Jr.*

CHAPTER 9

THE BEGINNINGS OF SOCIAL CHANGE, 1969–1973

On the afternoon of Friday, June 27, 1969, "John O'Leary" placed a sign in his print shop window that said, "CLOSED FOR THE WEEKEND DUE TO DEATH IN FAMILY." He had to leave work early to get ready, otherwise he would never make it to all of the evening events. The traffic in Manhattan was terrible, but John was intent upon his journey home. He showered and shaved while his wife, Susan, fixed dinner. Both John and Susan had been married several times before. In the early days of their courtship and marriage, Susan used to join John on his whirlwind weekends. It wasn't so novel or exciting for her now. Plus, after five days a week on her feet as a cashier in a grocery store, Susan looked forward to the weekends as a time to rest at home alone in front of the television with her feet propped up and comfortable. Besides, everyone would be upset tonight, so she wouldn't be missing a gala social affair.

Although John still wore pants to work, he was spending more and more of his free time wearing skirts and dresses. When his mother had died, he had kept some of her unusual outfits for himself. His favorite find, however, had been her large, feminine eyeglass frames. He'd had his prescription placed in each pair, and now wore these glasses exclusively.

John ate dinner carefully, trying not to smear his fingernails as they dried. Next, he spent almost two hours putting on his makeup and another hour choosing the right dress and accessories. While a black dress might have been appropriate for most memorial services, John didn't own one. His bright gold one would be fine. Besides, John couldn't imagine that Judy Garland would have wanted a somber farewell from her adoring followers anyway. Although her every gesture and the tone of her voice was imprinted in his mind, John wished he had known her better. Maybe if she knew how much she was adored, she wouldn't have killed herself. In many ways, it did seem like an important member of John's family had just died. Tonight they would say their farewells, although John knew that "Judy Garland" was such an icon in the gay and transgendered communities that she would remain in their lives forever.

After hours of preparation, John disappeared. In his place, in three inch high heels, stood "Sibhoan." At almost six feet tall and 250 pounds, with blond hair and an ear-to-ear grin, no one would mistake her for Judy Garland. But they would recognize Carol Channing in a second. Sibhoan was especially pleased that her outrageous gestures and raspy voice, made more so over the years from smoking and the effects of printing fumes, further complimented the effect. Carol Channing, in all of her theatrical glory, was ready to join her friends to mourn the loss of Judy Garland.

Greenwich Village had several gay bars, but the Stonewall Inn was most popular with drag queens and transgendered people. Sibhoan and her three gal pals shared a cab and arrived at the bar somewhat early for a typical Friday night. The place was already crowded with grieving, distraught people high on alcohol and drugs. Judy Garland's music played all night in tribute as people danced, drank, and cried in her honor. Given the crowd and the warm summer weather, the doors of the bar had been propped open, and some of the patrons stood in the street drinking and swaying to the music. For the patrons of the Stonewall Inn, that night was very different from their usual rowdy social events. On this night, despite the loud music and voices, the community was celebrating the life of one of its heroes. People also knew that precarious balance between surviving and death, so Garland's suicide was a painful reminder of their own vulnerability.

Because of their community expressions of grief, no one imagined that the New York City police would bother them on this evening. Police raids and harassment were common occurrences, especially if the politicians wanted to clean up the image of the City on some pre-election pretense. Drag queen bars were a favorite police target. Not only did you get to see all of the freaks, but none of them would cause any trouble out of fear that their double lives would make the morning papers.

When the lights started flashing — the signal that a police raid was happening — many of the patrons thought that it was part of the tribute to Garland. At first, instead of running out the door in fear and trying to evade the police, they looked around and cheered the show. However, as the officers started pushing patrons back into the bar and against the walls, some of the queens started screaming at the police and throwing drinks. In a matter of seconds, the entire bar erupted in violence. All the patrons started screaming and pushing the police out on to the streets. With cries of "Gay Power," the Stonewall patrons expressed their outrage at police harassment.

The violence lasted for five days, as more and more GLBT people joined the riots and for the first time asserted their collective entitlement to fair treatment. Susan, hearing the news reports of the rioting and violence, waited for the telephone call that would tell her where to go to bail Sibhoan out — not for the first time and certainly not for the last time.[1]

Since that date lesbians and gay men have been more visible and more vocal in their demands for social equality.[2] For example, special interest groups have been formed to lobby for gay, lesbian, bisexual and transgender (GLBT) interests, such as Gay and Lesbian Advocates and Defenders, The National Center for Lesbian Rights, and NGLTF. These organizations and others have sought political influence in addition to their efforts at legal change. They have been assisted in their undertakings by various organizations, such as the ACLU, that historically have championed the rights of minority people. But the example of support from the ACLU demonstrates the long struggle to gain social legitimacy.

As early as 1957, some chapters of the ACLU advocated due process protections for homosexuals, although they also supported laws criminalizing homosexual behavior.[3] By 1964, however, several chapters had reconceptualized homosexuality as a civil rights issue and actively supported lesbian and gay men's rights. Since 1969, the national office of the ACLU and its local chapters have been major forces in challenging discrimination on the basis of sexual orientation.[4] These gradual changes in perspectives mirrored social change occurring throughout a wide spectrum of American society.[5] In fact, one study was able to chart these attitudinal changes in American government documents.

Gerard Sullivan has searched for references to homosexuality in all documents, speeches, reports, and legislative actions in the House and Senate of the United States Congress. Sullivan discovered that those predating 1970 were openly hostile to homosexuality, often linking it with Communism, blackmail, obscenity, pornography, and other sexual perversions (very little mention was made of lesbianism). By 1975, however, with the increasing visibility of the gay rights movement, Congressional references started to be much more positive, including some attempts to prohibit discrimination on the basis of sexual orientation through the extension of the federal Civil Rights Act of 1964.[6]

These social changes also were reflected in the case law on gay and lesbian educators. On the one hand, from 1969 to 1973 most of the litigants still entered the dismissal and credential revocation process through an arrest for criminal sexual misconduct. Even in the Morrison case, that commenced without criminal behavior, the state board of education felt certain of its right to revoke his teaching credentials for minimal homosexual activity. On the other hand, in Morrison the California Supreme Court articulated a major challenge to the broad powers of the boards of education by requiring that a nexus be established between teacher misconduct and job responsibilities before any adverse action could be taken. Furthermore, the court declared that the status of being a homosexual was, of itself, insufficient basis for teacher dismissal or credential revocation without a detailed analysis of the complex legal and social factors involved in each case. Thus, with the Morrison decision, the absolute powers of school administrators was narrowed considerably, although the criminal arrest involved in most of the cases during this period acted as sufficient basis for dismissal or credential revocation even under the newly established Morrison requirements.

LANDMARK CRITERIA — MORRISON

For several years prior to 1964, Marc Morrison was employed as a school teacher by the Lowell Joint School District in California. In 1964 Morrison befriended a fellow school teacher, Fred Schneringer, and his wife. The Schneringers were having marital difficulties, and Morrison began to act as a counselor to the family. At some point, Morrison and Schneringer had four homosexual encounters with each other during a one-week period. The friendship cooled, and nothing occurred concerning the matter until more than one year later. Then, for some reason, Schneringer reported the nature of the relationship to the superintendent of the school district.[7] Morrison resigned his teaching position as a result of the report.

Almost two years later, the State Board of Education conducted a hearing and revoked Morrison's life teaching diplomas. The revocation was based on a finding that the sexual involvement with Schneringer constituted immoral and unprofessional conduct and moral turpitude, which were grounds for the revocation of the diplomas under Section 13202 of the California Education Code.[8] Morrison petitioned the Court for a writ of mandamus to review the revocations, and this request was denied.[9] He appealed that decision to the California Court of Appeals, which heard the case in early 1969.

Several facts of this case were positive for Morrison and distinguish it from the Sarac case as the legal community knows it. Although Morrison admitted to having homosexual urges since he was thirteen (he was 39 at the time of the incident), his only homosexual experience had been the one-week sexual involvement with Schneringer. The Board of Education could not automatically revoke Morrison's certificates because none of the sexual acts with Schneringer were criminal in nature under the California criminal code (because they had not engaged in oral copulation or sodomy) and because they had occurred between consenting adults in private. Furthermore, Morrison had sought psychiatric counseling since his youth because of his homosexual urges. And, importantly, Morrison's teaching record was exemplary.

Thus, the Court was called upon to determine whether the Board of Education had fairly revoked Morrison's diplomas by concluding that his brief, private, and non-criminal encounter was "immoral" and "unprofessional" within the meaning of Section 13202 of the Education Code. The term "immoral" was defined as "that which is hostile to the welfare of the general public and contrary to good morals."[10]

First, the Court of Appeals sought precedent by referring to the Sarac case, from which it concluded that Sarac,

> . . . squarely holds that homosexual behavior is clearly immoral conduct within the meaning of Education Code section 13202, and that constitutes evident unfitness for service in the public school system within the meaning of that statute.[11]

This reliance on <u>Sarac</u> demonstrates the powerful influence of legal precedent. It also demonstrates entrenched traditional perspective on the evil nature of homosexuality. The court did not even consider the need to balance the rights of Morrison against those of the school community. No further analysis of homosexuality was necessary, since, clearly in the minds of the Appellate judges, societal beliefs were bolstered by the power of case precedent.

The Court went on to determine that there was no direct evidence that Morrison's "homosexual character" had interfered with his "capacity, ability and willingness" to perform as a teacher, and that it had not affected his students. They concluded, however, that the School Board had a legitimate concern in protecting "impressionable pupils" from a teacher's conduct outside the classroom, because "a code of proper personal conduct" was especially essential in the teaching profession. Although Morrison's conduct was private, it became public knowledge, and in view of <u>Sarac</u> the Court concluded that it was certainly immoral. Thus, the Court of Appeals found for the State Board of Education. Morrison appealed his case to the Supreme Court of California.

Before discussing the Supreme Court of California's decision, it would be useful to delineate the specific aspects of Morrison's arguments against the revocation of his teaching diplomas. Morrison argued that the homosexual incident was a brief incident in the overall context of 39 years; the behavior was non-criminal; and it was private; between consenting adults; and did not affect his teaching or his students. Morrison's further legal arguments were that he had a right to privacy; the Education Code Section 13202 was "void for vagueness" because of the imprecise interpretations of "immoral," "moral turpitude," and "unprofessional;" the Court was essentially taking "judicial notice" by following the statement in <u>Sarac</u> that homosexuality was immoral and that homosexuals were implicitly unfit to teach and dangerous to children.[12] And finally he argued that by predicating their opinion on such unscientific, unsubstantiated prejudices, the Court was applying an unjust classification that deprived him of due process of law. The California Supreme Court held in favor of Morrison, although all of his arguments were not validated.

With their opinion in 1969, the California Supreme Court seemed to alter radically the legal status of GLBT educators as it radically altered the fitness tests for licensing of all professions. With specific reference to the failings in the <u>Sarac</u> decision, the Court called for a more rigorous analysis of such terms as "immoral" or "unprofessional."[13]

In an approach similar to that taken just prior to <u>Morrison</u> by the United States Court of Appeals for the District of Columbia in <u>Norton v. Macy</u>,[14] the Court determined that a mere labeling of conduct as "immoral" was no longer adequate cause for dismissal:

> A pronouncement of "immorality" tends to discourage careful analysis because it unavoidably connotes a violation of divine, Olympian, or otherwise universal standards of rectitude.[15]

Thus, "immoral," "unprofessional," and "moral turpitude" constitute mere "legal abstractions until applied to a specific occupation and given content by reference to fitness for performance of that vocation."[16] In <u>Morrison</u>, the California Supreme Court held that Education Code Section 13202 was not void for vagueness because it was possible to assess those terms in light of the specific demands and duties of a given profession. As an example of its thinking, the Court discussed the licensing and professional conduct issues involved in a wide variety of professions, and stated in a footnote:

> A particular sexual orientation might be dangerous in one profession and irrelevant to another. Necrophilism and necrosadism might be objectionable in a funeral director or embalmer, urolagnia in a laboratory technician, zooerastism in a veterinarian or trainer of guide dogs, prolagnia in a fireman, undinism in a sailor, or dendrophilia in an arborist, yet none of these unusual tastes would seem to warrant disciplinary action against a geologist or shorthand reporter.[17]

Each occupation's licensing standards must regard the "differing duties, responsibilities, and degree of contact with the public."[18] Furthermore, the Court felt that a reasonably stable consensus was possible concerning the type of behavior that would be harmful in the teaching profession and that this consensus would not "vary widely with time, location, and the popular mood."[19] One reason that the consensus would not vary widely is that the Court asserted that the test for unfitness was that the teacher's "retention in the profession poses a significant danger of harm to students, school employees, or others who might be affected by his actions as a teacher."[20] It was the duty of the School Board to prove affirmatively this harm was imminent; otherwise, "the right to practice one's profession is sufficiently precious to surround it with a panoply of legal protection."[21]

In assessing unfitness to teach, the Court offered a list of factors that the Board of Education could consider:

> . . . the likelihood the conduct may adversely affect students or fellow teachers, the degree of such adversity anticipated, the proximity or remoteness in time of the conduct, the type of teaching certificate held by the party involved, the extenuating or aggravating circumstances, if any, surrounding the conduct, the praiseworthiness or blame-worthiness of the motives resulting in the conduct, the likelihood of the recurrence of the questioned conduct, and the extent to which disciplinary action may inflict an adverse impact or chilling effect upon the constitutional rights of the teacher involved or other teachers. . . .[22]

The California Supreme Court affirmed the constitutionality of Education Code 13202, and at the same time rejected Morrison's arguments about an invasion into his privacy. Because of the nature of his occupation, the Board of Education did have a right to delve into aspects of Morrison's private life outside of his teaching duties. But such an inquiry had to have "a rational relation" to his teaching responsibilities and any possible harm to his students — a sweeping investigation was no longer acceptable.

This test of a nexus between Morrison's conduct and his duties was the important shift in licensing and occupational review begun by the United States Court of Appeals for the District of Columbia in Norton v. Macy. Now, with the apparent full weight of acceptance by the California Supreme Court in <u>Morrison</u>, the precedent seemed to be established which would further the rights of school teachers in general, and GLBT school teachers in particular.

Having established that the Board of Education was entitled to investigate the fitness of an individual to teach, and that the investigation had to focus on potential harm to the school community, the California Supreme Court went on in the <u>Morrison</u> decision and discussed whether Morrison's conduct, in fact, rendered him unfit as a teacher. Here the Court focused on the positive facts delineated by Morrison — that the brief act was between consenting adults, in private, had never been repeated after that week with Schneringer or any other male, and did not involve or impact students or other teachers. Because of these extenuating circumstances, and because of Morrison's positive teaching record, the High Court reversed the lower court decisions and remanded the case for a redetermination of the revocation of Morrison's certificates that focused on possible harm to school children if Morrison was reinstated. The Court was careful to point out that its holding did not mean that "homosexuals must be permitted to teach in the public schools of California."[23] Rather, the Court was asserting that there were strong constitutional and statutory requirements for a careful analysis prior to a decision of unfitness to teach. The <u>Sarac</u> decision was specifically held to be dicta, or past policy, in that homosexuality per se was not sufficient grounds to assume unfitness automatically and to abridge important rights involved in earning a living and privacy.

Another point on which the Court favored Morrison concerned the Board of Education's additional argument that even if Morrison was not unfit to teach because of his homosexuality under Education Code Section 13202, it was still correct in revoking his certificates under Education Code Section 13556.5. Under that Section, a teacher had an affirmative duty to "impress upon the minds of his pupils the principles of morality."[24] In reviewing the facts of the case, the Court again determined that there was no evidence that Morrison had failed in his responsibilities, but that the case would be remanded to the lower court for further consideration.

The Morrison decision seemed to reflect the Court's interest in protecting individual freedoms and personal expression that were consistent with the wave of civil liberationist ideology of the late 1960s. Given the strong position of the California Supreme Court as a leader in legal innovation, it was not improbable to think that the courts of other state and federal jurisdictions would soon be following the lead of the California Court as it advanced the rights of the individual in general and of GLBT people in particular.

In terms of Gusfield's analysis of status politics, the Morrison case reflected the changing social mores. It also served as a direct challenge to the norms and values of the status quo. A new minority group had emerged. It had reached a level of numerical significance and social influence that required the court to consider its presence in society. Additionally, this now visible subculture had emerged during the period of social change in sexual mores when the rights of the individual were receiving increased scrutiny and support. That period of "temporal injustice" when the law lagged behind social practice was mitigated by liberals in power in the institutions that regulated social behavior. Legal theorists, such as Justice Tobriner, expanded the rights of the individual, seemingly without seriously threatening or eliminating the powers of those people and institutions supported by more traditional perspectives. By upholding the constitutionality of the Education Code statutes, but modifying the tests for their applications, it seemed like a compromise might be possible within this cultural conflict. Unfortunately, although Morrison was a landmark opinion in terms of limiting the rights of employers and licensing agencies, and in terms of its attitude toward homosexuality, it fell victim to its own sense of compromise. The new tests and considerations had to be faced by administrators and judges, but in subsequent cases they were able to distinguish the facts in Morrison from other GLBT teacher circumstances.

Moreover, the Morrison opinion heightened the fears and concerns of administrators and parents in relation to their power and influence over the school setting. Not only was the broad power of the School Board and State Board of Education being limited in its application to hiring, retention, and licensing, but the court was requiring a new sensitivity to a previously stigmatized minority. Morrison deepened the concerns of parents and school administrators. At the same time, it raised the hopes of those who had been previously constrained under the status quo, living without hope their concerns would be supported.

With the Morrison decision, a social issue that had been present but relatively suppressed increased its visibility as both sides of the controversy struggled for power. Public awareness was heightened through this greater visibility and through increased coverage in the media. The controversy over the employment of GLBT educators was raised to an active level, where school boards felt the need to address it in case a situation arose in their own community. Thus, although the trend from Fountain and Sarac to Morrison suggested that one's non-heterosexual orientation could no longer serve as an automatic basis for dismissal, it did not end at Morrison with the policy resolution of the right of gay men and lesbians to teach. The trend traced the rise of the cultural conflict, but served more as a harbinger of a heated intensity in the conflict once the challenge to traditional powers had gained a foothold of legitimization.

EARLY 1970S: POST-MORRISON

With the Morrison opinion, the California Supreme Court established two major requirements that seemed forcefully etched in the case law of the 1970s. Those requirements were:

> . . . that a person may be barred from practicing a lawful profession only if he is unfit to do so, and, that unfitness is to be proved not by vague and unsupported prejudices but by evidence which reliably predicts behavioral consequences.[25]

Arguably, the mere status of being a homosexual was no longer sufficient grounds for job termination from school employment. With the Morrison and Norton decisions, it seemed that the incipient homosexual rights movement had gained some of the civil liberties it was demanding. Two legal opinions that immediately followed Morrison offered support for this perspective.

Shortly after Morrison, the California Court of Appeals, in Amundsen v. State Board of Education, ruled that the credentials of a teacher who had been arrested for a homosexual encounter could not be revoked without some assessment of his fitness to teach.[26] Because the opinion in Amundsen mirrored the prior decision in Morrison, it was presumed to be an insignificant addition to legal doctrine. The decision was not published, so it carried no weight as precedent, but the attitude of the California State Supreme Court concerning how these cases were to be handled seemed clearly established. Furthermore, other state courts were applying the Morrison standard, so a major trend in favor of teachers' rights and homosexual rights seemed secure.

For example, in 1971 in McConnell v. Anderson, a district court in Minnesota held in favor of a gay man whose contract to commence work as a university librarian had been revoked because school officials had learned of his public behavior as a homosexual, including his request for a same-sex marriage license.[27] The court found the university had violated McConnell's due process rights by automatically disqualifying him for employment based upon his status as a homosexual, his public behavior, and his private sexual conduct — none of which were relevant to employment duties as a university librarian. Upon appeal, however, the Eighth Circuit Court reversed the decision and held that to require hiring of a homosexual would "foist tacit approval of this socially repugnant concept upon his employer."[28] The Court determined that the employer should have greater discretion in the hiring process, although it acknowledged that had McConnell already been an employee, the university would have been required to demonstrate that his homosexuality negatively affected his job performance.

The initial ruling in the McConnell case, in addition to the holdings in Morrison, Norton, and Amundsen, was that the status of being a homosexual was insufficient grounds for job termination. Thus, standards of procedural due process would be required of employers in job termination situations and the private conduct of individuals did not automatically disqualify them from school employment unless it affected job performance.[29] All subsequent court decisions concerning employment dismissal in general, and GLBT employment dismissal in particular, would have to address the standards. But the anticipated wave of legal support for the GLBT educator did not occur, as evidenced by the discussion that follows.

The anticipated force of the Norton and Morrison trend was avoided by many judges deciding litigation in the early 1970s. Often it was argued that the facts of the case before them were so different from those in Morrison that the standards were not applicable. Even judges in the trend-setting jurisdiction of California were able to skirt the close scrutiny of the higher court because of personnel changes that neutralized the California Supreme Court's support of GLBT educators.

Two months after the decision, Chief Justice Traynor retired. The liberal majority of four justices became the minority of three. Together these three justices voted to hear certain cases, such as Moser, which will be discussed shortly, but they usually did not have enough votes to prevail. Consequently, the conflicting decisions of the Appellate Courts emerged because the clear standards established in Morrison lacked enforcement.[30]

Early in 1972, an Appellate Court in California once again took up the issue of the revocation of a teaching credential for unprofessional conduct relating to homosexuality. In Brent Moser v. State Board of Education,[31] the Appellate Court only briefly restated what it considered to be "the sordid details" of the testimony against Moser. Apparently, Moser had engaged in a mutual masturbation encounter in the public men's room in Long Beach and was convicted for the 1968 incident. Subsequently, the Board of Education determined that said conduct was an act involving moral turpitude, which was immoral and unprofessional under Section 13202 of the California Education Code. Moser's secondary education life teaching credentials were revoked. The Appellate Court concurred with the Board of Education's findings, and the State Supreme Court, by a vote of 4 to 3, refused to hear Moser's appeal despite the conflicting trends in case law emerging on the Appellate level.

Moser based his argument on the Morrison case by attempting to establish that his behavior was not related to his duties as a school teacher sufficiently to warrant the loss of his credentials. In its very brief opinion, the Court distinguished the facts of Morrison from those of Moser. One major difference was that Moser's behavior was criminal, and he had knowingly violated a law, which further suggested his unfitness to teach. Also, the Court noted that the sexual encounter occurred in a public place within view of a police or any other person entering the room. Thus, there was "tenuous security from public attention," which suggested that Moser was flaunting his lifestyle and was careless and notorious in his behavior.[32] Although the Court noted the Morrison opinion and the fact that the California Supreme Court had held that the Sarac case was dicta (no longer valid law), it contended that Moser's "sordid" behavior was similar to Sarac's and sufficiently immoral to warrant credential revocation.

The Court returned to two early California cases that had articulated the standards for judging the propriety of a teacher's conduct, Goldsmith v. Board of Education[33] and Board of Education v. Swan:[34]

> . . . the teacher is entrusted with the custody of children and their high preparation for useful life. His habits, his speech, his good name, his cleanliness, the wisdom and propriety of his unofficial utterances, his associations, all are involved. His ability to inspire children and to govern them, his power as a teacher, and the character for which he stands are matters of major concern in a teacher's selection and retention.[35]

Given the public and criminal nature of Moser's conduct, the Court easily affirmed the position of the Board of Education.

In 1973, another California Appellate Court reviewed another case of teacher credential revocation for homosexual acts that paralleled those of Moser. In Board of Education of the El Monte School District of Los Angeles v. Marcus Calderon,[36] Calderon was arrested for having oral sex with another man on the campus of Los Angeles City College. The Board of Education placed Calderon on a compulsory leave of absence without pay. Almost one year later, Calderon was acquitted of the criminal charge, so he requested reinstatement and back pay. The Board of Education refused both requests and dismissed Calderon. During the dismissal trial, the lower court supported the Board of Education conclusion that Calderon had engaged in the conduct for which he had been charged originally. The Board further determined that the conduct,

> . . . was indicative of corruption, indecency, depravity, dissoluteness, and shamelessness, showing moral indifference to opinions of respectable members of the community and an inconsiderate attitude toward good order and public welfare.[37]

Calderon did not deny the facts of the charges, but he argued that the legal doctrine of *res judicata* applied — having been acquitted of the criminal charges, the Board of Education was barred from any further adverse judgement.

Basically, the Appellate Court found that the Board of Education had several code sections that permitted it to dismiss Calderon despite his acquittal on criminal charges. Furthermore, Calderon's argument of *res judicata* failed because of the implication that no Board of Education could independently act on any civil matter that had also been considered by a criminal court. The Court pointed out that the criminal standard of proof beyond a reasonable doubt may have been a bar to a conviction, but that it did not mean that the acts had not been committed.[38] Furthermore, it might be that there was no risk of harm to students entrusted into Calderon's care from his sexual misconduct, but evidence of that conduct was sufficient proof that Calderon "would be unable to teach moral principles, to act as an exemplar for [his] pupils, or to offer them suitable moral guidance."[39]

Early in the 1970s, another criminal case arose that was not heard by the Court of Appeals until 1974. Much of the legal focus of <u>Governing Board of the Mountain View School District of Los Angeles County v. Frank Metcalf</u> revolved around whether the criminal evidence gathered against Metcalf in an unconstitutional manner could be used against him in the civil action to dismiss him from his probationary sixth-grade teaching position.[40]

Metcalf was convicted of engaging in an act of prostitution (lewd act between persons for money or other consideration) in violation of California Penal Code, Section 647(b). Apparently, he was caught engaging in oral sex in a doorless toilet stall of a public restroom of a department store. That conviction was later overturned on the grounds that the police had gathered the evidence against Metcalf in violation of his rights under the Fourth and 14th amendments to the United States Constitution and Article I, Section 19, of the California Constitution. Although the conviction was overturned, the Board of Education used the facts of that arrest as grounds to dismiss Metcalf for "immoral conduct and evident unfitness to teach."[41]

Since very little case precedent was before the Court with respect to the application of the exclusionary rule (requirement that illegally obtained evidence must be excluded from the prosecution's case) to civil cases, it resorted to a balancing of interests. The Court of Appeals concluded that although Metcalf's issues in the case were strong and based on constitutional criminal rights, the interests of the Board of Education and the students were of even greater concern. Although only a very few people in the school community knew about Metcalf's arrest, the Court feared that if it were to become known then Metcalf's effectiveness as a teacher would be destroyed. More important, the school environment would be disrupted. Also, the Court felt that the act of having engaged in public oral sex demonstrated Metcalf's moral unfitness to teach and be a role model for young children. Thus, to protect his students from his "serious defect of moral character, normal prudence and good common sense," the Court ruled in favor of the Board of Education.[42]

CHAPTER CONCLUSIONS

With its holding in the <u>Morrison</u> case, the California Supreme Court articulated the first inroad into the power of state and local school officials to dismiss teachers or revoke their credentials based upon a finding of immorality. Prior to <u>Morrison</u>, the concept of immorality was defined by offense to local sensibilities — anything that school officials found upsetting or inappropriate was immoral. This earlier perspective mirrored Lord Patrick Devlin's criteria of the basis for making law, as set forth in Chapter Six. This view relies on consensus. With collective agreement, no analysis is needed to explain why a behavior is offensive; mutual arousal and upset is sufficient basis for taking action against the inappropriate individual.

The <u>Morrison</u> decision marks the social change that took place in American society after World War II. New emphasis was placed on the rights of the individual as long as he or she did not harm others. A much wider range of expression was occurring in all facets of human behavior. Consensus about what was appropriate behavior began to break down, although the dominant majority could continue to enforce its code of conduct through their control over the legal, political, religious, and educational institutions.

The <u>Sarac</u> case discussed in Chapter Eight showed the power of the majority when it was challenged within the legal context it controlled. In the court's opinion, no analysis was necessary about Sarac's personal actions and whether homosexuality would affect his teaching responsibilities. On the other hand, by 1969 and the <u>Morrison</u> decision, a more liberal judiciary demanded that an analysis was needed of a person's behavior before punitive action could be taken against him or her. Immorality could still be defined within a community context, but a rational basis was needed to supplement the emotional reactions of those people who adhered to a traditional view.

In the <u>Morrison</u> decision the court was unwilling to eliminate the community's ability to define immorality by declaring homosexuality an acceptable form of behavior. Justice Tobriner and his colleagues seemed to believe that requiring a rational basis for action would protect individuals from the irrational actions of the traditional majority, so that personal freedom and collective governance could coexist.

Despite the court's best intentions, the compromise did not cause the majority to lift its constraints upon minority behavior. In fact, by establishing the link between the criminal justice and educational systems, traditionalists tightened their hold over the social definitions of appropriate behavior within the school teacher context. Anything that was criminal sexual misconduct was immediately considered immoral as well. With the additional power of the reporting statutes, the educational system was given tremendous autonomy in its power to define moral and immoral conduct. Eventually, because of the changing sexual mores and an increasing emphasis on individual rights, even the criminal justice system was required to accept the variations in sexual expression as long as people were not harmed. Thus, most of the cases discussed in this Chapter show a person initially drawn into the process through an arrest for criminal sexual misconduct. However, in these cases the criminal procedural context adhered to strict due process requirements and the possibility of rather lenient processing.

Regardless of the outcome in the criminal justice system, however, the police were required to inform state and local education officials of any teacher's arrest for sexual misconduct. Then the educational system was free to take any action it wished without the constraints of procedural due process or individual rights set forth in the federal and state constitutions as protections for the individual.

Essentially, in the <u>Morrison</u> decision the California Supreme Court offered the educational system a compromise that would permit it to continue to regulate itself with extraordinary powers, but required it to follow more rigorous analytical and procedural guidelines so it would be more responsive to changing social definitions of acceptable behavior. In most of the GLBT educator cases that immediately followed <u>Morrison</u>, the criminal behavior of the teacher offset any requirement for the educational system to be more flexible. In 1973, however, sex between consenting adults was decriminalized in seven states which adopted the American Law Institute's Model Penal Code.[43]   California followed that trend in 1975. Thus, the educational system was confronted with noncriminal GLBT educators. It remained to be seen whether the educational system was willing to bend with the times and broaden its definition of acceptable personal conduct by teachers or whether it would be broken by judicial intervention in the controversy over the employment of GLBT educators in particular. Chapter Ten begins the discussion of these major changes in legal and social attitudes towards homosexuality and how they affected teacher dismissal and credential revocation.

When I dare to be powerful —
to use my strength in the service of my vision,
then it becomes less and less important
whether I am afraid.

— *Audre Lorde*

CHAPTER 10

COMING OUT OF THE CLASSROOM CLOSET, 1973–1977

Cascade, Oregon: A teaching contract! Peggy Burton was thrilled that her job search was over. Now she was a member of the faculty at Cascade High School. Okay, so maybe most people would have second thoughts about the job. Between preparing a zillion new courses and running the girls' athletic program, she would be lucky to survive the first year. Teaching consumer education and business math would be a bit of a stretch for her. Biology and earth sciences would be fun, and the possibilities for field trips in the local area were endless. The mighty Hood River that divides Oregon from Washington, and the deep gorges cut by its waters, would provide a major class project. At some point they could go over to The Dalles and other rock outcrops to compare the rare geological formations.

While thrilled at the idea of teaching, Peggy also was aware of a drawback in accepting the Cascade contract. Since her teens, Peggy had grown in awareness that she had strong physical and emotional feelings for women.[1] By college she had explored those feelings, and now she was living with a lover. Peggy believed that her lesbianism was merely an alternative life — another variation on the human continuum of creating loving connections. Peggy knew many women just like herself — young, educated, athletic, women-oriented, and hard working. Her lesbian orientation just was, it wasn't any strident political statement. Sure, Peggy and her lover participated in community events. Certainly there was the bar scene, since there were few other places for GLBT people to meet. Like everyone else, Peggy made her share of trips into Portland to hit the lesbian bar. But now she was in a relationship — and a teacher! — so the odds were that she would be spending more time visiting with friends in their homes. God forbid that she run into one of her students at the bar! You hear so many stories of that happening. Or running into a student's mother! "Argh! I guess if they are at the bar, they are 'members of the faith,' " thought Peggy. "They probably wouldn't harm my teaching status. On the other hand, better safe than sorry. Some people haven't worked out their personal issues around their sexuality. Just what I need! Some kid dealing with their confusion over their lesbian feelings by turning in 'Miss Burton.' "

And, of course, there was the additional problem of being the new girls' athletic supervisor and referee. Perhaps, if she was stern and demanding of her students, no one would see through the facade of her feelings and her life. Maybe if she just kept very busy, she could become almost invisible. By being stern, aloof, committed, and talented, it would appear that she was much too focused to have a personal life. No time for becoming friends with her colleagues, no time for frivolous school social events, and no time for students with crushes on her!

Peggy supposed that she, too, would lead the schizophrenic life of the gay or lesbian educator. "Miss Burton, teacher" by day, "Peggy Burton, lesbian" during her free time. Merging the two seemed impossible, but the strain of keeping them separate also was impossible. Peggy knew that many gay men and lesbians taught school for a few years and then moved on. The strain of keeping a secret and worrying about being discovered haunted too many of their public and private moments. "How could something so simple and loving be the cause of so much pain and hatred," Peggy thought. Imagine being fired, or threatened, or called names merely because you loved someone. How could such a simple, very private matter cause parents and school administrators to rage hysterically and deny basic human freedoms to someone whom they admired five minutes before — before they knew . . . ?

Ironically, the deep division in her identity gave both parts of the equation much too much power over who she was as a person. Did anyone care that she had other interests, other words that she used to define who she was — daughter, sister, friend, athlete, scientist — that also were important. Why did "teacher" and "lesbian" take on such a power that they defined her employment security and social acceptance?

And, what if one day . . . those two labels merged at school? Maybe that day would never happen, if she was lucky. And if she wasn't? What if a student accused her of being a lesbian; what would she do? Would she lie about her life and her relationship? Or would she admit the truth and hope for the best? Maybe it would never come to that. "Certainly there have been tens of thousands of gay and lesbian teachers," she thought, "maybe I could just live my life in peace." Maybe it could just remain a non-issue in relation to her job. Peggy loved teaching and she knew she was good at it. Maybe that would be enough.

School had been in session for only a few months, yet everyone was feeling worn out and depressed. The cold winds off the Hood River gorges gave notice of the arrival of an early winter. Peggy's demanding teaching schedule was further complicated by long hours of coaching the girls' volleyball team and preparing for the basketball season. Already there was gossip about Miss Burton being a lesbian. Fortunately, tomorrow was Friday; her week was almost over.

Late that afternoon, Peggy received word that Mr. Frederico, the principal, wished to see her before she left for the day. Peggy assumed that he wanted to discuss her budget estimates for winter sports, so she was not prepared for trouble. But, it had happened; one of her students had brought Peggy's fears to life. The student had gossiped to her mother about Peggy's alleged lesbianism, and the mother was determined to make an issue out of it. Frederico had received the phone call earlier in the afternoon. "Mrs. Busibody" was concerned that Miss Burton might molest her child or convert her into a lesbian lifestyle. "Did Mr. Frederico know what kind of person he had working with these young, impressionable women?"

It didn't take Mr. Frederico long to decide that he faced a potential crisis. True, there was no accusation that Miss Burton had done anything wrong. And, she was a terrific teacher. But Mr. Frederico did not want trouble, and this was the start of trouble. Even if the accusations were not true, the damage had been done.

Mr. Frederico confronted Peggy Burton about her sexual orientation. Despite her upset over the whole incident, Peggy almost had to laugh as Mr. Frederico struggled to ask her if she was "a practicing homosexual?" This was probably no time for jokes about "practice makes perfect," she thought. Besides, she was much too upset to be funny as she faced this moment of truth. Peggy Burton answered, "Yes." That honest response left Mr. Frederico "with no alternative" but to suspend her from her teaching position pending a hearing before the school board. In the interest of all parties, Mr. Frederico felt that the gravity of the matter warranted an immediate special hearing that could be set up for the upcoming Monday school board meeting. Miss Burton was free to go. A permanent substitute would cover her classes until the matter was resolved, one way or the other.

By the early 1970s the issue of GLBT educator employment was squarely before the American public. This visibility was an outgrowth of several developments that influenced the ongoing debate.

The GLBT community had "come out of the closet" after the 1969 Stonewall riot and functioned as a reasonably well-organized political, social, legal, and educational lobbying group. There remained the problem of the invisible members who feared the threat of job loss, child custody defeats, physical violence, and other forms of discrimination. On the other hand, those who could afford to challenge the status quo worked to educate the public about homosexuality and remove it from the realms of sickness, immorality, and criminality. Often, their demands were in concert with other liberal social perspectives popular during the 1960s and 1970s, such as civil rights, due process, privacy, alternative lifestyles, and less intrusion by government into personal decision-making.

In 1973 several states adopted the Model Penal Code which, among other things, decriminalized sex between consenting adults in private. This major legal entitlement was passed because the entire Code was adopted with little discussion about specific sections. If state legislators had been required to vote specifically on the topic of decriminalizing sex between consenting adults, that section may not have been enacted because of pressure from constituents. These controversial sections were minimized within the context of the recommended changes, however, as numerous legislatures adopted the spirit and structure of the entire Code in a cohesive effort to overhaul their criminal system.

Adoption of the Model Penal code transformed the entire controversy over the rights of GLBT educators. As several states decriminalized sex between consenting adults, the previously-used argument that homosexual behavior was criminal and, therefore, obviously immoral, fell into disrepute. Thus, the scenario the plaintiff faced in GLBT school teacher cases dramatically changed from being both a homosexual and a criminal issue to being a purely social controversy over consenting sexual activity that was no longer prohibited by law.

In fact, since 1973, none of the litigants trying to retain his or her teaching credential or job has been regarded as both GLBT and criminal. All have been average-to-model citizens and educators who kept their sexual orientation out of their employment situation. Through various means, they became known as GLBT and confirmed that knowledge. Then, rather than resorting to the traditional response of quietly accepting termination of employment, they challenged the school or college system.

Also in 1973, lesbians and gay men successfully lobbied to challenge the label of homosexuality as a mental illness.[2] In that year the American Psychiatric Association (APA) voted to remove homosexuality from its list of mental illnesses. In March of 1975, Dr. John Spiegel, past president of the APA, went even further with APA support and spoke out on behalf of gay and lesbian school teachers, arguing that professional competence should be the only basis for teacher retention decisions and that the hostility against homosexual teachers should be eliminated. Otherwise, both the individual teacher and the educational system overall were harmed. The lesbian or gay male teacher was harmed by the psychological cost of living in secrecy to protect his or her livelihood. The school system was harmed by the loss of talent when these people left the system or never entered it because of discrimination. In 1977, when a conservative backlash against homosexual rights emerged, then-APA President, Jack Weinberg, reaffirmed Dr. Spiegel's position on homosexual teachers and added "that the efforts to frighten citizens into fear of the influence of homosexuals on our children are utterly without scientific foundation and the effort should be combated by all citizens of good will."

This pattern of successful enactment of pro-GLBT rights policies occurred in numerous other organizations, school settings, and state and local political arenas. For example, the Lutheran Church of America, with a membership of 3.2 million, issued a statement in support of homosexual rights.[3] Even the Catholic Church modified its position somewhat, as the Pope authorized proper burial for sodomites.[4] In 1970 election campaigns, several major gubernatorial candidates called for anti-discrimination protections for homosexuals.[5] And within the private sector, the *Wall Street Journal* reported that there was "a trend in private industry which suggests a cautious but noticeable shift in hiring and firing policies by companies towards employees it knows or believes to be homosexual."[6] The fact that more than 40 municipalities added "sexual preference" protections to the anti-discrimination clauses of their municipal legislation during the 1970s provided strong evidence that the nation's view of homosexuality was changing.[7] In numerous forums, homosexuality was being viewed as an alternative lifestyle rather than evil, sick, or criminal behavior.

With specific reference to the controversy over the employment of GLBT educators, two other significant developments enhanced the teachers' side of the debate. First, powerful lobbying groups concerned with either teachers' rights or GLBT rights joined forces with individual litigants. These organizations, such as the ACLU, the NEA, GRA, and the NGTF, added their legal expertise and fundraising ability to pursue litigation on behalf of GLBT educators that would have been prohibitively expensive on an individual basis. Second, GLBT educators had the strong precedent of the <u>Morrison</u> decision as a basis for their legal argument. They also asserted that they had rights under various federal civil rights statutes, which brought the federal courts into the legal debate. Inclusion of the federal courts, and the raising of the legal arguments from criminal to constitutional rights, changed the whole tenor of the cases by expanding beyond local impressions of acceptable behavior and morality. The arguments became more complex, the outcomes less predictable, and the courts' decisions influenced policy on a national level.

GLBT RIGHTS AND COMMUNITY ACTION

With the rising political visibility of GLBT people in the early 1970s, local advocates influenced city councils and school boards to add "sexual preference" to their ever-increasing list of anti-discrimination categories. The initial success of these lobbying efforts was impressive, especially in light of the low-keyed efforts necessary to influence local political and educational leaders. The lesbian and gay rights movement from 1972 to 1977 seemed in concert with the general mood of the country concerning privacy, personal freedoms, and civil rights. The lobbying efforts of a few gay activists and liberals convinced local officials that some good, and very little harm, would come from extending basic civil rights protections to the GLBT population.

Lobbying was not the only strategy used by GLBT educators. After the Stonewall riot of 1969, lesbians and gay men engaged in public demonstrations for their rights throughout the United States. GLBT educators were no exception. Their first protest against discrimination occurred early in 1971 in New York City.[8] They picketed the Board of Education and presented affidavits concerning discrimination against lesbian and gay male teachers. Chancellor Harvey Scribner convinced the group that the State Board of Examiners was responsible for the policies, so a sit-in was staged in Examiner offices during which five protesters were arrested.[9] This protest effort appears to be the first example of GLBT teachers collectively risking their jobs to assert their rights. In numerous other parts of the country, however, this extreme action was unnecessary.

In 1972, with little apparent fanfare, the District of Columbia became the first city in the country to bar discrimination against GLBT educators. The employment order stated:

> The District of Columbia Board of Education, after discussion and consideration hereby recognizes the right of each individual to freely choose a life style, as guaranteed under the Constitution and Bill of Rights. The Board further recognizes that sexual orientation, in and of itself, does not relate to ability in job performance or service.

236

Therefore it is resolved that henceforth it shall be the policy of all departments and services of the education system under the jurisdiction and control of the District of Columbia Board of Education to promote a policy of non-discrimination in hiring, employment, promotion, tenure, retirement and/or job classification practices, within its jurisdiction and control, relative to the sex or personal sexual orientation of any individual(s) regardless of past, present, and/or future status of such individual(s).[10]

Several other city councils followed suit, including St. Paul, Minnesota; Eugene, Oregon; and, Wichita, Kansas.[11]

Although the process of enactment was unique to each city, a typical pattern emerged. A small group of advocates favoring GLBT protections appealed to the city councilors and school board officials to add "sexual preference" to the increasingly viable anti-discrimination clauses. Although the vote to include "sexual preference" usually was not unanimous, a majority vote prevailed. Sometimes, there was a very brief, emotional outcry in the editorial pages of the local press, but the issue quickly faded from community awareness. For example, in St. Paul, Minnesota, the sexual preference protections enacted in 1974 were on the books for more than four years with little community attention. Advocates of GLBT rights made little use of the laws, and opponents were not upset by their official presence within the sanction of city policy.[12] The relatively quiet success of this pro-GLBT rights trend continued in various cities across the country. In fact, as late as 1978, "sexual preference" protections were added to city laws in Champaign, Illinois, and the conservative Bible-Belt city of Wichita, Kansas, with little initial opposition.[13]

The circumstances surrounding the issue in Palo Alto, California, were illustrative of a typical lobbying effort in support of anti-discrimination protections for GLBT educators. In October of 1975, the Board of Education of the Palo Alto Unified School District voted on the wording of a new non-discrimination policy drafted by the District's affirmative action committee. There was little debate over the inclusion of categories pertaining to sex, race, religion, color, or national origin. Some debate occurred over the inclusion of "handicap, political belief, and marital status," and these criteria were deleted from the original draft. The most intense debate surfaced over the inclusion of "sexual preference," and this criterion was deleted from the proposal by a vote of 4 to 1.[14] Those arguing against the inclusion of "sexual preference" maintained that the issue was highly personal and had no business in the employment setting. One board member feared that the provisions inclusion would result in overt homosexuality and advocacy in the schools.[15]

The local GLBT community, including students at Stanford University, responded to the Board of Education decisions by lobbying board members to change their vote.[16] More than 100 people met with board members and demanded that the categories be reinstated. Several people argued that, by refusing to include the criteria, the board inversely was encouraging discrimination. One noted gay psychologist, Don Clark, argued that homosexual youngsters needed role models just as much as did African-American students. The board's stand would send the message that great caution needed to be maintained by school employees.[17] Basically, the advocates tried to convince the board that by including "sexual preference" in the non-discrimination policy, it was preventing discrimination, not encouraging advocacy of homosexuality in the classroom.

Under pressure, the Board of Education agreed to reconsider its October vote. On November 18, 1975, by a new vote of 3 to 2, all of the previously-rejected categories were included in the district's non-discrimination policy. In his dissenting vote, Board member Royce Cole argued that by adding the words "sexual preference," the Board would soon be faced with a gay teachers organization, gay liberation student groups, issues of homosexuality in the classroom, and homosexual teachers who would gather a "coterie" of young homosexual followers with administration support.[18]

Although the new policy remained in effect, the inclusion of "sexual preference" created intense reaction, as reflected in the editorial pages of the local paper, *The Palo Alto Times*. The editorial board of the paper wrote that the Board of Education had "erred" in being swayed by the lobbying efforts.[19] It noted that sex between consenting adults had been legalized in California as of January 1975, but that did not mean that parents had to be blind to the role-modeling influences that their children were exposed to in school. The editorial also argued, without any documentation to support such statements, that molestation in the heterosexual community was "a more limited problem" but was a major issue in the homosexual community.[20] The opinion of the paper was supported by several emotionally-charged letters to the editor, but the controversy died almost immediately, probably because local opinion seemed to favor GLBT educators' rights and because local conservatives were not well organized as an opposition group.

GLBT Rights and Teacher Organizations

This pattern of successful enactment of pro-gay rights policies also occurred in the National Education Association during the 1974 annual convention in Chicago, Illinois.[21] No material is currently available concerning the lobbying efforts for the passage of the referendum to add "sexual orientation" to the non-discrimination statement of the organization, which had originally been adopted in 1969. The typical NEA procedure for passage of referenda involves the majority decisions of the more than 9,000 delegates to the annual convention. It appeared that the resolution was proposed by an ad hoc special interest group of GLBT teachers present at the conference. The resolution was proposed to the general voting body, passed by a majority vote, and entered into the body of documentation on the organization's policy positions. It remains in effect to this date, and states:

> The National Education Association believes that personnel policies and practices must guarantee that no person be employed, retained, paid, dismissed, suspended, demoted, transferred, or retired because of race, color, national origin, religious beliefs, residence,

physical disability, political activities, professional association activity, age, marital status, family relationship,
sex, or sexual orientation.[22]

With the adoption of this anti-discrimination policy for homosexuals, the NEA leadership faced the mandate to involve itself in
the GLBT educator issues of the union membership. Available
evidence from interviews and case law analysis suggests that the
NEA response to the issue has varied from state to state and from
administration to administration within the national office. For
example, the State of Washington's Education Association has
been very actively involved in homosexual school teacher litigation as evidenced by the cases of Gaylord v. Tacoma School
District No. 10[23] and Mercier v. Evergreen School District.[24] The
Maryland Education Association also has been active in
supporting lesbian and gay rights through the Acanfora litigation.[25]
Not surprising, several of the plaintiffs, such as Acanfora,
Gaylord, and Gish, in the GLBT educator litigation during this
period were NEA members.

The NEA situation concerning lesbian and gay teachers was
unique in that a national policy statement was adopted rather early
in the GLBT rights movement.[26] It appears that proponents of the
anti-discrimination policy for homosexuals successfully argued
that the "domino theory" pertained to all forms of discrimination,
meaning that if homosexuals were not protected by the organization, then African-Americans, women, Jews, and other minorities
faced possible discrimination as well. Once situations of discrimination arose on a local level, GLBT union members were free to
approach their local and state education association for legal and
financial assistance in their struggle to retain their teaching
employment. All initial and intermediate phases of the litigation
were handled by local attorneys who were experts in both GLBT
rights and teacher contract issues. Once the cases reached the state
supreme court or major federal courts, however, the national NEA
litigation experts stepped in and presented oral arguments. The
benefits to the teacher in this procedure were the financial involvement of the national office and the professional involvement of a
prominent team of litigation experts. The negative side of the

policy, according to the local attorneys who were upset by being replaced, was that the impassioned continuity of the case was lost by bringing in outside attorneys with general expertise in teachers' rights, but questionable loyalties in terms of GLBT issues.

When questioned about the attitudes of the national NEA offices towards GLBT educator litigation, several attorneys around the country were highly critical of what they considered to be ambivalent support. For example, several state education association attorneys stated that they had to pressure their own national organization to support GLBT educator rights, despite the national policy mandate. This pressure took the form of letters, mass mailings, and calls to other organizations around the nation interested in GLBT issues, encouraging them to lobby the NEA. Encouragement by state NEA affiliates and other national organizations, such as GRA, the NGTF, the NOW, the National Council of Teachers of English, the Speech and Communication Association, the American Association of University Professors, and the National Association of Social Workers was most evident in the correspondence to the NEA concerning the California and Oklahoma campaigns to prohibit homosexuals from teaching school. Despite the intense lobbying efforts, the NEA maintained a position of silence throughout most of the conflict.

In a letter dated 5 April 1981, Everett G. Sillers reminded then-NEA president, William H. McGuire, that not only did the NEA have a national policy mandating support of GLBT educator rights, but that at the 1978 Annual Convention in Dallas, Texas, the Representative Assembly had reaffirmed its support of that policy with passage of the following statement:

> The NEA shall reaffirm its opposition to situations as the Briggs initiative in California, and the recently passed law in Oklahoma which discriminates in the hiring and retention of teachers on the basis of sexual orientation. The Representative Assembly directs the NEA to use any and all appropriate legal and legislative means to defeat these and any other similar initiatives or discriminatory actions.

When questioned about the NEA's policy towards GLBT educators, Michael Simpson, assistant to the general counsel, and Al Erickson, manager of governance and policy support, stated that the NEA was determined to challenge any form of discrimination against teachers but that it would not characterize its perspective as "pro-gay." In fact, they both said that the NEA had been "pilloried" by the New Right for supporting individual homosexual teacher cases and for eventually filing an *Amicus* brief challenging the Oklahoma action against homosexual teachers. According to Erickson, comments and campaign material from the New Right alarmed NEA members across the nation, who wrote the organization demanding to know why it supported homosexuality. The NEA held special meetings to inform its membership about its stand in the Oklahoma case and its strong concern for teachers' rights, which at times must extend to less popular areas of individual freedom. But Erickson further noted that the NEA also supported very strong professional standards; and if a homosexual teacher deviated from those criteria the NEA would not participate in any challenge based upon homosexual discrimination.

Despite the conflicting support for the prevention of discrimination on the basis of sexual orientation, NEA leaders acknowledged that it was not a prominent issue for the organization because most teachers confronted with this discrimination did not take legal action because of the negative publicity and public condemnation. Furthermore, given the current AIDS crisis, they predicted that people interested in "going after" lesbian and gay teachers now had the ammunition that they needed to prevail. Much of the legal future of homosexual school teachers, in their opinion, was dependent upon federal and state policies towards sodomy and AIDS. If, for example, homosexual conduct between consenting adults in private was legalized in any given jurisdiction, then the NEA predicted eventual success in any homosexual school teacher litigation in that locale. Conversely, if laws became even more anti-homosexual because of AIDS, then the homosexual school teacher faced a difficult, if not unlikely, challenge to the authority of school leadership. In response to the AIDS crisis, in 1986 the NEA adopted a strong policy position against testing of all teachers and against questioning teachers about their sexual activity or their sexual orientation.

The position of the American Federation of Teachers, at least on a national level, mirrored that of the NEA until recently. In 1974, when the NGTF questioned AFT executive council president David Selden, he replied that the AFT had a policy in support of sexual preference protections for educators.[27] On the other hand, during the 1979 AFT convention in San Francisco, an amendment to prohibit discrimination on the basis of sexual preference was defeated. In a brief summation of the minutes of the 1979 AFT convention in San Francisco, it was noted that an "interesting floor fight" occurred over a proposed constitutional amendment to prohibit discrimination on the grounds of sexual preference.[28] Ultimately, the amendment was defeated by 20 votes short of the two-thirds majority needed. Apparently the policy was never formally adopted as an AFT guideline, which would explain why the current AFT leadership was able to withdraw from the controversy.

The current perspective of the AFT, as articulated in 1985 by its long-term president, Albert Shanker, is that the issues of homosexual school teachers are too marginal and controversial to merit much of its support.[29] AFT rejects the "domino theory" of teacher discrimination that maintains the commitment of the NEA. Shanker criticized the NEA for its naive support of an issue that was aversive to the American public. In his opinion, the NEA and the AFT could better use their influence to advance teacher causes that were of greater interest to their constituency and not in conflict with the values of many Americans. It should be noted, however, that the California Federation of Teachers was one of the first unions involved in the homosexual school teacher controversy, and it was very active in the campaign against the Briggs Initiative.[30]

CASE LAW — EARLY 1970S

The case law of the 1970s concerning GLBT educator litigation had a very different character from that of the 1950s and 1960s. After a few typical cases in the early 1970s, the phenomena of the criminal-origin and male-dominated litigants ceased. Litigants in the 1970s were male or female, and their homosexual orientation came to the attention of the school board through rumor, publicity, or political action rather than criminal behavior. Sex between consenting adults in private had been decriminalized in several states between 1973 and 1975, thus the traditional means of exposure to the dismissal process was invalidated.

Furthermore, the litigants no longer had to bear the financial and emotional costs of the proceedings alone. A politically astute GLBT community and its special interest groups became involved in the litigation with the belief that the success of one homosexual in combating discrimination benefited the entire group. They were aided in their efforts by legal advocates for homosexuals, civil rights, and teachers' rights. Given this wide-ranging support, it was apparent that a viable alternative social norm existed and that it was beginning to encroach upon the heterosexual cultural norms. In the sections that follow, the response of the majority and its traditional institutions will be explored.

COMPENSATION FOR TERMINATION — BURTON

Quite probably both Mr. Frederico and Peggy Burton had no realization about the hundreds of times their particular confrontation has taken place in American schools and colleges. The traditional script for resolving this situation called for Mr. Frederico to threaten to expose Miss Burton if she did not voluntarily sign a letter of resignation during their initial confrontation. In turn, Peggy Burton should have quietly signed her resignation, gone home, packed her belongings, and left town in shame. The official story about the incident would be that Miss Burton suddenly had to resign and leave the area for personal reasons. Of course, the rumors would circulate. In fact, they probably would be embellished to the point that Miss Burton had been fired for molesting students in the shower room. Mr. Frederico could take comfort in the fact that the incident was handled swiftly, with minimal challenge to his authority and with little parental interference. Miss Burton would waver between intense feelings of shame, loss, frustration, injustice, and relief. She could never teach again because any new school system would look to Cascade High School for an evaluation of her abilities and reputation. Besides, going through the daily struggle of hiding who she really was and fearing disclosure would be too costly in emotional energy and physical stress.

Mr. Frederico played his part perfectly. But Peggy Burton did something different. She became one of the first of numerous educators to both affirm her sexual orientation and assert her right to be employed as an educator. While there had been several prior cases of individuals asserting their right to retain their teaching credential in the face of accusations of homosexual activity, most of those individuals denied being homosexual or pleaded with the court for leniency because they sought to be "cured" of their homosexual urges through psychotherapy. Burton and this new wave of litigants challenged the authority of the school administration with a very positive perspective on their sexual orientation. In fact, the Burton case also became the first dispute of this type in which the educators argued that they were entitled to federal civil rights protections as lesbians and gay men.[31]

Previous cases had focused on the local arena of trying to limit the authority of school officials by arguing that social mores had changed in terms of the definition of "immorality" or that the incident did not affect the educator's teaching context. In the Burton case, an argument was made that, like African-Americans and other minorities, GLBT people deserved the protections of the strong civil rights legislation passed in the 1960s that implied an acknowledgement of the prejudice and discrimination inherent in mainstream, white, heterosexual America. As noted in Chapter Six, during the 1960s and 1970s there was an expansion of federal Equal Protection arguments at the expense of state authority. The primary intent was to force states to eliminate their role in perpetuating discrimination against African-Americans. As the Equal Protection concept gained in acceptance, however, women, aliens, elders, "illegitimate children," and numerous other minority groups sought protections under these federal laws. Ultimately, the boldness of these claims would arouse a powerful conservative backlash and Republican championing of state's rights over federal intervention. Gay and lesbian educators would be one of the first minority groups to feel this backlash with the 1977 Anita Bryant campaign against GLBT discrimination protections in Dade County, Florida. But for the moment, Burton's argument was both powerful and unique in the controversy over the employment entitlements of GLBT educators.

During the Cascade School Board meeting, the discussion over Peggy Burton's employment rights was quickly resolved in the minds of board members the minute Ms. Burton answered that she was a "practicing homosexual." Fearing public outcry, the board voted decisively to suspend Ms. Burton and terminate her contract "based on her admitting to be a homosexual." Later, on the advice of its attorney, the school board revised its resolution to read that "Peggy Burton be dismissed and the contract terminated as a teacher in the district because of her immorality of being a practicing homosexual."[32] This was done to comply more closely with the Oregon statute permitting the dismissal of a teacher on the basis of immorality. It also was done to diminish Burton's potential claims that her First Amendment freedom of speech entitlements were violated by being dismissed for answering a question about her sexual orientation.

Burton obtained an attorney and petitioned the District Court to reverse the school board's actions. In addition to federal civil rights arguments, Burton argued that the school board erred by not using the <u>Morrison</u> test to explore whether her supposedly inappropriate behavior or status as a lesbian directly affected her teaching performance. The District Court determined that the Oregon educational statute that permitted termination of employment on grounds of "immorality" was unconstitutionally vague in meaning because it did not define immorality or give fair warning of what conduct was prohibited. Judge Gus Solomon feared that the statute, as written, permitted "erratic and prejudiced exercises of authority." He felt that its interpretation was so dependent upon the "idiosyncrasies of individual school board members," that "every teacher in the state could be subject to discipline.[33] Judge Solomon also determined that the school board should be required to demonstrate a clear and direct harm to students from Peggy Burton's status as a lesbian before her job termination could be warranted.

Having ruled in favor of Burton, Solomon gave the attorneys 14 days to come up with a remedy acceptable to both parties. Apparently they did not do so because on appeal Solomon awarded Burton damages in the amount of the balance of her salary for that school year and half of her salary for the next year. She also received $750.00 in attorneys fees and the right to force the school board to expunge all of its documents about her dismissal. She was not reinstated in her job, however, so Burton appealed the decision.

Since the District Court ruling was a threat to the entire hiring, firing, and retention policies practiced by school administrators throughout the United States, it was little wonder that the higher courts that heard the appeals tried to restrict the Burton holding with respect to its larger implications. In March of 1975, for example, the United States Court of Appeals for the Ninth Circuit held that refusing to order a reinstatement of Burton "was not an abuse of discretion, where [the] teacher was awarded damages," especially since Burton had neither tenure or seniority to assure her of continued future employment with the school system.[34] Moreover, the Court of Appeals argued that Judge Solomon's failure to order Burton's reinstatement was accurately based upon his determination that to do so for the remaining months of her contract would disrupt the school community given the public nature of the controversy.

The Court also commented that refusing to reinstate Burton did not blemish her reputation as a school teacher, since all school board records were destroyed with respect to her dismissal and since she did win damages which demonstrated that the school board had acted inappropriately. It would not address the argument, however, that the Cascade School Board and other school boards might refuse to hire Burton based upon her status as an admitted, sexually active lesbian, which again raised constitutional concerns. The Court held that those arguments were speculative in the face of her uncertain future employment status.

Judge Lumbard's dissenting opinion argued that reinstatement was an appropriate remedy in light of the finding that Burton had been unconstitutionally removed from employment. His argument was that, to most courts, reinstatement was not an extraordinary remedy even in cases involving non-tenured teachers. Lumbard accused the majority in <u>Burton</u> of creating a hierarchy of constitutional rights so that people whose First Amendment or Equal Protection rights had been violated received the full benefit of the law, which in this case would be reinstatement. Rather than grant a lesbian that full protection, the majority fashioned a narrower remedy that contravened strong legal precedents.[35] All violations of constitutional rights of any minority should receive the benefit of the same redress, in Lumbard's opinion. He argued further that the disruptiveness of reinstatement should not be weighed against Burton's constitutional rights given the unconstitutional behavior of the school board. Finally, Lumbard questioned whether the monetary award to Burton would be adequate to deter the school board from removing other teachers for unconstitutional reasons. In Lumbard's opinion, only reinstatement would provide the appropriate remedy. Only a controversial issue like sexual orientation could explain the Court's retreat from accepted remedies in the face of unconstitutional action.

Out and Proud — Acanfora

Another case that did not involve criminal conduct and also demonstrated the increased political advocacy of the GLBT community was <u>Joseph Acanfora v. Board of Education of Montgomery County, et al.</u>[36] While Acanfora was a student at the Pennsylvania State University, he was active in a GLBT organization established to educate the public about homosexuality. Acanfora spoke publicly about his homosexual orientation and participated in a law suit against the university to allow his group official recognition on campus.[37]

After completing most of his coursework in education, Acanfora was suspended from his student teaching assignment by the Dean of the College of Education because of his homosexuality.[38] A state court promptly ordered Acanfora's reinstatement. Upon graduation, Acanfora applied for his teaching certificate, which the university forwarded to the Pennsylvania Secretary of Education for consideration rather than assume the responsibility for determining the requisite issue of "good moral character." A special six-member panel listened to Acanfora state his perspective on teacher professionalism and his intention never to discuss or encourage homosexuality in school. Acanfora also stated that he believed that homosexuals should have full legal rights and be free of societal hatred and fear. The panel failed to reach a decision because of a split vote, so the matter was turned over to the State Secretary of Education, John Pittenger.

In the meantime, Acanfora was granted his Maryland teaching certificate, probably without its knowledge of his public stance on homosexuality or his sexual orientation. He then was hired by the Montgomery County Board of Education in Maryland to teach junior high school science for the 1972-1973 school year. The school system also was unaware of Acanfora's personal and political GLBT stance. Several weeks into the school year, in a nationally publicized press conference, the Pennsylvania Secretary of Education announced his decision to grant Acanfora his Pennsylvania teaching credential. The deputy superintendent of the Montgomery County schools immediately removed Acanfora from his teaching post (with no reduction in salary) and transferred him to administrative work where he would have no contact with students. After requesting and being refused reinstatement, Acanfora commenced legal action pursuant to the federal civil rights statutes discussed previously in the Burton case. On the District Court level, Acanfora's case was funded by the Washington Gay Activist Alliance. On appeal, the ACLU and the NEA covered the expenses.[39]

Another controversial aspect of the Acanfora matter occurred shortly after the litigation commenced, when Acanfora granted a nationally-televised interview to "60 Minutes." When asked why he had taken such an activist stance, Acanfora replied:

> Many of my friends have asked me why I'm doing this, why I just don't go some place and be a teacher and not let the gayness enter into it at all. But the fact is that I'm gay, just like the fact is that other teachers are straight or heterosexual. But I'm sure a heterosexual teacher isn't going to live his life a complete lie and hide what he is and I have no intentions of doing that either. I have every right to be what I am. I have every right to be a teacher. And I plan on doing both.[40]

It was evident on the District Court level that Acanfora was transferred solely because of his homosexuality. In fact, the school system admitted that it would not have hired him had it known of his orientation, despite his tactful behavior at school and his fine teaching efforts. Acanfora's failure to disclose his GLBT political activity on his employment application was not addressed until the oral argument. It proved to be critical to Acanfora's case on an appellate level, as did his national television appearances.

The Acanfora case is significant in the development of GLBT educator case law for a number of reasons. For the first time, medical and psychological experts were allowed to testify on the potential impact a homosexual school teacher might have on his or her students. Allowing this testimony demonstrated that the issue of role modeling was open for debate, rather than presumed on the basis of traditional beliefs. Expert witnesses for the Montgomery School Board, Dr. Reginald S. Lourie, a pediatrician and child psychiatrist, and Dr. Felix P. Heald, a pediatrician, argued that preadolescence is a stage during which children with bisexual tendencies (approximately 3 percent of the population, in their opinion) chose their sexual orientation. Thus, a homosexual role model might encourage the child to be gay or lesbian. Because of the strong societal belief that homosexuality was abnormal and evil, the experts felt that the removal of GLBT teachers from the classroom was comparable to a vaccination program, whereby there was no direct evidence of how many children might have been affected, but that intervention helped prevent "infection." When asked in cross-examination if either expert knew of any literature, research, or incident in which a known homosexual teacher had an adverse effect on a student, both answered in the negative.[41] Both Dr. Lourie and Dr. Heald testified that harm arose when a teacher's sexual orientation became known, not that all homosexual school teachers pose a role-modeling danger to young children.[42]

All the experts who testified agreed that they did not know the determinants of homosexuality. Furthermore, expert witnesses for Acanfora argued that the limited amount of data showing either the positive or negative impact of a homosexual teacher on a child lead to the conclusion that such an impact would be minimal compared to the influence of parents, relatives, and the home environment. Dr. Stanford B. Friedman, professor of pediatrics and psychiatry at the University of Rochester Medical School, argued that having a homosexual role model would be of positive benefit to young children who might be bisexual or homosexual. And finally, several of the expert witnesses for Acanfora agreed that a child's sexual orientation is probably well predisposed by the age of five or six. Given this supposition, the influence of an eighth grade science instructor would be too late to cause a homosexual orientation and may, in fact, be of assistance to children and to the school community in combating negative stereotypes and prejudice about homosexuals.

The expert testimony in support of homosexuality prevailed. Although the District Court judge commented that "it would be premature to state definitively that Acanfora's presence in the classroom (on an eighth grade level) will have no deleterious effect," he did conclude that the danger was not as "great or as likely" as the defendants have assumed.[43] With reference to the overriding issue of whether a homosexual has a right to employment as a school teacher, the District Court judge ruled in favor of Acanfora. Judge Young noted that the 14th Amendment to the United States Constitution and the Bill of Rights provided the United States Supreme Court with the basis on which to recognize numerous protectable interests that had not been specifically designated.[44] Any impingement upon these constitutional rights required the Court to resort to an "especially careful judicial review" of the state action.[45]

For the first time in the history of GLBT educator cases, the Acanfora Court recognized certain homosexual rights as being protected under the developing constitutional doctrine of a right of privacy. Furthermore, Young also stated:

> As autonomous and rational beings, individuals are capable of reasoned decisions in pursuit of chosen goals. Given man's imperfect knowledge, full freedom of thought and association is imperative for individual self-development and social progress. So long as the freedoms of others are not affected, a government intended to promote the life, liberty and happiness of its citizens must abstain from interference with individual pursuits, no matter how unorthodox or repulsive to the majority. . . .
>
> In this context, the time has come today for private, consenting, adult homosexuality to enter the sphere of constitutionally protectable interests. Intolerance of the unconventional halts the growth of liberty.[46]

In discussing the historical development that led to his conclusion, Young noted that homosexuality was no longer regarded as an emotional disturbance, a genetic defect, or a character disorder. He further noted that, as early as 1967, a California court had ruled in a lesbian mother custody case that lesbianism per se was not a sufficient basis for the denial of custody of minor children, so he was following strong emergent legal precedent.[47]

Judge Young concluded that homosexuality per se did not hinder positive job or social performance.

Moreover, Young dismissed the idea that homosexuality was a threat to society. In particular, he noted the analysis of the Wolfenden Committee and that of the American Law Institute, both of which concluded that the criminal laws concerning private, adult sexual behavior should be revoked. Adding weight to his argument, Young noted that the Maryland sodomy statute had never been applied to private sexual behavior.[48] Thus, given its method of enforcement, even the State essentially agreed that sex between consenting adults was a private matter.

Judge Young's decision contained several other very radical comments. On the issue of religion and homosexuality, he stated that interference by organized religion violated the constitutional requirement of separation of church and state. He concluded that the constitutional right to privacy should extend to private, adult homosexual behavior and not affect other personal freedoms relating to career choice, freedom of association, and sexual freedoms. Most surprising were Young's brief comments that homosexuality should be considered a "suspect classification" similar to race and national origin under the federal Equal Protextion Clause, although he realized that the Supreme Court probably would not agree with him on this point.[49]

Having established a very radical benchmark in terms of the rights of homosexuals and homosexual educators, Young then went on in his opinion to weigh these strong personal freedoms against the strongly held societal value that school officials needed considerable discretion in their efforts to educate children and run the schools. Judge Young felt that had the facts of the case stopped with the public ruling by the Pennsylvania Board of Education, which exposed Acanfora as a homosexual to the public, and the subsequent transfer of Acanfora by the Board of Education of Montgomery County, then, said transfer would have violated Acanfora's constitutional rights. Ultimately, Young determined that the case analysis rested most strongly on the post-transfer publicity which Acanfora and others created around the issue.

Following a long analysis of freedom of speech in educational settings, Judge Young concluded that the Board of Education had the right to regulate speech that could be detrimental to the educational process. Because the instruction of young children carried with it numerous special responsibilities, Young determined that teachers not only had a right to privacy, but a duty of privacy, or, in other words, a duty to keep their personal lives and their sexual lives out of the school environment. Thus, even if school officials and parents were unreasonably intolerant, there was no question in Young's mind that the fear, anxiety, and conflict aroused by the notoriety of Acanfora's case interfered with the educational process. Having signed a contract to teach children, with all of the special duties entailed in that responsibility, any teacher, including a homosexual teacher, had a responsibility to go out of the way to keep his or her personal life from interfering with the educational process. Young ultimately relied on this reasoning in ruling for the Board of Education and concluded that Acanfora's public appearances, including "sensational" remarks on "60 Minutes," far exceeded his right to defend himself in the face of an injustice.

After writing the strongest pro-gay legal opinion in the history of GLBT educator case law — and possibly in the history of homosexual rights in general — it was ironic that Young would rule in favor of the Board of Education after determining that Acanfora had been removed unconstitutionally from his teaching position. Not surprisingly, Acanfora appealed the United States District Court opinion.

The United States Court of Appeals, Fourth Circuit, heard arguments in November of 1973 and rendered its ruling in February 1974. The Appellate Court overruled Judge Young on the issue of Acanfora's speech and held that it was indeed protected by the First Amendment. The Court stated that the proper standard by which to judge Acanfora's public statements was whether they were knowingly false, made with reckless disregard for truth, and impaired his performance of his teaching duties or the operation of the school.[50] Further, the Court determined that Acanfora's public comments about the difficulties he and other homosexuals encountered were matters of social interest and concern. In the Court's opinion, Acanfora did not advocate homosexuality in his speeches, and he approached the media interviews in a rational and appropriate manner. Since there was no direct evidence of the school being disrupted in any way by Acanfora's behavior, the Appellate Court determined that Acanfora's speech was protected and did not justify the transfer.

This holding was significant because previous discrimination against GLBT individuals was successfully characterized as a matter of curbing immoral and dangerous behavior, which is a strong interest of any state. With the holding in Acanfora, however, the constitutional focus shifted from the state's police and public safety rights to the very powerful personal freedom of speech. Ironically, failing to uphold Acanfora's First Amendment rights after asserting their existence, was a major step backwards in legal trends toward personal freedoms, even in 1974.

In an unusual move, however, the Court allowed the Board of Education to raise the previously undiscussed defense that Acanfora had failed to inform them of a material fact about himself in his application for the teaching job. The Board of Education argued that it had a right to transfer him upon finding out about the consciously withheld information. The Appellate Court agreed, citing the fact that the application requested detailed information about organizational affiliations and extracurricular activities, and that it required an oath of accuracy as well as an acknowledgement of the Board of Education's right to fire anyone who provided false information. The Court ruled that Acanfora had knowingly failed to inform the Board of Education of a material fact relating to his employment.

In his application, Acanfora made the following oath, and agreed to the following terms:

39. Read Carefully Before Signing:

The information as submitted on this application is accurate to the best of my knowledge. I concur in the above statements and requirements. I understand that falsification of any information submitted on this application shall be cause for dismissal from service. I have signed this application form in the presence of a notary public, whose signature and seal appear below.[51]

Following case precedent, the Court of Appeals ruled that Acanfora was barred from challenging the constitutionality of the Board of Education's disclosure policy and attitude about the employment of GLBT educators because he was guilty of fraud and misrepresentation in the face of potentially unconstitutional demands.[52] He "purposely misled the school officials so he could circumvent, not challenge, what he considered to be their unconstitutional employment practices."[53] The Court relied on the Dennis doctrine:

> The governing principle is that a claim of unconstitutionality will not be heard to excuse a voluntary, deliberate and calculated course of fraud and deceit. One who elects such a course as a means of self-help may not escape the consequences by urging his conduct be excused because the statute which he sought to evade is unconstitutional.[54]

This doctrine was further affirmed by the Supreme Court in Bryson v. United States, when it held:

> But after Dennis it cannot be thought that as a general principle of our law a citizen has a privilege to answer fraudulently a question that the Government should not have asked. Our legal system provides methods for challenging the Government's right to ask questions — lying is not one of them. A citizen may decline to answer to a question, or answer it honestly, but he cannot with impunity knowingly and willingly answer with falsehood.[55]

The Board of Education supported its argument by asserting that, had Acanfora honestly informed them of his personal and political affiliations, it would have had three criteria which would have caused it not to hire him. First, the Board admitted it would not have hired him if it had known he was a homosexual. Second, the Board argued that because of the involved consideration process by the Pennsylvania Secretary of Education, it was clear that Acanfora was certified "as being morally fit to teach children by the <u>barest</u> of margins."[56] And finally, the Board argued that had it known of Acanfora's political and legal activity, it would have been justified in not hiring him because he was "a litigious militant."

In its brief the Board of Education argued that, "militants are inevitably controversial, causing a factionalization of both the faculty and the students. Secondly, civil rights militants have the trait of being litigious."[57] Therefore, to protect itself from a disruptive influence that would involve the school system in expensive, "amorphous," and aggravating litigation, the Board would refuse employment had it known of Acanfora's past. Additionally, the Board stated that, in itself, militancy could be used by school authorities to evaluate fitness to teach in light of prior court holdings.[58] For a variety of reasons, then, the Board of Education felt it could have legitimately refused to hire Acanfora had he answered honestly about himself. By ruling in favor of the Board of Education on the grounds of Acanfora's fraudulent application, the Court of Appeals avoided the necessity of ruling on the constitutional status of homosexuals in educational employment. The United States Supreme Court refused to hear Acanfora's appeal, so the case was concluded in favor of the Board of Education.[59]

RESIDENTIAL RESERVATIONS

Shortly after <u>Acanfora</u>, the Supreme Court of Wisconsin decided a case by referring to the <u>Acanfora</u> holding and facts. In <u>Safransky v. Personnel Board</u>, the Court ruled that when one is employed as a school teacher or houseparent in a mental institution, the standard of conduct required many be higher than for other forms of employment.[60] Consequently, a tenured house parent/instructor at a home for moderately retarded teenage boys was appropriately fired for discussing his sexual orientation and personal life in front of colleagues and the institutionalized children. Safransky also allegedly wore make-up, called some of the female staff "lesbians," and in general made some outrageous comments. By informing his charges of his sexual orientation, the Court concluded that Safransky failed to provide an adequate role model for both appropriate sexual behavior and public social behavior. It was the specific duty of a houseparent (and a teacher) to "project to the patients an appropriate male image consistent with that experienced by the remainder of society."[61] Another significant duty was,

> . . . to direct the patients to a proper understanding of human sexuality. Such an understanding required the projection of the orthodoxy of male heterosexuality. Consistent with the projection of the normalcy of hetero-sexuality by the houseparent was the requirement that he not project the unorthodoxy of male homosexuality to the patients under his care.[62]

Given the overt behavior on Safransky's part and his responsibilities involving being housed with young male patients, it is probably not surprising that the Wisconsin Supreme Court would uphold his dismissal. But an equally extreme Court reaction and precedent was set in Washington State shortly after the Safransky opinion in James Gaylord v. Tacoma School District No. 10.[63] The Washington State Supreme Court seemed to take a step backward in the trend of legal decision-making to a pre-Morrison, pre-Norton belief that one's status as a homosexual was, in itself, significant and adequate grounds for teacher dismissal.

OLD DIRECTIONS — GAYLORD

In December of 1972, James Gaylord was fired from his high school teaching position when a letter by one of his former students was sent to the principal of his school accusing Gaylord of being a homosexual.[64] Apparently the student had been struggling with sexual orientation issues and another teacher had referred him to Gaylord for assistance, although no direct statement was made about Gaylord being a homosexual. In response to that letter, Gaylord, who had been teaching in the district for 12 years, admitted to his vice-principal and the school board to being "a publicly known homosexual."[65]

Despite his "consistently favorable," and "excellent," teaching record, the Tacoma School Board determined that Gaylord's status as a homosexual, in itself, evidenced immoral conduct under that State Educational Code and dismissed him from employment. Furthermore, the School Board argued that if Gaylord's homosexuality became public knowledge, it would result in "fear, suspicion, and parental concern and pressure,"[66] impair Gaylord's teaching efficiency, and cause injury to the school if he were allowed to retain his position.[67]

The trial judge ruled in favor of the school administrators and determined that Gaylord's firing was not unconstitutional, in part because the judge gave considerable weight to the expert opinion of the school administrators concerning the "conditions necessary to maintain the optimum learning atmosphere."[68] His decision was overturned by the Washington Supreme Court, and the case returned to the lower court. The High Court held that the greater burden of proof of disruption should rest with the school administrators, rather than allowing reliance upon their professional opinions concerning any potential disruption and its effects on the school environment.

From the partially dissenting/partially concurring opinion of Justice Ringold (who felt that Gaylord should be reinstated immediately), it is evident that the expert testimony concerning school disruption came from Tacoma School officials themselves. Some of the testimony is expressive of the administrators opinions about homosexuality and student development. For example, the high school vice-principal stated:

> I feel that homosexuality is out of place in a public school classroom. I feel that a student from his initial years as a six-year-old until he graduates from a high school, at about 17 years, is going through his formative stages, and a teacher, as well as a home or a church, but certainly a teacher is extremely instrumental in influencing a child in these developmental years. And I feel that consciously or unconsciously a teacher that is homosexual can do irreparable damage in these formative years. . . . If a homo-

sexual were on our faculty, a known homosexual, . . . I would have to defend his remaining there to other members of the staff. . . . [and] it would be extremely disruptive. . . . I have already operated under the assumption that homosexuality is an abnormality and would be classified as immoral, and as such don't believe that a homosexual meets the standards, the professional standards, the community standards, that we would expect of a classroom teacher.[69]

The Assistant Superintendent of Personnel testified:

I think there is a way of life that I have looked for in employing teachers . . . and fundamentally I don't think that homosexuality is a way of life that I can tolerate. . . . I've worked with adolescents a long time and adolescents do admire adults, and . . . if sometimes admire things that I don't think society accepts . . . . [So,] if the word was out that there was a homosexual teaching, . . . youngsters even with those tendencies could well accept them and say, this person is a fine man, he's a homosexual, I can't see what's wrong with it. . . . I think . . . that we've got to teach by examples as well as by discipline.[70]

Outside experts, however, differed with the school administrators' opinions. Two child psychiatrists, Dr. S. Harvard Kauffman and Dr. Jerman Rose, testified that in their opinion Gaylord's presence in the classroom posed no threat to the students and would not be disruptive to his teaching effectiveness. Although the psychiatrists felt that some students and parents might be upset, they concluded that a person's sexual orientation was acquired prior to high school and continued to be governed by free choice in terms of expression. Dr. Kauffman did feel that homosexuality was a deviation and a disease, so he would encourage Gaylord to change his orientation through psychiatric intervention. Gaylord, however, testified that he had been homosexual for 20 years, did not regard it as a problem, and did not wish to change.

Educational psychologist Dr. Stephen Sulzbacher testified that he consulted with every school district in the state and had first-hand knowledge of the effectiveness of homosexual school teachers in the State of Washington. In his opinion, even if parents and students learned of Gaylord's sexual orientation, it would not significantly disrupt his teaching or the school environment.

After sending the case to the lower court for further definition of immoral conduct, the Washington State Supreme Court was confronted again with Gaylord in early 1977. This time the High Court directly affirmed the lower court's finding that Gaylord was properly fired because his homosexual status was deemed immoral and thereby would impair his fitness to teach while also disrupting the school. The Court emphasized Gaylord's reluctance to reveal his homosexuality and inferred that Gaylord knew that such a revelation would result in the loss of his job and parental affection, otherwise he would not have been so secret. The Court noted that, "Gaylord's precaution for 20 years to keep his status of being a homosexual secret from his parents is eloquent evidence of his knowledge of the serious consequences attendant upon an undefined admission of homosexuality."[71]

The Court also re-opened the discussion of whether or not homosexuality, as a status and not an act, was immoral. Experts before that Court characterized homosexuality as an historically "frightening idea," and stated that "a majority of . . . adults in this country react negatively to homosexuality."[72]   The Court concluded that homosexuality "is widely condemned as immoral," and has been so condemned since biblical times. In fact, the Court referred to the *New Catholic Encyclopedia* for further material on the issue of the immorality of homosexuality.[73] Having concluded that homosexuality was immoral, the Court stated that homosexuals had a choice to not act on their desires. "Volitional choice is an essential element of morality. . . . . [Gaylord] has made a voluntary choice for which he must be held morally responsible."[74]   In response to the fact that the state of Washington had repealed its sodomy statute, the Court concluded that, "the fact that sodomy is not a crime, no more relieves the conduct of its immoral status than would consent to the crime of incest."[75]

Although at first not many people were informed of the reason for Gaylord's termination, the school board seems to have asked its teachers how they felt about the possibility of working with him. Three teachers apparently stated that his presence would be "objectionable," and the school administrators felt that it would "create problems." The Gaylord case is the first non-criminal homosexual teacher dismissal situation that provided overt evidence of hostility expressed by fellow teachers towards the litigant. In fact, even in the 1967 Sarac case involving supposed criminal conduct, Sarac enjoyed the support of his colleagues. On the other hand, the Tacoma Federation of Teachers was "incredibly supportive" of Gaylord, and provided him with employment after he was fired; Gaylord earned about one-third of his teaching income as an employee of the union. The tremendous expense of the Gaylord case was borne by the Tacoma Federation of Teachers (which is affiliated with the AFT), and the ACLU. At Gaylord's request, the homosexual community in Tacoma was not active in the case.[76]

The Court ultimately concluded that retention of Gaylord as a teacher would indicate approval of his homosexuality. Late in 1977, the United States Supreme Court refused to hear the Gaylord opinion, with only Justices Brennan and Marshall voting for review.[77] Upon the announcement of the Supreme Court's refusal to hear Gaylord, Anita Bryant, who was actively campaigning in Dade County, Florida, against anti-discrimination protections for gays and lesbians, commented, "Now I have greater hope that God has given America a space to repent and this will slow down the forces that are attempting to destroy the foundations of this country — the family unit."[78]

Proponents of rights for GLBT teachers expressed fear that by refusing to hear Gaylord, the Supreme Court had opened the door to unrestrained permission to fire allegedly lesbian and gay teachers. One New York activist called for an educational effort to inform the public that there had been gay teachers "from time immemorial, [since] Socrates, for instance."[79] With this information, it was hoped that the public would not feel so fearful of the homosexual teacher.

The <u>Gaylord</u> decision was an attempt by the Washington State Supreme Court to reiterate traditional beliefs about homosexuality and morality. To accomplish this outcome, the Court's majority reverted to old legal doctrines and ignored contemporary legal trends. In fact, the <u>Gaylord</u> majority placed themselves in the uncomfortable position of ruling against the Washington state legislature, which had just decriminalized sex between consenting adults. The traditional standard of morality had fallen, but the struggle to maintain its influence continued. The <u>Gaylord</u> decision would be followed, however, by another homosexual school teacher case, decided in Delaware, that emphasized the growing support for personal freedom in the area of sexual expression.

GROWING INFLUENCE — AUMILLER

Richard B. Aumiller was a non-tenured lecturer in the Fine Arts Department at the University of Delaware from 1973 to 1976.[80] His homosexual orientation was known by his immediate supervisors, but higher ranking university officials were unaware of this fact until three newspaper articles appeared in the local press. Aumiller also served as the faculty advisor to the gay student group on campus. This organization was permitted to form in 1971, despite administrative opposition, because university legal counsel advised that costly litigation might ensue if the group was prohibited.[81] After the third article appeared, University President Trabant wrote the Board of Trustees and informed them that after the first article he had ordered the Provost to inform Aumiller that he must stop speaking publicly about his homosexuality. Apparently the Provost had not acted on the request. As President Trabant stated:

> Speaking quite frankly, I don't really care what Mr. Aumiller does in his bedroom, but I consider it an effront [sic] to the University and to me as an individual that he insists in making his bedroom activities public information and a point of evangelistic endeavor to recruit more gays to his supposed case. . . . [Thus,] his private life was

his own business, but it had to be private and if he did anything to cause embarrassment to the University then something would have to be done.[82]

After the third article, President Trabant met with Aumiller and informed him that he could not speak publicly about homosexuality and remain employed by the University. Shortly after that meeting, Aumiller's contract was not renewed. When Aumiller filed a grievance against the university, President Trabant met with him again and this time informed him that he had not been rehired because he encouraged heterosexual undergraduates to experiment with homosexual sex.

In light of President Trabant's initial warnings to Aumiller to cease discussions on homosexuality, Aumiller filed suit charging an abridgement of his First Amendment freedom of speech. The U.S. Supreme Court's position at that time was that because of a state's strong interest in education, a teacher should exercise his or her constitutional rights only to the extent that they did not interfere with his or her professional duties. The criteria for balancing these competing interests was set forth in the case of Pickering v. Board of Education.[83] The school system would prevail if the teacher's behavior: (1) disrupted the effectiveness of the teacher's relationship to the school administration, (2) breached loyalty or confidentiality, (3) disrupted the educational process, (4) indicated unfitness to teach as derived from the content of the offending statement, or (5) failed to comply with established grievance procedures. The burden of proving that the teacher's speech violated the Pickering criteria fell upon the school board.

Based upon the Pickering criteria, U. S. District Judge Murray M. Schwartz found that the university had violated Aumiller's constitutional rights concerning freedom of speech and association. He wrote:

The Court fully recognizes that homosexuality is an extremely emotional and controversial topic and that Aumiller's opinions on the subject quite likely represent a minority view. But this unpopularity cannot justify the limitation of Aumiller's First Amendment rights by the University. The fundamental purpose of the First Amendment is to protect from state abridgement the free expression of controversial and unpopular ideas. The decision not to renew Aumiller's contract because of his public statements contravenes those most basic teachings of the First Amendment and cannot be tolerated.

Aumiller was granted back pay, reinstatement, and the university was ordered to pay him $10,000 for emotional distress and $5,000 in punitive damages for malicious and wanton disregard for his constitutional rights. The court was particularly supportive of Aumiller because he was not the instigator of the newspaper publicity and because of the flagrantly unconstitutional constraints articulated by President Trabant in his first meeting with Aumiller. Reinstatement was somewhat of a non-victory for Aumiller. The academic year had ended, so the court ordered that he receive his wages as if he had worked. On the other hand, since he did not have tenure, the university was free to not hire him for subsequent years. Aumiller may have prevailed in his request for reimbursement for attorney's fees and costs as well.

The Aumiller decision signaled that judges in many jurisdictions throughout the nation were willing to protect lesbians and gay men in the exercise of their First Amendment freedoms of speech and association, even within the sensitive context of the teaching profession. Since the facts in Aumiller took place at the collegiate level, the judge's decision was probably more favorable than if young, impressionable students had been involved. Nevertheless, the court's holding was unambiguous in mandating that it would not permit school authorities to abridge the constitutional freedoms of teachers. Not surprisingly, this growing judicial trend proved threatening to the traditional powers of school administrators and community members, who reacted strongly in 1977 and 1978 to oppose the changing of social norms. In the Gish case that follows, the 1977 decision demonstrates the attempt by school authorities to reassert their power over hiring and firing of teachers by resorting to medical criteria of fitness to teach. This effort appeared to be successful in 1977, but by 1981

Gish became litigation that toppled the previous, almost unlimited, authority of the New Jersey school boards.

TRANSITIONAL LITIGATION — GISH

During the long Gaylord litigation, and before the Aumiller decision, a gay teacher case was litigated in the Superior Court of New Jersey. In Gish v. Board of Education of Paramus,[84] the Court determined that Gish's "actions in support of 'gay' rights displayed evidence of deviation from normal mental health which might affect his ability to teach, discipline, and associate with students."[85]

John Gish taught in the Paramus High School for more than 10 years. In June of 1972, Gish became the president of the New Jersey Gay Activist Alliance, and he also was active in the annual gay caucus of the NEA. In these capacities, Gish was publicly visible as a leader in the New Jersey gay rights movement. Also in June of 1972, in response to knowledge obtained about Gish's political activities, the school board ordered him to take a psychiatric examination as an extension of the educational code statute pertaining to physical examinations.[86] At the board's request, a psychiatrist was asked to determine whether the "overt and public behavior of Gish indicated a strong possibility of potential psychological harm to the students."[87] The psychiatrist determined that Gish's behavior indicated potential harm.

Gish filed suit to test the constitutionality of the board's action. In response to that litigation, the board ordered another examination of Gish which was general in nature, rather than specific to his public, political action. Again the psychiatrist focused on his political behavior, that suggested "a significant deviation from mental health" which would "adversely affect his ability to teach."[88] At no time was Gish allowed to confront the psychiatrists during the litigation. This was one strong basis of Gish's appeal, since it was an aggregious unconsitututional violation of his Sixth Amendment rights.

After appealing the board's opinion to the Commissioner of Education and then to the State Board of Education, Gish's case finally came before the Superior Court. It concluded that Gish's constitutional rights had not been violated. Rather,

> School Boards are entrusted by our Legislature with the duty of determining the general issue of fitness of teachers. They are sufficiently equipped to conduct a fair and impartial inquiry whenever such issue legitimately comes into question. . . . Their obligation to determine the fitness of teachers is a reflection of their duties to protect the students from a significant danger of harm, whether it be physical or otherwise.[89]

The Superior Court relied on the 1952 U.S. Supreme Court decision in <u>Adler v. Board of Education of the City of New York</u>,[90] which supported the school board's traditional duty to protect the impressionable minds of children and support societal values:

> A teacher works in a sensitive area in a schoolroom. There he shapes the attitudes of young minds towards the society in which they live. In this, the state has a vital concern. That the school authorities have the right and duty to screen the officials, teachers, and employees as to their fitness to maintain the integrity of the schools as a part of ordered society, cannot be doubted.[91]

Although the New Jersey Superior Court could and probably should have relied on more recent precedent concerning the rights of teachers, it chose to revert back to a much older United States Supreme Court case to legitimize the outcome it wished to reach. The court concluded that since "human nature is such that beliefs and attitudes may not be shed by a teacher as he steps into the classroom," the school board had a right and a duty to fairly examine and then dismiss, if necessary, teachers who might cause harm of any nature to the school children. Failure to support societal norms would be one such potential harm.[92]

The United States Supreme Court refused to hear Gish's appeal in 1977, and he was dismissed from his teaching position. The case was a harbinger of the anti-homosexual backlash to come in 1977 and 1978. Four years later, however, a brief notice

267

in a GLBT community newspaper alerted this author that the outcome of the <u>Gish</u> litigation had changed radically. In 1981 the New Jersey State Board of Education reversed the previous decision of the State Education Commissioner in the <u>Gish</u> matter and announced a new policy that teachers could not be dismissed because they advocated controversial issues outside the classroom.[93] In language that echoed the <u>Morrison</u> nexus requirement, the new ruling stated that disciplinary action could occur only when the teacher's action resulted in "disruption of the school system or impairment of his capacity as a teacher." Since Gish had not mentioned his homosexuality in the classroom, the majority of the commissioners on the State Board of Education voted in his favor. Although the outcome provided Gish with the opportunity to sue the Paramus Board of Education for deprivation of his constitutional rights, he was not reinstated to his teaching position because the State Board of Education also held that he was appropriately dismissed for an arrest on possession of LSD and marijuana.

Apparently, during the initial litigation, Gish's apartment was raided by the police who seized the drugs. Gish maintained that they belonged to his roommate, and he was permitted to enter a drug rehabilitation program to have the charges against him dismissed. Despite this resolution of the criminal matter, the Board of Education was permitted to use the information about the arrest as additional grounds to fire Gish along with the homosexual political activities.

Members of the Paramus Board of Education responded by voicing traditional concerns that teachers, like clergy, should lead exemplary lives. "We might accept behavior from an actress that we wouldn't accept from a teacher." Another Board member stated, "For us to say we have to wait for the hazard to occur makes little sense. We do not wait for children to be killed before we require safety equipment on school buses or in school buildings."[94] This argument of prevention of harm to students became a strong force in the 1977 conservative backlash campaigns and continued to influence some school administrators in the 1980s.

Nevertheless, with decisions like <u>Aumiller</u> and <u>Gish</u>, a judicial and social trend was evident that constitutional freedoms could not be abridged based upon homosexual orientation, even within the teaching profession.[95]

CHAPTER CONCLUSIONS

The early 1970s was a period of legal conflict over the rights of the GLBT educators. Given the <u>Morrison</u> decision, one might have anticipated a sweeping series of cases that resolved the issue in favor of GLBT rights. In both the <u>Burton</u> and <u>Acanfora</u> litigation, for example, strong decisions in favor of homosexuals were rendered despite the ultimate holding in favor of the school boards. It appeared as though the next non-criminal GLBT educator case might be decided in favor of the teacher.

On the contrary, in 1977, one finds cases like <u>Gaylord</u>, in which the Court concluded that the status of being a homosexual was sufficient grounds for dismissal — which was a major step backward into the 1950s and 1960s legal mentality. This outcome was even more surprising in light of the expanding rights of the individual and the expanding protections being granted to minority groups.

One of the major reasons for this heated controversy was that the courts in the 1970s were being asked to confront and resolve a major social issue. Some courts successfully sidestepped the controversy altogether by focusing on tangential issues, as in the case of <u>Acanfora</u>, where one court ruled in terms of excessive public speech about homosexuality and the other court focused on failure to disclose significant employment details. What remained unresolved was whether or not it was legal to fire a teacher because of his or her sexual orientation. Part of the courts' reluctance to determine this issue was related to the potentially sweeping social and legal consequences if they ruled in favor of the GLBT educator. In these instances the judiciary was not prepared to advance new social policy and create a situation that paralleled the United States Supreme Court's highly unpopular stand on abortion in <u>Roe v. Wade</u>.

On the surface, the issue of employment of GLBT educators might not appear to be a critical aspect of the larger scheme of legal, social, or moral principles. Nevertheless, the issue embodied a wide range of points of disagreement between conservatives desiring to maintain the status quo, and liberals eager to alter the balance of power and resources within American society. Social definitions of family, child rearing, and morality might be redetermined if GLBT relationships were legitimized. Furthermore, control over one of the most influential institutions for cultural transmission was being threatened because of the challenge to the power of school administrators and community members to define morality.

From the early 1970s to the present, the entire debate over the employment of GLBT people as educators could be characterized as a struggle whereby each side was trying to assert a standard of morality which would serve as the operating definition in a wide variety of social realms. The perspective that succeeded would enjoy tremendous power and influence, not only in the schools, but in other American institutions such as politics, religion, and law. Specific to the schools, however, previously sacrosanct authority in hiring, firing, and retention decisions might no longer be assured. School administrators and parents faced the possibility of being ordered to work with individuals who, in their opinion, might further threaten their power, values, and lifestyle by being legitimized within the schools and allowed to influence the children.

By 1973, men and women who adhered to GLBT life asserted that their civil liberties extended to employment protection based upon sexual orientation. They were aided in their assertions by teacher unions and legal advocates who felt that there were issues within the GLBT educator controversy that were common to all teachers and minorities. Probably the most common theme was the right of individuals to live their lives without intrusion by government and employers, as long as the individual's behavior did not harm others. Not surprisingly, the courts were caught in this legal dilemma that has been an ongoing debate at least since 1859 when

John Stuart Mill articulated the perspective of individual freedom discussed in Chapter Six.

By the 1970s, the legal outcome was no longer predictable. In fact, the pendulum at first seemed to be swinging in favor of the GLBT educator. Community disapproval of victimless GLBT conduct seemed outweighed by emergent constitutional doctrines of equal protection, due process, privacy, and civil rights. In response to the legal conundrum, community leadership began to fear that the courts would eliminate the arguably subjective standards of immorality as being void for vagueness. The time had come for the traditional community spokespeople to appeal to other institutions to assure the continued pre-eminence of the traditional perspective. Thus, during the late 1970s state-wide legislative efforts developed to take the power of resolving this issue out of the hands of judges. In California, Oklahoma, and Florida various legislative and political actions were launched to articulate into law the traditional stance that homosexuality was immoral. Once established as a legal doctrine, the issues of vagueness and judicial discretion would be avoided, preventing more legal decisions in favor of GLBT educators.

An intelligent person is never frightened of knowledge, never frightened of education, never frightened of giving these opportunities to others.

— *Keith Lockhart*

(Boston Pops' conductor in response to question about Senator Jesse Helms' (R-NC) efforts to drastically cut federal funding for the arts, 1996.)

EPILOGUE

January 23, 1973. Every paper in the nation headlined the death of former President, Lyndon Baines Johnson. Lost as an aside was a brief announcement. The United States Supreme Court, ruling the day before in <u>Roe v. Wade</u>, had held as unconstitutional state laws prohibiting voluntary abortions during the first trimester of a woman's pregnancy. Supporters of the ruling hailed it as a profound statement of personal freedoms in our society, and very few voices of opposition were featured except the statements from a small number of Catholic leaders. The significance of this brief news story was not lost on Rev. Jerry Falwell.

"I don't usually let the newspaper interfere with my breakfast with my family, but on that day my coffee grew cold and my family ate alone. I sat there staring at the <u>Roe v. Wade</u> story growing more and more fearful of the consequences of the Supreme Court's act and wondering why so few voices had been raised against it. Already, leaders of the Catholic Church had spoken courageously in opposition to the Court's decision; but the voices of my Protestant Christian brothers and sisters, especially the voices of evangelical and fundamentalist leaders, remained silent."[1]

Falwell was the leader of the Thomas Road Baptist Church in Lynchburg, Virginia, which had been hailed as "the fastest growing church in the nation" by *Newsweek* magazine the year before. He was outraged by and fearful of the Supreme Court's curb on the power of the states. Images of the Civil War, with Northern troops invading the Southern states to impose Northern values concerning slavery on a soveriegn Confederate nation, were burned into his character. Essential to his Southern identity was the belief that every state should be free to determine its destiny. Majority rule should serve as the purveyor of personal entitlements.

This absolute identity with local values had placed Falwell in controversial positions already and had enhanced his following. With the advent of the Civil Rights Movement in the South in the early 1960s, for example, Falwell had forcefully preached that Northern liberals should mind their own business and stay out of the Southern debate over desegregation. Harsh attacks on the "arrogant, disruptive, and often violent wave of demonstrators arriving daily in the South," led Falwell to be labeled a racist and a segregationist.[2] In his autobiography, Falwell notes that as a Southerner, "I felt bullied and unjustly attacked by the army of white Northerners marching into the South, demanding that we follow their dictates in the running of our community and the ordering of our lives."[3] Clearly, Falwell's strong identification with his Confederate heritage was prominent in his beliefs.

Thus, the Supreme Court's holding in <u>Roe v. Wade</u> was just another example of Northern arrogance and curbs on local authority. Falwell made two vows to himself on that day in January of 1973. The first was that he would speak out against abortion at every opportunity so that local beliefs dictated political policy in each state. Second, Falwell vowed that he would build an evangelical movement so the next time a socially controversial situation arose, the national media would look to him to articulate the conservative religious perspective.

Four months after the <u>Roe v. Wade</u> decision, Falwell's aspirations were derailed temporarily. He and the other church leaders from the Thomas Road Baptist Church were charged with bond "fraud and deceit in twenty-five states" by the Securities and Exchange Commission (SEC) in relation to fundraising to expand their operations and build a religious college (Liberty University). Furthermore, the SEC maintained that the Thomas Road Baptist Church was insolvent and would never be able to repay its investors. Falwell wrote of this situation: "Whenever the people of God mobilize to win the world, Satan begins to plot against them."[4]

In August of 1973, the case went to trial in a local Lynchburg court. Although there was significant evidence of wrongdoing, the judge held that nothing seemed to have been done with criminal intent. In a brilliant move, Falwell suggested that a board of prominent local citizens who were not members of the Thomas Road Baptist Church be appointed to serve as overseers of the organization to make sure that things were done properly. Falwell previously had created a list of the men he wanted appointed, and each of them already had agreed to serve. Thus, provided with a gracious solution, the local judge ruled that no criminal actions were intended and dismissed all charges. Falwell would later admit in his autobiography that mistakes had been made in complying with bond measures and that "exaggerations" had occurred in the materials prepared for solicitation of investors. Falwell attributed the problems to "growing too fast."

With the SEC litigation behind him, Falwell launched his national television evangialism and educational efforts. In 1979, he formed the "The Moral Majority, Incorporated" to further his political efforts to create an organization of "sufficient numbers to turn back the tide of moral permissiveness, family breakdown, and general capitulation to evil and to foreign philosophies such as Marxism-Leninism."[5]

While Falwell was nationally prominent as a religious leader and television preacher by the late 1970s, it took a former Miss America contestant to "find the key to the conservative hearts."[6] Florida resident Anita Bryant would emerge as the spokesperson for traditional values during the Dade County struggle over GLBT rights. Shortly after her victory, conservative male political and religious leaders "cut her off at the knees," according to California State Senator John Briggs, who admitted to participating in this process. Anita Bryant had exposed a passionate, conservative political wellspring, and numerous male leaders rushed to claim the spoils. Nevertheless, few individuals are so indelibly linked to the struggle between personal liberty and majority rule in the arena of gay and lesbian educators as is Anita Bryant. An historical parallel comes to mind. When Abraham Lincoln was introduced to Harriet Beecher Stowe, the author of *Uncle Tom's Cabin*, Lincoln is said to have remarked, "So this is the little lady who started the big war." In may ways, for better and for worse, Anita Bryant holds that distinction in this more recent struggle between personal freedoms and public constraints.

Constitutional Provisions and Statutes

The First Amendment to the United States Constitution

Congress shall make no law respecting an establishment of religion, or prohibiting the free exercise thereof; or abridging the freedom of speech, or of the press; or the right of the people peaceably to assemble, and to petition the Government for a redress of grievances.

The Fourteenth Amendment to the United States Constitution

Section 1. All persons born or naturalized in the United States, and subject to the jurisdiction thereof, are citizens of the United States and of the State wherein they reside. No State shall make or enforce any law which shall abridge the privileges or immunities of citizens of the United States; nor shall any State deprive any person of life, liberty, or property, without due process of law; nor deny to any person within its jurisdiction the equal protection of the laws....

Section 5. The Congress shall have power to enforce, by appropriate legislation, the provisions of this article.

42 U. S. C., SECTION 1983
(THE CIVIL RIGHTS ACT OF 1871)

Every person who, under color of any statute, ordinance, regulation, custom or usage of any State or Territory, subjects, or causes to be subjected, any citizen of the United States or other person within the jurisdiction thereof to the deprivation of any rights, privileges, or immunities secured by the Constitution and the laws, shall be liable to the party injured in an action at law, suit in equity, or other proper proceeding for redress.

California's Proposition 6
The Briggs Initiative

Initiative Measure to be Submitted Directly to the Voters

The Attorney General of California has prepared the following title and summary of the chief purpose and points of the proposed measure:

School Employees — Homosexuality — Initiative Statute

Provides for filing charges against schoolteachers, teachers' aides, school administrators or counselors for advocating, soliciting, imposing, encouraging or promoting private or public sexual acts defined in sections 286(a) and 288(a) of the Penal Code between persons of same sex in a manner likely to come to the attention of other employees or students; or publicly and indiscreetly engaging in said acts. Prohibits hiring and requires dismissal of such persons if school board determines them unfit for service after considering enumerated guidelines. In dismissal cases only, provides for two-stage hearings, written findings, judicial review. Financial impact: Unknown but potentially substantial local cost to school districts depending on number of cases which receive an administrative hearing.

THE PEOPLE OF THE STATE OF CALIFORNIA DO ENACT AS FOLLOWS:

Section 1. Section 44837.5 is added to the Education Code, to read:

44837.5 One of the most fundamental interests of the state is the establishment and the preservation of the family unit. Consistent with this interest is the state's duty to protect its impressionable youth from influences which are antithetical to this vital interest. This duty is particularly compelling when the state undertakes to educate its youth, and, by law, requires them to be exposed to the state's chosen educational environment throughout their formative years.

A schoolteacher, teacher's aide, school administrator or counselor has a professional duty directed exclusively towards the moral as well as intellectual, social and civic development of young and impressionable students.

As a result of continued close and prolonged contact with schoolchildren, a teacher, teacher's aide, school administrator or counselor becomes a role model whose words, behavior and actions are likely to be emulated by students coming under his or her care, instruction, supervision, administration, guidance and protection.

For these reasons, the state finds a compelling interest in refusing to employ and in terminating the employment of a schoolteacher, a teacher's aide, a school administrator or a counselor, subject to reasonable restrictions and qualifications, who engage in public homosexual activity and/or public homosexual conduct directed at, or likely to come to the attention of, schoolchildren or other school employees.

This proscription is essential since such activity and conduct undermines that state's interest in preserving and perpetuating the conjugal family unit.

The purpose of Sections 44837.6 and 44933.5 is to proscribe employment of a person whose homosexual activities or conduct are determined to render him or her unfit for service.

Section 2. Section 44837.6 is added to the Education Code, to read:

44837.6(a) The governing board of a school district shall refuse to hire as an employee any person who has engaged in public homosexual activity or public homosexual conduct should the board determine that said activity or conduct renders the person unfit for service;

(b) For purposes of this section, (1) "public homosexual activity" means the commission of an act defined in subdivision (a) of Section 286 of the Penal Code, or in subdivision (a) of Section 288a of the Penal Code, upon any other person of the same sex, which is not discreet and not practiced in private, whether or not such an act, at the time of its commission, constituted a crime; (2) "public homosexual conduct" means the advocating, soliciting, imposing, encouraging, or promoting of private or public homosexual activity directed at, or likely to come to the attention of schoolchildren and/or other employees; and (3) "employee" means a probationary or permanent certified teacher, teacher's aide, school administrator or counselor;

(c) In evaluating the public homosexual activity and/or the public homosexual conduct in question for the purposes if determining an applicant's unfitness for service as an employee, a board shall consider the factors delineated in Section 44933.5(f).

Section 3. Section 44933.5 is added to the Education Code, to read:

44933.5(a) In addition to the grounds specified in Sections 44932, 44948 and 44949, or any other provision of law, the commission of "public homosexual activity" or "public homosexual conduct" by an employee shall subject the employee to dismissal upon a determination by the board that said activity or conduct renders the employee unfit for service. Dismissal shall be determined in accordance with the procedures contained in this section;

(b) For the purposes of this section, (1) "public homosexual activity" means the commission of an act defined in subdivision (a) of Section 286 of the Penal Code, or in subdivision (a) of Section 288a of the Penal Code, upon any other person of the same sex, which is not discreet and not practiced in private, whether or not such an act, at the time of its commission, constituted a crime;

public homosexual conduct" means the advocating, soliciting, imposing, encouraging, or promoting of private or public homosexual activity directed at, or likely to come to the attention of schoolchildren and/or other employees; and (3) "employee" means a probationary or permanent certified teacher, teacher's aide, school administrator or counselor;

(c) Notwithstanding any other provision of law regarding dismissal procedures, the governing board, upon the filing of written charges that the person has committed public homosexual activity or public homosexual conduct, duly signed and verified by the person filing the charges, or upon written charges formulated by the governing board, shall set a probable cause hearing on the charges within fifteen (15) working days after the filing or formulating of written charges and forward notice to the employee of the charges not less than ten (10) working days prior to the probable cause hearing. The notice shall inform the employee of the time and place of the governing board's hearing to determine if probable cause exists that the employee has engaged in public homosexual activity or public homosexual conduct. Such notice shall also inform the employee of his or her right to be present with counsel and to present evidence which may have bearing on the board's determination of whether there is probable cause. This hearing shall be held in private session in accordance with Govt. Code section 54957, unless the employee requests a public hearing. A finding of probable cause shall be made within thirty (30) working days after the filing or formulation of written charges by not less than a simple majority vote of the entire board.

(d) Upon a finding of probable cause, the governing board may, if it deems such action necessary, immediately suspend the employee from his or her duties. The board shall, within thirty-two (32) working days after the filing or formulation of written charges, notify the employee in writing of its findings and decision to suspend, if imposed, and the board's reasons therefor;

(e) Whether or not the employee is immediately suspended, and notwithstanding any other provision of law, the governing board shall, within thirty (30) working days after the notice of the finding of probable cause, hold a hearing on the truth of the charges upon which a finding of probable cause was based and whether such charges, if found to be true, render the employee unfit for service. This hearing shall be held in private session in accordance with Govt. Code section 54957, unless the employee requests a public hearing. The governing board's decision as to whether the employee is unfit for service shall be made within thirty (30) working days after the conclusion of this hearing. A decision that the employee is unfit for service shall be determined by not less than a simple majority vote of the entire board. The written decision shall include findings of fact and conclusions of law;

(f) Factors to be considered by the board in evaluating the charges of public homosexual activity or public homosexual conduct in question and in determining unfitness for service shall include, but not be limited to: (1) the likelihood that the activity or conduct may adversely affect students or other employees; (2) the proximity or remoteness in time or location of the conduct to the employee's responsibilities; (3) the extenuating or aggravating circumstances which, in the judgment of the board, must be examined in weighing the evidence; and (4) whether the conduct included acts, words or deeds of a continuing or comprehensive nature which would tend to encourage, promote, or dispose schoolchildren toward private or public homosexual activity or private or public homosexual conduct;

(g) If, by a preponderance of the evidence, the employee is found to have engaged in public homosexual activity or public homosexual conduct which renders the employee unfit for service, the employee shall be dismissed from employment. The decision of the governing board shall be subject to judicial review.

Section 4. Severability Clause.

If any provision of this enactment or the application thereof to any person or circumstance is held invalid, such invalidity shall not affect other provisions or application of this enactment which can be given effect without the invalid provision or application, and to this end the provisions of this enactment are severable.

OKLAHOMA STATUTE TITLE 70, SECTION 6-103.15

A. As used in this section:

1. Public homosexual activity means the commission of an act defined in Section 886 of Title 21 of the Oklahoma Statutes, if such act is:

    a. committed with a person of the same sex, and

    b. indiscreet and not practiced in private;

2. "Public homosexual conduct" means advocating, soliciting, imposing, encouraging or promoting public or private homosexual activity in a manner that creates a substantial risk that such conduct will come to the attention of school children or school employees; and

3. "Teacher" means a person as defined in Section 1-116 of Title 70 of the Oklahoma Statutes.

B. In addition to any ground set forth in Section 6-103 of Title 70 of the Oklahoma Statutes, a teacher, student teacher, or a teacher's aide may be refused employment or re-employment, dismissed, or suspended after a finding that the teacher or teacher's aide has:

1. Engaged in public homosexual conduct or activity; and

2. Has been rendered unfit, because of such conduct or activity, to hold a position as a teacher, student teacher or teacher's aide.

C. The following factors shall be considered in making the determination whether the teacher, student teacher or teacher's aide has been rendered unfit for his position:

1. The likelihood that the activity or conduct may adversely affect students or school employees;

2. The proximity in time and place of the activity or conduct to the teacher's, student teacher's or teacher's aide's official duties;

3. Any extenuating or aggravating circumstances; and

4. Whether the conduct or activity is of a repeated or continuing nature which tends to encourage or dispose school children toward similar conduct or activity.

STATUS OF SODOMY LAWS IN THE UNITED STATES — AUGUST 31, 1996

In the first column, M indicates misdemeanor, F indicates felony; a number indicates age of consent. In the state information, SS indicates same-sex only, while GN indicates gender neutral prohibitions.

	ALABAMA
M	§13A-6-65, Sexual Misconduct,
16	1 year/$2000; Does not apply to married couples.

	ALASKA
M	Repealed 1978, effective 1980.

	ARIZONA
M	§13-1411, Crime Against Nature
16	(anal intercourse), 30 days/$500
M	§13-1412, Lewd and Lascivious Acts, 30 days/$500.

	ARKANSAS
14	
M	§-14-122, Sodomy, 1 year/$1000, SS.

	CALIFORNIA
18	Repealed 1975, effective 1976.

COLORADO
15   Repealed 1971, effective 1972.

CONNECTICUT
16   Repealed 1969, effective 1971.

DELAWARE
12   Repealed 1972, effective 1973.

FLORIDA
M   §800.02, Unnatural and Lascivious Acts,
60 days/$500.

GEORGIA
F   §16-6-2, Sodomy, 1 to 20 years; GN;
M   §16-6-15, Solicitation of Sodomy,
14   1 year/$1000.

HAWAII
16   Repealed and effective 1973.

IDAHO
F   §18-6605, Crime Against Nature,
18   5 years to life; GN.

ILLINOIS
16   Repealed 1961, effective 1962.

INDIANA
16   Repealed 1976, effective 1977.

IOWA
14   Repealed 1976, effective 1978.

16   KANSAS
M   §21-3505, Sodomy, 6 mo./$1000, SS.

KENTUCKY
14   §21-3505, Criminal sodomy. No more than 6
M   months imprisonment.

LOUISIANA
F   §14.89, Crime Against Nature, 5 years with or
without hard labor/$2000, GN.
17   GN; Held unconstitutional by Orleans Parish
Court, appeal pending.

MAINE
14   Repealed 1975, effective 1976.

MARYLAND
F   Art.27-§553, Sodomy, not more than 10 years, GN.
F   Art.27-§554, Unnatural or Perverted Sexual
16 Practices, 10 years/$1000, or both, GN.

MASSACHUSETTS
F   G.L.c. 274, §34, Sodomy/Buggery (abominable and
18 detestable crime against nature, not more than 20
years in state prison.
G.L.c. 274, §35, Unnatural and Lascivious Acts, Fine
between $100 & $1000/state prison for 5 years or
hard labor for 2.5 years. Validity questionable.

MICHIGAN
F   §750.158, Crime Against Nature, 15 years;
16 GN; Held unconstitutional as applied to private,
consensual adult behavior. Michigan
Organization for Human Rights v. Kelly (Wayne
County Circ. Ct. 1990), only applies to Wayne
County; under appeal. Held consitutional by
Michigan Court of Appeals (People v. Brashier)
1992, effective outside of Wayne County.

16 MINNESOTA
M §609.293, Sodomy, 1 year/$3000.

18 MISSISSIPPI
F   §97-29-59, Unnatural Intercourse, 10 years; GN.

16 MISSOURI
M §566.090, Sexual Misconduct, 1 year/$1000, SS.

MONTANA
16 §45-5-505, Deviate Sexual Conduct,
F   10 years/$50,000, SS.

NEBRASKA
16 Repealed 1977, effective 1978.

NEVADA
F   §201-190, 1993 Amend. limits crime to anal or oral
16 sex in public, state prison 1 to 6 years.

NEW HAMPSHIRE
16 Repealed 1973, effective 1975.

NEW JERSEY
16 Repealed 1978, effective 1979.

NEW MEXICO
13 Repealed and effective 1975.

NEW YORK
17 Held unconstitutional by State Supreme Court,
People v. Onofre (1980).

NORTH CAROLINA
F §14-177, Crime Against Nature, 10 years/
16 discretionary fine; GN.

NORTH DAKOTA
M §12.1.20, Deviant Sex Acts, 1 year/$1000, or both.
F Repealed 1975, effective 1977.

OHIO
16 Repealed 1972, effective 1974.

18 OKLAHOMA
F Tit.21-§886, Crime Against Nature, 10 years.

OREGON
18 Repealed 1971, effective 1972.

PENNSYLVANIA
14 Invalidated by Commonwealth v. Bonadio (1980).

RHODE ISLAND
F §11-10-1, Crime Against Nature, 7–20 years;
16 GN. Includes "ordinary extramarital intercourse."

16 SOUTH CAROLINA
F §16-15-120, Buggery, 5 years/$500; GN.

SOUTH DAKOTA
16 Repealed effective 1977.

TENNESSEE
M §39-13-510, Homosexual Acts, 30 days/$50,
18 SS; Held unconstitutional 26 June 1996.

TEXAS
F §21.06, SS. Repealed with the dismissal of
17 Morales v. State (1994).
M Class "C" Misdemeanor created concerning anal and
oral sex, $500 fine, GN.

UTAH
M   §76-5-403, Sodomy, 6 months/$1000; does not
14   apply to married couples, GN.

VERMONT
15   Repealed and effective 1977.

VIRGINIA
F   §18.2-361, Crime Against Nature, 5–20 years in state
16   prison; GN.

WASHINGTON
18   Repealed 1975, effective 1976.

WEST VIRGINIA
16   Repealed and effective 1976.

WISCONSIN
18   Repealed and effective 1983.

WYOMING
18   Repealed and effective 1977.

U.S. POSSESSIONS

WASHINGTON D.C.
16   Repealed and effective 1993.

AMERICAN SAMOA
14   Repealed 1978, effective 1979.

GUAM
Repealed 1976.

NORTH MARIANA ISLAND
Repealed.

PUERTO RICO
F   Tit.33, §4065, Deviant Sexual Intercourse, SS;
     and Crime Against Nature, GN, 10 years in prison.

VIRGIN ISLANDS
F14 Tit.14, c103, §2061, Repealed 1984,
M16 effective 1985.

RESEARCH METHODOLOGY

In the preceding chapters, the controversy over the employment of homosexual school teachers was placed in its legal, educational, and historical contexts. This Appendix serves to overview the actual case law on lesbian and gay male teachers. Although several of the cases presented in this study are newly-found additions to the body of knowledge about homosexual teachers, it remains true that relatively few appellate cases have surfaced about the topic. Procedural mechanisms in the criminal law system have brought some of these cases to our attention, but they also have compounded the problems of studying this invisible population.

HIGHLIGHTED CASES

When the four LEXIS word searches were completed, more than 200 cases were highlighted for consideration. This large number was due to the nexus between terms for homosexuals and terms for teachers found within the body of the published opinion. Ultimately, most of these cases were excluded from this study because they offered very little insight into the relationship of being both a teacher and a GLBT person. In these court opinions concerning divorce, child custody, robbery, or murder, only one feature stood out as significant.[1] When the facts of each case were presented, the homosexual who was also a teacher invariably resided in a different county from the one in which he or she taught. This observation suggests that lesbian and gay educators frequently try to manage the information about their lifestyle by maintaining geographic distance between themselves and their community of employment.

If a highlighted but rejected case did not pertain to these legal difficulties, it referenced the landmark employment decision set forth by the California State Supreme Court in <u>Morrison</u> that is discussed in detail in Chapter Nine. With the <u>Morrison</u> precedent — that employers had to prove there was some nexus between the employee's offensive conduct and job responsibilities before termination was permissible — numerous heterosexual and homosexual individuals in education and other professions began to litigate their dismissals. After <u>Morrison,</u> a teacher who stole a motorcycle,[2] lived with a member of the opposite sex,[3] was a transsexual,[4] or engaged in "free love" and group sex[5] was able to argue that the Board of Education had to consider whether or not his or her out-of-school behavior seriously affected his or her teaching performance or effectiveness. For this reason, even when the case itself did not concern homosexuality, all of these employment cases were highlighted by the computer search because of their reference to the <u>Morrison</u> decision.

ANALYZED CASES TO 1987

After eliminating all the litigation that did not pertain directly to the experience of being a lesbian or gay school teacher or university professor, 39 cases in 17 states remained available for analysis up to 1987. Table 1 below lists the 17 states that were the loci for this litigation.

Each of the 39 cases commenced through one of four scenarios of discovery. Eight people (20 percent) were accused of having sex with students, so their litigation focused on criminal culpability or tort liability. Most of the cases before 1973 arose because of arrests for lewd sexual conduct, which was explained in Chapter Eight. Thus, 10 cases (26 percent) were initiated for criminal conduct (lewd sexual conduct) which served as grounds for school employment dismissal based upon immorality. After 1973, the case law arises because of discovery through rumor or a noncriminal incident (13 cases, or 33 percent), or because the teachers publicly asserted they were homosexual (8 cases, or 20 percent).

Table 1: States Involved In Litigation on Dismissal to 1987

Region	State	# Cases	Percent
West		**18**	**46%**
	1. California	11	
	2. Washington	3	
	3. Oregon	3	
	4. Alaska	1	
South		**8**	**20%**
	5. Florida	3	
	6. Louisiana	3	
	7. Maryland	1	
	8. West Virginia	1	
Central		**7**	**18%**
	9. Michigan	4	
	10. Illinois	1	
	11. Wisconsin	1	
	12. Ohio	1	
Northeast		**3**	**8%**
	13. Delaware	1	
	14. New Jersey	1	
	15. Massachusetts	1	
Midwest		**3**	**8%**
	16. Minnesota	1	
	17. Iowa	2	
Total		**39**	**100%**

Eleven (28 percent) of the 39 cases under consideration arose in California. As explained in Chapter Eight, this is because local police officials, particularly in the communities of Long Beach and Los Angeles, made active use of state legislation enacted after World War II aimed at ferreting out immoral educators.

Table 2: Dismissal Cases Minus "With Student" Incidents to 1987

Region	State	# Cases	Percent
West		**16**	**52%**
	1. California	11	
	2. Washington	2	
	3. Oregon	2	
	4. Alaska	1	
South		**7**	**22%**
	5. Florida	3	
	6. Louisiana	2	
	7. Maryland	1	
	8. West Virginia	1	
Central		**3**	**10%**
	9. Michigan	1	
	10. Illinois	0	
	11. Wisconsin	1	
	12. Ohio	1	
Northeast		**2**	**6%**
	13. Delaware	1	
	14. New Jersey	1	
	15. Massachusetts	0	
Midwest		**3**	**10%**
	16. Minnesota	1	
	17. Iowa	2	
Total		**31**	**100%**

The significance of the California legislation is even more evident in Table 2, which eliminates those cases involving sex with students. In this instance, more than 35 percent of the litigation can be attributed to these statutes. It may be the case that California represents a wider political spectrum than most states, and consequently it is an active arena for normative conflict.

On one hand the GLBT population in California has been large and increasingly visible since the 1940s. On the other hand, the sex crime panic of the 1950s provided police officials in that state with strong legal sanctions against same-sex conduct, especially as it pertained to educators, until the mid-1970s. To date, it appears that no other state required law enforcement officials to inform school authorities of teacher misconduct, as did California with Penal Code, Section 291. The only state that experienced a similar panic was Florida. All three Florida cases occurred because of an organized effort by state officials in 1959 to crack down on the "Communist, pinko, queer" element within the state by investigating the sexual orientation of public school teachers, as discussed in Chapter Eight.

Since appellate decisions concerned with criminal conduct often just cite the statutory reference and do not describe the incident, there may be many more cases involving homosexual school teachers that could not be retrieved under current search procedures. On the other hand, apparently only the state of California has actively sought to eliminate "immoral" educators by using the criminal legal system to enhance the powers of the Board Of Education, so the unavailable data may be relevant only to that state.

Because so many of the cases arose through criminal misconduct, the balance between male and female teacher representation has been distorted. Of the 39 individuals involved in GLBT educator litigation, only 10 (26 percent) were women. Up to 1987, none of them was revealed as lesbian through criminal misconduct. Chapter Eight offers a more detailed analysis of the reasons for this gender disparity.

TABLE OF CASE MATERIALS REFERENCED

* GLBT Educator Cases Used in Analysis. Page numbers are provided for cases cited in this book. Page numbers for some of the cases are missing; they are part of the upcoming sequel to this volume.

Abington School District v. Schempp, 374 U.S. 203 (1963).

* Acanfora v. Board of Education of Montgomery County, 359 F.Supp. 834 (D. Maryland 1973).

* Acanfora v. Board of Education of Montgomery County, 491 F.2d 498 (4th Cir., 1974). Cert. denied, 419 U. S. 839 (1974). (pp. 13, 115–116, 240, 248–257, 269, 316, 335, 358–360)
— Brief for the Plaintiff-Appellant (Acanfora).
— Brief for Appellees (Board of Education).
— Brief Amicus Curiae for the National Education Association in the Fourth Circuit.
— Reply Brief for Plaintiff-Appellant.
— Motion for Plaintiff-Appellant for Leave To File Post-Argument Memorandum and Memorandum.
— Brief Amicus Curiae of the American Civil Liberties Union in the Fourth Circuit.
— Exhibits to Plaintiff-Appellant's Brief.
— Joint Appendix.

Adler v. Board of Education of the City of New York, 342 U.S. 485; 72 S.Ct. 380 (1952). (pp. 267, 362)

* Amundsen v. State Board of Education, Civ. No. 37942 Cal. Ct. App. (2d Dist., 1971). (pp. 192, 221, 350, 354)

Andrews v. Drew Municipal, 507 F.2d 611 (1975).

Anonymous v. Kissinger, 499 F.2d 1097 (D.C. Cir., 1974).

Anonymous v. Macy, 398 F.2d 317 (5th Cir., 1968). Cert. denied, 393 U.S. 1041 (1968).

* Aumiller v. University of Delaware, 434 F.Supp. 1273 (D. Del. 1977). (pp. 263–266, 269, 361)

Barbier v. Connolly, 113 U.S. 27 (1885).

Beebee v. Haslett, 66 Mich. App. 718 (1976).

Bekiaris v. Board of Education of the City of Modesto, 6 C.3d 575; 100 Cal. Rptr. 16 (1972). (p. 355)

Blodgett v. Board of Trustees, 20 Cal.App.3d 183; 97 Cal.Rptr. 406 (1971).

* Blouin v. Loyola University, La.App., 325 So.2d 848 (1967). (pp. 362–363)

* Board of Education of El Monte School District of Los Angeles County v. Marcus Calderon, 35 Cal. App.3d 490; 110 Cal. Rptr. 916 (1973). Cert. denied, 419 U.S. 807 (1974). (pp. 223–224, 355)

* Board of Education v. Jack Millette, 19 Cal.3d 691; 139 Cal. Rptr. 700 (1977).

Board of Education v. Swan, 41 Cal.2d 546; 261 P.2d 261 (1953). (pp. 223, 355)

Board of Regents v. Roth, 408 U.S. 564 (1972).

Board of Trustees v. Judge, 50 C.A.3d 920; 123 Cal. Rptr. 830 (1975).

Board of Trustees v. Stubblefield, 16 C.A.3d 820; 94 Cal. Rptr. 318 (1971).

Board of Trustees of Mt. San Antonio Junior College District v. Hartman, 55 Cal. Rptr. 144 (1966). (p. 335)

Bowers v. Bowers, 257 Ark. 125; 514 S.W.2d 387 (1974). (p. 363)

Bowers v. Hardwick, 760 F.2d 1202; 765 F.2d 1123; 106 S.Ct. 342; 106 S.Ct. 2841 (1986). (pp. 94–95, 135, 140–141, 311, 337, 339)

* Bozarth v. Harper Creek, 94 Mich. App. 351 (1979).

Brandenburg v. Ohio, 395 U.S. 444 (1969). (pp. 91, 93, 330)

* Bradshaw v. State Board of Education, Fla., 149 So.2d 529 (1963). (pp. 24, 183–184, 319)

Brown v. Board of Education, 347 U.S. 483 (1954). (pp. 130–132, 138, 337)

Bryson v. United States, 396 U.S. 64 (1969). (pp. 256, 360)

* Burton v. Cascade School District, 353 F.Supp. 254 (D. Or., 1973). (pp. 229–233, 244–249, 269, 358)

* Burton v. Cascade School District, 512 F.2d 850 (9th Cir., 1975). Cert. denied, 423 U.S. 859 (1975).

* California Federation of Teachers v. March Fong Eu, Petition for a Writ of Mandate to the California Supreme Court, May 24, 1978. (pp. 326–327)

Chaffin v. Frye, 45 Cal. App.3d 39; 119 Cal. Rptr. 22 (1975).

Clark v. Ann Arbor, 419 Mich. 953; 21 Ed. Law Rep. 690 (1984).

Cole v. Arkansas, 333 U.S. 196 (1948).

* Commonwealth of Massachusetts v. Pilecki, Mass (1987).

Connick v. Myers, 461 U.S. 138; 103 S.Ct. 1684; 75 L.Ed.2d 708 (1983).

* Conway v. Hampshire County Board of Education, 352 S.E.2d 739 (1986). Rehearing denied, 17 February 1987.

Coupeville v. Vivian, 36 Wn. App. 728; 677 P.2d 192 (1984).

Curran v. Mount Diablo, 147 Cal. App.3d 712; 195 Cal. Rptr. 325 (1983).

Dennis v. United States, 384 U.S. 855 (1966). (pp. 256, 360)

Dept. of Education et. al. v. Gerald A. Lewis et. al., Supreme Court of Florida, No. 61, 4 February 1982.

Di Genova v. State Board of Education, 288 P.2d 862 (1955). (p. 335)

Doe v. Commonwealth's Attorney for the City of Richmond, 403 F.Supp. 1199 (E.D.,Va., 1975), aff'd., mem., 425 U.S. 901 (1976). (pp. 140, 338)

East Hartford Ed. v. Board of Education, 562 F.2d 838 (1977).

Epperson v. Arkansas, 393 U.S. 97 (1968). (p. 333)

* Ferndale Education Association v. School District No. 2, 67 Mich. App. 645 (1976). (p. 362)

Rex Fisher v. Fairbanks North Star, 704 P.2d 213 (1985).

* George Fountain v. State Board of Education, 157 C.A.2d 463; 320 P.2d 899 (1958). (pp. 191, 194–195, 220, 350)

Fricke v. Lynch, 491 F.Supp. 381 (1980).

* Galli v. Kirkeby, 398 Mich. 527 (1976).

Gay Alliance of Students v. Matthews, 544 F.2d 162 (4th Cir., 1976).

Gay Lib v. University of Missouri, 588 F.2d 848 (8th Cir., 1977). Cert. denied, 434 U.S. 1080 (1978).

* Gaylord v. Tacoma School District No. 10, 85 Wn.2d 348; 535 .2d 804 (1975).

* Gaylord v. Tacoma School District No. 10, 88 Wash.2d 286; 559 P.2d 1340 (1977). Cert. denied, U.S. 286 (1977). (pp. 86, 240, 258–263, 266, 269, 329, 358, 360–361)

In re Georgesen, No. 53359, Cal. Superior Ct., Humbolt County, 21 February 1974.

* Gish v. Board of Education, 145 N.J. Super. 96; 366 A.2d 1337 (1976). Cert. denied, 434 U.S. 879 (1977). (pp. 240, 265–269, 361)

Givhan v. Western Line Consolidated School District, 439 U.S. 410 (1979).

Glen West v. The State of Alabama, 57 Ala.App. 596; 329 So.2d 653 (1976). (p. 363)

Goldsmith v. Board of Education, 66 Cal.App. 157; 225 P. 783 (1924). (pp. 223, 355)

* Governing Board of Mountain View v. Metcalf, 36 Cal.App.3d 546; 111 Cal. Rptr. 724 (1974). (pp. 224–225, 355)

Griswold v. Connecticut, 381 U.S. 479 (1965). (pp. 139–140, 338)

In The Matter of Paula Grossman, 127 N.J. Super. 13 (1974). (pp. 354, 363)

Hoagland v. Mount Vernon, 95 Wn2d 424; 623 P.2d 1156 (1981). (pp. 354, 363)

Immerman v. Immerman, 176 Cal. App.2d 122; 1 Cal. Rptr. 298 (1959).

Isaacson v. Isaacson, No. D6867, Wash. Super. Ct., King County, December 22, 1972.

James v. Board of Education, 461 F.2d 566 (2d Cir., 1972).

Jame v. West Virginia Board of Regents, 322 F.Supp. 217 (S.D.W.Va. 1971). (p. 360)

In re Jane B., 85 Misc.2d 515; 380 N.Y.S.2d 848 (Sup. Ct., 1976).

Jarvella v. Willoughby-Eastlake City School District Board of Education, 12 O.Misc. 288; 41 O.O.(2d) 423 (1967). (pp. 191–192, 201–203, 206, 352)

Johnson v. Branch, 364 F.2d 177 (4th Cir., 1966). Cert. denied, 385 U.S. 1003 (1967).

Keyishian v. Board of Regents, 385 U.S. 589 (1967). (p. 333)

In re Koop, Nos. 28218-28219, Wash. Super. Ct., Pierce County, Juv. Dept., (February 6, 1976).

Kusper v. Pontikes, 414 U.S. 51 (1973).

* Lerner v. Los Angeles City Board of Education, 59 C.2d 382; 29 Cal. Rptr. 657; 380 P.2d 97 (1963). (pp. 191, 194–195, 349, 351)

* Lish v. Anchorage School District, Superior Court, Alaska (1978).

Los Angeles Teachers Local 1021 v. Los Angeles City Board of Education, 71 Cal.2d 551; 455 P.2d 827; 78 Cal. Rptr. 723 (1969).

Loving v. Virginia, 388 U.S. 1 (1967). (p. 338)

Lusk v. Estes, 361 F.Supp. 653 (N.D., Tes., 1973).

Don Ray Maupin v. Independent School District No. 26 of Ottawa County, Oklahoma, Sup. Ct. of Okla., 623 P2d 396 (1981).

* McConnell v. Anderson, 451 F.2d 193 (8th Cir., 1971). Cert. denied, 405 U.S. 1046 (1972). (pp. 221, 354–355)

McLaughlin v. Board of Medical Examiners, 35 C.A.3d 1010; 111 Cal. Rptr. 353 (1973).

* Mercier v. Evergreen School District, Superior Court, Washington (1985 and 1986). (pp. 240, 358)

Mitchell v. Mitchell, No. 240665, Cal. Super. Ct., Santa Clara County, June 8, 1972.

* Moe, Roe, Doe, Doe, Doe, and Moe v. The State Board of Education of the State of Oklahoma, Complaint of Plaintiffs', Filed August 31, 1979 in U.S. District Court. (pp. 83–89)
— Brief in Support of Filing Complaint, August 31, 1979.
— Brief in Support of Defendants' Application for Order of Dismissal, Filed September 18, 1979.
— Brief in Support of Defendants' Motion to Dismiss or, in the Alternative, Application for an Order of Abstention, Filed September 18, 1979.
— Brief by Plaintiff in Oppostion to Defendants' Motion for Order of Dismissal or Abstention.
— Response to Plaintiffs' Brief in Opposition to Defendants' Motion for Order of Dismissal or Abstention, October 19, 1979.
— Brief Amicus Curiae in Support of Plaintiffs', American Civil Liberties Union and The National Gay Rights Project, March, 1980.

* Morrison v. State Board of Education, 74 Cal. Rptr. 116 (1969).

* Morrison v. State Board of Education, 1 Cal.3d 214; 461 P.2d 365; 82 Cal. Rptr. 175 (1969). (pp. 24, 30, 164, 203, 213–223, 225–227, 235, 246, 258, 268–269, 294, 319, 346, 353–354)

* Moser v. State Board of Education, 22 Cal. App.3d 988; 101 Cal. Rptr. 86 (2d District, 1972). (pp. 222–223, 355)

Mount Healey Board of Education v. Doyle, 429 U.S. 274 (1977).

M.P. v. S.P., 169 N.J. Super. 425; 404 A.2d 1256 (App. Div., 1980).

Nadler v. Superior Court, 225 Cal. App.2d 523; 63 Cal.Rptr. 352 (1967). (p. 359)

* Naragon v. Wharton, 33 FEP Cases 61; 572 F.Sup. 1117 (1983).

* The National Gay Task Force and Stan Easter et. al. v. The Board of Education of the City of Oklahoma City, State of Oklahoma, United States District Court for the Western District of Oklahoma, Plaintiffs' Complaint, Filed October 14, 1980. (pp. 89–98)
— Brief by Defendant in Support of Motion to Dismiss, November 20, 1980.
— Brief in Opposition to Defendants' Motion to Dismiss, January 8, 1981.
— District Court Memorandum and Order, June 29, 1982.

* The National Gay Task Force v. The Board of Education of the City of Oklahoma City, State of Oklahoma, Brief of Appellant (NGTF), U.S. Court of Appeals, Tenth Cir., 18 October 1982.
U.S. Court of Appeals Memorandum and Order, 729 Fed.2d 1270 (10th Cir., 1984). 33 FEP Cases 1009 (1982). (pp. 22, 89–98, , 311, 318, 329–330)

* Neal v. Bryant, Fla., 149 So.2d 529 (1963). (pp. 183–184, 319)

William Newland v. Board of Governors of the California Community Colleges, 19 C.3d 705; 139 Cal. Rptr. 620; 566 P.2d 254 (1977).

In re Nicholson, Cir. No. withheld by mother's attorney, Iowa District Court, November, 1974.

Norton v. Macy, 417 F.2d 1161 (D.C. Cir., 1969). (pp. 216–217, 220–222, 258, 354)

Oakland Unified School District of Alameda County v. Eileen Barbara Ruth Olicker, 25 C.A.3d 1098; 102 Cal.Rptr. 421 (1972).

* Donald Odorizzi v. Bloomfield School District, 246 C.A.2d 123; 54 Cal. Rptr. 533 (1966). (pp. 196–197)

O'Harra v. O'Harra, No. 73-384E, Ore. Cir. Ct., 13th Jud. Dist., 18 June 1974.

Olmstead v. United States, 277 U.S. 438, 478 (1928). (p. 339)

Orloff v. Los Angeles Turf Club, 36 Cal.2d 734; 277 P.2d 449 (1951). (p. 353)

Paris Adult Theatre I v. Slaton, 413 U.S. 49 (1973). (p. 338)

People v. Andersen, 101 Cal.App3d 563; 161 Cal.Rptr. 707 (1980). (p. 363)

* People v. Mooney, 363 Mich. Rpts. 454 (1961).

* People of Illinois v. Gasner, 79 Ill. App.3d 964 (1979).

People of Illinois v. Deizman, 44 Ill. App.3d 829 (1976).

Perry v. Sindermann, 408 U.S. 593 (1972).

Pettit v. State Board of Education, 10 Cal.3d 29; 109 Cal.Rptr. 665; 513 P.2d 889 (1973). (pp. 354–355, 363)

Pickering v. Board of Education, 391 U.S. 563; 88 S.Ct. 1731; 20 L.Ed.2d 811 (1968). (pp. 264, 360–361)

Plessy v. Ferguson, 163 U.S. 537 (1896). (pp. 129–130, 337)

Poe v. Ullman, 367 U.S. 497 (1961). (p. 338)

* Poston v. State Board of Education, Fla., 149 So.2d 529 (1963). (pp. 183–184, 319)

Pryor v. Los Angeles Municipal Court, 25 Cal. 3d 238; 158 Cal. Rptr. 330 (1979). (p. 349)

Reineke v. Cobb County, 484 Fed. Supp. 1252 (1980).

Roe v. Ingraham, 364 F.Supp. 536 (1973). (p. 329)

Roe v. State of New York, 49 FRD 279; 8 ALR Fed 670 (1970). (p. 329)

Roe v. Wade, 410 U.S. 113; 93 S.Ct. 705; 35 L.Ed2d 147 (1973). (pp. 94, 137, 141, 269, 273–274, 311, 338)

Roy Romer, Governor of Colorado, et al. v. Richard G. Evans, et al. 116 S. Ct. 1620 (1996). Writ of Certiorari, U.S. Supreme Court, May 20, 1996, No. 94-1039. 64 USLW 4353; 70 Fair Empl. Prac. Cas. (BNA) 1180; 96 Cal. Daily Op. Serv. 3509; 96 Daily Journal D.A.R. 5730; 1996 WL 262293 (U.S.). See also Evans v. Romer, 882 P.2d 1335 (1994). (pp. 134–136, 311, 337)

* <u>Ross v. Springfield School District No. 19</u>, 56 Ore.App. 197; 641 P.2d 600 (1982).
  — Brief <u>Amicus Curiae</u> of the Oregon School Boards Association.
  — Revised Ultimate Findings of Fact and Conclusions of Law by the Fair Dismissal Appeals Board.

* <u>Ross v. Springfield School District No. 19</u>, 71 Ore.App. 111; 691 P.2d 509 (1984).
  — Brief of Respondent on Appeal.
  — Brief <u>Amici Curiae</u> of the Gay and Lesbian Alliance of the University of Oregon and the Eugene Chapter of the National Lawyers Guild.

* <u>Ross v. Springfield School District No. 19</u>, 294 Ore. 357; 657 P.2d 188 (1982).

* <u>Ross v. Springfield School District No. 19</u>, Decision of the Supreme Court of the State of Oregon dated 11 February 1986. (p. 320)
  — Brief of Respondent's Petition of Review.
  — Memorandum by Attorneys for the Fair Dismissal Appeals Board on Questions on Review.
  — Brief of Petitioner's Petition for Review.
  — Memorandum <u>Amicorum Curiae</u> of the Gay and Lesbian Alliance of the University of Oregon and the Eugene Chapter of the National Lawyers Guild.

* <u>Rowland v. Mad River Local School District</u>, Montgomery County, 615 F.2d 1362 (1980).

* <u>Rowland v. Mad River Local School District</u>, Montgomery County, 730 F.2d 444 (1984).
  — Brief for Plaintiff-Appellee.
  — Brief for Defendant-Appellant.
  — <u>Amicus Curiae</u> In Support of Rowland, by the National Gay Rights Advocates.
  — Reply Brief of the Defendant-Appellant.
  — Petition for Rehearing by Plaintiff.
  — Petition for <u>Writ of Certiorari</u> to the United States Court of Appeals for the Sixth District.
  — Petition for Rehearing From Denial of the <u>Writ of Certiorari</u>.
  — Petitioner's Reply Brief to Brief of Respondent in Opposition.

— Brief of Respondent in Opposition.
— Appellee's Updated List of Citations.
— Appellant's Citations of Supplemental Authorities.

* Rowland v. Mad River Local School District, Montgomery County, 84 L.Ed.2d 392 (1985). (p. 320)

* Safransky v. State Personnel Board, 62 Wisc.2d 464; 215 N.W.2d 359 (1974). (pp. 257–258, 360)

San Antonio School District v. Roderiquez, 411 U.S. 1 (1973). (p. 337)

* Sarac v. State Board of Education, 249 Cal. App.2d 58; 57 Cal.Rptr. 69 (1967). (pp. 27, 164, 197–200, 202, 214–216, 218, 220, 223, 226, 262, 319, 346, 351, 354)

Schuster v. Schuster, No. D6868, Wash. Super. Ct., King County, 22 December 1972.

Shelton v. Tucker, 364 U.S. 479 (1960).

Singer v. U.S. Civil Service, 530 F.2d 247 (1978).

Smith v. Smith, Cir. No. 125497, Cal. Super. Ct., Stanislaus County (February, 1978).
— Brief of Respondent's Reply on Appeal.
— Brief of Appellant's Closing Comments.

Society for Individual Rights v. Hampton, 63 F.R.D. 399 (N.D. Cal., 1973).

Solomitz et al. v. Maine School Administrative District No. 59 et al., 495 A.2d 812 (Maine, 1985).
— Brief for the Plaintiffs.
— Brief for the Defendants.
— Brief Amicus Curiae of the Christian Civic League of Maine, Inc., on behalf of Defendants.
— Brief Amicus Curiae of the Maine School Management Association.
— Brief Amicus Curiae of the Lambda Legal Defense and Educational Fund.

* State of Louisiana v. Frentz, La., 354 So.2d 1007 (1978).

* State of Oregon v. Chase, 613 P.2d 1104; 47 Or. App. 175 (1980).

* <u>State of Washington v. Forrest Bryant</u>, 3 Wn. App. 15; 472 P.2d 408 (1970).

<u>Stolberg v. Board of Trustees</u>, 474 F.2d 485 (2d Cir.,1973).

* <u>Strailey v. Happy Times Nursery School, Inc.</u>, 698 F.2d 327 (1979).
— Complaint.
— Opening brief for Appellant.
— Respondents brief.
— Consolidated Supplemental brief of Appellants.
— Consolidated Reply brief of the Appellants.
— Plaintiff's brief in Opposition to Motion to Dismiss.
— Deposition of Donald Strailey.

<u>Sun Company of San Bernardino v. The People</u>, 29 C.A.3d 815; 105 Cal.Rptr. 873 (1973).

<u>In the Matter of Tammy F.</u>, 1 Civil No. 32648, Cal. 1st App. Dist., Div. 2, August 21, 1973.

<u>Carl Thompkins v. United States</u>, 236 A.2d 443 (1967).

<u>Tinker v. Des Moines Independent School District</u>, 393 U.S. 503 (1969). (p. 311)

<u>Townend v. Townend</u>, 1 Family L. Rptr. 2830 (1975).

<u>United States v. Carolene Products Co.</u>, 304 U.S. 144 (1938). (p. 337)

<u>United States v. Kapp</u>, 302 U.S. 214; 58 S.Ct. 182; 82 L.Ed. 205 (1937). (p. 360)

<u>In re Volkland</u>, 74 Cal.App.3d 674; 141 Cal.Rptr. 625 (1977). (p. 363)

<u>Watson v. Memphis</u>, 373 U.S. 526 (1963).

<u>Glen West v. The State of Alabama</u>, 57 Ala.App. 596; 329 So.2d 653 (1976).

<u>Wieman v. Updegraff</u>, 344 U.S. 183 (1952).

* <u>Miss Marianne Woods and Miss Jane Pirie Against Dame Helen Cumming Gordon</u>, New York: The Arno Press, 1975. Photocopy of judges' transcript of original Scottish case. (pp. 170–171)

<u>Yanzick v. School District</u>, Mont., 641 P.2d 431 (1982). (pp. 354, 363)

<u>Zablocki v. Redhail</u>, 434 U.S. 374 (1978).

Time Line of GLBT Educators' Rights

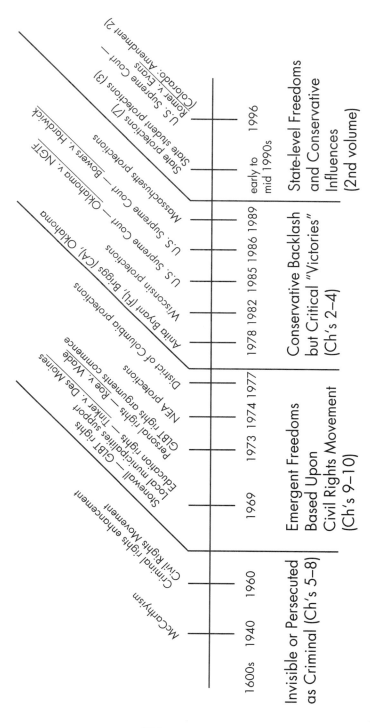

| 1600s | 1940 | 1960 | 1969 | 1973 | 1974 | 1977 | 1978 | 1982 | 1985 | 1986 | 1989 | early to mid 1990s | 1996 |

McCarthyism

Criminal rights enhancement
Civil Rights Movement

Stonewall — GLBT rights
Local municipalities support
Education rights — Tinker v. Des Moines
Personal rights — Roe v. Wade
GLBT rights arguments commence

NEA protections

District of Columbia protections

Anita Bryant (FL), Briggs (CA), Oklahoma

Wisconsin protections

U.S. Supreme Court — Oklahoma v. NGTF

U.S. Supreme Court — Bowers v. Hardwick

Massachusetts protections

State student protections (7)

U.S. Supreme Court —
Romer v. Evans
(Colorado: Amendment 2)

Invisible or Persecuted
as Criminal (Ch's 5–8)

Emergent Freedoms
Based Upon
Civil Rights Movement
(Ch's 9–10)

Conservative Backlash
but Critical "Victories"
(Ch's 2–4)

State-level Freedoms
and Conservative
Influences
(2nd volume)

311

ENDNOTES

INTRODUCTION ENDNOTES

1. Throughout this volume, the stories are true but sometimes the name of the individual involved in the incident has been changed to protect his or her identity. When names have been changed, they are printed in quotation marks at the first reference.

2. Bisexual is defined as an individual with the potential to feel sexually attracted to, and enjoy sexual contact with, people of either sex. The degree of attraction to either sex may differ in extent or time. See John Leland, "Bisexuality," Newsweek, 17 July 1995; and Marjorie Garber, Vice Versa: Bisexuality and the Eroticism of Everyday Life (New York: Simon and Schuster, 1995).

Transgender individuals are included in our view of sexual minority youth and adults because of their lack of visibility and political and emotional support in our society. The American Educational Gender Information Service's general information flier states, "Hundreds of thousands of human beings have a condition known as gender dysphoria ... characterized by a feeling of inappropriateness in the gender one is assigned at birth. It may manifest as crossdressing (called transvestite), which may be frequent or occasional, or, in the case of transsexualism, as a desire to change sex," (AEGIS, P. O. Box 33724, Decatur, Georgia 30033. Phone (404) 939-0244). Although most transgender individuals are heterosexual, they face much of the same invisibility and prejudice as do GLB people. Having worked with transgender youth in schools, many of us feel that their pain cannot be ignored. Imagine, for example, not being able to urinate between the hours of 7:30 a.m. and 3:00 p.m. on a daily basis because no private, single-person bathroom is made available to you in your school, and you do not feel safe or appropriate in either the boys' or the girls' bathroom. Similarly, many transgender youth drop out of school by 7th grade, rather than face the violence and hardships of dressing with their peers for physical education classes. Once educators become aware of these problems, accommodations are simple and cost-free, and the resulting consequences are extraordinarily positive. For additional information, see, Anne Fausto-Sterling, "The Five Sexes: Why Male and Female Are Not Enough," The Sciences, (March/April 1993).

3. Virginia R. Uribe and Karen M. Harbeck, "Addressing the Needs of Lesbian, Gay and Bisexual Youth: The Origins of PROJECT 10 and School-Based Intervention," ed. Karen M. Harbeck, in both Journal of Homosexuality (New York: Haworth, 1991) 22(3/4): 9-28, and Coming Out of the Classroom Closet: Gay and Lesbian Students, Teachers, and Curricula (New York: Haworth, 1992).

4. See, Commonwealth of Massachusetts, Massachusetts Governor's Advisory Commission on Gay and Lesbian Youth, Making Schools Safe for Gay and Lesbian Youth: Breaking The Silence in Schools and in Families (Boston: Governor's Advisory Commission on Gay and Lesbian Youth, 1993).

5. National Gay and Lesbian Task Force, Anti-Gay/Lesbian Victimization (New York: National Gay and Lesbian Task Force, 1984); and Gary Remafedi, "Male Homosexuality: The Adolescent's Perspective," Pediatrics 79 (1987): 326-330.

For legal information on youth homelessness, see Yvonne Rafferty, "The Legal Rights and Educational Problems of Homeless Children and Youth," Educational Evaluation and Policy Analysis, 17(1), (Spring 1995): 39-61.

6. United States, Department of Health and Human Services, Report of the Secretary's Task Force on Youth Suicide, (Rockville, MD, Department of Health and Human Services, 1989). See also, Gary Remafedi, ed., Death By Denial: Studies of Suicide in Gay and Lesbian Teenagers (Boston: Alyson, 1994).

7. Francine Shifrin and Mirtha Solis, "Chemical Dependency in Gay and Lesbian Youth," Journal of Chemical Dependency Treatment 5(1), (1992): 67-76.

8. Douglas Feldman, "Gay Youth and AIDS," <u>Gay and Lesbian Youth</u>, ed. G. Herdt (New York: Haworth, 1989). See also, Kevin Cranston, "HIV Education for Gay, Lesbian and Bisexual Youth: Personal Risk, Personal Power and the Community of Conscience," <u>Coming Out</u>, ed. Harbeck, pp. 247-259.

9. R. C. Savin-Williams, "Theoretical Perspectives Accounting for Adolescent Homosexuality," <u>Journal of Adolescent Health Care</u> 9(2), (1988): 95-104.

10. Uribe and Harbeck. See also, Anthony R. D'Augelli and Scott L. Hershberger, "Lesbian, Gay, and Bisexual Youth in Community Settings: Personal Challenges and Mental Health Problems," <u>American Journal of Community Psychology</u> 21(4), (1993): 421-448. Neil W. Pilkington and Anthony R. D'Augelli, "Victimization of Lesbian, Gay, and Bisexual Youth in Community Settings," <u>American Journal of Community Psychology</u>. See also, Gerald Unks, ed., <u>The Gay Youth: Educational Practice and Theory for Lesbian, Gay and Bisexual Adolescents</u> (New York: Routledge, 1995).

11. United States, National Center for Health Statistics, <u>Vital Statistics of the United States</u>, vol. 2: <u>Mortality, Part A</u> (Hyattsville, MD: National Center for Health Statistics, 1986). United States, <u>Report on Youth Suicide</u>. G. Remafedi, J. Farrow, and R. Deisher, "Risk Factors for Attempted Suicides in Gay and Bisexual Youth," <u>Pediatrics</u> 87(6), (1991): 869-876.

12. J. Jacobs, <u>Adolescent Suicide</u> (New York: John Wiley and Sons, 1971).

13. D'Augelli and Hershberger, 437-443.

14. Pawlowski, Wayne, Plenary Address at "Children of the Shadows I," University of Connecticut, Hartford, March 1994.

15. A. C. Kinsey, M. Pomeroy, and P. Gebhard, in both <u>Sexual Behavior in the Human Male</u> (Philadelphia: Saunders, 1948); and <u>Sexual Behavior in the Human Female</u> (Philadelphia: Saunders, 1953). R. Crooks and K. Baur, <u>Our Sexuality</u> (Redwood City, CA: Benjamin/Cummings, 1990). See also, Gary Remafedi, "Homosexual Youth: A Challenge to Contemporary Society," <u>Journal of the American Medical Association</u>, 258(2), (1987): 222-225; R. C. Sorenson, <u>Adolescent Sexuality in Contemporary America</u> (New York: Wark, 1973). B. Rensberger, "2.3% of U.S. Men in Survey Report Homosexual Acts," <u>Los Angeles Times</u>, 1 April 1993. S. Janus and C. Janus, <u>The Janus Report on Sexual Behavior</u> (New York: Wiley, 1993). Also see R. T. Michael, G. H. Gagnon, E. O. Laumann, and G. Kolata, <u>Sex in America: A Definitive Survey</u> (Boston: Little, Brown & Company, 1994).

Estimates of the current number of GLBT men and women in the United States ranges from 1 percent to 30 percent. Kinsey's 1948 estimate of 10 percent is still quoted widely, although it predates the emergence of visible, political GLBT subcultures, so 18 percent may reflect a more accurate estimate. Note, too, that 28 percent of the males and 17 percent of the females who participated in Kinsey's research reported engaging in one or more homosexual experiences between puberty and age 20. During adulthood, 37 percent of the individuals reported having at least one homosexual experience, while 10 percent of them had predominately homosexual experiences. In Sorenson's 1973 study of youth (ages 16-19) sexual behavior, 17 percent of the males and 6 percent of the females reported having at least one homosexual experience. The recent Janus Report estimates that 9 percent of men and 5 percent of women engage in ongoing or frequent homosexual activity. In terms of these men, 4 percent self-identified as homosexual and 5 percent as bisexual, while for the women, 2 percent self-identified as homosexual and 3 percent as bisexual. Further, 22 percent of the men and 17 percent of the women acknowledged having homosexual experiences. A 1990 study found that 11.6 percent of Americans reported same-sex behavior after age 15.

16. James T. Sears, "Educators, Homosexuality, and Homosexual Students: Are Personal Feelings Related to Professional Beliefs?" Coming Out, ed. Harbeck, pp. 29-79.

17. See Bianca Cody Murphy, "Educating Mental Health Professionals About Gay and Lesbian Issues," Coming Out, ed. Harbeck, pp. 229-246, for a discussion of the failings of education and health-related professional programs with respect to GLBT concerns.

18. For an extensive collection of articles that discuss how homophobia hurts everyone in our society, see Warren J. Blumenfeld, ed., Homophobia: How We All Pay the Price (Boston: Beacon, 1992).

19. Remafedi, "Homosexual Youth," 222-223.

20. D'Augelli and Hershberger, 430.

CHAPTER 1 ENDNOTES

1. Joseph Acanfora v. Board of Education of Montgomery County, 359 F.Supp. 834 (1973); 491 F.2d 498 (1974); Cert. denied, 419 U.S. 839 (1974). Hereinafter referred to as Acanfora. (See Chapter Ten.)

2. John Briggs, personal interview, Sacramento, CA, offices, 1989.

3. United States, National Center for Education Statistics, U. S. Department of Education, Digest of Educational Statistics (Washington: 1993): 13, 14, 73, 75. Because of the publishing schedule, the numbers referenced above pertain to 1991 data. The reader also should be warned that national census data on teachers varies based upon the data-gathering assumptions of each government agency.

4. Data obtained from <u>Educational Statistics</u>, 13-14. Numbers calculated by dividing the total number of teachers (2,787,000) by the total number of public and private elementary and secondary schools in the country (109,228).

5. I realize that in some parts of our movement it is politically incorrect to use the word "homosexual." Since it is a term that has both historical and contemporary significance, I have retained it in this volume. Moreover, using GLBT becomes depersonalizing and cumbersome. Please note that I include transgender individuals in the text where noted and transgender people as well in the larger context of freedom for sexual minorities. Also note that although I often refer to GLBT educators, I intend inclusion of our hetero-sexual allies in situations where their advocacy on behalf of sexual orienta-tion concerns places them in the same circumstances as GLBT individuals.

6. Numerous authors have documented the various reactions to homosex-uality, including, Walter Barnett, <u>Sexual Freedom and The Constitutionality of Repressive Sex Law</u> (Albuquerque, NM: University of New Mexico, 1973); Ellen M. Barrett, "Legal Homophobia and the Christian Church," 30 (4) <u>Hastings Law Journal</u> (March 1979): 1019-27; Vern L. Bullough, <u>Homosexuality: A History</u> (New York: Meridan, 1979); Bullough, "Homosexuality and the Medical Model," 1 (1) <u>Journal of Homosexuality</u> (1974): 99-110; Bullough, <u>Sexual Variance In Society and History</u> (Chicago: University of Chicago Press, 1976); Bullough, and Bonnie Bullough, "Lesbianism in the 1920s and 1930s: a Newfound Study," II <u>Signs</u> (1977): 895-904; Bullough and Bullough, <u>Sin, Sickness, and Sanity: A History of Sexual Attitudes</u> (New York: Garland, 1977); Lewis Crompton, "Homosexuals and the Death Penalty in Colonial America," 1 (3) <u>Journal of Homosexuality</u> (1976): 277-293; John D'Emilio, <u>Sexual Politics, Sexual Communities: The Making of a Homosexual Minority in the United States, 1940-1970</u> (Chicago: University of Chicago, 1983); Martin Ford, "Homosexuality: Description, Development, and Alternative Life Style," Unpublished paper, 1977; Lawrence M. Goldyn, <u>Legal Ideology and the Regulation of Homosexual Behavior</u>, Doctoral diss., Stanford University, August 1979; Jonathon Katz, <u>Gay American History: Lesbian and Gay Men in the U.S.A.</u> (New York: Thomas Y. Crowell, 1976); John Money, "Bisexual, Homosexual and Heterosexual: Society, Law, and Medicine," 2 (3) <u>Journal of Homosexuality</u> (Spring 1977): 229-233; Rhonda Rivera, "Our Straight-Laced Judges: The Legal Position of Homosexual Persons In the United States," 30 (4) <u>Hastings Law Journal</u> (March 1979): 799-955; Eric Rofes, <u>Socrates, Plato, and Guys Like Me</u> (Boston, MA: Alyson Publications, 1985; Vito Russo, <u>The Celluloid Closet: Homosexuality In the Movies</u> (New York: Harper & Row, 1981; and George Weinburg, <u>Society and the Health Homosexual</u> (New York: Anchor Press, 1973).

7. I am proud to have been an author of the changes to the Massachusetts Educational Personnel Certification Code that was passed rapidly by the Massachusetts State Board of Education in October of 1994, and made retroactive to the beginning of the new certification requirements. This mandate affects 60 programs housed at 35 institutions of higher education in Massachusetts. In an unprecedented arrangement, each program has been asked to appoint a liaison to the Massachusetts Governor's Advisory Commission on Gay and Lesbian Youth. Those of us on the Commission are working closely with these representatives to provide information and curriculum materials to the various programs to ensure successful compliance with the new regulations. Interestingly, it should be noted that religious institutions are normally exempt from federal or state anti-discrimination laws and are, therefore, able to discriminate on the basis of race, gender, or sexual orientation. If they wish to offer their graduates certification to teach in Massachusetts public schools, however, religious institutions must abide by all certification code requirements. In addition to changing the curriculum at all institutions, this change in the certification code requirements has provided powerful new arguments for GLBT student groups seeking recognition of their existence at religious institutions in the state, such as Boston College.

8. For an excellent discussion of emergent homosexual subcultures, see John D'Emilio, Sexual; and George Chauncey, Jr., "From Sexual Inversion To Homosexuality: Medicine And The Changing Conceptualization Of Female Deviance," Journal of Social History (1982): 114-146, and "Fairies, Pogues, and Christian Brothers: The Newport (Rhode Island) Homosexuality Scandal, 1919-1920," Among Men, Among Women: Sociological and Historical Recognition of Homosexual Arrangements, Gay-studies and Women's studies University of Amsterdam Conference, 22nd-26th June 1983, Oudemanhuispoort Amsterdam: 1-15. See also Jeffrey Weeks, Coming Out: Homosexual Politics in Britain from the Nineteenth Century to the Present (London: Quartet, 1977).

9. See David Rubin, The Rights of Teachers (New York: Avon, 1971): 108-109.

10. NGTF is now National Gay and Lesbian Task Force (NGLTF); GRA has folded; and LRP is now known as the National Center for Lesbian Rights (NCLR).

11. John Briggs, quoted in Ellen Goodman, "Proposition Fever," The Boston Globe, 28 September 1978.

12. The National Gay Task Force v. the Board of Education of the City of Oklahoma City, State of Oklahoma, 729 Fed.2d 1270 (10th Cir.1984); 105 S.Ct. 76 (1984); aff'd. 105 S.Ct. 1858 (1985). Hereinafter referred to as NGTF v. Oklahoma.

13. Oklahoma Statute 70, Section 6-103.15 (1978). See Appendix C for the full text of this statute.

14. "NGTF Wins Helms Appeal," NGTF Announcement (April 1985): 1. Shortly after the U.S. Supreme Court hearing, Oklahoma worked on alternative legislation, and other states, including North Carolina, Nevada, Texas, and Arkansas, considered taking similar action. Because of the powerful Constitutional protections of freedom of speech and association, these states found it difficult to draft alternative legislation that could be enacted. "Bill Against Gay Teachers Withdrawn," Gay Community News, 20 July 1985. George Michaelson, "Teachers Under Fire In Nevada," Gay Community News, 5 May 1979. "Gay Rights Backlash Repeals Local Ordinances," Gay Community News, May 1978.

15. People, 18 September 1995.

16. Harry F. Waters, "Teenage Suicide: One Act Not to Follow," Newsweek, 18 April 1994. See also, Governor's Advisory Commission, Making Schools Safe.

17. William Neal v. Farris Bryant, et. al.; Mary Frances Bradshaw v. State Board of Education; and Anne Louise Poston v. State Board of Education, Fla., 149 So.2d 529 (1963).

18. Morrison v. State Board of Education, 74 Cal. Rptr. 116 (1969); 1 Cal.3d 214; 461 P.2d 365; 82 Cal. Rptr. 175 (1969).

19. Internalized homophobia involves the negative belief system that society projects onto GLBT people and the subsequent internalization of that belief system into one's self-definition. Thus, many GLBT people believe that they are bad or worthless. Also, we internalize the negative images we hear of what others will do to us if they discover our sexual orientation, and we remain fearful of the consequences of such public disclosure.

20. Local-level District and Superior Court cases were not on file in LEXIS.

21. See Appendix E for a discussion of the cases used in this study or rejected as inappropriate.

22. Martindale-Hubbell Law Directory, Summit, NJ: Martindale-Hubbell (to 1994).

23. Sarac v. State Board of Education, 249 Cal.App.2d 58; 57 Cal.Rptr. 69 (1967). See Chapter Eight for additional details.

24. Morrison v. State Board of Education, 74 Cal.Rptr. 116; 1 Cal.3d 214; 461 P.2d 365; 82 Cal.Rptr. 175 (1969).

25. See, Kinsey, et al., Human Male, 277-279, 303-3-4, 332-334, 667. For a more complete discussion of the literature on sex with children, see Barnett, Sexual, (1973): 129-132. A. N. Groth and H. J. Birnbaum, "Adult Sexual Orientation and Attraction to Underage Persons," 7(3) Archives of Sexual Behavior (1978): 175-181. Carole Jenny, Thomas A. Roesler, and Kimberly L. Poyer, "Are Children at Risk for Sexual Abuse by Homosexuals?" Pediatrics 94(1), (July 1994). Ellen Gray, Unequal Justice: The Prosecution of Child Sexual Abuse (New York: MacMillan, 1993).

26. For examples, see Ross v. Springfield School District No. 19, 56 Ore.App. 197; 641 P.2d 600 (1982); 71 Ore.App. 111; 691 P.2d 508 (1984), and Rowland v. Mad River Local School District, Montgomery County, 615 F.2d 1362 (1980); 730 F.2d 444 (1984); 84 L.Ed.2d 392 (1985).

27. For an excellent overview of this literature, see Gregory M. Herek, "Beyond 'Homophobia': A Social Psychological Perspective on Attitudes Towards Lesbians and Gay Men," Bashers, Baiters, and Bigots: Homophobia In American Society, John P. DeCecco, ed. (New York: Harrington Park, 1985): 1-21.

CHAPTER 2 ENDNOTES

1. Some of the sources used in this section are: The Washington Star (1977); Gay Community News (1977); The Washington Post (1977); The National Enquirer (1977); The Miami Herald (1977); The Lincoln Nebraska Star (March 1978); The Chicago Tribune (1977); The Los Angeles Times (1977); The Miami News (1977); The Pittsburgh Post-Gazette (May 1978); Ken Kelley, "Cruising With Anita," Playboy (May 1978): 97, 232; The Times-Picayune (1977); The National Observer (1977); and The New York Times (1977).

2. Anita Bryant, The Anita Bryant Story: The Survival of Our Nation's Families and The Threat of Militant Homosexuality (Old Tappen, NJ: Fleming H. Revell, 1977): 13-14.

3. Bryant, Story 13.

4. Kelley, Playboy 73-95, 232-250.

5. Kelley, Playboy 74.

6. "Homosexuals: Anita Bryant's Crusade," Newsweek, 11 April 1977.

7. Bryant, Story 14-15.

8. Bryant, Story 26.

9. Legal conflicts with the Save The Children Federation forced Bryant's organization to select a new name, Protect America's Children, after the

Dade County referendum battle. Kelley, <u>Playboy</u> 74; and Anita Bryant and Bob Green, <u>At Any Cost</u> (Old Tappan, NJ: Fleming H. Revell, 1978): 23.

10. Bryant, <u>Story</u> 49.

11. Neil Miller, "Miami Gays Try To Pick Up $400,000 Vote Tab," <u>Gay Community News</u>, 2 April 1977.

12. Lindsy Van Gelder, "Anita Bryant On The March: The Lessons of Dade County," <u>Ms. Magazine</u> (September 1977): 100.

13. Miller, "Miami Gays."

14. More than $300,000 was raised. See B. Drummond Ayres, Jr., "Miami Votes 2 to 1 To Repeal Law Barring Bias Against Homosexuals," <u>New York Times</u>, 8 June 1977.

15. Bryant, <u>Story</u> 24.

16. Kelley, <u>Playboy</u> 250.

17. Kelley, <u>Playboy</u> 86, 87.

18. Bryant, <u>Story</u> 43, 100.

19. "Anita Bryant's Letter To Her Supporters," <u>Gay Community News</u>, 28 May 1977; and Bryant, <u>Story</u> 48.

20. Kay Zahasky, "Anita Bryant: Exclusive Interview," <u>Today's Student</u>, 6 February 1978.

21. Kelley, <u>Playboy</u> 248.

22. Ayres, "Miami Votes."

23. Bryant, <u>Story</u> 122.

24. "When Hearts Are Young and Gay," <u>Washington Star</u>, 16 February 1977.

25. Van Gelder, "Anita Bryant" 100.

26. Van Gelder, "Anita Bryant" 100.

27. For example, county ordinance supporters were able to raise five times the amount of money than was raised throughout the entire State of Florida for the ERA campaign.

28. Van Gelder, "Anita Bryant" 100.

29. Kelley, <u>Playboy</u> 247.

30. Kelley, <u>Playboy</u> 73.

31. Kelley, <u>Playboy</u> 75.

32. Kelley, <u>Playboy</u> 74, 78.

33. Kelley, <u>Playboy</u> 78.

34. Millie Ball, "I'd Rather My Child Be Dead," <u>The Times-Picayune</u>, 19 June 1977.

35. Kelley, <u>Playboy</u> 80.

36. Campaign material published in the <u>Miami News</u>, 4 April 1977.

37. Michael Bedwell, "Don't Buy This Book," <u>Gay Community News</u>, 22 December 1977.

38. Max Rafferty, "Should Gays Teach School?" <u>Phi Delta Kappan</u>, October 1977: 91-92.

39. Zahasky, "Anita Bryant."

40. Zahasky, "Anita Bryant."

41. Kelley, <u>Playboy</u> 74.

42. Kelley, <u>Playboy</u> 78-79.

43. Zahasky, "Anita Bryant."

44. Gloria Borger, "Gay Celebration Turns To Dirge," <u>Washington Star</u>, 8 June 1977.

45. "Gay Rights Supporter's Car Bombed," <u>San Francisco Chronicle</u>, March through May, 1977; "Youth Ruled 'Delinquent' In Miami Gay Shooting," <u>Gay Community News</u>, 10 October 1977.

46. The suit was later dropped. "Mother of Slain Gay Sues Anita," <u>San Francisco Chronicle</u>, 1 July 1977.

47. "Another Suicide Attempt; Hate Campaign Blamed," <u>Gay Community News</u>, 12 May 1977.

48. Bedwell, "Don't Buy."

49. "KKK 'Protects' Anita At Rally," Source Unknown, 23 July 1977.

50. SOC literature; see also, Zahasky, "Anita Bryant," and, Ball, "I'd Rather."

51. Bill Peterson, "Gay Rights Law Loses 2-1 in Miami," <u>The Washington Post</u>, 8 June 1977.

52. Borger, "Gay Celebration" (1977); Bryant, <u>Story</u>; and, "Enough! Enough! Enough!," <u>Time</u>, 20 June 1977.

53. Peterson, "Gay Rights."

54. David Hacker, "She's Against Gay Rights," The National Observer, 12 March 1977.

55. "My Holy War To Save Our Kids," Midnight Globe, 5 July 1977.

56. "Enough!"

57. "Gay Rights Showdown in Miami," Time, 13 June 1977.

58. Kelley, Playboy 248.

59. Zahasky, "Anita Bryant."

60. Chapter Three provides a detailed discussion of John Briggs' efforts to use the homosexual school teacher issue as a political stepping-stone in the California gubernatorial race.

61. William Safire, "For Anita, a Vote of Confidence," Richmond Times-Dispatch, 12 June 1977.

62. See, Gelbert, "Wichita" (1978); "Wichita Repeals Homo Law," New York Times, 10 May 1978; and, Hilda Bryant, "Seattle Reaction to Gay Rights Repeal In St. Paul," Seattle Post-Intelligencer, 27 April 1978. See also, "Laws Aiding" (1978); Nicholas von Hoffman, "Homosexuals Do Not Merit Special Laws," Richmond News Leader, 18 May 1978; "Avoiding A National Anti-Homosexual Crusade," The Providence Journal, 10 May 1977; and, "Editorial," The Milwaukee Journal, 12 May 1978.

As was the case in the Dade County campaign, members of the police force in Eugene provided additional leadership.

In several cities across the nation, fundamentalist leaders tried to repeal the gay rights ordinances, but they failed to gather much support. One good example is the city of Madison, Wisconsin. See "Minister Awaiting Child Abuse Trial Gets Into Repeal Act," Gay Community News, June 1978.

63. Johnson, "St. Paul."

64. Gelbert, "Wichita."

65. "Gay Rights Voted Down In Eugene," San Francisco Chronicle, date unknown.

66. Johnson, "St. Paul."

67. Yarnold, "Will Gay Rights."

68. "Don't Stay Home Tomorrow," VOICE, May 1978.

69. "Citizens of Eugene," Santa Clara Assembly Church of Eugene, Oregon (May 1978); "Vote Yes On Referendum #51," Concerned Citizens of Eugene

(May 1978); "Keep It Straight," <u>VOICE</u>, Eugene (May 1978); "Repeal Protection Of Offensive Conduct," <u>VOICE</u>, Eugene (May 1978).

70. Gelbert, "Wichita."

71. Hilda Bryant, "Seattle Reaction."

72. "National Enquirer Equates Mass Murder And Gay Teachers," <u>Seattle Gay News</u>, 2 February 1979.

73. "Eugene Voters Reject Gay Rights Law 2-1," <u>Arizona Gay News</u>, 26 May 1978.

74. Editorial, <u>Wichita Eagle and Beacon</u>, 23 April 1978.

75. Gelbert, "Wichita."

76. See, "The Eugene Campaign," <u>Lesbian Tide</u> (July/August 1978); "Bryant Organization" (1978).

77. "Avoiding" <u>Providence Journal</u>.

78. Rafferty, "Should Gays," 91.

CHAPTER 3 ENDNOTES

1. The Pride Legal Defense Fund, "Proposition Six," (San Francisco: The Pride Legal Defense Fund, 1978); see also, Johnson, "St. Paul."

2. "Proposition Six."

3. "Homosexual Issue At The Polls," <u>The San Francisco Examiner</u>, 17 May 1978.

4. "The Move to Ban Gay Teachers," <u>San Francisco Chronicle</u>, 12 January 1978.

5. <u>Proposition 6 Initiative</u>. See Appendix B for complete text.

6. Ronald Reagan, "Two Ill-Advised California Trends," <u>Los Angeles Herald Examiner</u>, 1 November 1978.

7. "Senator Briggs Refiles Anti-Gay Initiative In California," <u>Gay Community News</u>, November 1977.

8. "Senator Briggs Refiles."

9. "John Briggs Files Signatures for Anti-Gay Teacher Initiative," <u>Gaysweek</u>, 15 May 1978.

10. "Prop. 6, Senator Briggs Defends," <u>Coast To Coast Times</u>, 10 October 1978.

11. Rafferty, "Should Gays," 91.

12. "National Enquirer."

13. "National Enquirer."

14. "Gay, Gifted Yet Closeted In City's Classrooms," The San Francisco Examiner, 12 June 1975; see also, "Legal Memorandum to the Board of Education," by H.LeRoy Cannon, 17 June 1975.

15. "Gay, Gifted."

16. "Gay, Gifted."

17. "Gay, Gifted."

18. Much of the material for this chapter comes from my taped personal interview with Briggs, conducted in January of 1988 in his Sacramento, CA, office.

19. Ellen Goodman, "Proposition Fever," The Boston Globe, 28 September 1978.

20. McGrory, "Briggs."

21. "State's Probe of Briggs Spending," Source Unidentified.

22. "State's Probe;" "Briggs $167,000 in Debt: Paying Petition Circulators 35c Per Name," Gaysweek, 17 April 1978; "Poll Shows Californians Support Controversial Initiatives," Washington Post, 20 September 1978.

23. Briggs' daughter later carried on his conservative opinions when she sat on the California State Board of Education.

24. McGrory, "Briggs."

25. McGrory, "Briggs."

26. "Senator Briggs Attacks Gay Teacher," Gaysweek, 9 October 1978.

27. "Senator Briggs Attacks."

28. Randy Shilts, And the Band Played On: Politics, People, and the AIDS Epidemic (New York: St. Martin's, 1987); and Conduct Unbecoming: Gays & Lesbians in the U.S. Military (New York: St. Martin's, 1993).

29. Jerry Burns, "Brown's Vow On Briggs Initiative," San Francisco Chronicle (1978).

30. Judith Michaelson, "Briggs Submits Signatures For Anti-Gay Initiative," Los Angeles Times, 2 May 1978.

31. The actual number of reported signatures varied from 350,000 to 600,000, although it is agreed generally that a vast number of the signatures

were invalid. See, Judith Michaelson, "Briggs Submits Signatures;" and, "Briggs' Initiative on Gays Wins Ballot Spot," San Francisco Chronicle (1978).

32. Reagan, "Two Ill-Advised."

33. "After Low-Key Campaigns, Comeback Is Seen For Gay Rights," The Washington Post, 27 October 1978; and, "Homosexuality A Felony?" Lesbian Tide (July/August, 1978).

34. "Poll Shows."

35. "After Low-Key."

36. "After Low-Key."

37. "Couldn't Find Any Mountains," Gay Community News, 21 November 1981.

38. "Briggs Bill Gets Blah Reception," The San Francisco Progress, 26 May 1978.

39. "Stop Prop. 6," Californians Against The Briggs Initiative, San Jose, CA (1978).

40. "After Low-Key."

41. Ronnie Dugger, On Reagan, The Man and His Presidency (New York: McGraw, 1983): 264, 559.

42. "After Low-Key."

43. Reagan, "Two Ill-Advised."

44. "After Low-Key."

45. "Bryant Org." Quoting Reverend Murray Norris.

46. "Evidence of Fraud Uncovered In Briggs Anti-Gay Initiative Drive," The Boston Globe, 12 May 1978.

47. "John Briggs Files," Gaysweek.

48. "Briggs $167,000," and "John Briggs Files."

49. "Evidence of Fraud."

50. "Suits Hit Anti-Gay Initiative," The Recorder, 31 May 1978.

51. "Suits Hit."

52. Petition for a Writ of Mandate and Memorandum of Points and Authorities in Support Thereof, California Federation of Teachers et. al. v.

March Fong Eu, Secretary of State, and John Briggs, Supreme Court of the State of California, 24 May 1978.

53. "High Court Won't Remove Briggs Bill," Sentinel, 14 July 1978.

54. "Entitled To Redress," Gay Community News, 23 January 1982.

55. "Hundreds Protest Briggs Initiative After Attempt to Oust Teacher," Gay Community News, 9 September 1978.

56. "Senator Briggs Attacks."

57. "Senator Briggs Attacks."

58. "Entitled To Redress."

59. "Danger Seen in Support for Gays," Los Angeles Times, 15 September 1978.

60. "Donors Seek Secrecy," Lesbian Tide, September 1978; "Danger Seen."

61. Katy Butler, "Perils For Gays Fighting Briggs Initiative," San Francisco Chronicle, 26 August 1978. See also, R. Bowman, "Public Attitudes Toward Homosexuality In New Zealand," International Review of Modern Sociology 9 (1979): 229-238; B. Glasser and C. Owen, "Variations In Attitudes Toward Homosexuality," Cornell Journal of Social Relations 11(2), (1976): 161-176; G. Hansen, "Measuring Prejudice Against Homosexuality (Homosexism) Among College Students," Journal of Social Psychology 117 (1982): 233-236; Jim Millham, Christopher San Miguel, and Richard Kellog, "A Factor-Analytic Conceptualization Of Attitudes Toward Male And Female Homosexuals," 2(1), Journal of Homosexuality (Fall 1976): 3-10; and C. Weis and R. Dain, "Ego Development And Sex Attitudes In Heterosexual And Homosexual Men And Women," 8(4) Archives of Sexual Behavior (1979): 341-356.

62. Butler, "Perils."

63. Butler, "Perils."

64. "Poll Shows."

65. "Are Homosexuals Trying to Recruit Our Children?" California Defend Our Children, Yes On 6 (1978).

66. One disgruntled Proposition 6 supporter was mobilized into action by the threat of homosexuality in "our national pastime" — baseball. Mr. Edward Washatka, of Pasadena, CA, expressed his activism after witnessing the Los Angles Dodgers' 1978 winning of the national pennant. Mr. Washatka wrote:

"I have had it. As a concerned parent of two young impressionable boys I feel I must take a stand along side John Briggs and Anita Bryant.

"Time and time again our children witness grown men throwing their arms around each other after a score, patting one another's fanny after a free throw, dancing gayly (sic) together in the end zone. And now, we have seen them kissing after clinching a baseball pennant."

"Although that disgusting display was between consenting adults in the privacy of their clubhouse, it nevertheless was recorded on the front pages of The Times sports section. Such acts are against God, nature, and baseball. How can I tell my sons to act like men after scoring, when the men they idolize touch and feel one another at practically every turn at bat?"

"I want the 3.3 million people who paid to see the Dodgers to finally do the right thing and join with me in sponsoring an initiative to ban homo sexual activity from sports in California."

"We must save our children, save our Little Leagues, save our national pastime."

67. "Are Homosexuals."

68. Letter sent to organizations and individuals known to support homosexual rights (May 1977).

69. Andra Pearldaughter, "Employment Discrimination Against Lesbians: Municipal Ordinances And Other Remedies," 8 Women's Law Forum (1979): 553. In November of 1981, citing "job burnout" and the lack of "mountains to climb," Briggs announced that he would resign his senate seat. ["Couldn't Find."]

CHAPTER 4 ENDNOTES

1. Both Representative Monks and Senator Helm were members of the John Birch Society and active opponents of the Equal Rights Amendment.

John Greiner, "Homosexual Firing Bill Approved," The Daily Oklahoman, 7 April 1978; "State Senate Approves Bill On Homosexuality," The Oklahoma Journal, 7 April 1978; Ed Howard, "Anti-gay Bill Strips Teacher," The Oklahoma Daily, 9 February 1978; "Gay Teachers Bill Sent To Governor," Oklahoma City Times, 24 April 1978; Terry Maxon, "Helm Starts War On Gay Teachers," The Oklahoman Journal, 11 January 1978; and, "Okla. Teachers Face Firings," Gay Community News, April 1978.

2. "Senate OKs Resolution Hailing Anita," The Oklahoma Journal, 21 April 1977.

3. <u>Oklahoma City Times</u>, 25 May 1978.

4. "Klan Leader Affirms Oklahoma City High School Organizational Activity," Source Unknown; "KKK Head In UK On Recruiting Trip," <u>Gaysweek</u>, May 1977; "Klan Chapters Terrorize Gays In Oklahoma," <u>Gay Community News</u>, 11 February 1978; "Teens Turn To Klan To Combat Gays," <u>Washington Star</u>, 26 January 1978; and "High School Ku Klux Klan Terrorizes Gays In Oklahoma City," <u>Gaysweek</u>, 6 February 1978.

5. Maxon, "Anti-Gay" (1978).

6. <u>James Gaylord v. Tacoma School District No. 10</u>, 85 Wn.2d 348; 535 P.2d 804 (1975); 88 Wn.2d 286; 559 P.2d 1340 (1977). Hereinafter referred to as <u>Gaylord</u>.

7. "Okla. Teachers."

8. "Board Hears Gay," <u>The Norman Transcript</u>, 2 May 1978; "Request Snubbed," <u>Oklahoma City Times</u>, 2 May 1978.

9. Ironically, Mary Helm was defeated in her bid for re-election.

10. Howard, "Anti-Gay Bill" (1978). As mentioned later in this Chapter, leaders in the movements for teachers' rights and homosexual rights nationwide commenced a strong effort to force the National Education Association to articulate opposition to the Helm's Bill. The Oklahoma Federation of Teachers, a chapter of AFT, remained outside the struggle completely. [Personal correspondence, February 1986.]

11. Christine Guilfoy, "Court Overturns Anti-Gay School Law," <u>Gay Community News</u>, 31 March 1984.

12. Once the National Gay Task Force entered into the litigation, it publicly expressed annoyance that Gay Rights Advocates was more interested in immigration litigation than in the Oklahoma suit in their opinion. See "Litigation," <u>It's Time</u>, Newsletter of the NGTF (May/June 1980).

13. Information for this section was gathered from the records of the National Gay Rights Advocates, San Francisco, California, and from all of the briefs and motions filed by the litigants.

14. See <u>Roe v. State of New York</u>, 49 FRD 279, 8 ALR Fed 670 (1970); and, <u>Roe v. Ingraham</u>, 364 F. Supp. 536 (1973).

15. George Michaelson, "GRA Challenges Oklahoma Law," <u>Gay Community News</u>, 2 June 1979.

16. "NGTF Urges Letter Writing Campaign To Add Organizational Plaintiffs To Oklahoma Teacher Case," <u>It's Time</u>, Newsletter of the NGTF (January/February 1981), and "Litigation."

17. Paul Wenske, "Gay Oklahoman To Withdraw From Teaching Suit," The Daily Oklahoman, 10 March 1981.

18. Luther Eubanks, Memorandum Opinion and Order, 29 June 1982; 33 FEP Cases 1009 (1982).

19. See National Gay Task Force v. The Board of Education of the City of Oklahoma City, State of Oklahoma, 729 Fed.2d 1270 (1984). See also, Susan M. Fitch, "National Gay Task Force v. Board of Education of Oklahoma City," 19 (2) Akron Law Review (1985): 337-349.

20. A legal action undertaken to request that a higher court review the actions of a lesser court.

21. Oklahoma Stat. tit. 70, Section 6-103.15(A)(2). For text see Appendix C.

22. Brandenburg v. Ohio, 395 U.S. 444, 447; 89 S.Ct. 1827, 1829; 23 L.Ed.2d 430 (1969).

23. "NGTF Wins Helm Appeal," March 1985; "Homosexual Case Divides Top Court, 4-4," The Boston Globe, 27 March 1985; Tony Mauro," Gay Rights Case May Set Bench Mark," USA Today, 15 January 1985; "Supreme Court Deadlock Overturns Anti-Gay Law," Philadelphia Gay News, 4 April 1985; "Court Divided On Gay Case," Bay Windows, 4 April 1985. See also, Lesbian/Gay Law Notes, Bar Association for Human Rights, and all related briefs and memorandums.

24. See Nancy A. F. Langer, "A Moralistic Supreme Court Majority Keeps Sodomy Laws On The Books," Lambda Update, Newsletter of the Lambda Legal Defense and Education Fund, Inc. (Fall 1986).

25. Langer, "A Moralistic." See also Ethan Bronner, "Ex-Justice Powell Has 2nd Thoughts on Sodomy Case," The Boston Globe 26 October 1990; John Zeh, "Former Supreme Court Justice Calls Hardwick Decision a 'Mistake." Gay Community News, 3 November 1990.

26. Zeh, "Former."

27. "Homosexual Case."

28. "NGTF Wins."

29. Lesbian/Gay Law Notes, Bar Association for Human Rights (September 1985, April 1986).

30. "Bill Against."

31. Michaelson, "Teachers."

32. "Gay Rights Backlash Repeals Local Ordinances," Gay Community News (May 1978).

33. "Gay Rights Backlash."

34 Lesbian/Gay Law Notes, Bar Association for Human Rights (May, April 1986); "Idaho House Defeats Anti-Gay Bill," Gay Community News, 20 April 1985.

35. See Chapter 3 on California's Proposition 6.

CHAPTER 5 ENDNOTES

1. For example, see Louis Fischer and David Schimmel, The Civil Rights of Teachers (New York: Harper & Row, 1973): 1-13, and Dan C. Lortie, Schoolteacher: A Sociological Study (Chicago: University of Chicago Press, 1975).

2. David Tyack, Turning Points In American Educational History (Waltham, MA: Blaisdell, 1967): 4.

3. Howard K. Beale, A History of Freedom of Teaching in American Schools, Report of the Commission on the Social Studies — Part XVI (New York: Charles Scribner's Sons, 1941): 2.

4. Tyack, Turning, 4; and Beale, History, 2.

5. Beale, History, 14-15.

6. Beale, History, 8.

7. Howard K. Beale, Are American Teachers Free?, Reports of the Commission on the Social Studies - Part XII (New York: Charles Scribner's Sons, 1936): 9; and Tyack, Turning, 413.

8. Beale, History, 10-11, 13.

9. Beale, History, 12; and "Requirements Affecting Appointment, Retention, and Promotion of Teachers, VI National Education Association: Research Bulletin (September 1928): 213.

10. Beale, History of Freedom, 11.

11. Beale, History of Freedom, 12.

12. According to available statistics, just prior to the Civil War the procedure of boarding around the teacher on a weekly basis was so common that between 68 percent and 84 percent of teachers in various New England states reported living under these conditions. See Fischer and Schimmel, Civil Rights, 3.

13. Abraham Blinderman, American Writers on Education After 1865 (Boston: Twayne Publishers, 1975): 103.

14. See Joel Spring, The American School: 1642–1985 (New York: Longman, 1986): 112-132.

15. Willard Waller, The Sociology of Teaching (New York: John Wiley and Sons, 1932).

16. Fischer and Schimmel, Civil Rights, xi.

17. Fischer and Schimmel, Civil Rights, xi.

18. Rubin, Rights (1968): 117.

19. Quoted by T. Minehan, "The Teacher Goes Job-Hunting," 124 The Nation (1927): 606. Requoted in Fischer and Schimmel, Civil Rights, 2-3.

Male teachers were not exempt from similar restrictions in their contracts, although they were encouraged to seek a partner in marriage, as evidenced by the some of the rules for teachers in New York City in 1872:

"Men teachers may take one evening each week for courting purposes, or two evenings a week if they go to church regularly.

"After ten hours in school, the teachers spend the remaining time reading the Bible or other good books.

"Any teacher who smokes, uses liquor in any form, frequents pool or public halls, or gets shaved in a barber shop will give good reason to suspect his worth, intentions, integrity, and honesty." [Reprinted in "Echo," publication of the Alumni Association of Framingham State College, Framingham, Massachusetts.]

20. Rubin, Rights (1968): 109.

21. Rubin, Rights (1968): 117.

22. In all fairness to both the courts and school teachers, it should be noted that studies of public school litigation reveal that very few topics concerning personal freedom and minority rights reached the legal arena until the 1950s. Prior to that time, formal and informal mechanisms were adequate to address conflicts in relatively homogeneous communities. See David Tyack and Aaron Benavot, "Courts and Public Schools: Educational Litigation in Historical Perspective," 19 Law and Society Review (1985): 339-380.

23. School District of Fort Smith v. Maury, 53 Ark. 471; 14 S.W. 669 (1980).

24. Rubin, Rights (1968, 1971): 13.

25. Fischer and Schimmel, Civil Rights, 6.

26. See <u>Keyishian v. Board of Regents</u>, 385 U. S. 589, 605 (1967); and <u>Epperson v. Arkansas</u>, 393 U. S. 97, 107 (1968).

27. Fischer and Schimmel, <u>Civil Rights</u>, xiv-xv.

28. Margaret Cummings, "When To Stop Praying," <u>Unity</u> (September 1986): 6.

29. Beale, <u>History</u>; and Beale, <u>American Teachers</u>.

30. Willard S. Elsbree, <u>The American Teacher</u> (New York: American Book Company, 1939): 296.

31. David B. Tyack and Thomas James, "Moral Majorities and the School Curriculum: Historical Perspectives on the Legalization of Virtue," 86 (4) <u>Teachers College Record</u> (Summer 1985): 513-515.

32. Beale, <u>History</u>, xii.

33. Bruce D. Etringer, Erick Hillerbrand, Cheryl Hetherington, "The Influence of Sexual Orientation on Career Decision-Making: A Research Note," 19 (4) <u>Journal of Homosexuality</u> (1990): 103-112.

34. Albert Shanker, Lecture, University of Lowell, College of Education, October, 1986.

35. Shanker, comments made to author in response to post-lecture questions, University of Lowell, College of Education, October, 1986.

36. See Lortie, <u>Schoolteacher</u>, 10-13.

37. Deborah Rhode, "Moral Character As A Professional Credential," 94 <u>Yale Law Journal</u> (1985): 491-603.

38. Noah Webster, <u>A Collection of Essays and Fugitive Writings</u> (Boston: Thomas and Andrews, 1790); in Tyack, <u>Turning</u>, (1967): 96.

39. Bruce Biddle, <u>Role Theory: Expectations, Identities, and Behaviors</u> (New York: Academic Press, 1979): ix.

40. Jeanne Speizer, "Role Models, Mentors, and Sponsors: The Elusive Concepts," 6 (4) <u>Signs: Journal of Women In Culture and Society</u> (1981): 692-712.

41. For an extensive review of the literature, see Dorothy I. Riddle, "Relating To Children: Gays As Role Models," 34 (3) <u>Journal of Social Issues</u> (1978): 38-58.

42. Richard Green, "Sexual Identity of 37 Children Raised By Homosexual or Transsexual Parents," 135 (6) <u>American Journal of Psychiatry</u> (June 1978): 692-697. Richard Green, <u>The "Sissy Boy Syndrome" and the</u>

Development of Homosexuality (New Haven, CT: Yale University Press, 1987). R. Green, J. Mandel, M. Hotvedt, J. Gray, and L. Smith, "Lesbian Mothers and Their Children: A Comparison of Solo Parent Heterosexual Mothers and Their Children," 15 Archives of Sexual Behavior (1986): 167-184.

43. A. P. Bell, "Homosexualities: Their Range and Character," in J. K. Cole and R. Dienstbier, eds., 21 Nebraska Symposium on Motivation (Lincoln; University of Nebraska Press, 1973); A. P. Bell and M. Weinberg, Homosexualities (New York: Simon and Schuster, 1978).

44. M. Kirkpatrick, R. Roy, and K. Smith, "A New Look At Lesbian Mothers," Human Behavior (August 1976): 60-61. See also, Marilyn Elias, "Are Gays Fit Parents?" San Francisco Sunday Examiner and Chronicle, 2 September 1979; Steve Susoeff, "Assessing Children's Best Interests When A Parent Is Gay or Lesbian: Toward A Rational Custody Standard," 32 UCLA Law Review (1985): 852-903; Benna F. Armano, "The Lesbian Mother: Her Right To Child Custody," 4 (1) Golden Gate Law Review (1973): 1-18; Karen M. Harbeck, Mari Bush, and Karen Snell, "In The Best Interest Of The Child: Custody To Lesbian Mothers," Unpublished Paper (February 1980); Donna Hitchens and Ann Thomas, Lesbian Mothers and Their Children: An Annotated Bibliography of Legal and Psychological Materials (San Francisco, CA: Lesbian Rights Project, 1980); J. Bailey, D. Bobrow. M. Wolfe, and S. Mikach, "Sexual Orientation of Adult Sons of Gay Fathers," 31 Developmental Psychology (1955): 124-139; J. Bigner and R. Jacobsen, "Parenting Behaviors of Homosexual and Heterosexual Fathers," 18 Journal of Homosexuality (1989): 173-186; J. Bigner and R. Jacobsen, "Adult Responses to Child Behavior and Attitudes Toward Fathering: Gay and Nongay Fathers," 23 Journal of Homosexuality (1992): 99-112; F. Bozett, "Children of Gay Fathers," In F. Bozett (Ed.), Gay and Lesbian Parents (New York: Praeger, 1987): 38-57; F. Bozett, "Gay Fatherhood," In P. Bronstein and C. Cowan (Eds.), Fatherhood Today: Men's Changing Role in the Family (New York: John Wiley & Sons, 1988a): 214-235; F. Bozett, "Social Control of Identity by Children of Gay Fathers," 10 Western Journal of Nursing Research (1988b): 550-565; F. Bozett, "Gay Fathers: A Review of the Literature," 18 Journal of Homosexuality, (1989): 137-162; D. Cramer, "Gay Parents and Their Children: A Review of Research and Practical Implications," 64 Journal of Counseling and Development (1986): 504-507; D. Flaks, I. Ficher, F. Masterpasqua, and G. Joseph, "Lesbians Choosing Motherhood: A Comparative Study of Lesbian and Heterosexual Parents and Their Children," 31 Developmental Psychology (1995): 105-114; J. Gottman, "Children of Gay and Lesbian Parents," 14 Marriage and Family Review (1990): 177-196; M. Harris and P. Turner, "Gay and Lesbian Parents," 12 Journal of Homosexuality

(1986): 101-113; C. Patterson, "Children of Lesbian and Gay Parents," 63 Child Development (1992): 1025-1042; C. Patterson, "Families of Lesbian Baby Boom: Parents' Division of Labor and Children's Adjustment," 31 Developmental Psychology 115-123; J. Schulenburg, Gay Parenting (Garden City, NY: Anchor Books, 1985); American Journal of Orthopsychiatry (1996).

45. Joseph Acanfora v. Board of Education of Montgomery County, 359 F.Supp. 834 (1973); 491 F.2d 498 (1974); Cert. denied, 419 U.S. 839 (1974). Hereinafter referred to as Acanfora.

46. See Acanfora, Brief for the Appellant (1974): 27.

47. Acanfora, Brief for the Appellant (1974): 28-29.

48. California Education Code, Article 3, Section 44932. See also, Edwin M. Bridges, The Incompetent Teacher (Philadelphia, PA: Falmer Press, 1986).

49. John C. Davis, "Teacher Dismissal On Grounds of Immorality," 46 Clearing House (1972): 418.

50. Board of Trustees of Mt. San Antonio Junior College District v. Hartman, 55 Cal. Rptr. 144 (1966).

51. Di Genova v. State Board of Education, 288 P.2d 862 (1955).

52. See John C. Davis, Immorality and Insubordination in Teacher Dismissals: An Investigation of Case Law, Statute Law, and Employment Contracts, diss., University of Texas at Austin, 1971. See also, Davis, "Teacher Dismissal."

53. For additional information on teachers' rights litigation, see Peter J. Neckles, "The Dwindling Rights of Teachers and the Closing Courthouse Door," 44 Fordham Law Review (1975): 511-547.

54. Michael Willemsen, "Sex and The School Teacher," 14 Santa Clara Lawyer (1974): 846.

55. Lawrence M. Goldyn, Legal Ideology and the Regulation of Homosexual Behavior, diss., Stanford University (1979): 37.

56. "Woman Sues Judge," NOW Newsletter, San Francisco Bay Area Chapter (October 1981).

57. Joseph Gusfield, "Moral Passage: The Symbolic Process In Public Designation of Deviance," 15 Social Problems (1967): 175. Gusfield's analysis is similar to Robert Merton's, who argued that legal functions can be "manifest" or "latent." Manifest functions are explicit and intended,

while latent functions are unconscious. See Robert K. Merton, <u>Social Theory and Social Structure</u> (New York: Free Press, 1968): 118.

58. Lawrence Friedman, <u>The Legal System: A Social Science Perspective</u> (New York: Russell Sage Foundation, 1975): 96-98.

CHAPTER 6 ENDNOTES

1. Composite narrative of several gay and lesbian youth studied by Andi O'Conor. Andi O'Conor, "Who Gets Called Queer in School? Lesbian, Gay and Bisexual Teenagers, Homophobia and High School," In G. Unks, ed., 77(1/2) <u>The High School Journal</u> (1995): 7-12.

2. John Stuart Mill, <u>On Liberty</u>, (Northbrook, IL: A. M. H. Publishing Corp., 1947). First edition 1859.

3. Thomas Grey, <u>The Legal Enforcement of Morality: Essay and Materials In Law and Philosophy</u> (Chicago: American Bar Association, 1980): 1.

4. See Lord Patrick Devlin, <u>The Enforcement of Morals</u> (Oxford: Oxford University Press, 1965). See also Ronald Dworkin, "Lord Devlin and The Enforcement of Morals," 75 <u>Yale Law Journal</u> (May 1966): 986-1005. For a discussion of decisions pertaining to morality in American courts, see Martin Shapiro, "Morals and The Courts: The Reluctant Crusaders," 45 <u>Minnesota Law Review</u> (1961): 897-961.

5. Dworkin, <u>Rights</u> (1977): 241. See also, <u>Report of the Committee on Homosexual Offenses and Prostitution</u>, Cmd. no. 247 (1957): 9, 10, 24.

6, Dworkin, <u>Rights</u>: 241.

7. Dworkin, <u>Rights</u>: 240.

8. Dworkin, <u>Rights</u>: 242.

9. Dworkin, <u>Rights</u>: 243.

10. Dworkin, <u>Rights</u>: 199.

11. Dworkin, <u>Rights</u>: 255.

12. Dworkin, <u>Rights</u>: 255.

13. Dworkin, <u>Rights</u>: 85. See also, Richard D. Mohr, <u>Gays/Justice: A Study of Ethics, Society, and Law</u> (New York: Columbia University Press, 1988).

14. U. S. Const. Amendment XIV, Section 1. For text see Appendix A.

15. See, for example, U. S. Const. Amendment IV, Section 2: "The citizens of each state shall be entitled to all privileges and immunities of citizens in the several states."

16. 163 U.S.537 (1896).

17. 347 U.S. 483 (1954). Brown did not overturn all aspects of the "separate but equal" doctrines of Plessy v. Ferguson; only those aspects that had been applied to educational concerns.

18. Part of the reluctance to include homosexuals as a legitimate minority group has to do with the argument over whether or not homosexuality is inherent and immutable.

For additional information on strict scrutiny see San Antonio School District v. Roderiguez, 411 U.S. 1, 28 (1973). The Court also articulated the need for the group to act and be treated as a "discrete and insular" minority. See United States v. Carolene Products Co., 304 U.S. 144, 152-153, n. 4 (1938).

19. For a detailed, excellent analysis of whether sexual orientation legally warrants inclusion as a protected classification under the 14th Amendment, see Laurence H. Tribe, American Constitutional Law: A Structure for Liberty (Mineola, NY: The Foundation Press, 1978): 941-948; (1988 edition): 1394-95, 1420-35.

20. Roy Romer, Governor of Colorado, et al. v. Richard G. Evans, et al., 116 S. Ct. 1620 (1996). Writ of Certiorari, U.S. Supreme Court, May 20, 1996, No. 94-1039. 64 USLW 4353; 70 Fair Empl. Prac. Cas. (BNA) 1180; 96 Cal. Daily Op. Serv. 3509; 96 Daily Journal D.A.R. 5730; 1996 WL 262293 (U.S.). See also Evans v. Romer, 882 P.2d 1335 (1994).

21. Colorado Const., Art. II, 30c.

22. See reference to Bowers v. Hardwick later in this Chapter, p. 140. Michael Bowers v. Michael Hardwick, 760 F.2d 1202; 765 F.2d 1123; 106 S.Ct. 342; 106 S.Ct. 2841 (1986); rehearing denied 107 S.Ct. 29 (1986).

23. See p. 140 of this Chapter for discussion of the legality of statues criminalizing private sexual activity between consenting adult gays and lesbians.

24. Romer v. Evans, 116 S. Ct. 1628 (1996), quoting Shelley v. Kramer, 334 U.S. 1, 22; 68 S. Ct. 836, 846; 92 L.Ed. 1161 (1948).

25. Romer, 1628.

26. Romer, 1628–1629.

27. Romer, 1629.

28. See, for example, Massachusetts General Laws, Chapter 151B.

29. ENDA, introduced in June 1995, explicitly prohibits job discrimination on the basis of sexual orientation. Lead co-sponsors are Sens. James Jeffords

(R-VT) and Edward Kennedy (D-MA). This legislation was introduced with unprecedented bipartisan support.

30. "Gay Couples Get Canada Benefits," The Boston Globe, 14 June 1996. "Canadian Senate Passes on May 9 a Discrimination Bill," BayWindows, 20 June 1996.

31. For a detailed discussion of the application of strict scrutiny to homosexual issues, see Harris M. Miller, II, "An Argument for the Application of Equal Protection Heightened Scrutiny to Classifications Based on Homosexuality," 57 Southern California Law Review (1984): 797-836; Ellen Chaitin and V. Roy Lefcourt, "Is Gay Suspect?" 8 Lincoln Law Review (1973): 24-54; and, "Note: The Constitutional Status of Sexual Orientation: Homosexuality As A Suspect Classification," 98 Harvard Law Review (1985): 1285-1309.

32. Loving v. Virginia, 388 U.S. 1 (1967).

33. Griswold v. Connecticut, 381 U.S. 479 (1965).

34. Roe v. Wade, 410 U.S. 113 (1973).

35. Griswold v. Connecticut, 381 U.S. 479; 85 S. Ct. 1678; 14 L. Ed.2d 510 (1965) For a more complete discussion of emergent personal freedoms and the law, see J. Harvie Wilkinson III and G. Edward White, "Constitutional Protection for Personal Lifestyles," 62 Cornell Law Review (1977): 563-625.

36. The right of personal privacy arguably "springs from the First, Fourth, Fifth, Ninth, the penumbra of the Bill of Rights, or, as I believe, in the concept of liberty guaranteed by the first section of the Fourteenth Amendment. . . ." Dissenting opinion of District Court Judge Merhige, in Doe v. Commonwealth's Attorney for the City of Richmond, 403 F. Supp. 1199 (1975).

37. Morris L. Ernst and Alan V. Schwartz, Privacy: The Right To Be Let Alone (New York: Macmillan, 1962): 1.

38. Ernst and Schwartz, Privacy, 1.

39. Paris Adult Theatre I v. Slaton, 413 U.S. 49, 59 (1973).

40. Poe v. Ullman, 367 U.S. 497, 545-546 (1961).

41. Doe v. Commonwealth's Attorney (1975). See James J. Rizzo, "The Constitutionality of Sodomy Statutes," 45 Fordham Law Review (1976): 553-595; "The Constitutionality of Laws Forbidding Private Homosexual Conduct," 72 Michigan Law Review (August 1974): 1613-1637; and "Constitutional Protections of Private Sexual Conduct Among Consenting Adults: Another Look at Sodomy Statutes," 62 Iowa Law Review (1976):

568-590, for extensive discussions of the constitutional challenges to state sodomy statutes. Appendix D provides a state-by-state status report on sodomy laws as of August 31, 1996.

42. Grey, Legal: II-49.

43. Michael Bowers v. Michael Hardwick, 760 F.2d 1202; 765 F.2d 1123; 106 S.Ct. 342; 106 S.Ct. 2841 (1986); rehearing denied 107 S.Ct. 29 (1986). Hereinafter referred to as Bowers v. Hardwick. Lesbian/Gay Law Notes, Bar Association for Human Rights (February 1986): 7. See the discussion of this case and an interview with Michael Hardwick in, William B. Rubenstein, ed., Lesbians and Gay Men and The Law (New York: The New Press, 1993): 125-154.

44. For an analysis of the impact of decriminalization of homosexual acts see Gilbert Geis, Richard Wright, Thomas Garrett, and Paul Wilson, "Reported Consequences of Decriminalization of Consensual Adult Homosexuality In Seven American States," 1 (4) Journal of Homosexuality (Summer 1976): 419-426.

45. "Tenn. High Court Rules Sodomy Law to be Unenforceable," BayWindows, June, 1996.

46. Blackmun quoting from Olmstead v. United States, 277 U.S. 438, 478 (1928). Esteemed legal scholar Laurence H. Tribe, during a program on National Public Radio analyzing the legal impact of Justice Blackmun's career on the eve of his announced retirement, noted that Blackmun ultimately may be more famous for his powerful and well argued dissent set forth in Bowers v. Hardwick. April 7, 1994.

47. Erving Goffman, Stigma: Notes On The Management of Spoiled Identity (Englewood Cliffs, NJ: Prentice-Hall, 1963): i.

48. For a discussion of characteristics attributed to the homosexual population, see Gregory R. Staats, "Stereotype Content and Social Distance: Changing Views of Homosexuality," 4 (1) Journal of Homosexuality (Fall 1978): 15-27.

49. Goffman, Stigma, 2-3.

50. Goffman, Stigma, 4-5.

51. See Martin Levine, "Gay Ghetto," 4 (4) Journal of Homosexuality (Summer 1979): 363-377, for a sociological analysis of minority ghettos and their parallels in homosexual subcultures.

52. Goffman, Stigma, 7.

53. See Jerrold S. Greenberg, "The Effects of a Homophile Organization on The Self-Esteem and Alienation of Its Members," 1 (3) Journal of

Homosexuality (1976): 313-317. See also, Lawrence Wilson and Raphael Shannon, "Homosexual Organizations and The Right of Association," 30 (4) Hastings Law Journal (March 1979): 1029-1074.

54. Gusfield, "Moral": 179-182.

55. L. Friedman, Law: 151.

56. Edwin Schur, The Politics of Deviance (Englewood Cliffs, NJ: Prentice-Hall, 1980): 66-67. See also, Bernice Latt and Diane Maluso (Eds.), The Social Psychology of Interpersonal Discrimination (NY: Guilford Press, 1995). See also, Elisabeth Young-Bruehl, The Anatomy of Prejudice (Cambridge, MA: Harvard University Press, 1996).

57. Schur, Deviance: 132, 136.

CHAPTER 7 ENDNOTES

1. In Charley Shively, ed., Calamus Lovers: Walt Whitman's Working Class Camerados (San Francisco, CA: Gay Sunshine Press, 1987): 10-11.

2. See Staats, "Stereotype."

3. Barnett, Sexual: 75. See also, Bernard Sergent, Homosexuality in Greek Myth (Boston: Beacon Press, 1986).

4. C. S. Ford and F. A. Beach, Patterns of Sexual Behavior (New York: Harper and Brothers, 1951). For a discussion of problems with anthropo-logical studies of homosexuality in other cultures, see Thomas K. Fitzgerald, "A Critique of Anthropological Research on Homosexuality," 2(4) Journal of Homosexuality (Summer 1977): 385-397.

5. Ford and Beach, Sexual. See also, Marvin K. Opler, "Anthropological and Cross-Cultural Aspects of Homosexuality," in J. Marmor, ed., Sexual Inversion (New York: Basic Books, 1965): 108-123. See also, Walter L. Williams, The Spirit and the Flesh: Sexual Diversity in American Indian Culture (Boston: Beacon Press, 1986). Jan Bremmer, ed., From Sappho to DeSade: Moments in the History of Sexuality (New York: Routledge, 1989). Serena Nanda, Neither Man Nor Woman: The Hijras of India (Belmont, CA: Wadsworth Publishing, 1990). Bret Hinsch, Passions of the Cut Sleeve: The Male Homosexual Tradition in China (Berkeley, CA: University of California Press, 1990). Ihara Saikaku, The Great Mirror of Male Love (Stanford, CA: Stanford University Press, 1990). Reay Tannahill, Sex in History (New York: Stein and Day, 1982).

6. Barnett, Sexual: 77. Another useful source is Terry Calvani, "Homosexuality and The Law — An Overview," 17 New York Law Forum (1971): 273-303.

7. Barnett, <u>Sexual</u>: 77-79. See also, Martin Samuel Cohen, "The Biblical Prohibition of Homosexual Intercourse," 19(4) <u>Journal of Homosexuality</u> (1990): 3-20.

8. Barnett, <u>Sexual</u>: 79-80.

9. Barnett, <u>Sexual</u>: 81. For a more complete discussion of English laws about homosexuality see Barnett's chapter notes on "Establishment of Religion," 89-90. See also, Kent Gerard and Gert Hekma, eds., <u>The Pursuit of Sodomy: Male Homosexuality in Renaissance and Enlightenment Europe</u> (New York: Haworth Press, 1988).

10. See William Blackstone, <u>Commentaries on the Laws of England</u> (London: William Reed, 1811): 215. See also, B. R. Burg, "Ho Hum, Another Work of the Devil: Buggery and Sodomy in Early Stuart England," 6 (1/2) <u>Journal of Homosexuality</u> (1980): 69-78. Arthur N. Gilbert, "Conceptions of Homosexuality and Sodomy in Western History," 6 (1/2) <u>Journal of Homosexuality</u> (1980): 57-68.

11. Barnett, <u>Sexual</u>: 81. North Carolina Rev. Code c. 34, Section 6 (1837). See Louis Crompton, <u>Byron and Greek Love: Homophobia in 19th-Century England</u> (Berkeley, CA: University of California Press, 1985).

12. Louis Crompton, "Homosexuals and the Death Penalty in Colonial America," 1 (3) <u>Journal of Homosexuality</u> (1976): 278.

13. Crompton, "Death Penalty," 280-281. Crompton's essay provides an excellent analysis of the origins and application of colonial laws against homosexuality. See also, Crompton, "The Myth of Lesbian Impunity: Capital Laws From 1270 to 1791," 6 (1/2) <u>Journal of Homosexuality</u> (1980): 11-26.

14. Crompton, "Death Penalty," 282-283.

15. In his outline of criminal statutes and punishment written in 1777, Thomas Jefferson also maintained that sodomy should be punished by castration. See Crompton, "Death Penalty," 292-293. See also Julian P. Boyd, <u>The Papers of Thomas Jefferson, Vol. 2, January 1777 to June 1779</u> (Princeton, NJ: Princeton University Press, 1950): 663-664.

16. Crompton, "Death Penalty," 282-283.

17. Crompton, "Death Penalty," 282-283.

18. Crompton, "Death Penalty," 285.

19. Crompton, "Death Penalty," 288.

20. Lillian Faderman, "The Morbidification of Love Between Women by 19th-Century Sexologist," 4 (1) <u>Journal of Homosexuality</u> (Fall, 1978): 73-90, and "Lesbian Magazine Fiction in the Early Twentieth Century," <u>Journal</u>

of Popular Culture II (1978): 700-717. See also, Chanucey, Jr., "Sexual Inversion," 114-146; Bullough, "Medical Model," 99-110; D'Emilio, Sexual; and, Jeffrey Weeks, Coming Out: Homosexual Politics In Britain From the Nineteenth Century To the Present (London: Quartet, 1977).

21. Chauncey uses the plural of subculture to emphasize the diverse experiences of gender and sexuality based upon class, race, ethnicity, and religion. See Chauncey, Jr. "Sexual Inversion," 115-116. In his essay on "Fairies, Pogues," Chauncey demonstrates that the Newport homosexual subculture flourished with a complex social order that did not reference the labels and theories set forth by the medical profession concerning same sex relationships.

22. See Lillian Faderman, Surpassing the Love of Men: Romantic Friendships and Love Between Women from the Renaissance to the Present (New York: William Morrow, 1981).

23. Chauncey, "Sexual Inversion," 119.

24. One example of a typical study was the 1934 research, "Constitutional Factors in Homosexuality," 90 American Journal of Psychiatry (May 1934): 1249-1270, in which George Henry and Hugh Galbraith concluded that homosexuals were identifiable because of certain psychological characteristics. The homosexual male displayed a "feminine carrying angle of the arm, long legs, narrow hips, large muscles, deficient hair on the face, chest and back, feminine distribution of pubic hair, a high-pitched voice, small penis and testicles and the presence of the scrotal fold. Not uncommonly there is an excess of fat on the shoulders, buttocks and abdomen. Occasionally the penis is very large and the hips are unusually wide."[at p. 1265] The homosexual female exhibited "firm adipose tissue, deficient fat in the shoulders and abdomen, firm muscles, excess hair on the chest, back and lower extremities, a tendency to masculine distribution of pubic hair, a small uterus and either over-or under-development of the labia and clitoris. There is also a tendency toward a shorter trunk, a contracted pelvis, under-development of the breasts, excess hair on the face, and a low-pitched voice." [at p. 1265]

25. Chauncey, "Sexual Inversion," 132.

26. D'Emilio, Sexual, 15.

27. This perspective on homosexuality still exists to this date. A 1977 Gallup poll about homosexuality, completed after the Dade County referendum, revealed that some people who supported equal rights for homosexuals did so because they believed that "an abnormal twist develops in their [the homosexual's] growing process and they should not be punished all their lives for something beyond their control." See "Gallup Poll,"

Esplanade, 29 July 1977, and Jim Marko, "Gallup, Harris Polls Show Gay Rights Support," Gay Community News, 30 July 1977.

28. D'Emilio, Sexual, 15. See also, John D'Emilio and Estelle B. Freedman, Intimate Matters: A History of Sexuality in America (New York: Harper & Row, 1988).

29. The reader is referred to several of the following books and articles that discuss the psychological determinants of homosexuality. F. X. Acosta, "Etiology and Treatment of Homosexuality: A Review," 4 Archives of Sexual Behavior (1975): 9-29; I. Bieber, Homosexuality: A Psychoanalytic Study (New York: Basic Books, 1962); P.J. Fink, "Homosexuality: Illness or Lifestyle?," 1 Journal of Sex and Marital Therapy (1975): 225-233; M. Foucault, The History of Sexuality: An Introduction, trans. R. Hurley (New York: Pantheon Books, 1978); S. Freud, Three Essays on the Theory of Sexuality, trans. J. Strachey (New York: Basic Books, 1962); E. H. Gnepp, "Biology, Mental Illness, and Homosexuality: A Comment on Public Affairs," 12 Psychology (1974): 60-61; Kinsey, et al., Human Male; Kinsey, et al., Human Female; and C. A. Tripp, The Homosexual Matrix (New York: McGraw-Hill, 1975).

30. See I. Bieber, "A Discussion of Homosexuality: The Ethical Challenge," 44 Journal of Consulting and Clinical Psychology (1976): 136-166. See also, P. Wyden and B. Wyden, Growing Up Straight (New York: Stein and Day, 1968).

31. Ford, "Homosexuality," 8. See also W. Churchill, Homosexual Behavior Among Males (New York: Hawthorn Books, 1967); and Ford and Beach, Sexual Behavior.

32. Kinsey et al., Human Male.

33. Tripp, Homosexual. Since these factors are numerous and complex, behavioral therapists suggest that the failure of their mode of treatment is due to their failure to recognize the antecedents to homosexuality. See G. T. Wilson and G. C. Davison, "Behavior Therapy and Homosexuality: A Critical Perspective," 5 Behavior Therapy (1974): 16-28.

34. See Wyden and Wyden, Growing Up.

35. R. A. Farrell, and C. W. Hardin, "Legal Stigma and Homosexual Career Deviance," in M. Riedel and T. Thornberry, eds., Crime and Delinquency: Dimensions of Deviance (New York: Praeger, 1974): 128-140.

36. Daniel J. Kevles, "The X Factor: The Battle Over The Ramifications of A Gay Gene," The New Yorker, 3 April 1995. Richard A. Knox, "Gene May Help Explain the Origins of Homosexuality," The Boston Globe 16 July

1993. See also, Chandler Burr, "Homosexuality and Biology," The Atlantic Monthly, March 1993; David Wheeler, "Studies Linking Homosexuality to Genes Draw Criticism From Researchers," The Chronicle of Higher Education 5 February 1992; David Gelman, et. al., "Is This Child Gay?: Born or Bred: The Origins of Homosexuality," Newsweek 24 February 1992; and John P. DeCecco, David Allen Parker, eds., Sex, Cells, and Same-Sex Desire: The Biology of Sexual Preference, volumes I and II (New York: Haworth, 1995), published also in 28(1-4) Journal of Homosexuality (New York: Haworth, 1995).

37. M.I.T. Press, Cambridge, MA, 1994.

38. Dean H. Hammer and Peter Copeland, The Science of Desire: The Search for the Gay Gene and the Biology of Behavior (New York: Simon and Schuster, 1994). Also Hamer's keynote address to the Family Fellowship, Salt Lake City, Utah, 1995.

39. Family Fellowship, P.O. Box 9451, Salt Lake City, UT 84109, tel. 801/272-3806. Quarterly newsletter subscription is $10/year. Thanks to Sally Morse of Wichita, KS, for the Mormon faith information.

40. T. R. Clark, "Homosexuality and Psychopathology in Nonpatient Males," 35 American Journal of Psychoanalysis (1975): 163-168; W. R. Horstman, "MMPI Responses of Homosexual and Heterosexual Male College Students," 2 Homosexual Counseling Journal (1975): 68-76; J. E. Mundorff, Personality Characteristics of Selected College Male Heterosexuals, Homosexual Activists and Non-activists, diss., Northern Illinois University, 1973; and E. L. Ohlson, "A Preliminary Investigation Into the Self-disclosing Ability of Male Homosexuals," 11 Psychology (1974): 21-25.

41. M. Siegelman, "Birth Order and Family Size of Homosexual Men and Women," 41 Journal of Consulting and Clinical Psychology (1973): 164.

42. For studies of males, see Clark, "Homosexuality," and Ohlson, "Self-Disclosing." For studies of females see Bernard Riess, Jeanne Safer, and William Yotive, "Psychological Test Data on Female Homosexuality," 1 (1) Journal of Homosexuality (1974): 71-85.

43. G. Tourney, A. J. Petrilli, and L. M. Hatfield, "Hormonal Relationships in Homosexual Men," 132 American Journal of Psychiatry (1975): 288-290; and Tripp, Homosexual.

44. M. W. Ross, "Relationship Between Sex Role and Sex Orientation in Homosexual Men," 4 New Zealand Psychologist (1975): 25-29; Horstman, "MMPI Responses" (1975); N. L. Thompson, D. M. Schwartz, B. R. McCandless, and D. A. Edwards, "Parent-child Relationships and Sexual Identity in Male and Female Homosexuals and Heterosexuals," 41 Journal

of Consulting and Clinical Psychology (1973): 120-127; B. D. Townes, W. D. Ferguson, and S. Gillam, "Differences in Psychological Sex, Adjustment, and Familial Influences Among Homosexual and Non-homosexual Populations," 1 Journal of Homosexuality (1976): 266-272. See also, Joyce C. Albro and Carol Tully, "A Study of Lesbian Lifestyles In The Homosexual Micro-culture and the Heterosexual Macro-culture," 4 (4) Journal of Homosexuality (Summer 1979): 331-344.

45. Mark Freedman, Homosexuality and Psychological Functioning (Belmont, CA: Wadsworth, 1971). See also, William Parker, "The Homosexual in American Society Today," 8 Criminal Law Bulletin (1972): 692-695.

46. Ford, "Homosexuality," citing a study undertaken by H. B. Roback, R. Langevin, and Y. Zajac, "Sex of Free Choice Figure Drawings By Homosexual and Heterosexual Subjects," 38 Journal of Personality Assessment (1974): 154-155.

47. Judd Marmor and Richard Green, "Homosexual Behavior," in J. Money and H. Musaph, Handbook of Sexology (Amsterdam; Elsevier/North Holland Press, 1977): 1051-1052.

48. One study of children of homosexuals revealed that the major family problem was the societal reaction to the parent's lifestyle rather than the child's upset. See Martha Kirkpatrick's study of the psychological status of the children of lesbian mothers undertaken by the University of California at Los Angeles Medical School. Kirkpatrick et al, "Lesbian Mothers," 60-61; and, Riddle, "Relating," 38-58.

49. Chauncey, "Fairies, Pogues," 4-5, 8-9.

50. Personal discussion, source anonymous (1986).

51. See Laud Humphreys, Tearoom Trade: Impersonal Sex In Public Places (Chicago: Aldine-Atherton, 1970): 5. On the other hand, as the participant aged or gained weight, he was less likely to obtain sex within a context that permitted him to remain dominant.

Humphreys' study about the magnitude of casual sex with males by supposedly heterosexual males raises some serious issues concerning the spread of AIDS in our society.

52. Humphreys, Tearoom, 5.

53. Humphreys, Tearoom, 105.

54. Humphreys, Tearoom, 153.

55. Humphreys, Tearoom, 135, 147.

56. Kinsey et al., Human Male, 638.

57. Kinsey et al., Human Male; and Human Female.

58. Kinsey et al., Human Male, 651.

59. See Braden Robert Berkey, Terri Perelman-Hall, and Lawrence A. Kurdek, "The Multidimensional Scale of Sexuality," 19 (4) Journal of Homosexuality (1990): 67-88, for a recent study of determinations of heterosexuality, homosexuality, bisexuality, and asexuality. See also, John P. DeCecco and Michael G. Shively, eds., Bisexual and Homosexual Identities: Critical Theoretical Issues (New York: Haworth Press, 1983). Alan P. Bell and Martin S. Weinberg, Homosexualities: A Study of Diversity Among Men and Women (New York: Touchstone, 1978).

60. Marc Morrison v. The State Board of Education, 74 Cal.Rptr. 166; 1 C.3d 214; 82 Cal.Rptr. 175; 461 P.2d 375 (1969).

61. Sarac v. State Board of Education, 249 C.A.2d 58; 57 Cal.Rptr. 69 (2nd Dist., 1967).

62. Barnett, Sexual Freedom (1973): 81. North Carolina Rev. Code c. 34, Section 6 (1837).

63. Carroll Smith-Rosenberg, "The Female World of Love and Ritual: Relations Between Women In Nineteenth-Century America," 1 Signs: Journal of Women in Culture and Society (Fall 1975): 27. See also, Faderman, Surpassing.

64. Xenophon, Lacedaemonians 2, 13, trans. E. C. Marchant (London; William Heinemann, 1956).

65. Henri Marrou, "Pederasty In Classical Education," in A History of Education In Antiquity, trans. George Lamb (Madison, WI: University of Wisconsin Press, 1948): 31. See also, David M. Halperin, One Hundred Years of Homosexuality and Other Essays on Greek Love (New York: Routledge, 1990). John J. Winkler, The Constraints of Desire: The Anthropology of Sex and Gender in Ancient Greece (New York: Routledge, 1990).

66. Marrou, "Pederasty," 33.

67. In terms of the dis-esteemed status of teaching as a profession, it is worth noting the Greek perspective that any person who made a business of teaching any available student was a lowly and inferior educator. Only through careful selection of proteges could the intense bond develop that influenced a passion to excel. See Bullough, Homosexuality, 104.

68. Marrou, "Pederasty," 34.

69. Quoted by A. D. C. Peterson, <u>A Hundred Years of Education</u> (New York: Collier Books, 1962): 109; and cited in Bullough, <u>Homosexuality</u>, 106.

70. Bullough, <u>Homosexuality</u>, 106.

71. C. S. Lewis, <u>Surprised by Joy: The Shape of My Early Life</u> (New York: Harcourt, Brace and World, 1955): 88-89, 108-110; cited in Bullough, <u>Homosexuality</u>, 107-109.

72. Kinsey et al., <u>Human Male</u>, 625. If the national estimate of the homosexual population was 10 percent in 1948, prior to the gay and lesbian rights movement, it may be the case that the current figures could be as high as 20 percent of the population.

73. Bullough, "Lesbianism."

74. Kinsey et al., <u>Human Female</u>, 478.

75. <u>Miss Marianne Woods and Miss Jane Pirie Against Dame Helen Cummings Gordon</u>, The Arno Series on Homosexuality (New York: Arno Press, 1975). For additional information on the case, see Lillian Faderman, <u>Scotch Verdict: Dame Gordon vs. Pirie and Woods</u> (New York: Morrow, 1983).

76. Lillian Hellman, "The Children's Hour," in <u>Twenty Best Plays of the Modern American Theatre</u>, ed. John Gassner (New York: Crown, 1947): 561-598.

77. Much of this information was gathered by cross-referencing Abraham Blinderman's volumes on American writers on education with Jonathan Katz's volume on gay American history. The Blinderman volumes provided information on famous people who had been educators, while the Katz book revealed people who were attracted to members of their same sex. Unfortunately, the outcome of this research is of limited value to the study of homosexual educators because it often fails to elucidate the life experience of simultaneously being a school teacher and attracted to members of one's same sex. Blinderman, <u>American Writers After 1865</u>, and <u>American Writers on Education Before 1865</u> (Boston: Twayne, 1975). Katz, <u>Gay History</u>.

78. See Walter Harding, "Thoreau's Sexuality," 21 (3) <u>Journal of Homosexuality</u> (1991): 23-46.

79. Katz, <u>Gay History</u>, 658-659.

80. Madelon Bedell, <u>The Alcotts: Biography of a Family</u> (New York: Clarkson N. Potter, Inc., 1980). Most of the discussion on Alcott is from the Bedell biography, 17, 18, 175, 180, 189, 208, 227-230.

81. Gary Scharnhorst and Jack Bales, The Lost Life of Horatio Alger, Jr. (Bloomington, IN: Indiana University Press, 1985): 1.

82. Scharnhorst and Bales, Alger, 3.

83. Leviticus 20:13-14 states that: "[i]f a man also lie with mankind, as he lieth with a woman, both of them have committed an abomination: they shall surely be put to death; their blood shall be upon them."

Other relevant Biblical references include: Leviticus 18:22; Deuteronomy 23:18; Judges 19:22; I Kings 14:24, 15:12; II Kings 23:7; Romans 1:27; I Corinthians 6:9; and I Timothy 1:10.

84. Christian Register, 24 March 1866. See Scharnhorst and Bales, Alger , 3.

85. Katz, Gay History, 74-76.

86. D'Emilio, Sexual, 17.

CHAPTER 8 ENDNOTES

1. See for example, Nicholas von Hoffman, Citizen Cohn: The Life and Times of Roy Cohn (New York: Doubleday, 1988).

2. See D'Emilio, Sexual, 58; and Barnett, Sexual Freedom.

3. William Neal v. Farris Bryant, et al.; Mary Frances Bradshaw v. State Board of Education; and, Anne Louise Poston v. State Board of Education. Fla., 149 So.2d 529 (1962): 533. Hereinafter referred to as Neal v. Bryant.

4. Loughery, John, "Hunting Gays in Gainesville," The Harvard Gay and Lesbian Review (Winter 1996): 18.

5. Loughery, "Hunting Gays," 19.

6. See Bullough, Homosexuality, 103.

7. D'Emilio, Sexual, 112. See also Barnett, Sexual Freedom, 4, 5, 15, 16. The recommendations of the 1955 American Law Institute's Model Penal Code concerning legalizing sex between consenting adults was not adopted until 1973, when seven states ratified the entire Model Penal Code. This sweeping change to the penal codes of the states of Illinois, Connecticut, Colorado, Oregon, Hawaii, Delaware, and Ohio benefited homosexuals because the topic was not isolated for discussion and possible rejection. For an analysis of the impact of decriminalization of the sodomy statutes, see Geis et al., "Decriminalization," 419-426.

8. As will be noted throughout the case law discussion, in 1975 the State of California legalized private sexual acts between consenting adults. In

1979, the California Supreme Court rejected the traditional interpretation of the sexual solicitation and lewd vagrancy laws by demanding that the police prove that a person other than a vice-officer be present and offended by the solicitation conduct. Furthermore, the police must prove that the solicitation conduct was inappropriate for the setting, thus rendering police entrapment in gay singles bars a useless activity. Another significance feature of the holding in Pryor v. Los Angeles Municipal Court was that the High Court specified that their decision was retroactive, thus clearing the criminal records of tens of thousands of people. See It's Time: Newsletter of the National Gay Task Force, 6 (7), (November/December 1979): 3.

9. D'Emilio, Sexual, 46-47.

10. See D'Emilio, Sexual, Chapter Three: 40-53.

11. California Penal Code, Section 291 (West Supp. 1974) provides:

Every sheriff or chief of police, upon the arrest for any of the offenses enumerated in Section 290 or in subdivision 1 of Section 261 (essentially all sex offense crimes, such as rape, sodomy, solicitation, lewd and lascivious conduct, and sexual assault) of any school employee, shall do either of the following:

(1) If such school employee is a teacher in any of the public schools of this state, he shall immediately notify by telephone the superintendent of schools of the school district employing such teacher and shall immediately give written notice of the arrest to the Commission for Teacher Preparation and Licensing and to the superintendent of schools in the county wherein such person is employed. Upon receipt of such notice, the county superintendent of schools shall immediately notify the governing board of the school district employing such person.

(2) If such school employee is a non teacher in any of the public schools of this state, he shall immediately notify by telephone the superintendent of schools of the school district employing such non teacher and shall immediately give written notice of the arrest to the governing board of the school district employing such person.

12. Mark A Stodola, "The Homosexual's Legal Dilemma," 27 Arkansas Law Review (1973): 715-716. Interview of Eugene Warren, Counsel for the Arkansas Education Association, Little Rock, AR: 11 April 1973.

13. See Neal G. Horenstein, "Homosexuals in the Teaching Profession," 20 Cleveland State Law Review (January 1971): 129-130.

14. Lerner v. Los Angeles City Board of Education, 59 C.2d 382; 29 Cal.Rptr. 657; 380 P.2d 97 (1963). Hereinafter referred to as Lerner.

15. Amundsen v. State Board of Education, Civ. No. 37942, Cal. Ct. App. (2d District, 1971). Hereinafter referred to as Amundsen.

16. These cases are further obscured by the trial process itself, which usually provides for no public notice of the arrest, a hearing in private before the judge and a few necessary court personnel prior to regular court sessions, no actual probation reporting procedure, and sealed court records. [My experience in criminal practice with homosexual solicitation cases from 1982 to the present.]

Despite the rather considerate court procedures, in my trial experience, these types of arrests are devastating to the defendant. Usually, they have had no prior exposure to the criminal justice system, an institution which is designed to instill fear and respect. The complex emotions aroused by being arrested for one's homosexual behavior — including fear, shame, and anxiety — are heightened by the lack of someone to talk with about it. Their private tragedy does not change despite the outcome of the case — the mere fact that they've been charged is devastating. Further, the defendants fear the stigma of being a criminal and of making another mistake that could render the outcome of their original case much more serious.

17. Probation under these circumstances merely meant that the defendant must have had no further criminal instances during the period of probation, which usually lasted from 6 to 12 months. The defendant did not have to report to a parole officer.

18. George Fountain v. State Board of Education, 157 C.A.2d 463; 320 P.2d 899 (1958). Hereinafter referred to as Fountain.

19. For a complete analysis of the application of vagrancy statutes to homosexual arrests, see "The Consenting Adult Homosexual and the Law: An Empirical Study of Enforcement and Administration in Los Angeles County," 13 U.C.L.A. Law Review (1966): 643-832.

20. California Educational Code Section 12756 states, "Whenever the holder of any credential, life diploma, or document issued by the State Board of Education has been convicted of any sex offense as defined in Section 12011.7, the State Board of Education shall forthwith suspend the credential, life diploma, or document. If the conviction is reversed and the holder is acquitted of the offense in a new trial or the charges against him are dismissed, the board shall forthwith terminate the suspension of the credential, life diploma, or document. When the conviction becomes final or when imposition of sentence is suspended the board shall forthwith revoke the credential, life diploma, or document. (Added Stats. 1952, 1st Ex. Sess., c. 25, p. 340, Section 4. The Code Section was changed to 13207 at some later date)." Fountain (1958): 901.

21. Rehearing and hearing denied, <u>Fountain</u> (1958): 473.

22. <u>Lerner v. Los Angeles City Board of Education</u>, 59 C.2d 382; 29 Cal. Rptr. 657; 380 P.2d 97 (1963). Hereinafter referred to as <u>Lerner</u>.

23. In his dissent, Justice McComb stated the specific accusations against Lerner that were referenced as "lewd vagrancy" in the body of the court opinion. Lerner was charged with "lewd and lascivious acts in that he did... rub, touch and fondle the private parts of R. A. Cook, a person of the masculine sex, in a manner designed to arouse, excite and gratify unnatural sexual desires in R. A. Cook and the respondent; and, that the respondent did then and there further offer and attempt to then and there orally copulate the penis of R. A. Cook." <u>Lerner</u> (1963): 400.

24. Michael Willemsen, "Justice Tobriner And The Tolerance Of Evolving Lifestyles: Adapting Law To Social Change," 29 <u>Hastings Law Journal</u> (September 1977): 97.

25. Willemsen, "Tobriner," 75.

26. <u>Odorizzi</u> (1966): 127.

27. <u>Odorizzi</u> (1966): 135.

28. <u>Sarac v. State Board of Education</u>, 249 C.A.2d 58; 57 Cal.Rptr. 69 (2nd Dist. 1967).

29. Rudman, Norman G. (defendant's attorney), 20 February 1986, personal correspondence.

30. Rudman.

31. <u>Sarac</u> (1967): 61.

32. <u>Sarac</u> (1967): 61.

33. <u>Sarac</u> (1967): 63.

34. California Education Code, Section 7851.

35. <u>Sarac</u> (1967): 63.

36. See Goldyn, <u>Legal Ideology</u>, for a thorough analysis of the use of derogatory language in court decisions pertaining to some aspects of homosexual behavior.

37. Rudman.

38. Rudman did not think that the Sarac case was public knowledge or that there was community involvement in the matter.

39. Rudman.

40. Goldyn, Legal Ideology, 35.

41. Jarvella v. Willoughby-Eastlake City School District Board of Education, 12 O.Misc. 288; 41 O.O.(2d) 423 (1967). Hereinafter referred to as Jarvella.

42. Jarvella (1967): 425.

43. See Blackstone, Commentaries.

44. Nelson, John S. (defendant's attorney), 12 March 1986, personal correspondence.

45. Jarvella (1967): 425; First, Fourth, Ninth, and Fourteenth Amendments to the U.S. Constitution; Article I, Section 11 of the Constitution of Ohio.

46. Status of the American Public School Teacher, 1980-1981 (1982). National Education Association, Washington, D. C.

47. See the chapter on pedophilia in the next volume in this series.

48. For a more complete discussion of this topic see, Barnett, Sexual Freedom, 193-195. See also Susan E. [Reese], "The Forgotten Sex: Lesbians, Liberation, and The Law," 11 Willamette Law Journal (1975): 354-377.

49. In their essay review of the literature, "Coming Out: Similarities and Differences For Lesbians and Gay Men." 34 (3) Journal of Social Issues (1978), de Monteflores and Schultz described the differences in sexual behavior between male and female homosexuals.

50. See "Introduction," footnote 15 for more details.

51. See de Monteflores and Schultz, "Coming Out," 69, for a review of the research literature on reactions of men and women to lesbianism and male homosexuality.

52. See Barnett, Sexual Freedom for a discussion of the research pertaining to the relationship between homosexuality and an interest in sex with young children. See also, Groth and Birnbaum, "Adult Sexual," 175-181, and the next volume of this series.

CHAPTER 9 ENDNOTES

1. Many GLBT activists and historians argue that the death of Judy Garland was not a factor in the Stonewall riots. See Christopher Guly, "The Judy Connection," The Advocate, 28 June, 1994.

2. For example, in his study of homosexual awareness of and activism for civil rights, Fred A. Minnigerode has noted a significant change towards greater assertion of rights between pre-1970 and post-1970 attitudinal surveys. See "Rights or Repentance," 2 (4) Journal of Homosexuality (Summer 1977): 323-326. For additional information on the characterization

of homosexual issues as civil rights, see the symposium material presented in 2 (4) Journal of Homosexuality (Summer 1977); see also, Marcy R. Adelman, "Sexual Orientation and Violations of Civil Liberties," 2 (4) Journal of Homosexuality (Summer 1977): 327-330.

3. D'Emilio, Sexual, 112.

4. D'Emilio, Sexual, 212.

5. For additional documentation on the increasing tolerance for homosexuality around 1970, see Stodola, "Dilemma," 687-721.

6. Gerard Sullivan, "A Bibliographic Guide to Government Hearings and Reports, Legislative Action, and Speeches Made in the House and Senate of the United States Congress on the Subject of Homosexuality," in John P. DeCecco (Ed.), Bashers, Baiters and Bigots: Homophobia in American Society (New York: Harrington Park Press, 1985): 135-189.

Since 1977, however, the Sullivan information demonstrated increasing evidence of the influence of the conservative right that anticipates the analysis in the chapters that follow.

7. The record does not disclose what happened to Schneringer.

8. California Education Code, Section 13202 provides: "The State Board of Education shall revoke or suspend for immoral or unprofessional conduct, or for persistent defiance of, and refusal to obey, the laws regulating the duties of persons serving in the Public School System, or for any cause which would have warranted the denial of an application for a certification document or the renewal thereof, or for evident unfitness for service, life diplomas, documents, or credentials issued pursuant to this code." Among the causes warranting denial of such documents is the commission of "any act involving moral turpitude." (Cal. Ed. Code, section 13129, subd. (e). Morrison (1969): 217.

9. Black's Law Dictionary (Revised fourth edition, 1968, original edition 1891): 1113, defines a writ of mandamus as a mandatory precept in writing "which issues from a court of superior jurisdiction, and is directed to a private or municipal corporation, or any of its officers, or to an executive, administrative or judicial officer, or to an inferior court, commanding the performance of a particular act therein specified, and belonging to his or their public, official, or ministerial duty, or directing the restoration of the complainant to rights or privileges of which he has been illegally deprived."

10. Orloff v. Los Angeles Turf Club, 36 Cal.2d 734, 740; 227 P.2d 449,453 (1951).

11. Morrison (1969): 118.

12. "Judicial notice" is an act by the court during a trial or while formulating a decision that recognizes certain facts as true because of common knowledge. Morrison tried to argue that the court had erred in believing that homosexuality was evil based upon the Sarac decision.

13. After Morrison, a teacher who stole a motorcycle (Charles Hoagland v. Mount Vernon School District, 95 Wn.2d 424; 623 P.2d 1156 (1981)), or who lived with a member of the opposite sex (Tim Yanzick v. School District No. 23, Mont., 641 P.2d 431 (1982)), or who was a transsexual (In the Matter of the Tenure Hearing of Paula Grossman, a/k/a Paul Grossman, 127 N.J. Super. 13 (1974), or who engaged in "free love" and group sex (Elizabeth Pettit v. State Board of Education, 10 C.3d 29; 109 Cal.Rptr. 665; 513 P.2d 889 (1973) was able to argue that the Board of Education had to consider whether or not their out of school behavior seriously affected their teaching performance or effectiveness.

14. Norton v. Macy, (D. C. Cir. 1969) 417 F.2d 1161, 1165 (1969). Norton was a budget analyst for the National Aeronautics and Space Administration. He was arrested for a traffic violation and was accused of trying to solicit the arresting officer. Despite his admission of prior homosexual acts and his arrest details, the court held his dismissal was impermissible because a nexus was not established that demonstrated that his employment duties were impacted negatively by his homosexual conduct.

15. Morrison (1969): 214.

16. Morrison (1969): 228.

17. Morrison (1969): 226.

18. Morrison (1969): 216.

19. Morrison (1969): 217.

20. Morrison (1969): 230.

21. Morrison (1969): 237.

22. Morrison (1969): 240.

23. Morrison (1969): 240.

24. Morrison (1969): 236.

25. Willemsen, "Tobriner," 84.

26. Amundsen v. State Board of Education, (Civ. No. 37942); Cal.Ct.App.(2d District, 1971). Hereinafter referred to as Amundsen.

27. McConnell v. Anderson, 316 F.Supp 809 (D. Minn., 1970); Rev'd, 451 F.2d 193 (8th Cir, 1971); Cert. denied, 405 U. S. 1036 (1972). Hereinafter referred to as McConnell.

28. McConnell (1971): 196.

29. In a related case, Bekiaris v. Board of Education of the City of Modesto, 6 C.3d 575; 100 Cal.Rptr. 16, 493 P.2d 480 (1972), the California State Supreme Court held that school authorities had not followed standards of due process when they refused to rehire a probationary teacher because he presented positive views of homosexuality, sexual expression, and use of marijuana to his classes. Arguably, discussing these topics was an exercise in constitutionally protected free speech, although school authorities maintained that Bekiaris was an ineffective teacher who did not comply with administrative requirements. Although the case was remanded to a lower court for a determination of the real reasons for the Bekiaris firing, the final outcome of the litigation is not known.

30. Willemsen, "Sex," 849.

31. Brent Moser v. State Board of Education, 22 C.A.3d 988; 101 Cal.Rptr. 86 (1972). Hereinafter referred to as Moser.

32. Moser (1972): 990.

33. Goldsmith v. Board of Education, 66 Cal.App. 157, 168; 225 P. 783 (1924).

34. Board of Education v. Swan, 41 Cal.2d 546, 553-554; 261 P.2d 261 (1953).

35. Moser (1972): 991.

36. Board of Education of the El Monte School District of Los Angeles v. Marcus Calderon, 35 Cal.App.3d 490; 110 Cal.Rptr. 916 (2d Dist. 1973); Cert. denied, 419 U.S. 807 (1974). Hereinafter referred to as Calderon.

37. Calderon (1973): 918.

38. Calderon (1973): 920.

39. Calderon (1973): 921, quoting from Pettit v. State Board of Education, 10 Cal.3d 29, 36, fn. 7; 109 Cal.Rptr. 665; 513 P.2d 889 (1973).

40. Governing Board of the Mountain View School District of Los Angeles County v. Frank Metcalf, 36 Cal.App.3d 546; 111 Cal. Rptr. 724 (2d Dist., Div. 3, 1974). Hereinafter referred to as Metcalf.

41. Metcalf (1974): 726.

42. Metcalf (1974): 727. Metcalf's attorney, Hirsch Adell, of Los Angeles, stated that the files had been destroyed. The case was handled quietly and did not receive any public attention. The State Board of Education did not remove Metcalf's teaching credential after his job termination, but he did

leave the teaching profession. Metcalf at all times denied being a homosexual despite the criminal conduct for which he was arrested. Adell, Hirsch (defendant's attorney), 6 February 1986, personal correspondence.

43. The seven states were Illinois, Connecticut, Colorado, Oregon, Hawaii, Delaware and Ohio. For an analysis of the impact of decriminalization of the sodomy statutes, see Geis et al., "Decriminalization," 419-426.

CHAPTER 10 ENDNOTES

1. Since I was unable to locate Peggy Burton for an interview, the details of this story are gathered from the court records and judicial opinions. The thoughts and feelings ascribed to Peggy Burton are my own interpretations based upon her behavior and comments, and the experiences of other GLBT educators in similar circumstances. I hope that Peggy Burton understands and approves of the details as written.

2. Marmor and Green, "Homosexual," 1051-1052.

3. New York Times, 3 July 1970.

4. Saturday Review, 12 February 1972.

5. New York Times, 27 October 1970.

6. M. Thorp, "Last Minority? With Little Fanfare, More Firms Accept Homosexual Employees," Wall Street Journal, 1 July 1974.

7. "Laws Aiding Homosexuals Face Rising Opposition Around Nation," New York Times, 27 April 1978; "After Low-Key."

8. For a history of GLBT school teacher political efforts in New York City, see Marc Rubin, "Gay Teachers Association — New York City," 1 (2) Gai Saber (Summer 1977): 89-92. Rubin points out that one of the most successful accomplishments of the organization was to make ongoing contact with Frank Arricale II, the Executive Director of the Division of Personnel for the New York City Board of Education.

9. Marotta, Politics, 206.

10. "Gay Teacher Support Packet," National Gay Task Force.

11. The St. Paul ordinance passed in 1974, while Eugene and Wichita enacted similar legislation in 1977. For information about the St. Paul ordinance see Jim Marko, "Rights Measure Repealed in St. Paul Vote," Gay Community News, 6 May 1978; Nathaniel Sheppard, Jr., "Vote To Repeal St. Paul Homosexual Law Leads 2-1," New York Times, 26 April 1978; Orv Johnson, "St. Paul — What Went Wrong?," Seattle Gay News, 12 May

1978; "What Both Sides Are Saying," Today's Student, 24 April 1978; Jim Coleman, "Homosexual Lifestyle Challenged In St. Paul Election," Today's Student, 24 April 1978; "Gay Rights Law Upset In St. Paul," Milwaukee Journal, 26 April 1978; and, "City Voids Gay Rights Law," Source Unidentified. For information about the Seattle ordinance see, Hilda Bryant, "Seattle Reaction"; "Bryant Organization Gives $3G To Seattle Anti-Gay Initiative Drive," Gaysweek, 12 June 1978; Jim Arnold and Steve Mettner, "SOME Hands In Signatures," Source Unidentified, 4 August 1978; "Anti-Gay Drive Finally Comes Out," Seattle Sun, 5 April 1978; "Initiative Against Gay Rights Wins Validation," Seattle Times, 16 August 1978; and, "Seattle Battles On," The Advocate, 9 August 1978. See also, Paul Yarnold, "Will Gay Rights Spell Anything Goes?," Voice of the People of Eugene, Oregon Human Rights Ordinance 51 (May 1978).

12. Johnson, "St. Paul."

13. Bruce Michael Gelbert, "Wichita: The Next Miami?," Gaysweek, 6 February 1978.

14. "School Board Refuses Specific Protection For Homosexuals," Palo Alto Times, 22 November 1975.

15. Rob Lence, "PA School Board Ends Anti-Gay Ban," The Stanford Daily, 19 November 1975.

16. Donald C. Knutson, Letter to Rebecca Morgan, 12 November 1975. See also, Newman M. Walker, Letter to Donald C. Knutson, 24 November 1975.

17. "Palo Alto School Board To Reconsider Bias List," Palo Alto Times, 17 November 1975.

18. Joseph Honig, "Sexual Preference In Hiring Outlawed In School Policy," Palo Alto Times, 19 November 1975.

19. "Trustees Err In Policy Stand," Palo Alto Times, 20 November 1975.

20. "Trustees Err." For a more complete discussion of the molestation issue, see upcoming volume.

21. The information in this section was obtained from interviews with attorneys around the country who wished to remain anonymous, and with two officials in the national offices of the NEA, Michael Simpson Assistant to the General Counsel (5 March 1986), and Al Erickson, Manager of Governance and Policy Support (10 March 1986).

22. In 1974-1975 Book of Resolutions adopted in Chicago, Illinois (1974): 252.

23. Gaylord v. Tacoma School District No. 10, 85 Wn.2d 348; 535 P.2d 804 (1975); 88 Wash.2d 286; 559 P.2d 1340 (1977); Cert. denied, U.S. 286 (1977). Hereinafter referred to as Gaylord.

24. Mercier v. Evergreen School District, Superior Court, State of Washington, (1985, 1986).

25. Acanfora v. Board of Education of Montgomery County, 359 F.Supp. 834 (1973); 491 F.2d 498 (1974). Cert. denied, 419 U.S. 839 (1974).

26. The reader will recall that in the ACLU, for example, state and local offices of the organization repeatedly lobbied the national office for years to take a pro-homosexual rights stand on the issue. Despite the national office's refusal, these state organization's used their resources to involve themselves in the litigation. See Chapter Nine.

27. Letter from David Selden to Dr. Bruce Voeller, 4 March 1974. A similar statement was obtained from the United Federation of Teachers as well.

28. See Myron Lieberman, "Demography and the Economy Chill the AFT Convention," Phi Delta Kappan (September 1979).

29. Shanker questioning, 1 November 1986.

30. See Chapter Three for further details about the participation of the California Federation of Teachers. Their resolution in support of homosexual educators was passed in December of 1969.

31. Civil Rights Act of 1871, 42 U.S.C. Section 1983, founded upon 28 U.S.C. Section 1343(3), 1343(4), and 1331.

32. Burton v. Cascade School District Union High School No. 5 et al., 353 F.Supp. 254 (1973). Hereinafter referred to as Burton (1973). Burton v. Cascade School District Union High School No. 5 et al., 512 F.2d 851 (1975); Cert. denied, 423 U.S. 859 (1975). Hereinafter referred to as Burton (1975).

33. Burton (1973): 254, 255.

34. Burton (1975): 850-851.

35. For a more complete discussion of the Ninth Circuit Court's resolution in Burton in the context of case precedent on redress and reinstatement, see "Remedial Balancing Decisions and the Rights of Homosexual Teachers: A Pyrrhic Victory," 61 Iowa Law Review (1976): 1080-1098. See also, "Civil Rights — Remedies — Case Notes," Brigham Young University Law Review (1976): 531-548.

36. Joseph Acanfora v. Board of Education of Montgomery County, et al., 359 F.Supp. 843 (1973); aff'd 491 F.2d 498 (4th Cir. 1974); Cert. denied, 419 U.S. 836 (1974). Hereinafter referred to as Acanfora. See Kenneth H. Ostrander, "The Teacher's Duty To Privacy: Court Rulings In Sexual Deviancy Cases," 57 Phi Delta Kappan (1974): 20-22.

37. See Michael LaMorte, "Recognition of Homosexual Organizations," 5 (1) NOLPE School Law Journal (1975): 48-52, for a discussion of the case law on the recognition of homosexual organizations at universities. See also Rhonda Rivera, "Our Straight-Laced Judges: The Legal Position Of Homosexual Persons In The United States," 30 (4) Hastings Law Journal (March 1979): 799-955; and, Rhonda Rivera, "Recent Developments In Sexual Preference Law," 30 Drake Law Review (1980): 311-346.

38. Dr. Patricia Graham, formerly Dean of the College of Education at Harvard University, and currently the Director of the Spencer Foundation, mentioned to me that when she worked in New York in the mid-1970s, she had a similar situation of having to decide the fate of a male student teacher who was gay. She decided that one's sexual orientation was not detrimental to one's teaching responsibilities, so she directed that gay and lesbian education students be free from extraordinary scrutiny because of their sexual orientation. Personal communication, about 1985.

39. Acanfora was a member of the NEA and of its annual lesbian and gay caucus.

40. Transcript of "60 Minute" interview, broadcast on 25 February, 1973, 8.

41. Acanfora, Brief for the Plaintiff-Appellant (1974): 28.

42. Acanfora, Joint Appendix, Dr. Lourie: 41, 50, 51, 53, 59, 65; Dr. Heald: 78-79.

43. Acanfora (1973): 849.

44. See discussion in Chapter Two.

45. Acanfora (1973): 850.

46. Acanfora (1973): 850-851.

47. See Nadler v. Superior Court, 255 Cal. App.2d 523 (1967).

48. Maryland Sodomy Statute, Article 27, section 553 Md. Anno. Code, 1971 Repl. Vol.

49. Senior U.S. District Judge Joseph H. Young had to decline an interview concerning Acanfora because of tangentially-related pending litigation. Judge Young recently delayed any discharge of Navy Lt. Richard Selland so that Selland's appeal of the military's policy of dismissing openly gay and

lesbian military personnel could be decided. See personal correspondence with Judge Young of 2 February 1996 and 22 March 1996. See also "Navy Must Delay Removal of Gay," The Boston Globe, 10 November 1995.

50. Based on Pickering v. Board of Education, 391 U.S. 563; 88 S.Ct. 1731; 20 L.Ed.2d 811 (1968).

51. Acanfora, Joint Appendix: X-4.

52. United States v. Kapp, 302 U.S. 214, 217, 58 S.Ct. 182, 82 L.Ed. 205 (1937); Dennis v. United States, 384 U.S. 855 (1966).

53. Acanfora (1974): 504.

54. Dennis (1966): 866-67.

55. Bryson v. United States, 396 U.S. 64 (1969): 72.

56. Acanfora, Brief for the Appellees: 5. Emphasis in the original.

57. Acanfora, Brief for the Appellees: 15.

58. James v. West Virginia Board of Regents, 322 F.Supp. 217 (S.D.W.Va. 1971), aff'd, 448 F.2d 785 (4th Cir. 1971) — no duty to hire a militant.

59. Cert. denied, 419 U.S. 839 (1974).

60. Safransky v. Personnel Board, 62 Wis.2d 464 (1974). Hereinafter referred to as Safransky.

61. Safransky (1974): 475.

62. Safransky (1974): 475.

63. James Gaylord v. Tacoma School District No. 10, 85 Wn.2d 348; 535 P.2d 804 (1975); 88 Wn.2d 286; 559 P.2d 1340 (1977). Hereinafter referred to as Gaylord.

64. Gaylord (1975): 354. See also, "Gay Teachers Banned, Latents O.K.," Source Unidentified, 23 February 1977; and, Michael D. Tewksbury, "Gaylord and Singer: Washington's Place In The Stream of The Emerging Law Concerning Homosexuals," 14 Gonzaga Law Review (1978): 167-196.

65. "Gay Teacher Looks To Court," Gay Community News, September 1977.

66. "Gay Teachers Banned."

67. Gaylord (1975): 350.

68. Gaylord (1975): 350. Pursuant to Educational Code RCW 28A.58.1011.

69. Gaylord (1975): 362.

70. Gaylord (1975): 363.

71. Gaylord (1977): 294-295.

72. Gaylord (1977): 295.

73. New Catholic Encyclopedia (1967): 116.

74. Gaylord (1977): 296.

75. Gaylord (1977): 297.

76. Young, Christopher (Gaylord's attorney). Personal correspondence, 18 February 1986; and, "Supreme Court Permits Firing of Gay Teachers," 320 Civil Liberties (November 1977): 7.

77. "Supreme Court Permits."

78. Grace Lichtenstein, "Teachers on Coast and In Jersey Lose Disputes Over Homosexuality," New York Times, 4 October 1977.

79. Lichtenstein, "Teachers."

80. Aumiller v. University of Delaware, 434 F.Supp. 1273 (D. Del., 1977). Hereinafter referred to as Aumiller. See also Tewksbury, "Gaylord."

81. See Robert Steinbrook, "Gays Battle Prejudice, Keep Low Profiles," The Sunday Bulletin, 1 June 1975; Jan de Blieu, "Gays: There's No Need To Deny Fact, Says A Homosexual Activist At U. D.," Wilmington Sunday News-Journal, 2 November 1975; and, Timothy O'Shea and Gwen Florio, "Gays Seeking Campus Acceptance," The Review (University of Delaware), 4 November 1975.

82. Aumiller (1977): 1283. See also, Philip W. Semas, "Homosexual Professor Wins $27,000 in Damages," Chronicle of Higher Education, 5 July 1977.

83. Pickering v. Board of Education, 391 U.S. 563 (1968).

84. Gish v. Board of Education of Paramus, 145 N.J.Super. 96 (1976). Cert. denied, U.S. (1977). Hereinafter referred to as Gish.

85. Gish (1976): 104.

86. N.J.S.A. 18A: 16-2. Physical examinations, requirement: Every board of education shall require all its employees, and may require any candidate for employment, to undergo a physical examination, the scope whereof shall be determined under rules of the state board, at least once in every year and may require additional individual psychiatric or physical examinations of any employee whenever, in the judgment of the board, an employee shows evidence of deviation from normal, physical or mental health. [Gish (1976): 99.]

87. Gish (1976): 101.

88. Gish (1976): 101.

89. Gish (1976): 104.

90. Adler v. Board of Education of the City of New York, 342 U.S. 485; 72 S.Ct. 380; 96 L.Ed. 517 (1952).

91. Gish (1976): 105.

92. Gish (1976): 105.

93. Jil Clark, "New Jersey Ruling Protects Teachers' Freedom of Speech," Gay Community News, 18 July 1981.

94. Clark, "New Jersey."

95. In 1976, a case similar to Gish came before the Michigan Appellate Court, Ferndale Education Association v. School District No. 2 (Ferndale Education Association v. School District No. 2, 67 Mich. App. 645 (1976). Hereinafter referred to as Ferndale. Gordon Ostrowski applied to teach in the Ferndale School System, commenced teaching, and as a part of the hiring process took a required physical. The doctor who gave Ostrowski the physical concluded that he had nervous problems, probably stemming from homosexual tendencies, although Ostrowski maintained that homosexuality had not been discussed. The school board immediately fired Ostrowski based on the medical report, and the teacher's union moved to assert due process and procedural rights. It was the school board's position that until all of the requirements for employment were satisfactorily completed, no new teacher had any rights in the job situation pertaining to notices, hearings, and other procedural aspects, even if they had been teaching for several months. The Michigan Appellate Court remanded the case back to the lower court for a hearing in which Ostrowski could refute the medical testimony, in part because of "the potentially great harm of the allegations of homosexuality and resultant dismissal" on Ostrowski's reputation and future employment possibilities (Ferndale (1976): 652.). To date, no information on the outcome of the case has been discovered.

Also in 1976, the state of Louisiana ruled on a university teacher case that was concerned with procedural issues as well, rather than actually focusing on the homosexual school teacher. In Michael T. Blouin v. Loyola University et al., the Fourth Circuit Court of Appeals held that Blouin's suit against the university for slander and libel was barred because it was not commenced within the statutory period. Blouin was dismissed from his teaching job at Loyola University in 1969 because, according to their termination letter, "he was a homosexual, made anti-Catholic remarks, made anti-Jesuit remarks, he frequented bars, and that he dealt in or used illegal drugs." The Court held in the university's favor, despite Blouin's argument that he delayed litigation in order to resolve the matter within the university appeal procedure. (Michael T. Blouin v. Loyola University et al., La.App., 325 So.2d 848 (1976).)

EPILOGUE ENDNOTES

1. Falwell, Jerry, Strength for the Journey: An Autobiography (New York: Simon & Schuster, 1987): 335.

2. Falwell, pp. 290–291.

3. Falwell, pp. 290–291.

4. Falwell, p. 303.

5. Falwell, p. 361.

6. Briggs (January 1988). Personal interview.

APPENDIX E ENDNOTES

1. For example, see Bowers v. Bowers, 257 Ark. 125; 514 S.W.2d 387 (1974); Glen West v. The State of Alabama, 57 Ala.App. 596; 329 So.2d 653 (1976); and, In re Volkland, 74 Cal.App.3d 674; 141 Cal.Rptr. 625 (1977). The one excluded case that seemed somewhat related to employment as a teacher was People v. Lori Andersen, 101 Cal.App.3d 563; 161 Cal.Rptr. 707 (1980). In Andersen, a female college tennis instructor at California State University, Northridge, was murdered by a jealous student who was romantically involved with the victim's lesbian live-in lover. The Court directly, and in great detail, discussed the lesbian lifestyle and relationships of all concerned parties. In fact, they quoted the Appellant as stating that "at Northridge, tennis and homosexuality went hand in hand."

2. Hoagland.

3. Yanzick.

4. Grossman.

5. Pettit.

INDEX